The House of Frohman

A view of the revered Empire Theater in the early twenties. This playhouse
was opened by Charles Frohman in 1893 (Empire Theater Collection—
Photo White Studio).

Matinee Tomorrow

FIFTY YEARS OF OUR THEATER

by Ward Morehouse

WHITTLESEY HOUSE

McGraw-Hill Book Company, Inc.   New York   London   Toronto

MATINEE TOMORROW

THIRD PRINTING

Published by WHITTLESEY HOUSE

A division of the McGraw-Hill Book Company, Inc.

PRINTED IN THE UNITED STATES OF AMERICA

To
W. M. III, aged four,
who will know the theater of the
next half century. I hope that it
will be as exciting for him as it
has been for me.

PREFACE

In the writing of this book I have made an effort to put an informal history of the New York theater of the past half century into a single volume; to present an examination and, to some extent, an interpretation, of the Broadway stage from the days of Lillian Russell to Mary Martin, from the time of Clyde Fitch to that of Tennessee Williams.

I have sought to write of the theater's turbulence and excitement, its gusto and warmheartedness, and have concerned myself with its plays and its people, its trends and its crazes, its triumphs and its disappointments, its errors and its hysteria.

It has been my purpose to give the pageantry of the New York stage in a panoramic chronicle, and if there is revealed a certain reverence for the subject matter, it's a reverence that was inescapable. Something that has been with me since an afternoon in the long ago when I was taken to a matinee performance of *Mrs. Wiggs of the Cabbage Patch,* given by an undoubtedly road-weary company that was trouping the South.

My own playgoing experience has been a source of impressions and memories without number, and I have talked with, and have had correspondence with, scores of people of the theater—actors, actresses, managers, playwrights, composers, house managers, stage managers, road agents. I'm grateful to them all for assistance in my fact-finding, and for helpfulness in supplying details and anecdotical material.

Some very special acknowledgment must be made—it is now being made—for the assistance rendered by the staff of the Theater Collection of the New York Public Library, and by that of the library of the "New York Sun." I am particularly grateful to the "Sun's" reference chief, Charles Stolberg, and to the patient and cooperative Johnson Briscoe, whose memory is infallible, and whose stimulating love for the theater is unsurpassed in our time.

I am also deeply indebted, for counsel and encouragement and undiminishing interest, to Keats Speed, executive editor of the "New York Sun"; to John Mason Brown, critic, essayist, author, and lecturer; to Lois Dwight Cole of Whittlesey House; to Joan Marlowe and Betty Blake

vii

of the Theater Information Bulletin, and to Medora Field Perkerson and Angus Perkerson, old friends from Atlanta.

It's in the tradition of the stage that a vast number of plays have been written in hotel rooms, and perhaps it's now in order for me to report that every line of *Matinee Tomorrow: Fifty Years of Our Theater* was done in long hours of hotel-room writing, and with room service at the other end of the telephone.

So there is now a word of thanks to the understanding and hospitable managements of several of our better inns—the Ritz-Carlton in Boston, the Chalfonte-Haddon Hall in Atlantic City, the Atlanta Biltmore in Atlanta, the Algonquin in New York, and the Monticello in Alexandria Bay, N.Y. It's my notion that protests about my early-morning typewriter pounding from in-the-next-room neighbors went unheeded at intervals throughout two years. At least, I was never asked to cease the clatter or to throw the portable out the window. So I kept on writing. Hence this book.

WARD MOREHOUSE

FANCY ROCK
ST. LAWRENCE RIVER
THOUSAND ISLANDS
JULY, 1949

CONTENTS

LIST OF ILLUSTRATIONS

MATINEE TOMORROW

CHAPTER I

1898 — and Before

MRS. LESLIE CARTER had swung from her bell in *The Heart of Maryland* and Mrs. Fiske had trouped the land in *Tess of the D'Urbervilles* when the fifty-year period of which I am writing began. Nat C. Goodwin had died a hero's death (in Chicago) in *Nathan Hale;* Francis Wilson had been astride a comic camel in *The Little Corporal;* Ada Rehan had gone cycling in England, and Sarah Bernhardt had told the world of scorching her eyebrows by peeking into the crater of Vesuvius. They will all, along with a multitude of others, find their places in the pages of this chronicle of the New York stage as it goes its way for a half century from the final months of 1898 through the late fall of 1948.

In November of 1898, an orchestra seat for a Broadway hit was sold for $2 and a gallery perch was to be had for 50 cents. The sum of $1 down and $1 weekly would buy a shiny new bicycle. A two-story house in Flushing, Queens, could be purchased for $27.50 monthly; first-class fare to England was obtainable for $50, and a round trip to Niagara Falls, via the West Shore Railroad, called for an outlay of $8. Apartments in Manhattan's West 80th Street, seven rooms and bath (all improvements), were available at from $40 to $60 monthly. Men's fall and winter suits started at $10, the finest shoes cost $5 and $6, and Macy's, Sixth Avenue and 14th Street, sold men's overcoats at prices ranging from $9.49 to $16.24. A woman could buy an attractive hat for $1.98, a taffeta waist for $5, and imported suits at the Lord & Taylor store, Broadway and 20th Street, for $28.50.

The Brevoort House, at Fifth Avenue and 8th Street, "a homelike hotel of established reputation," provided rooms on the European plan at $1 up. Brentano was the bookseller of the time, Eaves the theatrical costumer, Sarony the stage photographer, and Lietz the wigmaker; and Stein's make-up was in every actor's dressing room. The bicycle craze was on,

1

and the "New York Sun," fully aware of it, carried a regular column bearing the heading, "News of the Wheelmen."

It was an era of clanking Broadway cable cars, ungainly Hudson River ferryboats, and somber brownstone mansions along Fifth Avenue. The early automobiles, with all of their uncertainties and perversities, were being driven through the city's streets to the accompaniment of chuckling and muttered abuse from the pedestrian multitude. The Spanish-American War (April 21–July 26, 1898) had been fought and won, and Lieutenant Colonel Theodore Roosevelt of the Rough Riders, one of its colorful heroes, had been elected Governor of New York in a whirlwind campaign against Augustus Van Wyck, brother of Robert A. Van Wyck, New York City's first Mayor under the new five-borough consolidation. The five municipalities, Manhattan, Brooklyn, Queens, the Bronx, and Staten Island, were merged, and not without protest, into a gigantic and fabulous entity, the sprawling city of Greater New York.

New Yorkers chewed Beeman's (Original) pepsin gum, they drank Hunter's Baltimore Rye, they took steamers to Albany, Troy, and Old Point Comfort, and they went to the Studebaker shop at Broadway and Prince Street for their carriage repairs. It was a day and time of wasp waists, high button shoes, matinee idols, dimpled chins of the Gibson girls, and testimonials bearing the signatures of famous stars of the stage—Viola Allen came out for Johann Hoff's malt extract; DeWolf Hopper endorsed Paine's Celery Compound, and Ada Rehan gave her approval (for a price) to Vin Mariani as a body-building tonic. Sousa and his band were in the news, as were William Jennings Bryan and the Klondike. Matineegoers had their crushes on John Drew, leading light comedian of the era, and Maude Adams, already something of a legend and rising to an enduring stardom. New Yorkers were still reading "Quo Vadis," which had been the delight of the rocking-chaired America, and were turning to such new best sellers as "Hugh Wynne," "Caleb West," and "When Knighthood Was in Flower." The theater of the day was the theater of the star system, of the romantic play, of the dramatized novel, and of plays slavishly written, or tailored, to fit the requirements of famous players. Civil War plays, including such pieces as *The Heart of Maryland* and *Secret Service,* coming along after *Shenandoah* and *The Girl I Left Behind Me,* were in great favor.

New York's theatrical life was centered in the Twenties and the Thirties. Daniel Frohman operated a fine stock company at the Lyceum, Fourth

Broadway Stars of Yesteryear

1. Henrietta Crosman 2. Viola Allen 3. Maxine
Elliott 4. Lillian Russell 5. Eleanor Robson
6. Sarah Bernhardt 7. Eleanora Duse 8. John
Drew 9. Anna Held 10. Clara Bloodgood
11. Mrs. Leslie Carter 12. Maude Adams

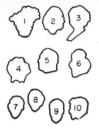

Great Names, Turn of the Century

1. Mrs. Fiske   2. Amelia Bingham   3. Mary Mannering   4. Julia Marlowe   5. E. H. Sothern   6. Otis Skinner   7. William Hodge   8. David Warfield   9. Nat Goodwin   10. William Gillette

Avenue between 23d and 24th Streets; Viola Allen had her most popular play, *The Christian*, at the Knickerbocker; Annie Russell played *Catherine* at the Garrick. Daly's, the Herald Square, and Weber & Fields' were among the leading playhouses of the Thirties, and the Grand Opera House, at 23d Street and Eighth Avenue, assured the world that cable cars passed its very door. The reigning vaudeville houses were Keith's Union Square (continuous performances from noon to 11 P.M.), Proctor's 23d Street, Koster and Bial's, and Tony Pastor's, 14th Street between Irving Place and Third Avenue, whose prices were 20 and 30 cents, and whose patrons were urged to "come in any hour of the day." Vaudeville headliners of the time included the Four Cohans, Marie Dressler, Mr. and Mrs. Edwin Milton Royle, and Tony Pastor himself. There was also a vogue for burlesque, and it found refuge at such establishments as Sam T. Jack's (Broadway and 29th Street), the Olympic, and Miner's Bowery.

In that fall of a half century ago the handsome Mary Mannering, the Rose Trelawny of Pinero's *Trelawny of the Wells*, was married to the actory actor, James K. Hackett; Maxine Elliott was the wife of Nat C. Goodwin and was co-starring with him; Virginia Harned was leading woman for her husband, E. H. Sothern; and the dainty Grace George Dougherty, just then starting in the theater, became the bride of the colorful, hardheaded Irishman, William A. Brady, former train butcher, actor, and fight manager, at the Roman Catholic Church of St. Thomas the Apostle. The same Brady, of course, who had startled Broadway with his daily telephone calls—at $15 a call—to his New York office from West Baden Springs, Indiana, to which he had gone for a rest. And Richard Mansfield, versatile and flamboyant actor, a man of cultivated perversity, born on the island of Heligoland, in the North Sea—his mother was a dramatic soprano and his father a violinist in her company—put his production of Rostand's *Cyrano de Bergerac* into the Garden Theater just as Augustin Daly was presenting Ada Rehan in his own version in Philadelphia.

Daly, in the interest of the redoubtable Rehan, enlarged the part of Roxane and reduced that of Cyrano, and remained undisturbed when charges of mutilation of the text were brought against him. The "New York Herald," devoting a great deal of space to theatricals in that day, had its respectful reservations as it paid tribute to Mansfield's Cyrano:

3

Unfortunately, Mr. Mansfield has an unconquerable desire to assume all the hues of the chameleon and so it comes that he presented himself not only as Bergerac but also as the leading comedian of the French stage. He was M. Coquelin first, always, and as Cyrano de Bergerac afterward. Not until the battle scene did we catch a true glimpse of Mr. Mansfield, while in the finale he again demonstrated that he is gifted with the very rarest histrionic talents.

And the "Herald" spoke thus of the company's Roxane:

An unknown young woman of the name of Margaret Anglin will wake up this morning to find herself famous. She possesses no great personal beauty but in all other ways is lavishly endowed by nature to play an important part in the history of the American stage.

This was the Margaret Anglin who was engaged at $60 a week and chosen from many for Roxane. When she met the keen-eyed Mansfield he asked, "Do you think you could make yourself pretty enough to play Roxane?"

"Yes," she replied quickly, "if you could make yourself ugly enough to play Cyrano." The part was hers.

During that fall of '98 souvenirs were given, in accordance with the custom of the day, to playgoers at the time of fiftieth and one hundredth performances—hand-painted and imported China teapots were distributed on the occasion of performance Number 100 for *The Village Postmaster* at the 14th Street—theatrical folk were making Atlantic crossings on such popular liners as the *Kaiser Wilhelm der Grosse* and the *Augusta Victoria,* and the world was in wax at the Eden Musée. Charles H. Hoyt's farces were then all over the map; Charles Klein and George Broadhurst were applying themselves to their early playwriting labors; the beautiful and ample-busted singer, Lillian Russell (born Helen Louise Leonard, of Clinton, Iowa), who had not yet joined Weber & Fields, was given a divorce in the Chancery Court of Jersey City from Signor Perugini, her third husband. And the theater was then experiencing a widespread change—a turnover—in the personnel of stars, dramatists, and managerial giants.

The day of the great managerial trio, Augustin Daly, A. M. Palmer, and Lester Wallack, was gone. Lester Wallack, son of James William Wallack, was a dominant figure as an actor-manager-playwright in the New York theater for nearly forty years. Black-haired, handsome, temperamental, dashing, he played nearly three hundred roles. He made his farewell appearance as an actor at the Grand Opera House in 1886. He was without a theater and with no money at all when death came to him in 1888. Augustin Daly, North Carolinian and one-time dramatic critic, an idealist, egotist, and disciplinarian, was through after thirty years of distinguished activity as a producer-playwright. The curtain was falling on the internationally known showman who had made many adaptations from the French and German and who had managed Rehan, Otis Skinner, and John Drew. And Palmer was on his way out—Albert Marshall Palmer, of the large, expressive eyes, the full side whiskers and white tie, a man of culture and refinement, son of a Presbyterian clergyman, who turned to the theater after serving as a public librarian, and who made many productions during his years as proprietor of the Union Square Theater. Palmer accumulated considerable wealth, but, like so many of the theater's celebrated managers —such as Dillingham and Ziegfeld and George C. Tyler—he died insolvent. He lost his theater, his health failed, he went to Florida, and returned as manager for Richard Mansfield, for whom he had done so much. But his status was merely that of an employee of the star. In 1904, just prior to his death, Palmer was manager of the Herald Square Theater at $100 a week, an apologetic position for a once powerful showman.

Let's flash back, for the moment, to New York's theatrical tumult in the decades of the 1870s and 1880s. The playhouses of the middle nineteenth century were scattered over downtown Manhattan, to the north of Chambers Street, in lower Broadway and environs, and they were, in the majority, dreary, ill-kept theaters. The drama gradually moved northward, settling and centering around Union Square, which held its place for twenty years as the city's Rialto. In the mid-fifties James William Wallack's Lyceum, at Broadway and Broome Street, was the most celebrated playhouse in New York. In the sixties Wallack, sensing the northbound trend, moved to Broadway and 13th Street, and two decades later the restless Lester Wallack opened a new theater at Broadway and 30th.

The mid-century favorites of the American stage included Lotta Crabtree, the comedienne, daughter of a Scotsman; the Vokes family, English comedians; John T. Raymond, William J. Florence, E. A. Sothern, Dion Boucicault, the Dublin-born actor-dramatist, who specialized in romantic Irish plays; Maggie Mitchell, who found great success with *Fanchon, the*

5

Cricket, adapted from the French; Madame Rachel, the French trage-dienne, who failed to the extent that Sarah Bernhardt later succeeded, and Joseph Jefferson, who made a life's work of *Rip Van Winkle.* There were such indomitable players as Edwin Booth, Lawrence Barrett, John McCul-lough, Tommaso Salvini, the Italian tragedian, and Helena Modjeska, the Polish star. Booth was the greatest actor of his time; he distinguished himself as Hamlet, Iago, Richelieu, Romeo, Shylock. He exerted a great influence in raising the standards of the stage in this country, and his earn-ings were enormous. Notwithstanding many financial reverses, he left a fortune when he died in 1893, and his home in Gramercy Park became the home of the Players, which he founded.

Augustin Daly came along at the start of the seventies; his most cele-brated star, the Ireland-born Ada Rehan, who played a great variety of roles, was with him from the mid-seventies until his death in 1899. A. M. Palmer opened his Union Square Theater, 14th Street, between Broadway and Fourth Avenue, early in the decade—his biggest success was *The Two Orphans,* in which Kate Claxton played the blind girl for a generation— and the New York playgoers, in the seventies and eighties, paid their homage to Adelaide Neilson, Louis James, Jeffreys Lewis, Clara Morris, from out of the West, a mannered actress of great power, and Fanny Lily Gipsy Davenport, born in London, educated in Boston, tall and beautiful, whose roles ranged from Camille to Nancy Sykes in *Oliver Twist.* And to Mary Anderson, the California-born convent girl who made her spec-tacular debut as Juliet at the age of sixteen at the historic Macauley's Theater in Louisville, Kentucky. The 1880s brought about the emergence of Mrs. Fiske, Julia Marlowe, Viola Allen, John Mason, Richard Mansfield, Henrietta Crosman, Herbert Kelcey, Nat C. Goodwin, Henry Miller, Mrs. Thomas Whiffen. The decade brought on Charles Frohman and David Belasco, and it gave increased prestige to such dramatists as Arthur Wing Pinero, Henry Arthur Jones, C. Haddon Chambers, Oscar Wilde, R. C. Carton, and Jerome K. Jerome. The native playwrights were then strug-gling for recognition; there was widespread managerial inclination to give preference to the imported plays and to the foreign writers. The American dramatists were not being taken seriously. Gradually, very gradually, the labors of the pioneering Bronson Howard and Steele MacKaye, along with the playwriting activity of Clyde Fitch, James A. Herne, Augustus Thomas,

6

Charles H. Hoyt, and William Gillette, wore down the resistance of the producers.

Augustin Daly's company flourished in the New York of the eighties; so did the Madison Square Theater company, and Daniel Frohman's company at the Lyceum, a playhouse of many fine performances but one that never achieved the distinction of Wallack's and Daly's. Union Square, as the nineties came along, still had the Union Square Theater, the Star Theater, the Academy of Music, and Tony Pastor's, but it was yielding its place, however reluctantly, to Madison Square, nine blocks to the north, as the city's new theatrical center. There was then vast tranquillity in that pleasant Madison Square area. Life flowed leisurely. There were no subways, no motor cars; the Fifth Avenue stagecoaches were slow and horse-drawn. Leading actors of the day strolled the area of the Square without molestation—the frightening era of the autograph hoodlums was still many years away—and they frequented the bars of such establishments as the Hotel St. James, the Hoffman House, Delmonico's, and the Lambs Club, then in West 26th Street.

Madison Square, fringed by such playhouses as the Garden, the Lyceum, and the Madison Square, had its day, but it was comparatively brief, for the drama was moving relentlessly northward. And in 1893, with the opening of a beautiful new playhouse, the Empire, as the showshop of Charles Frohman, the corner of Broadway and 40th Street became the heart of New York's Rialto.

The powerful Theatrical Syndicate, a phenomenon that was also known as the Theatrical Trust, was an alliance of six men—A. L. Erlanger, Marc Klaw, Al Hayman, Samuel F. Nirdlinger, J. Frederick Zimmerman, and Charles Frohman, and it was vigorously in operation in the closing years of the nineteenth century. The Syndicate, which became a monopoly of power, wealth, and frightening influence, was started in '96 when the six showmen got together at a luncheon at the Holland House to standardize cross-country theatrical bookings, to systematize them, and to make possible the booking of consecutive tours through a central agency. The Syndicate gained control of the great majority of the playhouses of America, its operations extending from New York to New Orleans, from New Orleans to California. The road theaters were put into one great national chain. Numerous cities became so tightly controlled that nonsyndicate attractions could not enter. Philadelphia was the first of the large cities to become Syndicate-dominated. Managements unwilling to accept the terms of the Syndicate—and tough terms they generally were—had the alternative of booking in independent houses, and these were generally nonexistent.

Newspapers throughout the country attacked the monopoly, with the "New York World" the most outspoken. Conflict developed between the Syndicate and famous stars who were accustomed to making their own bookings; the great stars, such as Nat Goodwin, Joseph Jefferson, Richard Mansfield, Francis Wilson, and Mrs. Fiske, were in open revolt. And the Syndicate drew spirited battle from some of the producers: Belasco, Harrison Grey Fiske, and Henry W. Savage, and later—and to a major degree —from the wily brothers Shubert, Sam S. and Lee and J. J., who did not begin their New York operations until after the turn of the century. The individual stars, one by one, made peace with the Syndicate when convinced that a cessation of resistance would work out to their advantage, but Mrs. Fiske, steadfast and alone, fought on, and the country later witnessed the spectacle of her playing in lodge halls and skating rinks and of Sarah Bernhardt playing in tents. The lively opposition that had developed from the Syndicate's foes brought forth scornful comment from members of the so-called Trust but only expressions of considerable admiration from Charles Frohman, then becoming the outstanding figure in the New York theater. He was a passive member of the combination. The Syndicate needed Frohman's name; he needed its money. He frequently remarked that all he ever got from his participation was trouble.

Nathaniel Carl Goodwin, affectionately known to the world of the theater as "Nat," was in the news of the day; Nat Goodwin, for whom Clyde Fitch had written *Nathan Hale*—Goodwin, the five-foot-seven actor with a Roman nose and penetrating blue eyes, who occasionally used a comic stutter and who talked five beautiful women into becoming Mrs. Goodwin. And there were many other personalities of the time—Colonel W. F. Cody (Buffalo Bill) on tour with *Wild West in Arkansas;* George Fuller Golden, monologue comedian and vaudeville headliner; Lincoln J. Carter, king of melodrama, who was giving the road such thrillers as *The Fast Mail* and *The Heart of Chicago;* Joseph Jefferson, still valiantly trouping in his enduring *Rip Van Winkle.* Also Tony Pastor, who frequently headlined his own variety bill; Jobyna Howland, tall and slender with a graceful neck, who had posed for Charles Dana Gibson; Corse Payton, occasionally billed as "The World's Worst Actor," who traveled in his private railway car. And such practitioners of the art of dramatic criticism as the white-mustached, highly opinionated William Winter of the "Tribune," the petulant Alan Dale of the "American," the scholarly J. Ranken Towse of the "Evening Post," and the "Times'" Edward A. Dithmar, a resolute student of the drama, and Franklin Fyles, critic of the "Sun." Winter, full of knowledge, was the dean; independent-minded Norman Hapgood was the youngest of the clan. He wrote for the "Commercial Advertiser." Most of the critics of the day were inclined to verbosity; plots were recited in seemingly unendurable detail.

It was an era of theatrical partnerships—Hurtig & Seamon, Sothern & Harned, Goodwin & Elliott, Stair & Havlin, McIntyre (James) and Heath (T. K.), in blackface together for twenty-four years, and Primrose & Dock-stader, also blackface specialists. And there was the dauntless team of Weber & Fields, who had just come into their Music Hall with their extravaganza, *Hurly Burly.* The New York "Dramatic Mirror" made this passing comment:

Weber and Fields fooled the audience with the Fregoli trick. Two men made up like them entered, looked around and bowed while everybody applauded. They went off and the real Weber and Fields entered from the other side. When those in the audience saw through the trick, they laughed for a full minute before the comedians got a chance to speak, and they laughed again at the mixed-up talk of the popular team of actor-managers.

It was an era, too, of touring companies roving the land, from Tuscaloosa, Alabama, to Grand Forks, North Dakota; from San Diego, California, to Oswego, New York. There was real theater in such places as Laconia, New Hampshire; Live Fork, Pennsylvania; Paris, Kentucky; Owosso, Michigan; and in Yakima and Grand Rapids and Carson City. There were many road playhouses, with distinction and individuality of their own, that were known far beyond the sections in which they flourished. Such

9

theaters as Macauley's in Louisville, the Coates Opera House in Kansas City, the Hyperion in New Haven, Parsons in Hartford, the Van Curler Opera House in Schenectady, English's in Indianapolis, Boyd's in Omaha, the Savannah in Savannah, the Alvin in Pittsburgh, the Star in Buffalo, the St. Charles in New Orleans, the Euclid Avenue Opera House in Cleveland. And such institutions as the old Academy of Music in Baltimore, the Great Southern in Columbus and Ming's in Helena, capital of the thinly populated state of Montana.

It was a day of short runs, short indeed in comparison with the three- to eight-year engagements of the Broadway of a later day, and stars were given to dropping plays, however successful, and turning impulsively to new ones. A run of one hundred New York performances was generally satisfactory to star and to manager; a stay of fifty to sixty performances, such as Nat Goodwin had in *Nathan Hale,* was by no means calamitous. The star was always thinking more of his next play than the one in which he was appearing. The restless Goodwin—an actor who could make playgoers laugh while tears were still in their eyes—was talking of and planning for *The Cowboy and the Lady,* which Fitch was writing for him, as he played the same author's *Nathan Hale.* The latter drama followed the career of the patriot from a New London schoolhouse to his heroic death as a spy.

The capricious, Celtic, gray-blue-eyed Ada Rehan, educated in Brooklyn, whose flamboyant scarlet gown was necessary to every performance she ever played as Shakespeare's Katherine, gave up *Cyrano de Bergerac* for Sardou's *Madame Sans-Gêne;* the fragile and girlish Maude Adams turned from *The Little Minister* to *Romeo and Juliet;* the unpredictable Mrs. Fiske quit on *Frou Frou* and took over *Becky Sharp,* and with fine results. Ada Rehan, of the great manner and authority, an actress who had been hypnotized by Daly, drew harsh comment from the "Dramatic Mirror" for her *Sans-Gêne:*

Miss Rehan has two great faults that are apparent in everything she does, and both faults are exaggerated when she is not sure of herself. One of these is a restless activity that has no artistic meaning, an absolute lack of artistic repose, and the other, which has all the tokens of a habit so long followed that it seems hopelessly inveterate, is seen in her frequent addresses to the audience and a tendency to take the audience into her confidence.

10

And the same publication, reviewing Miss Adams's Juliet of the same year—we've gone over into 1899—said:

Every good wish was hers, but yet it may be said only that Miss Adams cannot play Juliet. She spoke the Bard's words of passions but shows them not in voice, action or gesture. Even her personality ill befits the part. Her reading of Shakespeare's lines seldom rang true or certain. It was vague, almost aimless, and she suffered apparently from quite pardonable nervousness.

And this was Miss Adams's Juliet to the Romeo of William Faversham and the Mercutio of James K. Hackett.

Notwithstanding her defeat as Juliet, the Utah-born Maude Adams, daughter of the Kiskaddens, was making a place for herself in the theater. So were Ethel Barrymore, John Drew's radiant niece, and Minnie Maddern Fiske. Mrs. Fiske, of the chopped-off sentences and the fluent, brisk, head-tossing style—an actress with an economy of gesture and an intellectual approach—had come a long way since her teen-age appearance in the monstrous melodrama called *Fogg's Ferry*. She now gave the nineteenth century's final year one of its distinctive productions when she brought forth *Becky Sharp*. That was also the year of a curious assortment of Broadway offerings—Ada Rehan in *The Great Ruby*, Julia Marlowe in Fitch's Civil War story, *Barbara Frietchie*, William Gillette in his own *Sherlock Holmes*, the Klaw & Erlanger large-scale production of *Ben Hur*, John Drew in *The Tyranny of Tears*, and Mrs. Leslie Carter in the then sensational *Zaza*, a melodrama of the *Camille* and *Sapho* school, one of torrid love scenes, in which Zaza, a girl of humble origin, brought up by a drunken aunt, is taught to sing by an adoring journeyman musician.

There was also James A. Herne's moving Civil War play, *The Reverend Griffith Davenport*, a story of a devout Virginian, a Methodist circuit rider, who was bitterly opposed to slavery. It was undoubtedly Herne's strongest play, but it was a failure to as great a degree as *Shore Acres* and *Sag Harbor* were popular successes. Herne, as a playwright, was a realist ahead of his time.

Herne and Gillette were two of the gallant figures of the period. Herne's work was done with the writing of *Griffith Davenport* and *Sag Harbor*—he died in 1901—but Gillette remained an active and brilliant worker in the theater for another two decades and a stimulating force for more than

11

three. Herne was a Catholic, something of a radical, and an ardent supporter of William Jennings Bryan. He was, like Gillette, an actor-playwright-director. He was quiet and unassuming, a genial storyteller and a man with a deep vein of melancholy. In his playwriting, he emphasized character rather than plot, he liked quiet curtains; and his plays, in breaking away from the accepted conventions, were human, atmospheric, untheatrical. He had years of heartbreaking reverses until he established himself with *Shore Acres,* which opened in Boston in 1893. He played it for five seasons.

Shore Acres was a play that never failed to cast a spell over its audience; proof of this quality came with an incident early in its career. The final scene of *Shore Acres* takes place in an old Maine farmhouse on Christmas Eve. The benevolent old Uncle Nat has reunited the family and has saved the farm from foreclosure. The members of the household, tired and happy, have gone to bed. Old Nat remains on stage, puttering about, putting out the fire, winding the clock. He finally lights his candle, clumps up the stairs to his own attic bedroom, and the curtain slowly descends as he reaches the top step. Not a word has been spoken during the scene, which was one audiences would watch in dead silence. One night in Boston, however, and during the run at the Boston Museum, just as Herne started up the stairs, a man in the gallery cried out "Good night, old man—God bless you!" Herne was stunned. He was sure the outburst would bring a laugh and that the scene would be ruined. But there was not a sound from the audience. That man had voiced the thoughts of everybody in the house. The curtain fell to enormous applause.

In the closing months of 1899, New Yorkers talked of the marriage of Florenz Ziegfeld, Jr., and Anna Held, the French music hall singer, which had taken place in Paris two years earlier; they debated the Jeffries-Sharkey fight at Coney Island, won on points by Jeffries after twenty-five rounds; they paid their tributes to the beauty of Maxine Elliott and the art of Julia Marlowe; and they stormed the Broadway Theater to see the whopping *Ben Hur,* dramatized from the novel of General Lew Wallace, and destined to become one of the theater's greatest all-time money-makers. *Ben Hur,* coming along before the stage had achieved the mechanical proficiency of later years, and before the Hippodrome had introduced its gigantic spectacles, was a sensation because of its chariot race, with carefully trained horses running over the treadmills in the face of blinding

12

stage lights. And because of the multitudinous cast, the enormous orchestra, the ingenious creation of the Star of Bethlehem, and the rebuilding of the theater to make possible the use of the tons of equipment that were necessary for the production.

The opening night, November 29, 1899, was one of New York's most exciting *premières* of the decade. General Lew Wallace, who had refused for ten years to permit the dramatization because of religious scruples, and who had finally yielded to Joseph Brooks, representing Klaw and Erlanger, came from his home in Crawfordsville, Indiana, to attend the first performance. He looked on as Edward J. Morgan, a popular leading man of the time, played Ben Hur; as William S. Hart, later to gain renown on the silent screen, played Massala, and as the faithful stage version of his famous book, in all its pageantry, was unfolded. There were thunderous calls for "Author!" at the close of the fifth act, and the General, palpably nervous, rose in his box and bowed and then appeared on the stage. *Ben Hur* was an enormous hit. It stayed in New York six months for that first engagement, and in the American theater for the next fifteen years.

So these were the people of the New York stage of the passing nineties . . . the brothers Frohman and Klaw & Erlanger, Gillette and Herne and Fitch, Mansfield and Goodwin and John Drew, Ada Rehan and Mrs. Leslie Carter, Viola Allen and Mrs. Fiske and Maude Adams. And, to be sure, Julia Marlowe and Weber & Fields and Augustus Thomas and the beauteous Lillian Russell. The Shuberts of Syracuse were extending their up-State holdings and planning for their descent upon the big city, and George M. Cohan was still wearing his jaunty straw hat and doing his crazy dance in the variety houses. But their time was to come.

CHAPTER II

Belasco, Fitch, Gillette, and C. F.

DAVID BELASCO, of the dreamy eyes, the chalk-white face, the clerical collar and the somber garb of a priest; Charles Frohman, short, compact, pudgy, with a pleasant face, a good brain, and a big heart; Clyde Fitch, of the black, bristly, well-kept mustache, an Amherst graduate, aesthete, raconteur, and world traveler, and William Gillette, a New Englander of culture, courtesy, and unfailing humor—these were men of the theater who contributed vitally to the bustle of the American stage in the final years of the nineties.

Belasco, of English-Portuguese-Jewish stock, came on from the West at the age of twenty-nine and took a job as stage manager of the Madison Square Theater at $35 weekly. He had played scores of parts in California and had written numerous plays. He had been greatly impressed in his youth by a parish priest, one Father Maguire in Vancouver, British Columbia, and once he had begged for, and had obtained, a suit like the good Father's, it became his costume for life. He went from the Madison Square Theater to Daniel Frohman's Lyceum and by the time the year of 1898 came around he had given the New York stage, as a playwright, *Lord Chumley, Men and Women, The Girl I Left Behind Me,* and *The Heart of Maryland.* Belasco had a positive worship for the theater; he was a man whose talents combined those of manager, director, playwright, scenic designer, electrician, costumer. Notwithstanding his abundant success throughout a long and eventful career he was a worrier and a whiner. He always insisted—generally as he caressed his thick, white, silken forelock—that he was a poor man. "All I have in the world are my antiques," he said to me in one of my many talks with him. "I don't own a yacht. I never dreamed of such a thing. I don't own a bond. I have no real estate. My theater? Yes, that's mine, with a heavy mortgage behind it."

He stroked that forelock and went on: "In all my productions I've never had the assistance of a dollar from the outside. I wonder if people know that, or will believe it. When I was young and in the Far West I longed to come to New York and get my finger into the big Eastern pie. When I arrived I found that Augustin Daly, Palmer, and Wallack presented an iron ring against invaders. But I stayed in New York and fought Klaw and Erlanger and the Syndicate, and got my own theater. . . . Some of these new critics don't like me. But they come to see my plays and they know that I shall be doing plays as long as there is breath in my body."

Belasco was a showman without an appreciation of writing. His thoughts were always on what he could do for a play and not on the quality of the play itself. He enjoyed the theater most when blood was dripping from the ceiling in *The Girl of the Golden West,* when real tulips were growing in Peter Grimm's garden, when sizzling wheatcakes were being served in the Childs restaurant scene in *The Governor's Lady.* The dark-haired, willful, intelligent Jane Cowl, about whose acting ability Belasco had considerable doubt at the outset of her career, recently gave me this summing up of "the great wizard of 1888" (as Alexander Woollcott once called him):

"Belasco did wonderful things for the theater in many ways, such as in lighting and in the training of actors. He really represented a theater twenty years ahead of its time. He had one great fault: he would not put on good plays. His passion was finding poor plays and doing them beautifully."

And the astute John Mason Brown, in a consideration of Belasco in his book "Upstage," wrote thus: *

As a technician he [Belasco] has been one of the great influences of our stage, as well as one of its great pathfinders, but, as is the sad fate of the leaders of the new tendencies, the times passed beyond him for the definite well-being of our theater. . . . And, as the years have slipped by, it has become increasingly clear that, in spite of Mr. Belasco's fidelity to realism and his fondness for truth, his first allegiance has been neither to truth nor realism, but to what he thought his audiences would accept as truth. Accordingly, he has been more realistic about his box office than he has ever been on the stage.

* Reprinted from *Upstage: The American Theater in Performance,* by John Mason Brown, by permission of W. W. Norton & Company, Inc. Copyright, 1930, by the publishers.

But Belasco was never a man to be deterred by his shortcomings, if he ever admitted for an instant that he had any. The new century was coming on, and he was writing plays, casting plays, directing plays, reading plays. There was time needed for bringing forth Blanche Bates in *Naughty Anthony,* for buying fabrics and effects for *Zaza,* for getting David Warfield started as an East Side clothing dealer in *The Auctioneer,* for attending to Mrs. Carter's thousand-odd whims, and for making plans for the running of the New York theater as he thought it should be run. He well knew that in Charles Frohman he had a resolute and resourceful competitor.

Charles Frohman was one of three sons of Henry Frohman, a German peddler, who had turned to cigar making after settling in Sandusky, Ohio. Charles's brothers were Daniel and Gustave. Charles got his early theatrical experience with Callender's Original Georgia Minstrels, later acquired by J. H. (Jack) Haverly, and served in varying capacities—advance man, treasurer, manager. He began his New York activities at the Madison Square Theater, the pride of Steele MacKaye, whose *Hazel Kirke* had played there for the then extraordinary run of 486 performances. Frohman gained tremendous knowledge of road conditions in a theater-minded America by taking charge of companies that resulted from the Madison Square productions, and he began quietly planning for a producing career of his own. He and Belasco had been friends in San Francisco, and it was Belasco's *The Stranglers of Paris,* a ghastly melodrama, that Frohman did in 1883 as his first New York production, and while still in the employ of the Madison Square. The most important native dramatist at the close of the eighties was Bronson Howard, who had given the theater such successful pieces as *Young Mrs. Winthrop, Saratoga,* and *The Banker's Daughter.* Frohman went to Boston to see Howard's Civil War melodrama, *Shenandoah,* which featured Sheridan's ride. The play was a Boston failure, but Frohman liked it and acquired it for New York, thereby achieving his first New York success. He celebrated the opening by passing around twenty-five-cent cigars.

In the early nineties Frohman, who had known a great deal of financial distress, had his own theater, the Empire, and John Drew as his biggest star. Drew, who had made his first New York appearance in 1874, after serving an apprenticeship with his mother, Louisa Lane Drew, in the famous Arch Street Theater of Philadelphia, was brought to New York by Augustin Daly. For twelve years he was leading man at Daly's Theater.

But as the nineties came along he was uncertain and concerned as to his future under Daly's management; he had met Frohman and liked him enormously, and when Frohman offered him a three-year contract, and stardom, he took it. Daly had only scorn for the upstart Frohman and he was severely jolted by Drew's desertion. The news was something of a Broadway sensation.

Charles Frohman was always "C.F." to those closely associated with him and to many who were not. He had urbanity, humor, a talent for mimicry, and was often given to practical jokes. His schooling had been scant, but he had a sense of good taste, great feeling for the theater, and he was also an extraordinarily good businessman. He was a resolute advocate of the star system and was generally inclined to prefer the writings of foreign dramatists to the plays of native authorship. However, he did develop an enduring enthusiasm for the works of William Gillette, Augustus Thomas, and the oncoming Clyde Fitch. He brought forth Arthur Pinero's *The Gay Lord Quex* and *Mrs. Dane's Defense* of Henry Arthur Jones; he gave his eager sponsorship and production dollars to C. Haddon Chambers's *The Tyranny of Tears* and R. C. Carton's *Lord and Lady Algy*. But, to present evidence of his increasing appreciation of the home product, he also produced Gillette's *Sherlock Holmes,* Fitch's *Captain Jinks of the Horse Marines,* and Thomas's *Colorado.* And *David Harum,* dramatized from the popular novel of Edward Noyes Westcott, found its way into his crowded schedule. Playwrights and stars had no contracts in writing with Frohman; his word was all that was ever asked.

"When I was with him," said Marie Doro of the lovely profile and large bright eyes, in talking of her years in the theater, "I never knew what my salary was in any play until I got my pay envelope. For years I was hypnotized by two men—Frohman and William Gillette. Frohman had a fey quality—he was unique. He had a genius for exploiting personalities. He was a gentleman; he hated vulgarity and he stood for the fundamentals. In all my association with him we never spoke of money. I really had some dreadful plays, generally those that Maude Adams and other Frohman stars had turned down."

American dramatists, working full time at their trade, were increasing in the late nineties, it having been demonstrated by Bronson Howard that playwriting could be an attractive profession, and one decidedly worth

17

while financially. Howard was rapidly becoming a legend toward the close of the final decade of the century, and he was off for England for some bicycle riding and speechmaking on the chances of the drama in the States. But there was frenzy in the labors of some of his fellow playmakers. Charles H. Hoyt, a specialist in farces, was a one-man play factory. Belasco was taking his playwriting as seriously as he did his producing. Clyde Fitch was revealing a positively startling talent for high-speed production. Denman Thompson was starring in his own *The Old Homestead,* which he had expanded into a full-length play from his sketch called *Joshua Whitcomb,* and Lottie Blair Parker was in the news as the author of *Way Down East,* a play based on New England types that she knew so well. Augustus Thomas, who was to have a long and profitable career as a dramatist, if never to achieve actual distinction, was improving steadily in his technical skill. George Broadhurst, a former bookkeeper in Chicago and theater manager in North Dakota, was busily engaged with the *Why Smith Left Home* type of farce.

A young New Englander, Owen Davis, who had studied Greek at Harvard and who had turned to the writing of blood-and-thunder melodrama, was on his way to becoming the most prolific playmaker the theater had ever known. He was ineligible for the New York theater of the Frohmans. His specialty was the Bowery-type thriller, his trade the writing, under his own name and five names that were fictitious, of 10-20-30-cent fables of the triumph of love over lust, good over evil, virtue over vice. For fifteen years the amazing Davis, goaded on by Al Woods for several seasons, turned out such pieces as *Nellie, the Beautiful Cloak Model* and *Driven from Home,* finishing two and three of them a week, until he suddenly decided to change his ways and go out for uptown recognition. He went on to write *The Detour* and to win the Pulitzer Prize with *Icebound,* but his pride on that occasion was certainly no greater than he experienced in the late nineties when Gus Hill, once a juggler, and holding forth at 105 East 14th Street, put on his *Through the Breakers.* This was, according to the billing, "a drama in real life, produced with a carload of elaborate scenery, two sensational scenic effects, the height of mechanical realism, in addition to being a play of real strength and originality, with a cast of New York favorites." Owen Davis, at the time, was a playwriting contemporary of Pinero and Jones, of Barrie and Gillette, just as he was to be a vigorous competitor in the theater of three decades later, with such men as Eugene

18

"Tell Me, Pretty Maiden"

The Famous Sextette, with beseeching escorts, singing the song hit of *Florodora*, the toast of New York in 1900 (Photo by Byron).

INSET   Evelyn Nesbit, who joined the *Florodora* company during its run. Six years later she was in the front-page headlines of the nation (Daniel Blum Collection—Photo by Sarony).

Scene of gaiety from the shocking (to some, early in 1900) *Sapho,* which caused Olga Nethersole's arrest, and brought her to trial as an offender against public morals.

They Wrote the Popular Plays in the Early 1900s

1. Edgar Selwyn   2. Owen Davis   3. Charles Klein
4. Booth Tarkington   5. Channing Pollock
6. Clyde Fitch   7. Rachel Crothers   8. Avery
Hopwood   9. Eugene Walter   10. Wilson Mizner
11. Paul Armstrong   12. George Broadhurst
13. Edward Sheldon   14. Augustus Thomas
15. Winchell Smith

O'Neill and Robert E. Sherwood and Maxwell Anderson as his fellow craftsmen.

Now consider the case of Clyde Fitch, who wrote sixty-odd plays (including adaptations) in a comparatively short career of less than twenty years. Notwithstanding his many and definite shortcomings as a dramatist, Fitch was, for more than a decade, the most active, the most talked about, and the most successful playmaker in the American theater.

Fitch, born in New York in 1865, was five feet eight, unusually cultivated, and inclined to conspicuousness in his clothing. He was frequently something of a dandy in his dress. He liked tweeds, fur coats, plaid mufflers, in a day when the American male was given to plain, conventional attire. His suits were well made, many of them bought in London. In his boyhood he had great fondness for a bright blue suit that he still had when he went to Amherst. It was an outfit that always brought forth jeers from his fellow students, but he stuck to it throughout his freshman year. He enjoyed travel and spent his vacations roaming the Continent. He had a multitude of friends and acquaintances in London, and was never happier than when visiting an old bookshop in Charing Cross Road.

Fitch had a craving for beautiful things. He collected brocades, old China, Venetian glass, tapestry, porcelains, statuary, and rare books, vases, and furniture. He built his famous house at 113 East 40th Street—a small, square entrance hall and a little stairway of marble—and acquired a beautiful country home at Greenwich, calling it "Quiet Corner"; later he came to own "The Other House" at Katonah, which would have been converted into a palatial estate had he lived. He was a charming host, he entertained constantly, and despite the great amount of work that he turned out, he maintained a voluminous correspondence, writing with disciplined regularity to such friends as Virginia Gerson, Robert Herrick, Robert Hitchens, Maude Adams, and John Corbin. There was a bond of close friendship between Fitch and Corbin, but some of the sharpest criticisms of Fitch's plays were done under the Corbin by-line. Fitch's letters were generally gay and effusive, but several times he wrote tartly, even bitterly, in reply to Corbin's charges of faulty construction and artificiality in his playmaking.

Clyde Fitch, as a dramatist, was undeniably superficial; he was always too careless, too hasty. He was so extraordinarily prolific, he once had five plays—*Lovers' Lane, The Climbers, Captain Jinks, Sapho,* and *Barbara*

19

Frietchie—running in New York simultaneously. He was a playwright with an ear for the speech of the day, an observant eye, and a keen relish for the writing of the social foibles of his time. He was definitely at his best when giving his sly and penetrating attention to the imperfections of the feminine sex. Few of his characters had any reality—certainly two of his best were Johnny Trotter in *The Climbers*, superbly played by Ferdinand Gottschalk, and Jinny Austin in *The Girl With the Green Eyes*, created by Clara Bloodgood—but he was a man with an unending zest for creative work. He was stung, but never halted, by the taunts of many critics, by the persecution of William Winter. He believed, at the time he completed his last play, *The City*, that he was on his way to a new power and to far greater importance as a dramatist—and perhaps he was. It was in 1903 that James Huneker, in an appraisal in the "New York Sun" of Fitch's merits and his limitations, wrote thus:

Mr. Fitch is seldom sentimental. It is not his forte. He can paint fashionable life with its monkeys, its dolls, its occasional tragedies . . . he has shown us several highbred men and women and a wilderness of apes and wantons. . . . He is evidently overworked; his talents are too good to spoil in perpetual hack work. . . . Go to Switzerland, Mr. Fitch. Forget all about your promises to Charles Frohman, your promises to your bankers, and think only of the artistic future of Mr. Clyde Fitch. . . . You have one foot in the stirrup. Get both. And then gallop on to a hazard of new fortunes and fame that shall be permanent.

William Gillette, another dramatist-director of great stature in that period, was an industrious and skillful craftsman and, as an actor, he had a style of underplaying that was so effective he could steal a scene with an inflection, a glance, a nod, a shrug. And he could hold an audience as he stood motionless and in complete silence—tall, dignified, impassive, imperturbable.

Gillette was a man of many fascinating eccentricities. He had a great fondness for using his stage costumes as his regular, off-stage wearing apparel. One of his leading women, invited by him to lunch, was greatly impressed by a bluish-gray coat that he wore, a coat that had a jaunty, military air and was lacking only in brass buttons. She later learned that he had had the buttons removed and that he had used the coat in *Held by the Enemy*. And when he again invited her to lunch the shock of his cos-

EMPIRE THEATRE, BROADWAY and 40th STREET

(ERECTED AND OWNED BY FRANK W. SANGER AND AL HAYMAN.)

CHARLES FROHMAN, - - - - MANAGER.

Also Manager of the Criterion and Herald Square Theatres, New York City and the
DUKE OF YORK'S and VAUDEVILLE THEATRES, LONDON, ENG

Evenings at 8.   Matinee Saturday at 2.

MR. CHARLES FROHMAN PRESENTS

William Gillette

IN THE FOUR-ACT DRAMA ENTITLED

SHERLOCK HOLMES

FOUNDED UPON A HITHERTO UNPUBLISHED
EPISODE IN THE CAREER OF THE GREAT
DETECTIVE, AND SHOWING HIS CONNECTION
WITH THE

STRANGE CASE OF MISS FAULKNER

CHARACTERS IN THE PLAY	COMPANY APPEARING IN THE CAST
SHERLOCK HOLMES	WILLIAM GILLETTE
DOCTOR WATSON	WILLIAM COURTLEIGH
JOHN FORMAN	SIDNEY HERBERT
SIR EDWARD LEIGHTON	FRANK ANDREWS
COUNT VON STAHLBURG	ALFRED S. HOWARD
PROFESSOR MORIARTY	GEORGE W. WESSELS
JAMES LARRABEE	RALPH DELMORE
SIDNEY PRINCE	QUINTON McPHERSON
ALFRED BASSICK	GEORGE SUMNER
JIM CRAIGIN	W. R. WALTERS
THOMAS LEARY	JULIUS WEYMSS
"LIGHTFOOT" McTAGUE	HAROLD HEATON
JOHN	HENRY S. CHANDLER
BILLY	HARRY McARDLE
PARSONS	SOLDENE POWELL
ALICE FAULKNER	JANE LAUREL
MRS. FAULKNER	JULIA THOMAS
MADGE LARRABEE	HILDA SPONG
THERESE	SYBIL CAMPBELL
MRS. SMEEDLEY	MAUDE GIROUX

THE PLACE IS LONDON   THE TIME ELEVEN YEARS AGO

William Gillette's most popular characterization in all his years in the theater was that of Conan Doyle's omniscient and unconquerable Sherlock Holmes.

tume almost destroyed her appetite; he called for her in his clothes from *Sherlock Holmes.*

Gillette disapproved of the women of his companies being seen in public places; he wanted them always to remain aloof, elusive, and mysterious. He liked supper after his performances, and would consume two dozen raw oysters at a sitting. He had a passion for Chopin, particularly the *Raindrop Prelude,* and he enjoyed reading O. Henry aloud. Cats were sacred to him—alley cats or pedigreed, it didn't matter. He liked tinkering with things, such as old clocks; and he often rescued a clock that had been pronounced beyond repair by jewelers, putting it to ticking and to perfect timekeeping. He collected old bird cages for years—his associates always wondered why, but they never asked him.

He was a star who never forgot his manners and seldom lost his temper. He did lose it completely, however, near the close of a performance of *Secret Service.* He was delivering his big, final-act speech when an actor playing a Confederate soldier sneezed, and a gigantic sneeze it was. Nearly every player on the crowded stage broke up; they all turned from the audience, but shaking shoulders were beyond their control. When the curtain fell Gillette was white with rage. He glared at his company and spoke in a low voice, "You people have no right to stand on this side of the curtain. You are only useful out front. That's where you belong." He turned and walked away.

He was an actor who was witty in conversation, charming in correspondence, and given to the writing of notes, with black and red ink, that were precise, laconic, incisive, and frequently profane. For all of his attractive qualities, he had a reputation among his co-workers for being stingy. His "nearness," as they called it, particularly amused Charles Frohman, who was devoted to him. On one occasion, during a trans-Atlantic voyage early in the century, Jessie Busley, a member of his company, had a headache, and Gillette gave her two powders. In telling Frohman that her headache was relieved, Miss Busley said, "Willie G. gave me two headache powders." And then Frohman, with a twinkle, said simply, "Not *two.*" But there was also the story of "Matches Mary," who used to peddle her matches outside the New York theaters. During Gillette's revival season at the Empire in December of 1910—he was doing five of his famous plays— he invited Mary and her family to occupy a box for the Christmas Eve performance of *Secret Service.* Mary's party had the box bulging with humanity of all ages and sizes, and after the performance Gillette entertained his guests with refreshments backstage. There were tears in the eyes of Matches Mary when the evening was over—and in her hand was her host's check for one hundred dollars.

Gillette's best play, written when he was recovering his health in the mountain air of Tryon, North Carolina, in the nineties, was the soundly constructed *Secret Service*. This tells the story of the love of a Southern girl for a Northern spy, with its big scene in the War Department telegraph office, in which Lewis Dumont, posing as Captain Thorne, a Confederate officer, renounces his duty as he places love above patriotism. But Gillette's most memorable performance came with his playing of Sherlock Holmes in the play he wrote from the stories of A. Conan Doyle, and to which he brought his compelling stage figure and a voice that was dry, crisp, metallic, almost shrill. *Sherlock Holmes* opened at the Garrick Theater on the evening of November 6, 1899—a burlesque skit, *Round New York in Eighty Minutes*, with Jim Jeffries, Tom Sharkey, and Jim Corbett in the final scene, opened the same night at Koster & Bial's—and one of the congratulatory messages that Gillette received was a cablegram from Conan Doyle in London. In the year that followed another cablegram from Doyle arrived, but it had nothing to do with the theater. The Boers and the British were then at war in South Africa, with fierce fighting centered about the town of Ladysmith. Dr. Doyle, a surgeon as well as a storyteller, was off to the Dark Continent, to do what he could for his country and countrymen.

So the decade ended, with Charles Frohman's star-machine in full-time operation. Gillette and John Drew were under his management; he had made a star of Maude Adams, and he was seeking plays for the tall, willowy Ethel Barrymore, whose freshness and beauty had just enchanted the playgoers of London. . . . We now dim the lights to denote a lapse of time. Our curtain is slowly lowered. It will rise again upon a new year, a new era and a new and incredible century.

CHAPTER III

Turn of the Century

THE DAWN of 1900 found a confident McKinley in the White House, a jubilant Roosevelt in the Governor's chair at Albany, and a frequently perplexed Van Wyck in New York's City Hall. Maurice Grau was blandly presiding over the affairs of the Metropolitan Opera, and Mrs. Langtry was preparing to come into the Garden Theater while her officer-husband remained in South Africa, fighting the Boers. Heavy-eyed New Yorkers, recovering slowly from New Year's Eve festivities—an evening celebrated, decorously and otherwise, in such institutions as Sherry's, Rector's, Delmonico's, Reisenweber's, the Hotel Metropole, the Café Boulevard, and Luchow's—learned from their turn-of-the-century newspapers that the stubborn Boers had been cheered in an anti-British demonstration at the Academy of Music; that William Jennings Bryan was coming on in mid-January from Lincoln, Nebraska; that the books and manuscripts of Augustin Daly—he had died in Paris in '99—were to be sold at auction; that Richard Croker, the Tammany chief, had broken his leg in trying to mount his horse in London. And that Kid McCoy, scaled at 168, had knocked out Peter Maher in the fifth round at the Coney Island Sporting Club. These same New Yorkers, if they included the newspaper advertisements in their breakfast-table reading, were duly reminded of the virtues of Royal Baking Powder, Cuticura Soap, Old Crow Rye and Maryland Club, Syrup of Figs, Dr. Lyons Tooth Powder, Paine's Celery Compound, and the Pianola.

How *was* the American theater at the turn of the century? It was the day of the romantic actor, of the drawing-room comedy, and of stage success for popular novels turned into plays. There were many musical comedies, numerous farces, and many plays adapted from the French and the German. The classic drama, as represented by Shakespeare, was getting considerable attention from celebrated players, but the theater was still cautious in its experimentation with Ibsen and George Bernard Shaw. There was a trend toward historical characters, such as Nell Gwyn and Du Barry. The American Revolution was a subject that appealed to the native dramatist; the success of *Nathan Hale* and *Janice Meredith* stimulated interest in Colonial times. The entire country, from ocean to ocean, was road-show territory, and the touring projects, as the new century began, included Olga Nethersole in *Sapho,* E. H. Sothern and Virginia Harned in *The Sunken Bell,* Henry Miller in *The Only Way,* Mrs. Leslie Carter in *Zaza,* John Drew in *The Tyranny of Tears,* Sarah Cowell Le-Moyne in *The Greatest Thing in the World,* James K. Hackett in *The Pride of Jennico,* Julia Arthur in *More than Queen.* There were stock companies in the American cities, and there was vaudeville throughout the land. The motion picture, flickering, grotesque, and tentative, was struggling for a beginning, with such pioneering devices as the cinematograph and the kinetoscope booth in the penny arcades and the Edison Mutoscope, which was like a shooting-gallery slot machine, with a crank for separate action photographs for the customer's gaze.

New York City, serving as the American theater's show window, as the supply depot for the playhouses of the Continent, had twenty to thirty theaters in use for stage plays, dramatic and musical, as of January 1, 1900. The minimum price for a ticket to an attraction having a Broadway run— the standard scale was up to $2—was 50 cents, but speculators were brazenly plying their trade and were getting from $1.50 to $3 for 50-cent seats. Second-run plays were available at the Harlem Opera House and the Academy of Music in 14th Street at prices ranging from 25 cents to $1. New York City's theatrical district had spread into the Forties, and the march was still northward. Theatertown was dominated by Klaw & Erlanger and the mighty Syndicate, but the Shuberts were preparing to move in, via a lease on the Herald Square. Charles Frohman was, by now, the leading producer and the best play-buying customer in the market of the Continent and the British Isles. Several playhouses, such as the Empire, had built up established clienteles and were assured of a response from playgoers regardless of their bookings. When the Empire suggested that carriages be ordered for ten-forty the carriages were there, and in glittering array.

As the year of 1900, greeted by horns, rattles, chimes, and general pandemonium in the vicinity of lower Broadway's Old Trinity, became an actuality, the peripatetic Four Cohans were having a romp at Proctor's (15 cents to 50) in George M.'s sketch, *Running for Office;* Maude Adams was playing a return engagement in *The Little Minister, Ben Hur* was booming along at the Broadway Theater, corner of 41st Street, and the piquant Anna Held was surprising everybody, even husband Florenz Ziegfeld, with her mastery of English in *Papa's Wife.* Henry V. Donnelly was presenting popular-priced stock at his Murray Hill Theater in 42d Street—matinees at 25 cents—and Viola Allen had moved up to Harlem with *The Christian.* The Alabama-born Miss Allen had appeared with some notable players and held a secure place with the Empire Theater stock company when she suddenly gave it up, disrupting her association with Charles Frohman, to accept the offer of stardom under George C. Tyler's management. It was just at this time that Elizabeth Marbury, a play agent, asked her to read *The Christian,* which had been dramatized by Hall Caine from his popular novel and rejected by Charles Frohman as being worthless. Miss Allen read the play, decided that changes were necessary, but did not get them until she had spent the summer with the author and his wife on the Isle of Man. She returned jubilantly, with the play just as she had wanted it. Her success as Glory Quayle—*The Christian* became one of the great money-makers of the nineteenth century—gave her new prestige and gave George C. Tyler of Chillicothe, son of a country newspaper editor, new importance in the managerial field.

The bustling new year was not two months old when Olga Nethersole, born in London and educated in Germany, ran into trouble with the police. Miss Nethersole had a certain exotic beauty and dramatic force and was an actress of indisputable talent, although she was seldom praised for the delicacy of her style. She was successful in all phases of her profession, as Lawrence Reamer observed, except one—the public just did not come to see her. They did come for a time, however, after she opened at Wallack's, Broadway and 30th Street, in early February with *Sapho,* produced with her own money, and given pre-Broadway presentation in cities that had seen her in *Camille* and *Carmen* and Pinero's *The Second Mrs. Tanqueray.* *Sapho* was Clyde Fitch's dramatization of the Alphonse Daudet novel.

Some of the newspapers of the day, easily shocked, reacted with scare headlines to the scene in which Miss Nethersole was carried up the stairway by Hamilton Revelle, her leading actor. Those headlines turned the police into playgoers. Miss Nethersole was arrested in her apartment at the Hoffman House on the charge of violating the section of the penal code relating to public morals. Protesting regally and indignantly, in a purple gown, purple hat, and mink muff with boa, she was taken by cab to the Centre Street Police Station. Miss Nethersole was paroled in the custody of her attorney, the undersized, bald-headed, black-mustached, black-garbed Abraham Hummel, of the fantastic law firm of Howe & Hummel, which took great relish in its theatrical business and had countless actors and actresses among its clients. She was later given a magistrate's hearing, along with Hamilton Revelle, Marcus R. Mayer, her manager, and Theodore Moss, proprietor and manager of Wallack's. The case of Public Morals *versus* Olga Nethersole finally reached trial in the criminal part of the Supreme Court, with scenes and incidents of *Sapho* being described to the jury, and with the proceedings being given acres of space in the daily press. The jury, after several days of testimony in a courtroom jammed at every session, returned a quick verdict of not guilty. Miss Nethersole was cheered. She smiled and slipped into the beaming Attorney Hummel's hand a plain gold ring as a talisman of good luck.

Well, *Sapho* reopened at Wallack's as hawkers sold copies of the novel outside the theater. There was a tremendous ovation from a packed house when Miss Nethersole made her first appearance in the ballroom scene at Dechelette's, and later a breathless silence as Jean Gaussin, played by Revelle, took her up in his arms and started up the stairway. The curtain fell to wild applause. When the performance was done Miss Nethersole made a speech, Abe Hummel smiled his approval from a box, and she returned to the Hoffman House to find her quarters overflowing with floral tributes. The police and press lost in their bout with *Sapho*. But there were other years and other plays, such as *Mrs. Warren's Profession* and *The Lure* and *The Captive* and the offerings of Mae West, to come. The constabulary has always enjoyed these brushes with art, regardless of whether it wins or loses.

Olga Nethersole never married. In the summer of 1945, at the age of seventy-five, she was making her home on her 193-acre estate in north Cornwall. Out of the theater for many years, she talked with me in her small hotel in London of *Sapho* and her Broadway seasons.

"I could never," she said, fumbling with her dark-rimmed glasses, "understand all that uproar over *Sapho*. It was not an offensive or immoral

27

play. The novel was a classic, and the play merely followed the novel. . . .
The American audiences were very kind to me and so were the managers
in New York. I knew the Frohmans, and the Shuberts, who were just starting about the time I did *Sapho*. All that does seem so very long ago. I'm
now very happy in Cornwall; my country is beautiful, and my house is
more than four hundred years old. I grow oats and potatoes and wheat and
barley. I've had the place for about twenty years and I love it. The Atlantic
comes right into my little bay."

Sapho was a play—actually, not much of a play, and its New York career
was comparatively brief—that became a news story, and another piece of
the year of 1900, the legendary *Florodora*, found its way to the news pages
because of the tumult brought on by the girls of the famous Sextette. The
production opened at the Casino Theater, November 12, 1900. It was
mildly received by the press, and if the Sextette beauties had not been
taken up by the wealthy beaux of the town, *Florodora* might have gone its
way as just another musical comedy, and as a costly failure, at that. Ned
Wayburn wrote in later years:

It was Thomas W. Ryley, of Fisher, Dunne and Ryley, who turned failure into a classic success. He did it by his energetic publicity for the girls
of the Sextette. Those six goddesses were the first of their class to immortal-
ize the lure of the chorus girl. They were perhaps the most beautiful women
on the stage of their time and they passed from the front row, to the pleasant oblivion of wealth and retirement.

The commotion created by the Sextette was such that *Florodora*, after
some uncertain early weeks, began selling out, and it stayed for a remarkable run of 505 performances. There were many Sextette replacements as
the engagement continued, but the original six, some of whom really did
marry millionaires, were Margaret Walker, Marjorie Relyea, Daisy Greene,
Vaughn Texsmith, Marie Wilson, and Agnes Wayburn. They all had style
and a certain distinction; they had been picked from hundreds. Marie
Wilson and Vaughn Texsmith, who took her stage name from her native
state of Texas, were the prettiest of the lot. It's one of the Broadway legends that Marie Wilson made $750,000 from Wall Street tips during the
engagement.

The original *Florodora* cast included Willie Edouin (brought on from
London), Cyril Scott, R. E. Graham, Edna Wallace Hopper (Lady Holy-

rood). Evelyn Nesbit, who was to make the front page headlines of the nation in another few years, joined the company during the run. The Sextette members—the boys in the "Tell Me Pretty Maiden" number were George De Long, Lewis Hopper, Edward Gore, Joseph Welsh, Thomas A. Kiernan, and Joseph S. Colt—got $30 weekly at the time of the opening and were later given $50. Edna Goodrich, who became Mrs. Nat Goodwin number four, joined the Sextette as a $50 cast member.

How true are the stories that have come down through the years of the crush of New York millionaires at the Casino stage door during the *Florodora* run? Well, take the report of the ageless and buoyant Edna Wallace Hopper, with whom I talked recently. "Yes," she said, "a great many of the wild tales were absolutely true. We did get wonderful presents; there was a mob at the door every night. It was all very fantastic. I was there from the beginning and saw it all. The boys came in broughams—there were no motor cars handy in those days—and they came in tails and white ties, and it was always a scream to go out and see which was coming for which. We were taken up and taken out. Sherry's, at Fifth Avenue and 44th, was the smart place. Rector's, if you weren't dressed. We were all chased, as it were, and I suppose I had my share of the beaux. *Florodora* was a show that always brought in repeaters, and that was one reason it was so popular. Men would buy tickets ten and twenty times just to come in to hear the 'Tell Me Pretty Maiden' number.

"All that's been told about the wonderful presents for the Sextette girls was true—a great deal of it. They did get them; I know because I saw them. They got jewels and ropes of pearls and scarves and furs and coats and horses and houses. One of the original girls got two hundred fifty thousand dollars in securities from an admirer. There were often jewels in the flowers, there was always champagne, and cost never counted. That was the day of flowers being thrown across the footlights, and if there was ever a performance when I didn't get them I'd think something was wrong. It was always fun doing the show because the audience made it that way. The same faces were out front night after night. It was the fashion around town to brag about the number of times you had seen *Florodora*.

"I got two hundred dollars·a week—it was later raised to five hundred—only because I had ten thousand dollars to invest in the show before it opened. John C. Fisher—he was the same man who built a theater in San Diego without any dressing rooms—was the money man and the producer, along with Thomas Ryley and John Dunne. Things were in a bad way, he needed cash in a hurry, when I took him across the street and drew out ten thousand dollars. In the early weeks, when we were doing no business, he offered me a percentage of the show, thinking he could never pay back the ten grand, but soon we were all right. There were several *Florodora* companies; and the show must have made a couple of million. . . . Fisher? What happened to him? He died broke."

New careers in the theater were taking shape as the century turned. Grace George, guided cautiously and always devotedly by William A. Brady, was on her way to a guaranteed stardom. She learned her business and acquired brilliance by the time of *Divorçons,* but in her early plays she was somewhat distressing. Ethel Barrymore was moving ahead; so were Eleanor Robson, David Warfield, Clara Bloodgood, William Collier, and Elsie Ferguson and Marie Doro, both of whom were taken by Charles Frohman from small parts in the musical comedy, *The Girl from Kay's.* A minor musical play, *The Defender,* introduced a new young singer, Blanche Ring. Gay, good-looking, the daughter of an actor, she took the show for her own with the singing of a new song hit, "In the Good Old Summertime," written for her by George (Honey Boy) Evans and Ren Shields. She sang it first in Boston, and before leaving Boston for a New York engagement at the Herald Square in the summer of 1902 she had put in eighteen extra chorus verses on the topics of the day. And there was the musical piece, *The Wild Rose,* that reached New York in the spring of 1902 with a remarkable cast—Irene Bentley, Marie Cahill, and two lovely young players, Marguerite Clark and Elsie Ferguson. During the engagement at the Knickerbocker, Cornelius Vanderbilt imported the entire *Wild Rose* company to Newport, at a cost of $7,500, for a performance in a private theater built at the rear of his house.

The new century brought on increasing activity from producers and playwrights in the native field. The debonair Charles B. Dillingham was making his plans to enter the New York competition; the big city was beckoning to Lincoln A. Wagenhals and Collin Kemper, stock managers at Binghamton. The boyish, natty Sam S. Shubert, less than five feet and weighing 105 pounds, formerly a house treasurer and house manager in Syracuse, had come on to New York after having proved himself a bright young showman with his up-State operations. Such playwrights as Langdon Mitchell, George Broadhurst, the London-born Charles Klein, Augustus Thomas, and Fitch—always Fitch—were competitors in an active field. Newcomers in the playwriting ranks included Richard Harding Davis, war correspondent and novelist, who turned to playmaking with considerable success—*Soldiers of Fortune, Ranson's Folly, The Dictator, The Galloper,* and *The Yankee Tourist,* for Raymond Hitchcock.

There were also those two gentlemen from Indiana, George Ade and Booth Tarkington. Ade took up the theater as a side line and stayed in it to make a fortune; Tarkington, with the publication of his first book, had committed himself to a career as a novelist and was reluctant to try the theater. He never felt sure of himself in it, not even after Richard Mansfield had excitingly produced his *Beaucaire* at the Herald Square. There was early indication of Tarkington's indifference to theatrical acclaim, coming with the opening of *Beaucaire.* Shrieks for the author on the opening night went unanswered. Mansfield stepped forward and told the audience that the young dramatist was not in the house. But when Louis V. De Foe, critic of the "Morning World," hurried from the theater at the play's conclusion he found, as he later reported, Tarkington standing at the curb, "nonchalantly sharing a banana with a grateful cab horse."

Langdon Mitchell, raconteur, poseur, and gentleman by birth, turned to the theater, with all his subtlety and wit, somewhat condescendingly. He demonstrated his abundant talent in his writing of *Becky Sharp,* dramatized from Thackeray's "Vanity Fair," and he revealed his ease with dialogue and sharp characterization in his comedy of manners and divorce called *The New York Idea,* which has been in playwriting courses ever since. But Mitchell did little playmaking in the years that followed *The New York Idea,* so adroitly played by Mrs. Fiske. He lived thereafter by the device of writing first acts. He would take to the producer bright first acts and then seldom bother to finish the plays.

The playwriting contagion had spread, it seemed, to all the garrets of the land in the early 1900s. Young and unsung dramatists, having heard of the fabulous returns from successful plays (mere pennies as compared with a dramatist's earnings when talking pictures began bidding for the hits), were turning up in the ranks of bank clerks, drug clerks, department store employees. Playwriting was being taken up by college students and university professors, by actors and lawyers and theatrical advance men,

31

this category including Eugene Walter and James Forbes. But there was no man, young or old, obscure or famous, who was practicing the trade with the enthusiasm and tenacity of William Clyde Fitch, pride of Amherst. He was often working on two plays simultaneously; it was no trick at all for him to have two Broadway openings in the same month. And there came an evening in 1907 when two of his plays opened the same night! Harsh reviewers did not deter Fitch any more than short runs, and in the twenty-two successful productions that he achieved before he was thirty-eight he got some long ones—long for that day. On January 21, 1901, New York playgoers were summoned to the Bijou for the first-night performance of *The Climbers,* and two weeks later the first-night contingent turned up at the Garrick to greet *Captain Jinks of the Horse Marines.* And to greet Ethel Barrymore in the role of the opera singer, Mme. Trentoni.

Ethel Barrymore—daughter of Maurice Barrymore and Georgiana Drew, niece of John Drew, and sister of John and Lionel Barrymore—had played minor roles and had served as an understudy in New York in the late nineties. She went to London to appear in *Secret Service.* Upon her return, following an engagement with Henry Irving and Ellen Terry, Charles Frohman—vastly delighted with her voice, her grace, her bearing, her humor, and her beauty—gave her two New York engagements, sent her touring in *His Excellency the Governor,* and told her that he would have some exciting things for her. Later, with great excitement, he invited her to come to see him at the Empire.

She hurried to the theater from her boardinghouse in 32d Street, and Frohman, his eyes shining, said, "Ethel, I have a good part for you at last." The part was that of Mme. Trentoni. Well, the opening night of *Captain Jinks of the Horse Marines* was one of triumph for the convent-educated Miss Barrymore. She read the next day's press and told her landlady that she would be moving immediately from her top-floor room to a larger room on the second floor. And several nights later she arrived at the Garrick and became transfixed as she stood at the curb. Her name was in lights—there it was, blazing above her, spelled out in glorious refulgence. Tears welled in her eyes. Charles Frohman had made her a star.

This same Frohman turned down *The Climbers,* one of the best of the Fitch plays. It was a drama that began with a funeral and ended with a suicide. Several important producers refused it. Nobody seemed to want it until the blond, buxom, and handsome Amelia Bingham, just back from

London and determined to have a company of her own, suddenly appeared. She bought the play when she finished reading the second act and she engaged an impressive cast—Frank Worthing, Robert Edeson, Madge Carr Cook, Minnie Dupree, Clara Bloodgood, and Ferdinand Gottschalk, who became famous for the catch line, "I'm no Dodo bird!" which he spoke in the role of Johnny Trotter.

Gottschalk was a frail, undersized actor who made a hit as Dodson Dick in a relic called *The Silver Shield,* at the Madison Square Theater back in 1891—a meticulous, fussy, old-womanish Englishman with a genius for characterization. He was never a star during all of his fifty-odd years on the stage and he never wanted to be. He was always content to get the little parts—and the big notices. He went his way serenely, unconcernedly, from management to management, play to play, star to star. They used to say in the lounge of The Players that Bruce McRae had thrown his strong arms about more leading women of the American stage than any other actor. It was also agreed that Ferdie Gottschalk had played with nearly all of the great ladies of the drama but that he had never embraced any of them, except when a play called for his doing so for purposes of comedy, as in a father-daughter scene in *The Truth.*

Amelia Bingham, whose faith in *The Climbers* was completely justified by its reception from press and public, stayed in the headlines pretty steadily throughout her life. Born Amelia Smiley in Hicksville, Ohio, she attended Ohio Wesleyan and made several New York appearances prior to coming forth, and as an actress-manager—she was the first since Laura Keene of the 1850s—in *The Climbers.* Miss Bingham had her troubles with the press from time to time. She received severe reviews in Clyde Fitch's *The Frisky Mrs. Johnson* (1903), and when she opened in April of 1907 in *The Lilac Room,* a comedy by Evelyn Greenleaf Sutherland and Beulah Marie Dix, the critics dismissed it with considerable scorn. The opening took place on Wednesday evening. No performance was given on Thursday. But on Friday night, Miss Bingham did appear and in a curtain speech she said that illness, and not the shock of the notices, had caused her absence the night before.

"When I took this play," she said, "I thought I had a good property. But I have no right to complain, for out of six plays I have selected five money-makers. No one can ever tell just what a play will be—or Charles Frohman would never have refused *The Lion and the Mouse.* The critics have said

33

that this play is bad and that I'm bad and that the production is bad. Well, I have the theater for three weeks and I'm going to play the engagement." But Miss Bingham had trouble with her authors—*The Lilac Room* expired after four performances.

Miss Bingham's husband was Lloyd Bingham, hot-headed actor, who became engaged in frequent brawls. He had a fist fight with Robert Hilliard in Boston and later, in January of 1904, he selected a critic, the blond, rotund Acton Davies, as an opponent. Davies, after seeing the first act of James K. Hackett's production of *The Secret of Polichinelle* at the Madison Square Theater, went into the café of the Hoffman House for a drink. He was in a chair when Bingham came up to him and punched him in the face, knocking him and the chair to the floor. Davies, bleeding freely, wanted to continue the fight, but Bingham was led to the door. Davies had suffered a bitten finger when he grappled with Bingham on the floor and when he rose, brushing himself and nursing his injured finger, he said, "Mr. Bingham is a magnificent cannibal. My only regret is that this will serve to advertise the rotten show [a four-act drama called *Olympe,* in which Amelia Bingham was appearing] that is at the Knickerbocker."

Two of the most restless players of the first decade of this century were Nat Goodwin and Minnie Maddern Fiske. Goodwin never hesitated to drop any play in which he was losing interest; he was always ready to try a new role, melodramatic, farcical, or classical. He failed utterly as Shylock in *The Merchant of Venice,* giving only three performances—but it is also a fact that he had previously announced a three-performance showing—and he fared little better when he took over Bottom in *A Midsummer Night's Dream.* He changed his plays even more rapidly than he did his wives, and in all his roles after *Nathan Hale* he found only two or three that he liked until he came upon Fagin in George C. Tyler's 1911 revival of *Oliver Twist.* Nat Goodwin turned to character acting in *Oliver Twist,* as he had to sentiment and heroics in *Nathan Hale,* but he was always at his greatest ease when he was playing comedy, as in *When We Were Twenty-one.*

"Goodwin's comedy," relates Katherine Grey, a Broadway star of yesterday, "depended upon the expression on his face, the irresistible twist he could give to words; he seemed instinctively to strike the right note. Yet it was not a case of hit or miss with him, for he had the accuracy that is fundamental in all art, touched as he was by the wand of genius."

Captain Jinks of the Horse Marines

Ethel Barrymore, playing the bewitching Mme. Trentoni in Clyde Fitch's
comedy of 1901, is shown here at the New York pier upon her arrival from
Europe (Culver Service Collection—Photo by Byron).

Celebrated Producers of the Early Century

1. Charles Dillingham 2. A. H. Woods 3. Sam H.
Harris 4. William A. Brady 5. Florenz Ziegfeld
6. Sam Shubert 7. A. L. Erlanger 8. Henry W.
Savage 9. Winthrop Ames 10. Henry B. Harris
11. F. Ray Comstock 12. Harrison Grey Fiske

This was the same Miss Grey who appeared with Goodwin in *Wolfville*, the dramatization of the Alfred Henry Lewis stories. There was a scene in which Faro Nell—played by Miss Grey—is left alone in a saloon. She has just learned that Cherokee—played by Goodwin—is in love with another woman, and she starts to drink to forget it all. Clyde Fitch, who was directing, took great interest in the scene. He wanted the audience to get Nell's feelings from the things she did, and arranged for her to go behind the bar, get a bottle of whisky and a small glass, pour out a stiff drink, and then lean on the bar, drinking sip by sip, thinking everything out. Nat Goodwin, upon seeing the scene rehearsed for the first time, yelled at Miss Grey, "Hell, Kate, that isn't tea you're drinking. You can't sip straight whisky. You've got to toss it down." He demonstrated, with a quick turn of the wrist, and turned to Fitch for approval. The dramatist smiled, paused, and said quietly, "I bow, Nat, to your superior knowledge and experience."

Mrs. Fiske went on the stage at the age of two and was actually a star at sixteen. She turned to Ibsen in the mid-nineties, later found success with *Tess of the D'Urbervilles* and *Becky Sharp*. She revealed her gift for high comedy in the urbane and ironic satire, *The New York Idea*, which had a remarkable cross-country tour after a comparatively brief showing on Broadway. Mrs. Fiske never had beauty but she had magnetism. She had, with all of her nervous, jerky manner, subtlety and finesse, and she was as much at ease in light-handed drawing-room comedy as she was in the problem plays of Ibsen. She was an actress who was eloquent in silence, as demonstrated when she sat for ten minutes without moving and without uttering a word, in the first act of Edward Sheldon's *Salvation Nell*, holding her drunken lover's head in her lap. Mrs. Fiske's style of playing had many champions—Alexander Woollcott was the most excitable, the most explosive, and certainly the most devoted—but there were also numerous detractors. Such as the pedantic J. Ranken Towse, who entered this dissent in the "New York Evening Post":

In all her "creations" she presented her own identity without any substantial modification of speech, gesture, look or manner. Situations, circumstances differed, not the personality. . . . Her ambition, which was more active and dauntless, inclined her to the more serious and emotional dramas, for which she had not the necessary histrionic or artistic qualifications. Her elocution was faulty and did not lend itself readily to emotional expression. She could be imperious, sarcastic, fiery and angry, but the deeper notes of passion she could not sound, and her pathos was hard and hollow, without the true ring.

Mrs. Fiske was always of the theater, whether behind scenes or entertaining at tea in her apartment in the old Murray Hill Hotel, and in time of crises her sense of the theatrical never left her. It was during her tour in *Mis' Nelly of New Orleans* that her train, in leaving Salt Lake City en route to Los Angeles, struck an open switch. The locomotive and four cars left the rails. The car in which Mrs. Fiske and her principal players were riding was not overturned, but all persons in it were thrown out of their seats, and it finally came to a stop with a terrific jolt. It was then that Mrs. Fiske's drawing-room door flew open and, as if she were speaking a well-rehearsed line, she called out, "Courage, dear children, courage! We are all in the hands of God!"

Minnie Maddern Fiske and her intelligent and theater-wise husband, Harrison Grey Fiske, who became editor and publisher of the "Dramatic Mirror," fought the Theatrical Syndicate relentlessly. In her touring she was always ready to play under canvas or any handy BPOE hall or vaudeville house because of the unavailability of Syndicate-controlled theaters, and she was actually without a New York stage until Fiske, after considerable manipulation, got control of the Manhattan Theater at Sixth Avenue and 33d Street. There, elated to have a roof over her head, she went ahead blithely with productions of *Becky Sharp, Mary of Magdala, Hedda Gabler, Miranda of the Balcony,* and C. M. S. McLellan's skillfully written but overlong melodrama, *Leah Kleschna,* the story of the regeneration of a girl thief. It was at the Manhattan that Harrison Grey Fiske broke away from the prevailing $2 scale with a reduction to a $1.50 top for the engagement of Dustin Farnum, something of a matinee idol of the time, in *The Virginian,* a big success. Here was a novel (Owen Wister's) that was turned into a play, and that became as big a money-maker as the dramatization of George Barr McCutcheon's *Brewster's Millions. The Virginian* lived again, and prosperously, in the silent movies and still again when the screen began to talk.

The Fiskes, Belasco, Otis Skinner, Sarah Bernhardt, Richard Mansfield, and other leading players enlivened the theatrical world of the time with their warfare against the Syndicate, but the choleric, pompous, and powerful Abe Erlanger, who thought of himself in terms of Napoleon, was contemptuous of such foes. Abraham Lincoln Erlanger was Buffalo-born and spent his boyhood in Cleveland. He was in charge of the cloakroom and opera-glass stand at the old Academy of Music and later served as call boy, usher, assistant stage manager, treasurer, and as advance agent. His partnership with Marc Klaw began in 1889 with their production of *The Great Metropolis,* and in 1896 the powerful Syndicate, which controlled about forty theaters during the first year of its operation, came into being. Ten years later, when the Syndicate was at the height of its power, its theaters totaled nearly seven hundred.

The Syndicate's opposition that counted, opposition that became a brazen challenge as the years went by, was supplied by the brothers Shubert, three uneducated boys from Syracuse who had quick minds and notions of a theatrical empire of their own. From almost the very beginning the canny Erlanger sensed that the Shuberts represented an actual threat to his monopoly, and it was after they had taken over the Herald Square Theater, and had moved on to get control of the Casino, the Lyric, and the Princess, that he remarked, "I'd break the Shuberts except that they're Jews: I don't want to hurt the Jews."

The Shuberts—Lee was the oldest, J.J. the youngest, and Sam S. the smartest, according to the opinion prevailing in their youth—were the sons of David and Catherine Shubert, who came to this country from Russia. The family settled in the old Seventh Ward of Syracuse. David Shubert was a pack peddler, and the family was very poor. The boys had some public school education and also attended Rabbi Levy's Hebrew school, but from their early years they worked industriously to contribute to the support of a large family, selling candy, fruit, and peddling handbills for the Grand Opera House. Thus they started in the theatrical business.

Sam S., while employed at the Bastable Theater in Syracuse, met Charles H. Hoyt, the prolific farce writer, and was soon a producer on his own account with road sponsorship of Hoyt's *A Texas Steer,* subtitled *Money Makes the Mare Go.* When Sam left Syracuse for New York, Lee Shubert, who, for a while, had been in the haberdashery business, was managing the Grand Opera House in Syracuse, and J.J., who had worked as a train butcher, was managing the Baker Opera House in Rochester. Sam S., bringing along some limited up-State financial backing, obtained the lease on the Herald Square, went to New London and there, in an impulsive call

37

at Richard Mansfield's yacht, talked the actor into playing the house with Tarkington's *Beaucaire*.

Later, deciding that the time had come for him to make his bow as a Broadway producer, he found a supposedly uproarious farce called *The Brixton Burglary*, written by one Frederick W. Sidney, and began casting it. He engaged the formidable Elita Proctor Otis, Jessie Busley, and the character actor named W. J. Ferguson, who was in the cast of *Our American Cousin* the night of the Lincoln assassination, and who bade his farewell to the stage in Jules Eckert Goodman's *Treasure Island* in 1915. On the evening of May 20, 1901, *The Brixton Burglary* had its *première*, and the house boards of the Herald Square bore the legend, "Sam S. Shubert Presents——." The farce, one of harum-scarum complications, wasn't much of a play, but the Shuberts had made their start.

Lee came on from up-State, and they achieved their first hit with the musical piece, *A Chinese Honeymoon*, following it with such productions as *The Emerald Isle, The Night of the Party, There and Back* (a comedy by George Arliss), *Winsome Winnie, The Girl From Dixie*. And finally, in January of 1905, they put on a big popular success in *Fantana*, a musical piece with an absurd book, a routine score, and some good-looking girls and scenery. It was done at the Lyric, with the players including Adele Ritchie, Jefferson De Angelis, an asset to any musical production, and the young and breezy Douglas Fairbanks, Colorado-born, who was on his way to a million. Sam S. Shubert was, by now, a young producer to be reckoned with: he controlled three New York playhouses and eight in other cities. *Fantana* brought to him and to brother Lee—J.J. was still up-State—a new and definite prestige. The year of 1905 was, then, one of triumph for twenty-nine-year-old Sam S.—but it was also to be one of tragedy.

Sam's lawyer and inseparable companion of his early New York years was William J. Klein, the first Jew ever admitted to membership in the Manhattan Club, and admitted after he had been proposed by an Irishman. There came the time when a trip to Pittsburgh to close the lease on the Duquesne Theater—the Shuberts' interests were spreading—was necessary, and Sam decided to go, with Klein accompanying him. They went by ferry to Jersey City and boarded the train, Sam taking lower 3 and Klein lower 1. Klein got out at Philadelphia to buy some cigars, and then, en route westward, they talked for two hours of the theater, astronomy, the booking situation, and the Russian-Japanese war. Both were in bed when, near Harrisburg, their train crashed into a freight. Klein was badly bruised and shaken; Sam Shubert was horribly burned and mangled.

"All of a sudden," Klein now relates, "the head of my berth was on fire and the foot was smoldering. The man above me fell out of his upper, dead at my feet. I yelled for Sam and he said, 'Here I am, Billy.' He was badly hurt; he was crying. He said, 'Get out, Billy, and save yourself.' I managed to get Sam through a window that had been blown out. I spoke to the conductor who was standing there. 'Isn't this awful?' I said. He fell dead. . . . Somehow they got hold of Sam and took him to the hotel. I found myself wandering down to the river. There was a woman there with only a nightgown on. She took it off and gave it to a man who had been cut like a zebra. When I finally got to the hospital that fellow was in bed alongside of me. He died with my coat around him. I found Sam at the Commonwealth Hotel. He looked up at me and said, 'Billy, are you here?' Those were his last words."

Sam S. Shubert's shocked brothers, making a pledge never to ride on a train together for the rest of their lives, took over operation of the firm, began giving the name of the Sam S. Shubert Memorial Theater to their multiplying cross-country playhouses, and went ahead with their play producing and the extension of their empire.

It was on Christmas night of the year 1901, the year that brought George M. Cohan bounding into the Savoy in his first Broadway play, *The Governor's Son*, and David Warfield into the Bijou in *The Auctioneer* as a Belasco star, that Mrs. Leslie Carter, of the flaming red hair, born as Caroline Louise Dudley of Louisville, Kentucky, had a spectacular success. Her play was the gaudy *Du Barry*—actually a melodrama, written by Belasco and produced with every trick he had mastered up to that time—the story of Jeanette Vaubernier, nobody's child, working in a milliner's shop, who became a courtesan and a court favorite of Louis XV and who finally, after being condemned to death, went shrieking to the scaffold. Mrs. Carter, something of a manufactured actress, came through with the emotional performance of her life as the King's mistress who hid a lover in her bed as the King searched for him, and she had the advantage of being the queen of an extraordinarily able company. Hamilton Revelle, an actor of many interesting engagements in the New York theater, had an important role. Revelle had been engaged after he had received a letter from Acton

Davies, the critic, who was, oddly enough, closely associated with the operations of the Belasco office. The *Du Barry* experience stays in the memory of Hamilton Revelle, as indicated in a letter of reminiscence that he wrote to me in 1949 from his home in Monte Carlo:

Belasco had everything against him on the opening night of *Du Barry* in New York. He was fighting the Trust, and the Criterion was the only theater he could get. The stage was too small for the huge production and carpenters had worked night and day, making a double stage, a kind of elevator, for the change of scenery. Christmas night was cold and snowy. The house was packed as the play began. Mrs. Carter's ability as an actress was a revelation in *Du Barry*. She made a personal triumph and the play ran all season, until the end of June. Meanwhile, Belasco had acquired the old Republic Theater in 42d Street and had spent a lot of money altering the stage and building new dressing rooms. We opened this house in September as the Belasco Theater and stayed on for another run before going on the road. . . . While the play was in New York we would all have supper almost every night at the old Fifth Avenue Hotel—supper with Mrs. Carter and her mother, Mrs. Dudley, and Belasco. When Mr. B. and I left we would get on the Broadway cable car and Mrs. Carter would always stand at the window of her suite, waving to us until we were out of sight. . . . And on Saturday nights there would be poker parties at my hotel—William Dean, Billy Elliott, Acton Davies and Mr. Dave, of course. Poker he adored.

Mrs. Carter trouped the land with *Du Barry,* alternating it with *Zaza,* and three years later she came forth in *Adrea,* written by Belasco and John Luther Long. When *Adrea* was done she turned again to *Du Barry* and *Zaza* for brief revivals. The Mrs. Carter–Belasco association had been an exciting and profitable one, and it was expected to last for a lifetime. Perhaps that would have been the case if Mrs. Carter, while resting at her summer home at Shelter Island, New York, had not decided to go on a motoring trip with a party of friends through New England. The tour paused at Portsmouth, New Hampshire, and there in mid-July of 1905, in St. John's Episcopal Church on placid State Street, Belasco's foremost star became the bride of a younger player, William L. Payne. When New York reporters went to Belasco with the news he refused to believe it and reached Mrs. Carter-Payne by telephone in Boston. She denied the report, but a few hours later Belasco, to his anger and chagrin, learned how very true it was. He never forgave her; she never again appeared under his

40

How Many of These Do You Remember?

management. In the fall of that year, on the opening night of *The Rose of the Rancho*, Hamilton Revelle received a note from Mrs. Carter and a bunch of violets; she asked that he give them to Belasco for her, wishing him every success. Violets had been the motif of *Du Barry*. Just before the curtain rose that night on the pictorial *Rose of the Rancho*, a night that was to mean so much to Frances Starr, Belasco called on Revelle, who delivered the flowers and Mrs. Carter's message. Belasco was touched, but did not speak. He hesitated an instant and then handed the bouquet back to Revelle. The withered violets remained in the actor's dressing room throughout the long run of the play.

Mrs. Carter floundered during the years that followed; the disruption of her association with Belasco brought her great days to an end. It became apparent, as the seasons went by, that she needed Belasco more than he had ever needed her. She lost standing as a star, but she remained in the news—she was always suing or being sued, or she was delivering a tirade against her former great friend and employer, or she was breaking with her new manager, Charles Dillingham.

There was competition, however, for news-column space from such experienced campaigners as Sarah Bernhardt and Eleanora Duse, the Italian actress of the beautiful hands, big black eyes, heavy eyebrows, and face of tragedy. Neither Bernhardt nor Duse was ever handicapped by diffidence. Signora Duse and her repertoire of plays by the Italian poet, Gabriele D'Annunzio—*La Gioconda, La Citta Morta* and *Francesca Da Rimini*—were brought to this country late in 1902 by Liebler & Company.

The German-born Theodore Liebler, who resembled William Howard Taft and lived to be ninety, was considerably annoyed because no one connected with the firm could deal with the famous visitor in her own tongue. Certainly his partner, George C. Tyler, couldn't. Tyler, showman out of Chillicothe, and producer of two hundred and more plays, spent his summers abroad for years. He had a way of motoring from Paris to Italy; he liked to sun himself at Sorrento with Tarkington and Harry Leon Wilson. But he refused to learn Italian or French or anything else, contending, illogically, that it might place him at a disadvantage in negotiations with foreigners. So Liebler went to his own son, Theodore, Jr., then in college, to find a spokesman for the firm in its dealings with Duse.

The *Signora* received him with great effusion, spoke with excitement of her coming tour and her appearances in New York, and said that she dreaded only one thing—the atrocious American weather. She pleaded to be protected against it and asked that the temperature of her dressing room be kept at an even temperature—say, 72 degrees Fahrenheit. She declared, in fact—and here her glorious voice lost all of its velvety texture —that if she entered her dressing room at any time and found that the temperature was *not* 72 she would refuse to go on the stage. The ultimatum alarmed the Lieblers; they well knew that the dressing rooms of those days were notoriously drafty. Liebler, Sr., took the problem to the ingenious master carpenter, who listened, grinned, and cried, "I fix!" He fashioned a thermometer that registered precisely 72 under all conditions, and hung it in the *Signora's* dressing room. It went with her everywhere, and no more was heard from her until her final New York matinee.

The d'Annunzio plays were not well received on tour, and the Lieblers were sixty thousand dollars in the red by the time the great Duse agreed to play a single farewell performance of scenes from *Camille* and *Magda*. The Metropolitan Opera House was engaged and could have been sold ten times. Duse's reception was more or less a continuous ovation, and she returned to her dressing room in great elation. The Lieblers were there on an invitation from Madame to tea. Suddenly, Duse's maid entered with a large pitcher of ice water; chunks of ice floated in the pitcher. The maid placed the pitcher on the table, and Duse, indicating the wall, cried triumphantly,

"Bring to me de termometer!"

The maid did so. Duse smiled, looked at it, plunged it into the icy water, and then began to serve tea. For once Duse's beautiful hands did not hold the attention of her audience; all eyes were upon the thermometer. Then Duse began to speak, charmingly and gaily. Everybody in America had been so kind. Even our atrocious weather had been kind. "It renn and it snow," she said. "It frizz and it blow hard. It is hot, it is cold, but de termometer"—and then she quickly took the thermometer from the ice water and looked at it once more—"he is always seventy-two!"

CHAPTER IV

The Early 1900s

SARAH BERNHARDT was a woman of no beauty at all. She had frizzly, red-gold hair, a thin, pale face, and a frail body. But her voice was beautifully modulated; she had sinuous grace in movement and in gesture, a compelling stage presence, and an emotional power that kept American playgoers clamoring for the sight of her, with two legs or one, for nearly four decades. She was a creature of whims and wild extravagance and self-indulgence; she was generous and she was penurious; she was kindly and understanding; and she was calculating and grasping. And she was money-mad throughout her years. Something of a blind passion for money-making explained, to a certain extent, her willingness to go on those periodic, 25,000-mile jaunts across America.

Bernhardt, of the unconquerable spirit and limitless courage and energy, was born of French, Dutch, and Jewish blood in Paris in 1844. Her real name was Rosine Bernard and she was the eleventh of fourteen children. She was an actress with her voice, her body, her hands, her eyes; and her genius asserted itself in her early school years. She made her first appearance in America in 1880, earning $180,000 in 156 performances on a seven-months' tour, and she was so delighted with her reception—and with her earnings—that she vowed that she would come back again and again—and she certainly did. She appeared in this country in the nineties and in 1900, in 1901, in 1905, in 1906, and on through the years, playing her final engagement in 1918. She toured with dozens of trunks and a swarm of maids, and through these tours, always highly Barnumized, she got to know the American road cities as few of our own actresses knew them. Other foreign stars failed dismally in this country. Duse was ignored in many cities. Mme. Simone, the Parisian actress, had a bitterly unprofitable tour, and it was said of Gabrielle Rejane that she never once drew into the theater enough

44

money to pay her salary for a single performance. But the amazing Bernhardt was nearly always "box office," although she always spoke in French, a language incomprehensible to the great majority of her American audiences, and regardless of whether she was playing the Maid of Orleans or Hamlet or Camille or Roxane or Magda.

Bernhardt was a trouper. She signed a contract with Sam S. Shubert for a coast-to-coast tour, but the death of that able young showman created difficulties. When she was told, with considerable hesitation, that because of the booking warfare between the Shuberts and the Syndicate many theaters would be unavailable and that she would have to do much of her playing in a tent, she accepted the situation calmly, even gaily. It was a new adventure for her, and she called her tent her canvas temple. One of the great nights of her lifetime came when she made her first appearance under canvas in Dallas, Texas, in March of 1906, playing *Camille* to an audience of 8,000. There was a gross in excess of eleven thousand dollars for the performance. She collected her share of that eleven thousand dollars—and quite a share it was—and she departed, with her tent, for Waco and Austin.

Lee Shubert always chuckled quietly when he talked of "the Divine Sarah." "We paid her a thousand dollars a performance," he once said, "and she was as willing a worker as you ever saw. She spoke very little English but she always understood you when the talk was about money."

And there is the testimony of Broadway's J. H. Del Bondio, who used to be associated with that wonderful old vaudeville house, the Orpheum Theater in New Orleans. "Bernhardt," he relates, "was in Havana and was coming to New Orleans. We got a wire asking us to meet her at the dock with a lavender touring car. That wasn't easy to find but we finally got it. I'll never forget her hair, dyed a bright red. She was carried down the gangplank—she had lost her leg by this time—put into the lavender car, and we paraded her down St. Charles Avenue. She was with us two weeks in scenes from *Camille* and *Madame Sans-Gêne*. We paid her off nightly. Every evening I'd go back and give her eight hundred and eighty-three dollars in cash, often in gold. I must say that she always seemed glad to see me."

Bernhardt was excitingly recurrent in New York and America in the early-century years, years in which the playgoers of our country were becoming increasingly familiar with the works of foreign dramatists. Barrie, with his *Little Minister,* took a firm hold upon the affections of American audiences and held his place from season to season; when he didn't want to work Charles Frohman prodded him into doing so. Such London playwrights as C. Haddon Chambers, H. V. Esmond, and Louis N. Parker, wrote for American representation with enormous relish. There was vast respect in our theater for the plays of Henry Arthur Jones and Pinero, who found New York his most satisfying outlet. Oscar Wilde delighted New York in the nineties with *The Importance of Being Earnest,* and Frohman now tried it again with good effect, putting it on with a glossy cast. Here was a comedy of manners with qualities of imperishability, a timeless bit of theatrical bric-a-brac certain to outlive any and everyone inclined to tamper with its farcical nonsense.

Ibsen was still being handled somewhat gingerly by the American acting profession in the pre-Nazimova era, but the resolute Mrs. Fiske did *A Doll's House* with considerable success and turned later to *Rosmersholm.* The George Bernard Shaw vogue did not really start until two young men of the theater, Arnold Daly and Winchell Smith, decided to do something about it. And to do it with *Candida,* a play which, as Alexander Woollcott wrote later in the "New York World," had been tossed into the dusty scrap basket by Richard Mansfield "after three scornful rehearsals eight years before."

Daly, an actor with a mind and heart for the stage, made his Broadway start as an office boy in the employ of Charles Frohman. He did not have the advantage of even a common school education, but he was a man of charm and wit and wistfulness and an Irish voice of lilting cadence and great variety of tone. He had done numerous minor roles and several rather important ones at the time he and Smith got together on *Candida.* Smith was a shrewd showman, a New Englander with an extraordinary sense of the theater, an actor-director-playwright who became the most astute play-fixer of the stage for a period of two decades, from *Brewster's Millions* through *The Last of Mrs. Cheyney.* He shared Daly's enthusiasm for *Candida,* and they set about engaging a cast for a trial matinee performance.

Daly talked to Hilda Spong about creating the title part for New York, and she agreed to do it, but after a week of watching Daly rehearse only himself and his scenes she withdrew. Dorothy Donnelly took over the role, Dodson Mitchell was the Morell, and Louise Closser the Prossy, and *Can-*

dida, put on for $398, had its first Broadway performance at the Princess Theater on the afternoon of December 9, 1903. The notices were by no means as favorable as *Candida* received in later years, the "Herald" complaining that "there is too much of a muchness in *Candida*—of talk, for instance" and that "Mr. Daly walked up and down the stage like a caged animal."

But *Candida* thrived. It moved later into the Madison Square Theater and into a regular run, and it came to be a play to tempt and to challenge some of the theater's finest players from decade to decade. Daly was the first of a long line of poets who told his Candida that in another hundred years they would be the same age and that the night outside was growing impatient. The Candidas have included Hilda Spong, who never quite forgave herself for walking out in 1903. The same Miss Spong, a native of Melbourne, Australia, stood at the window of her mid-town New York apartment on a morning in 1927 and watched firemen rescue two girls from a ledge of an apartment building just across the street. A few minutes later the body of a man who had been burned to death was borne from the building upon a stretcher. Miss Spong's maid came rushing in to her with the news: the man on the stretcher was Arnold Daly. A dreadful ending to a turbulent career.

The year in which New York discovered Shaw, via *Candida,* brought forth Enrico Caruso's spectacular debut at the Metropolitan; he became a part of New York life and just as much a part of the world that centered around the Hotel Knickerbocker as Diamond Jim Brady, or Wilson Mizner, or Charles Dillingham ever were. And 1903 brought hearty acceptance of the musical comedy team of Montgomery (Dave) and Stone (Fred); it revealed the slim and lovely Eleanor Robson as a star in Zangwill's *Merely Mary Anne;* it found Al Woods presenting *For Her Children's Sake* and *Queen of the White Slaves,* a twenty-thousand-dollar production in nineteen scenes and six acts; and it put William Gillette to playing in Barrie's delightful *The Admirable Crichton.* This was the whimsical comedy of the aristocratic family shipwrecked on an island, with the butler taking command for the emergency and returning to his former status after the rescue.

The New York theater, which had had its beginnings below Canal Street a hundred years before, and which had moved from Union Square into the Twenties and then into the Thirties and on into the Forties, now made

47

a stand in 45th, just to the east of Broadway. This came about with the opening of the new Lyceum Theater with E. H. Sothern in *The Proud Prince*. The man who built the theater and who produced the play was the showman who had given the drama valiant service at the old Lyceum and at the Madison Square. His name was Daniel Frohman, whose orchestra had played "Auld Lang Syne" on the final night of the downtown Lyceum just the year before.

Daniel Frohman was tall, gaunt, sociable, and often embarrassingly punctual. I don't believe he was two minutes late to an appointment in fifty years. He had a sparse chin beard, a mustache of sorts, and wore the highest collar ever made for man. He was a mixer, he liked the hubbub and the jostle of teas and cocktail parties, and he was as accessible as his more celebrated brother Charles was elusive. During the last three decades of his life Daniel, as president of the Actors' Fund, attended a merciless round of luncheons and dinners; he also entertained frequently in his famous studio atop the Lyceum Theater, its walls covered with autographed portraits of the great of the drama's past.

Uncle Dan, as Broadway got to calling him, lived a busy life that took him into his middle eighties; for a half century he devoted himself to the interests of the Actors' Fund. In his youth he was an office boy for Horace Greeley at the "New York Tribune"; he became a theatrical advance man and later business manager for the Madison Square Theater. He gave New York some excellent productions after establishing his famous stock company at the old Lyceum Theater in Fourth Avenue, but he was never the showman that Charles was, and after opening his new theater in 45th Street he was a negligible factor in the New York managerial field, actually retiring with the production of *Seven Sisters* (with Laurette Taylor) in 1911. But he became, more and more as the years went on, a personality in the life of New York. His favorite way of seeing a play was to draw up a chair beside the little door that opened in the north wall of his Lyceum studio and look down upon the stage. The audience could be heard but not seen; all that was visible through the chutelike opening was a small rectangle of the stage.

In the late November of 1903 Frohman married Margaret Illington. Her real name was Maud Light (of Bloomington, Illinois), who later became the bride of Edward J. Bowes, and who gave her most impressive performance in *Kindling*, a play that failed. Miss Illington and Frohman made

48

practical use of that trick door high above the Lyceum's stage. They arranged a set of signals for use during her engagement in Henri Bernstein's *The Thief*. When she became too overwrought in the emotional scenes in the powerful second act—the act in which she and Kyrle Bellew, of the classic profile, the silvered hair, and heart-appealing voice, were the only players—Frohman would wave his handkerchief to calm her down. They never got their signals mixed.

Dan Frohman, dean of the theater during his last decade, seemed to grow leaner (or his collar grew higher) as the seasons went by, and he often remarked, with his accustomed affability, that he was not only the oldest man in the theater but quite the tallest man alive. In the mid-thirties he went back to his home town of Sandusky on a sentimental journey of exploration and rediscovery, but he came away disappointed. He prowled the city, which had become gauche and overgrown and somewhat terrifying, in quest of boyhood playmates, but in Sandusky he was a complete stranger. He saw nobody he knew; nobody knew him. He wandered all over the place, revisiting the old circus grounds where he had once carried water for the elephants, without ever being recognized. Finally, and in tears, he took a train for Cleveland.

Frohman watched the theater's passing parade for sixty-odd years; it was always his notion that Mary Anderson, who had startled the playgoers of Louisville with a fine performance of Juliet at the age of sixteen, was "the first lady of the theater." "Mary Anderson," he said somewhat sadly when I called upon him on his eightieth birthday, "fell in love with her husband, and quit the stage." Mary Anderson (she married Antonio F. De Navarro in England in 1890) belonged to the pre-nineties beauties of the American theater; she vanished from the native stage in '89. But there were two women of comparable magnificence who were very much in the scene at the time Uncle Dan opened his trim playhouse late in 1903—Lillian Russell and Maxine Elliott, of Rockland, Maine, once known as Jessica, and daughter of a doughty sailing ship captain by the name of Thomas Dermot.

The legendary Lillian Russell, of the satin skin, bright-eyed and big-bosomed, was given to impromptu marriage and to impulsive generosity. She once had a dressing room maid named Lizzie, and Lizzie's duties included the care of the Russell pay envelope, which was delivered nightly, and in cash—no checks. There came a time when it was discovered that the figures written on the pay envelopes and the deposits made in the bank

49

did not correspond, and Lizzie was instantly suspected. The fair Lillian remained unperturbed as it was revealed that Lizzie had been appropriating sums of twenty dollars and thirty dollars with each delivery of her employer's pay and that she had something like five thousand dollars on deposit in her own name.

Miss Russell, in speaking later of her maid's systematized thieving, merely said, "It was all my fault. I had no right to expose her to that temptation and I never scolded her. I told her that I thought we had been together too long and I believed she understood why she was being dismissed." Several years later the quite solvent Lizzie found herself a man and sent Miss Russell a notice of her wedding. The prima donna immediately responded with a gift of a silver coffee service.

Lillian Russell had a passion for vegetable-growing and for the collection of Chinese porcelains. She was a woman of a serenity uncommon to the stars of her time. On one occasion, on a long ride to Los Angeles, her train was delayed some five hours. She realized that she would be late for her opening but she accepted the situation, sat quietly at the bridge table in her private car, and was the calmest person in the house when she made her appearance at her Los Angeles theater at eleven o'clock in the evening, finding that many of the audience which had assembled three hours earlier were still waiting to receive her—an experience not unlike that which was to be Katharine Cornell's when she began an after-midnight performance in *The Barretts of Wimpole Street* in Seattle nearly thirty years later.

Maxine Elliott, characterized by Nat Goodwin as a "Roman senator" in a casual summing-up of the virtues of his five beautiful wives, was never a brilliant actress. Not even a good one in many plays. But, besides her incredible beauty, she had definite charm, warmth, and womanliness. "Cold" was a word frequently applied to her as an actress; "limited" was another. But she was tremendously convincing in her tears, and it was always Clyde Fitch's contention that she could outsob any actress he had ever known. There was a scene in his *Nathan Hale* in which she had some emotional lines as she walked across the stage. When, during the course of rehearsal, these lines seemed devoid of feeling, Fitch struck them from the script—and only the sobs remained. They were enough. In a play of later seasons— Rachel Crothers's *Myself Bettina*, Daly's Theater, 1908—the radiant Miss Elliott shed tears that had never been written into the play. She had produced the play with her own money, opening it on a Monday night. The

"My Mother Thanks You—"

The Four Cohans, George M., Helen F., Josephine, and Jerry J., as they were when they were vaudeville headliners at the beginning of the century, and as they turned to the Broadway stage in *The Governor's Son*— Savoy Theater, 1901 (Ward Morehouse Collection).

Peter Pan, of Course

BELOW Here's lovely Maude Adams, duelling unconcernedly with the ferocious Captain Hook in James M. Barrie's immortal fantasy (Culver Service Collection).

The Drama's Ladies of the Century's First Decade

1. Minnie Dupree   2. Marie Doro   3. Jessie Busley
4. Laura   Hope   Crews   5.   Margaret   Anglin
6. Grace George   7. Elsie Ferguson   8. May Irwin
9. Marie Dressler

reviews appeared Tuesday. On Wednesday a trade paper, which must have had something of a grudge, printed a conspicuous article, with a photograph of Miss Elliott, purporting to give the gist of the criticisms of the previous day. But the presentation was venomous, using only the comment that had been harsh and omitting that which had been favorable. Miss Elliott was shocked by the unfairness of the article, and it was on her mind when she made her appearance at the Wednesday matinee. She went along well enough until she reached the middle of the first act. Then, as she was seated in the center of the stage, her voice broke and she burst into a spasm of uncontrollable sobbing. The curtain was rung down.

Before that disastrous matinee came about Maxine Elliott had appeared in two other plays by Fitch—*Her Own Way* and *Her Great Match*, both presented by an extraordinary young showman named Charles Bancroft Dillingham. Here was a man of the theater who seemed to take life and himself none too seriously. He was a *bon vivant, boulevardier*, and practical joker—courtly, jovial, and expansive, a showman who knew prosperity and poverty, who remained a gentleman during the last penniless years of his life, years in which he lived at the Astor by the courtesy of the hotel, and on money given him by his faithful valet. The magnificent Dillingham, of the pink shirts and the precisely clipped mustache, was born in Hartford, the son of a minister. He worked as a cowboy and as a reporter before entering the theater. He was ever given to pranks. When he was on the staff of the "Chicago Tribune" and assigned to the hotel run he was berated by his City Editor for missing some big stories and was quietly advised to get a few exclusives of his own. A few days later he turned in a story of the arrival of a Russian prince, who had come to Chicago to purchase ten million dollars' worth of farming equipment for use in Russia. The Palmer House lobby was soon thronged with eager salesmen in pursuit of the prince. When the infuriated "Tribune" learned that it had been the victim of a hoax a call was sent out for Dillingham, but he had prudently vanished. The pipe dream of the visiting prince represented his farewell to journalism; he was on a train bound for New York.

There were later many revelations of Dillingham's impishness, generally in his association with his great friend, Charles Frohman. Dillingham accompanied Frohman on many trips to London and the Continent. One day at the Savoy Frohman upbraided him for his apparent neglect of business. "You're wrong, Charlie," protested Dillingham. "I work while you're asleep.

I'm always working when you're in bed." The next morning, at six o'clock, Frohman was awakened by a violent clatter in the living room of the suite they shared. He got out of bed, went into the other room, and found Dillingham, in overalls, washing the windows. On another occasion—we're now back in America—Frohman wanted to see a play in a Jersey City theater and made the mistake of telling Dillingham of his intention of taking a ferry ride. He went to the pier in a cab and just as he was about to step onto the ferry a messenger boy rushed up to him, asked if his name was Frohman, and handed him an enormous basket of fruit. There was a card in the basket. It read, "Bon voyage—Charlie."

Another vital, if somewhat less elfin, young man of the early 1900s, was Sam H. Harris, short, slight, wiry, Jewish, who grew up in the tumultuous New York East Side that produced Irving Berlin, Al Jolson, George Jessel, and Eddie Cantor. In his knockabout youth Sam Harris, a showman of whom I have never heard an ill word spoken, did a little of everything—he sold newspapers, ran up and down the stairs of tall buildings as a telegraph messenger, delivered hats for a Grand Street firm, worked as a cash boy in a department store, operated a steam laundry, and broke into the theatrical business by putting the cyclonic fighting machine known as Terry McGovern into two Bowery-type melodramas, the productions of Paddy H. Sullivan and Al Woods. He became a partner in the firm of Sullivan, Harris & Woods, purveyors of such thrillers as *The Road to Ruin* (by Theodore Kremer) and *The Fatal Wedding*, in which Mary Pickford, as a child actress with beautiful golden curls, made her first appearance. Finally, Sam Harris met George M. Cohan. They liked each other instantly. They went on a Sunday outing to Staten Island, played a game of baseball, and by the time their ferry returned them to the tip of Manhattan Island they had formed a partnership that was to endure for sixteen years.

From the beginning of the century until 1905 the most industrious man in the New York theater, with the possible exception of Clyde Fitch, was the tall, lanky, likable Hoosier, George Ade, who turned from Midwestern newspaper work to the more exacting, and frequently more profitable, profession of the stage. He wrote a flock of hits—*The Sultan of Sulu, Peggy from Paris, The County Chairman, The Sho-Gun, Just Out of College,* and *The College Widow. The County Chairman* was a valid satirical study of small-town politics, quite the best piece of playwriting of Ade's career, and

The College Widow, an enduring comedy, gave a picture of American undergraduate life as Ade had seen it, lived it, known it. This play was an enormous success of the 1904–1905 season, and toured throughout the land. It was one of the popular stock company plays of the decade; it became a popular musical comedy (*Leave it to Jane,* with score by Jerome Kern); it was done as a silent picture and also as a talkie—and it is still performed by amateur organizations.

Dorothy Tennant was the original Widow, but the performance that did most for the play was that of Gertrude Quinlan in the role of Flora Wiggins, the wisecracking waitress. The role of Ade's hero, Halfback Billy Bolton, was created in New York by Frederick Truesdell and was played on tour the following year by Thomas Meighan, who later became one of the leading stars of the silent screen. But when *The College Widow* came into my consciousness, and into my town (the year was about 1913), the man who was the star of the show was the greatest baseball player of all time— Ty Cobb. It was the custom of the day for touring companies to recruit extras from local talent in towns along the route, and the management of that "Widow" company turned to the high school for its football team. The Savannah boys were engaged for two performances, matinee and evening, but they appeared for the matinee only because one of the group, going in early for dramatic criticism, made the observation that as an actor Ty Cobb was a wonderful ballplayer. Cobb overheard the remark, threatened to lick the entire team, and threw the S.H.S. eleven out of the theater. Middle-aged stage hands, electricians, carpenters, and bewildered passers-by yanked in from the street, grotesquely attired in football togs, went on that evening in *The College Widow.*

The George Ade plays were in vogue in the Broadway theater at the time the playgoers were responding to impressive productions from numerous managements. Belasco presented a swarm of interesting players, the youthful Jane Cowl included, in *Sweet Kitty Bellairs* and in support of Henrietta Crosman, a brilliant, West Virginia–born comedienne, who ruined her career by her temper and arrogance. Miss Crosman was, actually, the outstanding actress of the New York season of 1900–1901 through her playing as Nell Gwyn in George C. Hazelton's play, *Mistress Nell,* a part that came to her after she had worked for all of the great managements in her earlier years. Her press notices on the Nell Gwyn performance were so overwhelmingly favorable she couldn't go on for the matinee

53

following the opening. During her *Sweet Kitty Bellairs* engagement Miss Crosman became hostile to a member of the cast and went to Belasco with this ultimatum: "Either that woman goes or I go." So what happened? Neither went.

Those funny men, McIntyre and Heath, set the town to laughing in the musical piece called *The Ham Tree*, and Fred Stone and Dave Montgomery did likewise in *The Wizard of Oz*. John Drew pleased his following with *The Duke of Killikrankie*, and his nephew, young John Barrymore, made his first Broadway appearance in Clyde Fitch's *Glad of It*, done for a short engagement by Charles Frohman at the Savoy, with such players as Zelda Sears, Lucile Watson, Grant Mitchell, and Hassard Short in the cast. The homey *Mrs. Wiggs of the Cabbage Patch* came into the same theater for a long run and immediately became something of a national institution, with the performances of Madge Carr Cook, Helen Lowell, and William Hodge, creator of the role of Mr. Stubbins, taking their places with the outstanding characterizations of the time.

Arnold Daly and Mary Shaw got into the headlines and into court because of their production of George Bernard Shaw's *Mrs. Warren's Profession*. Victor Herbert, an Irishman with melody in his soul, increased his prestige immeasurably with his score for *Babes in Toyland*. Johnston Forbes-Robertson, an English actor of distinction, who had first appeared in this country with Mary Anderson, played *The Light That Failed* to critical appreciation and no business at all. David Warfield, who had won considerable attention with his Jewish peddler characterizations—in such make-up he convulsed a crowd at a charity ball game at the Polo Grounds by selling cracked ice—turned to a serious and sentimental role, that of Anton von Barwig in Charles Klein's emotional claptrap, *The Music Master*, and registered a huge success. The spry new producing firm of Cohan & Harris got away to a good start with Cohan's *Little Johnny Jones*, and undoubtedly because of the presence of the waggish and nimble Cohan in the role of the American jockey. And the eventful partnership of E. H. Sothern and Julia Marlowe began with their appearance at the Knickerbocker in Shakespearean repertoire. The date was October 17, 1904.

Julia Marlowe, of the cleft chin and the long black hair, was a disciplined, studious, and good-looking woman with a voice of unearthly beauty. Born in England as Sarah Frances Frost, she began her stage career as an

54

GARDEN THEATRE

Madison Square Garden—Madison Avenue and Twenty-Seventh Street.

MADISON SQUARE GARDEN COMPANY, - - - - Proprietors
CHARLES FROHMAN, - - - ~ - - - - - . Manager

Also Manager of the Empire, Criterion, Garrick, Savoy and Madison Square Theatres, N. Y. City,
and the DUKE OF YORK'S and VAUDEVILLE THEATRES, LONDON, ENG

Every Evening at 8 P. M., Sharp.
Matinee Saturday at 2 P. M., Sharp.

E. H. SOTHERN

Management DANIEL FROHMAN

IN

IF I WERE KING

By JUSTIN HUNTLY McCARTHY.

Cast of Characters.

FRANCOIS VILLON	E. H. SOTHERN
LOUIS XI	GEO. W. WILSON
TRISTAN L'HERMITE	STEPHEN WRIGHT
OLIVIER LE DAIN	JOHN FINDLAY
THIBAUT D'AUSSIGNY	WILLIAM HARRIS
NOEL DE JOLYS	HENRY J. CARVILL
RENE DE MONTIGNY	SYDNEY C. MATHER
GUY TABARIE	ROWLAND BUCKSTONE
COLIN DE CAYEULX	CECIL De MILLE
JEHAN LE LOUP	STEWART CAMERON
CASIN CHOLET	GORDON JOHNSTONE
ROBIN TURGIS	RICHARD PITMAN
TROIS ECHELLES	MALCOLM BRADLEY
PETIT JEAN	FREDERIC KAUFFMAN
DU LAU	PERCY G. MOORE
PONCET DE RIVIERE	NEIL MORAN
DE NANTOILLET	PEDRO De CORDOBA
AN ASTROLOGER	MALCOLM BRADLEY
TOISON D'OR, (Burgundian Herald)	CHAS VANE
MONTJOYE, (French Herald)	RICHARD PITMAN
CAPTAIN OF THE WATCH	CHAS REDMUND
CARDINAL	EDWIN VARREY
KATHERINE De VAUCELLES	CECILIA LOFTUS
MOTHER VILLON	FANNY L. BURT
HUGUETTE DU HAMEL, (The Abbess)	MARGARET ILLINGTON
JEHANNETON LA BELLE HEAULMIERE	LENORE CHIPPENDALE
BLANCHE	OLIVE MURRAY
GUILLEMETTE	ROSE HUBBARD
ISABEAU	IVY TROUTMAN
DENISE	MARGARET CORCORAN
QUEEN	NORMA HOBSON

E. H. Sothern found one of his favorite roles in the romantic drama pro-
duced at the Garden Theater in 1901.

awkward chorus girl in *The Chimes of Normandy*. She acquired her knowledge of Shakespearean roles by assiduous study, and she had distinguished herself in the poetic drama when she went under Charles Frohman's management, giving her talents to some decidedly inferior but commercially successful productions. But when she joined Sothern, who brought suavity and charm and intelligence to his Shakespearean readings, she was again in the theater that she knew and loved, and they worked together in a partnership that was extraordinarily rewarding to themselves and to the American theater. Sothern was a scholarly actor, unremitting in his discipline and tireless in his labors. He would play a matinee performance of *Romeo and Juliet*, an evening performance of *Hamlet*, and then never hesitate to call his company together for a midnight rehearsal of *Twelfth Night* or *The Taming of the Shrew*. "He drove us, he tired us, he killed us," says Atlanta's Gladys Hanson, who was with him in seven productions, "but we loved it. Sothern wears a halo for everybody who ever worked with him."

The first decade of the century brought popularity to numerous women of the theater—to such players as Frances Starr, Irene Bentley, Minnie Dupree, Grace Van Studdiford, Charlotte Walker (beautiful, but no actress), Mabel Taliaferro, Elsie Janis, Jessie Busley, and Blanche Ring, and increased prestige to some of the more mature ladies of the drama—to Virginia Harned, who had sex, vitality, dignity, and beauty, for one. And Marie Cahill, of the song-and-dance stage, for another. Miss Cahill stopped the show in *The Wild Rose* when she brought her humor and clear enunciation into her singing of "Nancy Brown." Where did it come from—and who wrote it? Well, it was the composition of a young man who was a pro golf instructor at a club near Boston. He had written the song for a club smoker. His name was Clifton Crawford. He went on the stage, became a popular comedian in musical comedy, and died in a fall from a window of a London hotel.

Other successful women of the period knew stage fame that was comparatively brief. Josephine Cohan, a beautiful dancer and pride of the Four Cohans, died before she was forty. Clara Bloodgood's short but brilliant career ended in tragedy. Margaret Illington demonstrated her skill in emotional roles in *The Thief* and again in *Kindling*, but she had less success in later plays and she was dead at fifty-three. Rose Stahl, a thin-faced, nasal, Canadian convent girl, came to Broadway after extensive stock company and vaudeville experience, and won the town's cheers with her spectacular characterization of Patricia O'Brien in James Forbes's *The Chorus Lady*. She fared well enough as a department store clerk in Charles Klein's moderately popular *Maggie Pepper*, but she did little after that. The lovely Marie Doro, daughter of a Kansas City lawyer, had earned her stardom by the time she appeared in George C. Tyler's impressive revival of *Oliver Twist*, and she contributed to the excitement of Frohman's revival of Sardou's *Diplomacy*, but a few seasons later she suddenly lost interest in the theater and took up residence abroad. Eleanor Robson was one of the theater's leading players when she gave up her career for marriage. Grace Elliston distinguished herself with her performance in *The Lion and the Mouse*, but another role of equal strength never came her way.

Consider, for the instant, the careers of Eleanor Robson and Grace Elliston. The dark and slender Miss Robson, daughter of Madge Carr Cook (of "Mrs. Wiggs" fame) went all the way from New York to San Francisco to enter the theater via the Daniel Frawley stock company. Playgoers of New York later saw her in the original cast of Augustus Thomas's *Arizona*. She played with Kyrle Bellew in *A Gentleman of France*, and she charmed playgoers in *Merely Mary Ann*, which would never have been written at all had she not gone for a bus ride to London's ghetto with Israel Zangwill, fiery critic and lecturer turned dramatist.

During that afternoon Zangwill gave her a pamphlet which contained his story of a London slavey who inherited a great fortune. Miss Robson was impressed with the stage possibilities of the story and upon returning to New York she went immediately to George C. Tyler, then a man of action. Tyler sent this cablegram to Zangwill:

CAN YOU DELIVER A PLAY ON "MERELY ANN SMITH" WITHIN A MONTH?

Zangwill cabled back:

WILL TRY. STARTING WORKING AT ONCE.

Playwrights worked rapidly in those days. They seldom required more than a month or two to complete a job; they occasionally wrote their plays—and well-constructed plays they were, in accordance with the fashion of the times—in a week, or less. In exactly a month Zangwill mailed the manuscript of the gentle, innocuous and human little comedy that was *Merely Mary Ann*. Tyler put the play into rehearsal, and presented it at the Garden Theater, giving Miss Robson the big moment of her career up to that time. She later did Paul Armstrong's *Salomy Jane* and

Frances Hodgson Burnett's *The Dawn of a Tomorrow* (critic Burns Mantle had told her there was a play in Mrs. Burnett's story). And it was while she was playing *The Dawn of a Tomorrow* that she gave up her career to become the bride (in 1910) of August Belmont—and to become a valiant worker for the Red Cross and a leader in civic and patriotic movements. "I knew when I quit," Mrs. Belmont said last year, in talking with me of her years in the theater, "that I had quit for good. And I've never really missed the stage because I've been too busy."

Miss Robson was done with *Merely Mary Ann* (except for a revival for matinee performances) and had not yet gone into *The Girl Who Has Everything* (by Fitch, and not so good) when *The Lion and the Mouse*, with Grace Elliston playing its fighting heroine, became something of a sensation at the Lyceum, notwithstanding scornful treatment by some critics. It was a play of frenzied finance, written by Charles Klein, who had a way of turning to the front pages of the daily papers for his dramatic themes. It had been rejected by Charles Frohman; other managers refused it on the theory that the public did not want, and would not support, big business plays. The manuscript finally reached Henry B. Harris, who had experienced instantaneous failure with Robert Browning's tragedy, *A Blot in the 'Scutcheon*, with Miss Elliston and Sarah Cowell LeMoyne in the cast. The Klein play had come to Harris from Daniel Frohman, whose interest in it vanished when Margaret Illington decided against playing it. Harris had been pleased with Miss Elliston's performance in the short-lived *Blot in the 'Scutcheon* and went to her about playing Shirley Rossmore, Klein's heroine.

"I read the play," Miss Elliston now relates—she has been living for years at Stockbridge, Massachusetts, serene in her retirement—"and I knew that it was sure-fire. It was the time of Teddy Roosevelt's fighting the trusts, and the villain of the drama, John Burkett Ryder, was supposed to be John D. Rockefeller and the heroine Ida Tarbell. Mr. Harris said he would produce the play for me if I would put up part of the money. I could not do this but the play finally went into rehearsal, with Richard Bennett as the juvenile and Edmund Breese playing Ryder. When we opened near New York we had to paper the house to get an audience. The play was such a hit the manager of that house wanted it for a second night. We went to New London and to the Park Theater, Boston, where we played four weeks, selling out. Then to the Lyceum in New York. Again great success.

58

I asked Mr. Harris about his promise to star me, as I was getting only $200 a week. He finally told me that his father or someone had the bright idea of sending out four road companies and that he could not make me a star because the road companies would not accept the play without my name. So I had to take the salary I was getting or leave. If I had been starred I would have made one hundred thousand dollars, for we played two years in New York. . . . *The Lion and the Mouse* was not really a good play. It was just timely and I was never proud of my success in it. I got very tired, whereas in *The Blot in the 'Scutcheon* I knew I had done a beautiful thing in a play of distinction. . . . Oh, yes—something else. Richard Bennett ate onions, and I disliked the odor when we played our love scenes. I scolded him about it and found a small bunch of scallions on my make-up table. I ate strawberry jam to sweeten my breath, but Dick went on eating onions."

Notwithstanding the dissent of Miss Elliston, the role of Shirley Rossmore was one that was to be played by a multitude of actresses during the next few years. It brought some of them a measure of stock and road company fame and for one of them, the handsome Marie Shotwell, it won a husband. Miss Shotwell was the road star of the company that was sent into the Southeastern states. When *The Lion and the Mouse* reached the river port of Savannah, Georgia, the stalwart Chief of Police Austin was in the opening night audience. He liked the play; he thought Miss Shotwell the fairest creature he had ever seen. When the curtain fell he went backstage, introduced himself to the actress, and proposed marriage. A short time later Miss Shotwell quit the theater and went to Savannah to live. She had become Mrs. W. G. Austin.

Henry B. Harris's production of *The Lion and the Mouse* reached Broadway in November of 1905, the month that yielded two other plays that have stayed in the memory of playgoers of the era. One was James M. Barrie's *Peter Pan*, with which Maude Adams captivated a nation; the other was David Belasco's *The Girl of the Golden West*. This was a roaring and flavorful melodramatic piece, whose big moment—around which Belasco built his play—comes when the blood of the wounded outlaw, who has been hidden in the loft by the girl, drips down upon the wrist of the pursuing sheriff, Jack Rance. Blanche Bates, who had started in the New York theater under the bland and magical guidance of Augustin Daly, and who had increased her following with her performance as the tragic Cho Cho

59

San in *The Darling of the Gods,* was the Girl of the Belasco production. Frank Keenan played the Sheriff and Robert Hilliard was the dashing outlaw.

It was another personal success for the dark, animated, San Francisco–born Blanche Bates, who became Mrs. George Creel in 1912 and who had never, in her long career, encountered rudeness in the theater until it came from Katharine Hepburn during the disastrous engagement of *The Lake* in 1933. Miss Bates forgave the pretty Kate, left the stage, went back to the Golden Gate, and there, in her lovely San Francisco home, she died after a quiet Christmas reception in the year of 1941. Blanche Bates was an actress of considerable power, if no great distinction; as a woman, she was warm, kindly, and outspoken. She had a quick mind. During the early 1920s, when she was appearing in Philadelphia, there was a fire scare in the theater. She stepped out of character, went downstage, and said, "There is no fire here. And if there were, what the hell would you do about it?" Her stunned audience stopped dead in its tracks. The play went on.

The Girl of the Golden West was undoubtedly the play for which Belasco had deepest affection. He told me several times that he hoped to revive it, and there were also murmurings from him about *The Return of Peter Grimm.* "But I tell you, dear Ward Morehouse," he would say, " 'The Girl' would go today. I'm going to write dear Blanche Bates and ask her what she thinks. I'll certainly write her." I don't believe he ever did.

In the 1904–1905–1906 era of the New York stage the well-to-do of the drama, including Nanette Comstock, Digby Bell, Frank Gillmore, Henrietta Crosman, George Fawcett, Isabel Irving, and Frederick Perry, flocked to Siasconset, Island of Nantucket, to join the actors' summer colony; players were rehearsing six, eight, ten and twelve weeks without pay; chorus girls were still getting $18 a week and paying for their own stockings, and there was jubilation at the Lambs Club over the success of the stagey, popular and handsome William Faversham in Edwin Milton Royle's *The Squaw Man,* which had first been done as a short play at a Club Gambol. . . . The bustling, firm-jawed, and hefty May Irwin found a serviceable vehicle in George V. Hobart's farce, *Mrs. Black in Back.* . . . Robert B. Mantell thundered into the Princess in overpowering Shakespearean repertoire. . . . The Hippodrome, calling itself the largest and safest and costliest playhouse in the world, built by Thompson & Dundy—Frederic W. Thompson, spectacular showman with energy and ideas, and Elmer Scipio

Dundy, better known as Skip Dundy, founders of Luna Park at Coney Island—opened with the spectacle, *A Yankee Circus on Mars*. And Ethel Barrymore with dramatic timing intoned the words, as she finished reading a letter, that ran, "That's all there is; there isn't any more."

The play was *Sunday* and her role was that of a girl named Sunday who, by the terms of a will, was left in the care of three Western cowpunchers. The producer was Frohman, the theater was the Hudson—and the author? The name of Thomas Raceward appeared upon the playbills and upon the house boards, but Raceward was as fictitious a fellow as George Spelvin was to be in later years. *Sunday*, a flimsy and ingenuous concoction, was actually written by three actors—T. Wigney Percyval, Horace Hodges, and Edward Irwin. The play was quickly forgotten, but that line spoken by Miss Barrymore has achieved a certain immortality. The Messrs. Percyval and Hodges refrained with great difficulty from using it again when they wrote the comedy hit, *Grumpy*, for Cyril Maude a decade later.

CHAPTER V

Enter the Poetic Drama

MAUDE ADAMS went on the stage at the age of nine months; she was still on it, playing Portia, when she was sixty, having returned to the theater after a long retirement to make a harrowing, across-America tour in *The Merchant of Venice*. Greatness, as an actress, was never attributed to Miss Adams as it was to Bernhardt—she was never the "actress" that Ada Rehan was—but the daughter of Annie Adams and James Kiskadden had something of a spiritual quality that made her appeal universal. The rippling laugh, the lilting voice, the odd toss of her head—these were attributes that endeared her to playgoers. On the practical side, she was the theater's star with the greatest box-office power from the time of *The Little Minister* in 1897 until *What Every Woman Knows*, eleven years later. Her name sold seats! It packed theaters. The evidence was incontestable. People went to see her who never entered a playhouse at any other time. A week's receipts of twenty thousand dollars for an Adams play in a road stand was a normal gross, and that was the day and time of the $2-top ticket.

Charles Frohman was fully aware of Maude Adams's potentialities when he put her into *The Masked Ball* with John Drew. He was quietly exultant when she again succeeded with Drew in *Rosemary*, and when she brought her girlishness and ineffable loveliness to the role of James M. Barrie's Lady Babbie in *The Little Minister,* he was certain that she could be sure of a devoted following for all the years that she cared to give to the stage. Miss Adams was in *Rosemary* at the Empire when Barrie, on his first visit to this country, saw her performance. He was enchanted with her playing and returned to London and wrote the role of Lady Babbie for her. And then Frohman presented her as a star.

Maude Adams had her failures. Juliet, for instance. She was far from im-

CHARLES FROHMAN

—PRESENTS—

MISS MAUDE ADAMS

In a Play, in Five Acts,

PETER PAN

Or, THE BOY WHO WOULDN'T GROW UP

By

J. M. BARRIE.

PETER PAN...............................Miss MAUDE ADAMS
MR. DARLING................................ERNEST LAWFORD
MRS. DARLING................................GRACE HENDERSON
WENDY MOIRA ANGELA DARLING.............MILDRED MORRIS
JOHN NAPOLEON DARLING....................WALTER ROBINSON
MICHAEL NICOLAS DARLING....................MARTHA McGRAW
NANA..CHARLES H. WESTON
TINKER BELL.....................................JANE WREN
TOOTLES........ }   { ....VIOLET RAND
NIBS............ | | ....LULA PECK
SLIGHTLY....... | | ..FRANCIS SEDGWICK
CURLY.......... } Members of Peter's Band. { ....MABEL KIPP
FIRST TWIN.... | | .KATHERINE KEPPELL
SECOND TWIN.. }   { ....ELLA GILROY
JAMES HOOK, the pirate captain..................ERNEST LAWFORD

SMEE............... | (..........THOMAS McGRATH
STARKEY.......... | | ....WALLACE JACKSON
COOKSON.......... | | ....WILLIAM HENDERSON
CECCO............. } Pirates.   } .....·..............PAUL THARP
MULLINS.......... | | ....THOMAS VALENTINE
JUKES............. | | ....HARRY GWYNETTE
NOODLER.......... }   (.......FREDERICK RAYMOND
GREAT BIG LITTLE PANTHER.. } Redskins. } ...LLOYD CARLETON
TIGER LILY.................... }   { .MARGARET GORDON
LIZA, author of the play..........................ANNA WHEATON
    Redskins, Pirates, Crocodile, Ostrich, Lion, Pack of Wolves, etc.

Here was the original New York cast of Barrie's enduring fantasy—Empire Theater, November 6, 1905.

pressive in the exacting role of the Duc de Reichstadt, the weakling son of Napoleon, in Rostand's *L'Aiglon,* and she was no more suited to Chanticler of the comb, spurs, and tail feathers than she would have been to Lady Macbeth, but these defects were not counted, and certainly not remembered, by her worshiping public. She was beloved for her Babbie and for her Phoebe of the Ringlets in *Quality Street;* for her charming Spanish heroine in *The Pretty Sister of José;* for her delightful playing as the indispensable Maggie Wylie in *What Every Woman Knows;* and for the most memorable performance of her life, given at the Empire on the evening of November 6, 1905, when she came forth as Barrie's Peter Pan. Barrie had great misgivings about *Peter Pan* when he sent his manuscript to America; he frankly told his producer that he did not have much hope for it as a commercial property, but Frohman did not share the Scotsman's doubts. He was elated with the play and talked of little else for weeks. He predicted that Miss Adams would be irresistible in her suit of leaves and that Peter of the treetops and the Never-Never Land would become her most popular role. And during the long run at the Empire, as playgoers from six to sixty came swarming into his theater, he had reason to be pleased with his foresight, but he was a man too free of pretensions and self-importance to go in for self-congratulation. And he was too busy. He was planning to send his star and her Barrie fantasy to every corner of America.

Maude Adams was an actress of good judgment and intelligence and with a sense of obligation to her public. She was always interested in reaching the young people of America. There were the playgoers of the future to be considered, and she insisted upon having a good number of seats selling at 50 cents available at every stand. There came an evening during one of her tours in *Peter Pan* when the line for the gallery box office in an Eastern city was a block long at 7:40 P.M. The regular admission price to the gallery was 50 cents but the house manager, knowing that he could get more for this performance, gave his orders, "Open up, and charge everybody one dollar." When Miss Adams reached the theater a few minutes later there was a teen-age girl sobbing near the stage door. The girl tearfully confided that she had saved up her fifty cents and had been planning for many weeks to see *Peter Pan* but that she didn't have a dollar and didn't know where to get it. Miss Adams summoned the house manager to her dressing room, told him what she thought of his actions, and demanded that there be a refund of fifty cents to every person who had paid a dollar to get into the gallery that evening. And if he did not do so there would be no performance. What happened to the young girl who had been crying? She saw the performance in a box seat as the guest of the star.

At the time the Empire first shook with cheers for the daughter of the Kiskaddens in *Peter Pan* (which was, as John Gassner observed in his *Masters of the Drama*,* "perhaps the most escapist play ever written"), there was commotion of sorts in New York's Thirties and Forties. The Gilsey House, a sporty theatrical hotel at Broadway and 29th Street, was still a favorite meeting place for people of the amusement world; theater folk also flocked to the Holland House and to Considine's and to Jack's and the Metropole. The Astor, in all its magnificent bulk, had reared itself at Times Square. Playgoers were discovering Sixth Avenue via the mighty Hippodrome. William Faversham, who had learned his trade with the fine Lyceum and Empire stock companies, had a solid success in *The Squaw Man* at Wallack's. Robert B. Mantell was roaring as King Lear at the Garden. Lillian Russell, still highly paid but on the downgrade artistically, was singing twice daily at Proctor's 125th Street. Viola Allen was engaged with a minor comedy, Fitch's *Toast of the Town.* Margaret Anglin was at the Princess in *Zira.* The long-legged and frequently funny Richard Carle was in *The Mayor of Tokyo* at the New York, and another laugh specialist, Eddie Foy, had *The Earl and the Girl* at the Casino. "Variety," the theatrical weekly, founded by the sagacious Sime Silverman, was preparing to come forth with its first issue. Burns Mantle, from out of Denver, was covering plays for the "Chicago Inter-Ocean." Ashton Stevens was the outspoken critic of the "San Francisco Examiner"; George Jean Nathan, Cornell '04, was about to enter journalism via the "New York Herald." And the brassy, flag-waving George M. Cohan, of the crazy dance and the kangaroo walk, had opened his *Forty-five Minutes from Broadway* out of town and had a booking for the New Amsterdam. He brought it in as his New Year's gift to Broadway, on the very first evening in 1906. It had been Cohan's intention to make it a show for Fay Templeton, who played the housemaid, Mary Jane Jenkins, but by the time the production reached the 42d Street the reformed vaudeville actor, Victor Moore, in the role of the slangy Kid Burns, had completely taken over.

The vogue of the dramatized novel continued. Numerous plays based

* Gassner, John, *Masters of the Drama,* Random House, New York, 1940.

65

on novels of the period—such plays as *The Virginian* and *Mrs. Wiggs* and *Janice Meredith* and *The Pit*—had been successful. *The Man on the Box* did well, as did *Zira* and *The Pride of Jennico*. *St. Elmo* and *The House of a Thousand Candles,* which were to come along later, had enormous stock company popularity. But *The Spoilers,* taken from Rex Beach's rugged novel, collapsed quickly as theater fare. *The Marriage of William Ashe* and *The Clansman* had brief New York engagements. *Graustark* and *The Firing Line* were road-circuit rubbish.

The Clansman, failing as a New York play (it became the sensational *Birth of a Nation* of the screen ten years later) introduced the novelist, Thomas Dixon, Jr., to the ranks of professional playmakers at a time when the names of many new dramatists were appearing upon the house boards. Rida Johnson Young, never to do a play of any consequence, turned out a popular college piece in *Brown of Harvard,* starring Henry Woodruff, a reigning matinee idol. Channing Pollock, of the bushy hair and the boundless energy, followed *The Pit* with a negligible comedy, *The Little Gray Lady;* then, in collaboration with young Avery Hopwood, a tall, gangling, yellow-haired University of Michigan alumnus, he brought forth *Clothes,* played with some success by Grace George, with Douglas Fairbanks in the cast at $40 a week. Edgar Selwyn, then an actor, took to playwriting as a part-time job, and it was definitely full-time work for such newcomers to the craft as James Forbes, Rachel Crothers, and Richard Walton Tully. Forbes, a newspaperman and press agent with a talent for pungent dialogue, who went on to write a sound and sobering play in *The Famous Mrs. Fair,* contributed a money-making hit in the trashy *Chorus Lady,* expanded from a vaudeville sketch. And Rachel Crothers, native of Bloomington, Illinois, a one-time instructor in a school of acting, revealed an understanding of character in *The Three of Us,* a play of a girl in a Nevada mining camp who looked after her two younger brothers. Carlotta Nillson was the leading woman in the play; she was a good actress, and one who definitely knew her own mind. It was her feeling that a seven-performance week was all that she could do and give her best service to the play, so she positively refused to appear eight times weekly. Laura Nelson Hall, her understudy, went on at the Wednesday matinees throughout the run. It was predicted at the time of *The Three of Us* that Rachel Crothers could expect a lifetime career as a dramatist if she stuck to her job. She stuck and she got it.

The Squaw Man

Climactic moment in Edwin Milton Royle's popular play, with William Faversham, as Jim Carston, being clutched by his devoted Indian maiden, Nat-u-rich, played by Mabel Morrison. The body is that of William S. Hart, who became the famous silent-picture actor (Culver Service Collection).

The Girl, the Sheriff, the Road Agent

BELOW Frank Keenan, playing Jack Rance, the relentless Sheriff; Blanche Bates, as the Girl, and Robert Hilliard as the dashing outlaw in David Belasco's play of the Old West, *The Girl of the Golden West,* a success of 1905 (Robinson Locke Collection).

Murder in Old Kentucky

Tense scene in Augustus Thomas's *The Witching Hour,* in which John Mason, in the role of the Louisville gambler, Jack Brookfield, bends over the body of a man who has just been killed with an ivory paper cutter (Culver Service Collection).

New Yorkers were still talking of the big murder story of the decade, the killing of the celebrated architect, Stanford White, by Harry K. Thaw, heir to a steel fortune and married to Evelyn Nesbit, erstwhile Broadway chorus beauty—a murder that took place on the roof of Madison Square Garden near the close of a second-rate musical revue called *Mamzelle Champagne* —when the theater received a drama of dignity and importance, a disturbing and beautifully written play called *The Great Divide,* which arrived unexpectedly at the Princess Theater, located atop a shoeshop at Broadway and 29th Street. Here was a play literary in its composition and imaginative in its ideas, not the work of any New York–trained dramatist, not written by anybody working for Frohman, but by a man from Chicago—by an Indiana-born teacher and poet named William Vaughn Moody. It came into the Princess on the evening of October 3, 1906, with Henry Miller and Margaret Anglin in the cast—but let's revert to the Chicago beginnings.

Margaret Anglin, who had played *Zira* in New York and the East, was doing this play in Chicago when Donald Robertson, an Art Theater leader in that city, sent her Moody's manuscript, which then bore the title of *A Sabine Woman.* It was Moody's good luck—and hers—for the script to be on the top of the pile beside her bed at her hotel—as she propped herself against the pillows for some midnight supper following an evening's *Zira* performance.

"I just took the first script off the pile," Miss Anglin told me some months ago, "and began reading. I got fascinated and couldn't put the damn thing down. My eggs got cold; the fuzz went off my Guinness' Stout. I read and read until I was through and I knew something had happened to me. I was crazy about the play."

The next day Miss Anglin reached Robertson; she wired Lee Shubert and called Henry Miller by telephone, telling him about the play and asking his approval of a Chicago tryout. "Who's Moody?" asked Miller. And later, when she was talking with the author in Chicago, after he had been yanked from the gangplank of a Europe-bound liner and told the good news, it was Moody who asked, "Who's Miller?"

Miss Anglin was now full of action. She asked Moody for a letter giving her a six weeks' option, he promised to write it immediately, and then she gave her thoughts to her cast, to be selected from the company members of *Zira.* The play was put into rehearsal on a Thursday, and the opening performance, amazingly enough, was given Sunday evening. Before the curtain rose Miss Anglin again asked Moody for his promised letter of option and urged him to write it quickly, with an eyebrow pencil, but he didn't. She played the first act and the second and then she struck—no letter, no third act.

"Mr. Moody," the actress recalls, "came rushing backstage, the color of an oyster. They all went searching for a lawyer, and who do you suppose they found? A Shubert lawyer! They went into a huddle below stage. We were all waiting on stage. I was called down to see the agreement and there it was, with Moody's signature. I got the thing and pushed it down into my dress and it came popping up during the third act, which we began playing after a delay of an hour and ten minutes. Moody came back after the play and said he was terribly sorry for what had happened. There was no applause at the end of the play. The audience just sat there, impressed and kind of stunned. We gave only four performances. Lee Shubert never saw it in Chicago. Jack Miller (as she always called Henry Miller) never saw it, but the next season he was ready to play it in New York."

So that was the Chicago story of *A Sabine Woman*. Moody rewrote parts of the play, the title was changed to *The Great Divide*, some new players were engaged, and some scenery built—scenery was just built and painted in those days and the theater somehow got along without the services of the specialist to be known as the scene designer—and the play was taken to Washington and to Pittsburgh on a pre-Broadway tour. Henry Miller came to regret those bookings; the press of both cities was hostile. All of the Pittsburgh critics were violent in their disapproval; so were those of Washington with the exception of Frank P. Morse, who covered the drama for the "Times." The "Post's" critic went to the play in no condition to write about *The Great Divide* or anything else, but he did put together a notice that bristled with offensive personal remarks about Miller and Miss Anglin and others of the cast. The infuriated Miller spent the better part of the week trying to find the "Post's" critic, it being his announced intention to beat him up. The "Post" reviewer was fired a short time later; Morse was hired from the "Times" to take over the job. And it was his Washington review of the Moody drama that led to a lifelong friendship with Henry Miller.

Margaret Anglin was disturbed, of course, by the Washington and Pittsburgh notices, but they did not upset her as did the apparent unconcern of playwright Moody, who would sit for hours upon the porch of Pittsburgh's Schenley Park Hotel, rocking, smoking his pipe, meditating, and stroking his auburn beard. *The Great Divide*, a drama of conflict between the Puritanism of New England and the freedom of the Great West, was brought into New York quietly by an apprehensive management and opened at the Princess the same night that Nat Goodwin and Edna Goodrich (the beautiful and then current Mrs. Goodwin) arrived at the Bijou in a scanty farce, *The Genius*, written by William and Cecil B. de Mille. *The Great Divide* was acclaimed by the New York press, being accepted as a drama of deep and vital passions, of technical grace and dramatic strength. The "Sun" paid this tribute:

It is abundantly clear that no play of the present season has equalled it either in calibre or execution, except only Pinero's *His House in Order*, and even this strikes less true and deep into the wells of human impulse and passion. . . . To say that it is the best product of the American drama thus far would doubtless be extravagant; yet the fact remains that it is inspired by precisely that fullness and wholesomeness of feeling and accomplished with precisely that technical firmness, the lack of which has thus far proved the cardinal defect of our most vivacious and amusing playwrights.

Margaret Anglin and Henry Miller came through magnificently in the roles of Ruth Jordan and Stephen Ghent. The rush of playgoers to the box office of the Princess began early the next morning. *The Great Divide* was Miller's biggest success over a long career, and for Miss Anglin it was the play of a lifetime. They had a run of eight months in New York. They were devoted friends, with vast respect for each other's abilities. But the next season, on tour, they weren't speaking. The theater is like that.

During that fall of 1906 the Princess, jammed for the regular performances of *The Great Divide*, was the scene of additional commotion as a remarkable young Russian actress, Alla Nazimova, who had learned English in five months, came forth in a series of matinees of Ibsen's *Hedda Gabler*. Ibsen had never been a success in New York, and Henry Miller, who sponsored Nazimova, planned only four matinees, but she so fascinated her audiences that the performances were continued for two months. After the first of the year she turned to *A Doll's House*, which had been done by Mrs. Fiske and Ethel Barrymore.

Nazimova was born in a little town on the Black Sea. Self-educated, she was the daughter of a druggist. She had blue-black hair, large black eyes, white skin, a soft voice; and she could double herself up like a snake. She frequently gave the impression of great height on the stage. She came to New York with a company of Russian players and startled some discovery-minded New York playgoers, including Grace George and Margaret Anglin, as she presented the viciousness, the mystery and desperation of Hedda, the girlishness and spontaneity and introspection of Nora. Grace George went back to William A. Brady with words of great excitement about the young Russian. Miss Anglin gave a similar report to Miller, who got to Nazimova as Brady was thinking it over. Nazimova's company returned to Russia but she stayed, learned English under the tutelage of Caroline Harris, the mother of Richard Barthelmess, an actress engaged by Miller for the job. Then, as curious and skeptical New York critics sat in judgment in the upstairs Princess, she made her English-speaking debut. In less than a decade she was established as the first Ibsen actress of America.

Alan Dale, the critic, first saw Nazimova when she was Nasimoff, playing with her Russian co-workers in something quite incomprehensible, and it was after her success at the Princess that he made these appreciative observations in the "Green Book," a famous theatrical monthly of the period:

Unlike most New York critics, I don't know a word of Russian (my colleagues are, of course, very fluent and at their ease in the language of the ski and koff and vitch), but in spite of that degrading fact, I spotted an enigmatic personality in that company's leading woman. I loved the way she wept in *The Chosen People*. Our emotional actresses weep from their temples and their foreheads. Afraid to ruin their make-up. Nazimova shed her tears from her eyes, mopped them with a handkerchief, and at the end of her grief, she actually had a red nose.

The human play factory that was Clyde Fitch continued operations. He became busier and busier and richer and richer. He won critical approval with some of his plays, notably *Captain Jinks of the Horse Marines* and *The Girl with the Green Eyes*, but he was frequently blasted by the reviewers. Consider the severity of this report from the critic of the "New York Press" in that publication's issue of January 31, 1905:

Another of Clyde Fitch's salacious, talky, preposterous and futile plays was brought into Broadway last night. In the Herald Square Theater Blanche Walsh appeared in *The Woman in the Case*, a pretense at "refined" melodrama that was hideously vulgar. Lest the impression might obtain

70

that Mr. Fitch was not entirely responsible for the work it is said in the programme that all was "new and original." That was superfluous. No one could mistake the source of the piece. It was the Fitch of *The Coronet of the Duchess*. He has been going from bad to worse. He seems to be possessed with the same craze as Pinero. He has no more thought of the bright and diverting themes of his early days, which brought him fame and fortune, but, like the Englishman, besmirches his reputation and strikes at his popularity by keeping his characters in immorality. It was a remarkable first night. It saw the star outplayed in the climax by Dorothy Dorr and the audience cheering the minor player while it limited itself to handclaps for Miss Walsh. There was plenty of applause, but it came from a set of men who warmed at the sight of the willful blonde drinking herself stupid, uttering picturesque curses and hiccoughs, and fondling a fat politician who, when slapped on the cheek, returned the insult by writing a check.

The happiest incident of the evening was at the end of the third act, when Mr. Fitch announced he was "going away" and that it would be a long time before he would appeal to playgoers again. Reflection ought to do Mr. Fitch much good. Should he resolve to turn himself again to the bright side of life, and not grind out "plays" as a grocer's clerk would a pound of coffee or spice, then he will be a favorite as of old.

Fitch shrugged, went ahead with his labors, and by the time January 7, 1907, came around *The Woman in the Case* was something that he had quite forgotten. That mid-winter evening of 1907 brought the simultaneous opening of two of his plays—*The Straight Road*, with the same Blanche Walsh, daughter of a well-known politician who was the one-time warden of the Tombs, and *The Truth*, written for Clara Bloodgood. Fitch attended the performance of *The Truth* at the Criterion, occupying a box with Virginia Gerson, his great friend through many years, and when the last curtain fell he went upon the stage and made a speech. He was then told that there were calls for him at the Astor and he rushed across the street and made a second speech. The next morning he did not shrug off the indifferent reviews accorded *The Truth;* the dissent of the critics fairly overwhelmed him. He favored *The Truth* above nearly everything else he had ever written.

During the theatrically tumultuous year of 1907 George M. Cohan, divorced by Ethel Levey, married a Catholic girl, Agnes Nolan, in a ceremony at Freehold, New Jersey; John Drew introduced a new leading woman in the Continent-trained Billie Burke; Walter Hampden turned to

71

Biblical drama with *The Servant in the House*, playing a character that was a counterpart of Christ; Irving Berlin, a skinny East Side boy with a genius for melody, became a singing waiter at Nigger Mike's in Chinatown; and death came to Richard Mansfield after he had played a farewell engagement in repertoire at the New Amsterdam. His final performance as Peer Gynt, the legendary Scandinavian, was one of the most impressive of his life.

And it was in 1907 that Paul Armstrong was accepted as a dramatist, Augustus Thomas went in for telepathy and hypnotism, and Oscar Hammerstein sat back contentedly on the roof of his famous Victoria theater, Broadway and 42d Street, enjoying his garden and fresh milk from his cow, which was kept in a roof stall.

Things were then going well with the Victoria, a variety house of sensational acts, and with the Manhattan Opera House, built by the one-time cigar maker to give competition to the Metropolitan, a New York institution since 1883. He had no directors and no subscription list, and his first season was not expected to last a month, but he introduced many new and beautiful voices and he brought music-lovers surging into 34th Street. When he eventually sold out to the Metropolitan he was broke, but he bluffed his competitor into the belief that he would continue for another season. He signed an agreement that he would not give grand opera in New York for ten years and he had difficulty concealing his exuberance as he got a fancy price, $1,200,000.

Augustus Thomas's interest in telepathy, to which he had given many months of study in his home at New Rochelle, was revealed in his drama, *The Witching Hour*. Thomas, upon completion of the play, went instantly to his friend Charles Frohman and read the play in Frohman's apartment in the old Sherry building at Fifth Avenue and 44th Street. Frohman expressed great enthusiasm when the dramatist finished, and they talked immediately of a cast, deciding that John Mason was the man to play Jack Brookfield, the gambler. But when Thomas, as he recorded in his autobiography, "The Print of My Remembrance," * saw Frohman several days later the producer had cooled off. His brother Daniel had read the play and hadn't liked it. And Dan, with that report, cost C.F. a quarter of a million. *The Witching Hour* was probably the strongest play the brothers Shubert ever did.

* Charles Scribner's Sons, New York, 1922.

Paul Armstrong was a subject of controversial discussion in the Broadway area, from his days in sports writing under the name of Right Cross to his death from a heart attack in 1915. The legend of the man persists to this day, and there is still talk of him at the bar of The Players, in the grill of the Lambs, in corners of Hollywood where erstwhile folk of the New York stage, solvent but discontented, gather for reminiscence about the glory of the theater. Sharp-tongued appreciation of Armstrong is also to be had in the state of Maryland and from H. L. Mencken, the sage of Baltimore, and an authority on Armstrong & Mizner and practically everything else. It was from Mencken, as we strolled along Charles Street, that I got such comment as this:

"Armstrong? He had a place at Annapolis and he used to stop over in Baltimore on his way to and from New York. I thus saw him often and got to know him well. He was a fellow of somewhat burly make-up, with broad shoulders, and he wore a dreadful little goatee that gave him a fierce aspect. This was helped by a large black felt hat that he commonly sported. He was actually, however, a very sentimental man and I have seen him shed tears at his own dinner table over the sufferings of the heroines of his plays. He had an enormous facility and could write a three-act play in not more than six days. If he had lived he would have been one of the greatest of all movie writers. His thoughts were turning in that direction, and he had some magnificent ideas."

It was George C. Tyler who went to Armstrong with a volume of Bret Harte stories, as he was to do later with a book of O. Henry stories, and told him to shut himself in and read it. Armstrong did and came out with an outline for *Salomy Jane*, a vigorous tale of romantic Western life, a story of hate and love and a heroine's faith. Tyler approved and told him to write it into a play. He did this in ten days. Tyler submitted the manuscript to Eleanor Robson, offering her the title role, which she accepted. He then engaged H. B. Warner, Holbrook Blinn, and Ada Dwyer, hired the experienced Hugh Ford to do the staging, and put the play into rehearsal. It opened at the Liberty and sold out the second night. Paul Armstrong was on his way.

Florenz Ziegfeld, a man with an engaging smile and hawklike nose, son of the one-time president of the Chicago Musical College, and Henry W. Savage, tall, heavy, harsh, and impressive, formerly a Boston real-estate operator, were musical show competitors of the time. Ziegfeld's first *Follies*, that of 1907, actually marked the beginning of the American revue as the theater was to know it for the next quarter of a century. Ziegfeld, with considerably more temperament than anybody he ever managed, all the way from Sandow the Strong Man and Anna Held to Will Rogers and Marilyn Miller, squandered money (not necessarily his own) on his productions and on his whims and affectations, such as imported lavender shirts, thousand-word telegrams, hour-long talks by long distance, dinners of quail and venison and terrapin, private cars and royal suites on ocean liners, priceless collections of jade and glass elephants, a private zoo for his daughter (Patricia Burke Ziegfeld) at Hastings-on-Hudson, greenhouses and swimming pools and a fleet of motor cars that included two Rolls Royces and a Mercedes. He thought nothing of having terrapin brought from Baltimore by messenger, after being cooked to order there by a special chef, or of sending to South America for a rare orchid, or to Africa for a baby elephant. When a stage setting was presented to him in its entirety for the first time at rehearsals he would casually order all of it scrapped if a detail or two displeased him, and at a cost of thousands of dollars, but he was also very quick to insist that unnecessary electric lights be turned off, and he complained about the cost of spring water, and the size of his telephone bill.

He had a remarkable memory and a vexatious way of recalling the price of a pair of last year's silk stockings. In selecting girls for his shows he always insisted that the trimness of ankles was as important as beauty of face and instructed his faithful Goldie (Mathilda Golden Stanton, his secretary for years) to observe an applicant's ankles before showing her into his presence.

"When he dictated to me," says Goldie, in her description of the Ziegfeldian nightmare, "it was usually when he was lying in bed and I was on the telephone. He would run practically the entire letter together in one sentence, though it be pages long, but when the letter was done his urgency was emphasized. And then, after dictating a letter or a telegram, he would write it all out in longhand, and have it taken to the person for whom it was intended, with the messenger riding in his Rolls Royce."

Ziegfeld was cordially disliked by many of his fellow showmen, as well as by several of his immediate associates, but it was readily conceded that he was a master in putting together the stunning Ziegfeld-type revue. His

74

ingredients included, first, beautiful girls, second, good comedians, and third, lush backgrounds. His *Follies* were eye-filling spectacles, but he was showman enough to realize that girls, costumes, and scenery weren't enough—that laughs were also needed. Hence the presence, as the years went by, of such funnymen as Will Rogers, Bert Williams, Andrew Toombes, Leon Errol, Frank Tinney, Ed Wynn, Eddie Cantor, and W. C. Fields—the finest talent in the way of comedians that the theater afforded.

The first *Follies*, only a moderate success and actually a minor entertainment in comparison with Savage's bountiful *Merry Widow*, came along in a time of such musical pieces as *Top o' the World, Knight for a Day*, and George M. Cohan's *The Talk of New York*, in which Victor Moore, again appearing as Kid Burns, proved his right to stardom. But *The Merry Widow* was the sensation of the day. The shrewd, austere Henry W. Savage, who was never a handshaker, had a facility for putting the right people in important parts—a casting skill which deserted him momentarily when he engaged Edwin Stevens for the title role in Molnar's *The Devil*.

Savage was preparing a production of *The Devil* just as the same play, in another translation, was being secretly rehearsed over a firehouse by George Arliss and a company assembled by Harrison Grey Fiske. Savage was in a mid-town New York barbershop when his barber, in the course of rambling comment, told him of the imminent Fiske production. The haircut was not completed. Colonel Savage, determined not to let Fiske beat him to town with the Molnar play, rushed out and began sending telegrams to members of his company, some of whom were then motoring in New England. Edwin Stevens was reached by wireless at Nantucket Island. He instantly gave up his plans for a holiday, chartered a steamer that took him to Woods Hole, Massachusetts, and from there he went to Providence as fast as the finest motorcar available would carry him. And in Providence he got aboard a train for New York. He and the Colonel, however, suffered a defeat for all of the frantic, last-minute rush. The two productions of *The Devil* reached Broadway on the same night—August 18, 1908—and the Arliss-Fiske production had the better of it. Arliss got a longer run. He used a sharper translation, and it was also true that Edwin Stevens wasn't in his class as an actor.

Colonel Savage refused to be hurried in his choosing of the players for the roles of Sonia and the jaunty Prince Danilo for the introduction to New York of *The Merry Widow*, which had been the rage of Vienna under the title of *Die Lustige Witwe*. Savage finally hired Donald Brian away from Cohan & Harris to create the part of the Crown Prince of the impecunious state of Marsovia and took a chance on the dark and handsome but obscure singer, Ethel Jackson, as Sonia. They were felicitous selections. Miss Jackson made her entrance in a floppy lace hat topped by a bird of paradise with a rise under the brim, a hat she got for $50 in Paris, paying for it herself. The Colonel bought her a $400 costume, but she supplied her own shoes and stockings. The Colonel had a reputation for being tight—very tight—and there was evidence of his parsimony in the fact that Miss Jackson, the outstanding prima donna of the 1907–1908 season, was shockingly underpaid—$125 a week. But she took it without protest, accepted the acclaim that the role brought her with an extraordinary calm, and gave up the role of Sonia after a few months, turning to the dramatic stage, in which she had little success. The first of a vast multitude of Merry Widows fancied herself in love with the profile of Dustin Farnum, but never did anything about it.

The Merry Widow score, written by Franz Lehar, erstwhile bandmaster of an Austrian regiment, was a New York success the instant Brian and Miss Jackson went into their waltz on the first night at the New Amsterdam October 21, 1907. Seven prima donnas sang and danced the role of Sonia during the long run. There was a matinee-goers' riot on the occasion of the 275th performance when 1,300 women scrambled for 1,200 two-feet-in-diameter souvenir Merry Widow hats, and real champagne was served in the scene at Maxim's, the habitat of such charmers as Jou-Jou and Clo-Clo and Lo-Lo, on the final night of the engagement. *The Merry Widow* became Big Business. Companies were organized to take the production to every state in the union. Merry Widow hats became the universal vogue in millinery. A nation was soon humming the Lehar music, which was to be heard everywhere in New York in that fall of '07 as playgoers applied themselves to other, and perhaps lesser, excitements—to the seeing of the dainty Mabel Taliaferro in Margaret Mayo's *Polly of the Circus*, to the contemplation of the fragile and spiritual beauty of Marie Doro in *The Morals of Marcus*, and to the appreciation of the suavity of John Drew and the delightful ways of the new Billie Burke in *My Wife* at the Empire.

And how did the redheaded Billie Burke, who had made her music hall debut at the age of fifteen singing two American songs, "Honeysuckle and the Bee" and "Nancy Brown," outside of London, get to be John Drew's leading woman? She had once gone, ever so pertly, to the Frohman table in London's Carlton grill as he sat at luncheon with Sir James Barrie, and she chattered on ever so brightly as he calmly looked up from his favorite dessert, melon filled with ice cream and sprinkled with cherries and slices of peaches. But she got scant encouragement. Later, however, when she was appearing in London in *Mrs. Ponderbury's Past* with Charles Hawtrey, a note written with a heavy blue pencil came backstage. It read, "I would now like to take you to America in a beautiful little comedy called *My Wife*, and to be John Drew's leading lady." The note was signed "C.F."

John Drew remained a fad and a fixture in the theater of New York. The revered Empire was Drew's theater, and there was always a crush of carriages in the vicinity of Broadway and 40th Street when his annual fall opening came along. He changed his leading women from time to time— Ada Rehan, Maude Adams, Isabel Irving, Ida Conquest, Margaret Dale, Billie Burke, Mary Boland—but he himself was changeless through the years. Drew was Drew—and what was that? A man of grace and humor, a polished, expert comedian who contributed mightily to the dignity and the stability of the American stage for a full half century. He set the style for the playing of drawing-room comedy; he had a great influence in forcing the taste of the playgoing public, in improving the manners of the American actor on stage and off.

Drew never had a glass eye, notwithstanding the legend that persisted for years—on several occasions he felt himself called upon to enter a good-humored denial. He was a star who married but once; Josephine Baker of Philadelphia became his bride in a ceremony at Long Branch, New Jersey, in the fall of 1880. He maintained an affectionate, paternal attitude toward his beautiful niece, Ethel Barrymore, and his brilliant nephews, John and Lionel, and for many years there was always an apple from Uncle John on their opening nights. Drew, a man of average height, with a somewhat large head, fine nose, and carefully kept mustache, was the theater's Beau Brummel. He wore imported shirts, ties, and suits, and he was one of the few actors to be admitted to the membership of the gentlemen's clubs. He belonged to the Brook and to the Racquet and Tennis, and to the Players and the Lambs. He came of a great line and he took his playing easily and effortlessly, his openings casually. So casually, in fact, that on the first night of *The Second in Command,* during a scene in which he was supposed to feign sleep, he actually fell asleep. Hassard Short, the juvenile of the play, turned from a love scene to find the great man snoring.

Mary Boland, in the years after she had made the transition from leading woman to character comedienne, paid to her former star this tribute: "John Drew was the very first of the completely natural school. I was with him in *Smith* and in *A Single Man* and knew him about as well as anybody ever did. He was a gentleman, a man of many kindnesses, and a great actor."

By now William A. Brady, who had sold newspapers on the streets of San Francisco as David Warfield peddled matches, was very much in the Broadway scene, buying plays, directing plays, putting on plays, looking for plays for Grace George—always looking for plays for Grace George. And going in for Shakespeare with Robert B. Mantell. By now Brady was standing on the 34th Street curb in front of the Savoy Theater, chewing a cigar, a contented grin on his face. His play in the Savoy was selling out. It was George Broadhurst's *The Man of the Hour,* the story of a young man, elected Mayor of a big city, who resisted corruption by the political bosses. The friendly and aggressive Henry B. Harris had reluctantly turned down *The Man of the Hour* after trying to interest members of his theatrical family—Rose Stahl, Robert Edeson, James Forbes—in a reading of it during a cruise aboard a Hudson River steamer, and the script had fallen into the eager and appreciative hands of San Francisco Bill, who once hired Warfield out of a dime museum on Eighth Avenue.

"Sure," said Brady, in talking with me of those early days, as he so frequently did during twenty-odd years, "Warfield worked for me. I gave him his first engagement on the stage in New York, and Maude Adams worked for me, too. She danced in my dramatization of Rider Haggard's *She* at the Alcazar Theater on San Francisco's O'Farrell Street. I think I paid her the magnificent salary of six dollars a week. She earned every dime of it."

CHAPTER VI

Walter, Sheldon, the New Theater

CLARA BLOODGOOD was a stage-struck New York society woman who thought she could act and went about proving it to herself and many dubious friends. "She was a person of wit and charm and culture," recites Grant Mitchell, Yale man and actor. "She always looked fresh, crisp, and well groomed. Her love for the stage was something to be respected. She was a hard worker and unsparing of herself. I suppose you know of her tragic end—do you?"

Clyde Fitch and Amelia Bingham, in their casting of *The Climbers*, selected Clara Bloodgood for the role of the caustic-tongued Miss Godesby. Fitch was so enchanted with her performance that he wrote a play for her —*The Girl with the Green Eyes*, a dramatization of jealousy—and her success as the tormented Jinny Austin led to his writing of *The Truth*. Mrs. Bloodgood went to the playwright's Greenwich house, Quiet Corner, to hear him read *The Truth*, and she left Greenwich, as he later wrote Virginia Gerson, "in a wild state of excitement." The New York failure of *The Truth* was as great a disappointment to Mrs. Bloodgood as it was to Fitch, but in the fall of 1907, encouraged by Fitch and Charles Frohman, she took to the road. The out-of-town reviewers were far kinder to the play than those of New York had been, but the road business was disappointing. Mrs. Bloodgood was frequently despondent, and it was a despondency certainly not lessened by the news that Marie Tempest, light-opera singer turned dramatic actress, had scored an enormous success in *The Truth* in London. Fitch, in a letter from Paris to Mrs. John Corbin, wife of the dramatic critic, made his own comparison of the Bloodgood and Tempest performances, saying that Tempest "does three times with the part what our Clara does except in the last act—there I prefer Clara. But in acts one, two, and three Tempest is brilliant, perfection."

79

The Truth opened its Baltimore engagement at the Academy of Music on a Monday evening. That night, or on the following day, John Emerson, who was stage manager for the production, was told that Mrs. Bloodgood had bought a pistol. He took her for a long drive and asked her about the weapon. She admitted having purchased it. She had it with her at that very moment, and she gave it to him. The greatly relieved Emerson then drove his star back to the Stafford Hotel and thought that he had saved a life. The next afternoon Mrs. Bloodgood attended a performance of Paul Armstrong's play, *Society and the Bulldog* at Albaugh's Theater, occupied a box seat, and apparently enjoyed the play. She returned to the Stafford and went to her room. At 7:40 P.M. John Emerson knocked upon the door of her theater dressing room; she had not arrived. Emerson waited nervously for ten or fifteen minutes and then he called the hotel. No, Mrs. Bloodgood had not come down; they were positive she was still in the hotel. But her room telephone did not answer. A bellman was rushed upstairs, and just as he was about to knock upon the door he heard a shot. The door, bolted from the inside, was forced open. The star of *The Truth* lay dead upon the bed. She had put the muzzle of a .38 caliber revolver into her mouth and had pulled the trigger. A small pamphlet, "How to Shoot Straight," was found upon a table. It was later learned that Mrs. Bloodgood, after giving her pistol to John Emerson, had returned to the same shop to purchase another. The Baltimore suicide, which was column one, page one news in New York, brought tears streaming down the face of Clyde Fitch. He refused to accept the theory that his dedication of the published version of *The Truth* to Marie Tempest had caused Clara Bloodgood to end her life.

Tidings reached New York's theater-town, during the early-century years, of the up-State operations of two friendly showmen, Lincoln A. Wagenhals and Collin Kemper, who were succeeding in modest fashion with low-priced, summertime stock, paying their actors $15 weekly, plus room and board, and satisfying both their players and their patrons. Binghamton was all right, but these men had big-time notions.

"One thing that was in our favor," the hearty Ohio-born Wagenhals told me a year before his death, "was that we liked actors. Genuinely liked them, and never owed one of them a dime. We tried to treat them right. When they went broke or died we looked after them. During our years as partners we buried forty-one players and sent their bodies home, and there was a lot of fine talent in that forty-one. Kemper and I spent a lot of time making friends. We wanted friends, but not partners. We never had any partners and we never borrowed any money to put on a show. We made a hell of a lot of money out of Broadway, a couple of million, but we were in it because we loved it."

Those amazingly successful showmen—they later brought forth such big-money wonders as *Seven Days* and *The Bat*, both written in collaboration by Mary Roberts Rinehart and Avery Hopwood—began their Broadway activity with a lease on the new and beautiful Astor Theater, erected by Meyer R. Bimberg, who was called "Bim the Button Man" because of the fortune he had made in campaign buttons. The house was to have been leased to the Shuberts, but the brothers had a row with Bimberg, and the Astor's control went to the young men from Binghamton. They opened the Astor with Annie Russell in *A Midsummer Night's Dream*, which was pleasantly successful for a month, and then booked Raymond Hitchcock's *A Yankee Tourist*, until they struck gold with their own production of a seven-character, colloquial drama that was called *Paid in Full*.

Eugene Walter now comes into these pages—and into the American drama. He was a swashbuckling adventurer, a one-time Army sergeant, Alaskan prospector, sailor, reporter, and theatrical advance man. He wrote a piece called *Sergeant James* in a boardinghouse in New York's West 51st Street as Edgar Selwyn paid his room and board, but nobody liked it and it never got to Broadway. Walter later, and notwithstanding alcoholic misadventures, wrote *Paid in Full*, the story of Joe Brooks, the thieving collector for a steamship line who, to keep out of jail, was quite willing for his pretty wife to give herself to his employer.

The writing of *Paid in Full*, Arch Selwyn now recalls, went along easily enough until Walter reached the third act scene between the gruff sea captain, owner of the line, and the wife of the embezzler. There he got stuck and stayed stuck for a week. Then, in the middle of the night, he woke, screaming "I've got it! I've got it!" He grabbed pencil and paper, the act was finished before sunup, and the entire play completed in another week.

The manuscript was sent to Dillingham, who turned it down. Then to Frohman, who read it and summoned the author. Yes, he said, beaming, he liked *Paid in Full*. It revealed good writing. It revealed great talent as a dramatist. "But," he said, using words that have been ringing dolefully in the ears of playwrights since the beginning of time, "it's not my kind of play." But would Mr. Walter—and Frohman was still beaming—be sure to bring in his next play?

Walter reacted like an enraged, wounded animal. "No!" he screamed. He advanced a step toward the short-legged, short-armed producer behind the great desk in the big, luxurious office on the third floor of the sacred Empire. He spat upon the rich carpet. He denounced Frohman as an old-fashioned fogy, snatched up the manuscript, and strode in a fury from the room. The incident so upset Frohman that he broke a luncheon engagement with Maude Adams.

Two days later the play was bought by Wagenhals & Kemper and they gave it out-of-town presentation, Walter going to Albany on railway fare borrowed from Frank Case of the Algonquin. Wagenhals lost some of his enthusiasm during the tryout and offered to sell the production, in its entirety, to Lillian Albertson, who created the role of the wife, Emma Brooks. Miss Albertson had faith in the play but not the ten thousand dollars, and during the time between the first and second tryouts she had many arguments with Walter, pleading with him to keep the play uncompromising, and frequently offering to bet her Merry Widow hat that she was right in every point she was making.

"Gene Walter," says Miss Albertson, "was a rambunctious little guy with a deep inferiority complex and a remarkable talent. I nearly broke his heart because I wouldn't tear into Joe Brooks in the final scene, the scene in which I was walking out on him, but it was my feeling that no audience would want to see a worm dissected. . . . Oh, there were a lot of battles, especially when Gene got tight in Rochester and I shoved him out of my dressing room and his finger somehow got caught in the door. He was always afraid no one would know he was the author unless he threw his weight around. But it was good clean fun, even when the company was not speaking to him in dining cars and hotels."

Lillian Albertson stuck to her convictions, refusing to make her readings melodramatic, and she was still the Emma Brooks of *Paid in Full* when the play was given its second tour. In Toronto the Arkansas-born Oza Waldrop, named for the Ozark mountains, joined the company as ingénue, and had the somewhat dismaying experience of playing to audiences of from thirty to fifty persons. Wagenhals and Kemper were now somewhat pan-

82

Kokomo (Indiana) vs. Old World Culture

The uninhibited ways of Daniel Voorhees Pike (William Hodge), home-spun lawyer from the Hoosier state, are more than mildly shocking to some fortune-seeking titleholders on a terrace at Sorrento in the opening act of the Booth Tarkington–Harry Leon Wilson comedy, *The Man from Home* —Astor Theater, 1908 (Hall).

Salvation Nell

Ornate barroom scene from the famous first act of Edward Sheldon's drama of the New York slums, showing Mrs. Fiske as Nell, the charwoman, pleading with Jim Platt (Holbrook Blinn), her sullen and drunken lover (Culver Service Collection—Photo by Byron).

C. F. and Mr. Dave

Charles Frohman and David Belasco
on a Boston stroll early in 1915, during
the tryout of their joint production
A Celebrated Case (Culver Service
Collection).

Clyde Fitch's *The City*

BELOW Hannock, the dope fiend, played by Tully Marshall (right),
struggling to retrieve the gun which he used in killing his sister. Walter
Hampden appears as George Rand, Jr.—Lyric Theater, 1909 (Robinson
Locke Collection).

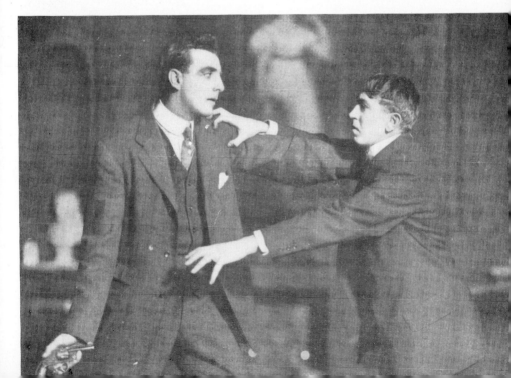

icky. Was their play worth bringing to New York—or wasn't it? They decided to leave the decision up to the critics and invited a few of the metropolitan reviewers on an all-expense visit to Toronto. Acton Davies of the "Evening Sun" was among those who made the trip. The New York jury turned in a verdict of unanimous approval.

Paid in Full won critical cheers as a drama of vigor and realism, Eugene Walter was accepted as a playwright of tremendous promise, and the firm of Wagenhals & Kemper, for which there was already a great deal of good will, was conceded to have a million-dollar property in its possession.

"Yes," Wagenhals told me in his recital of the days of his fabulous partnership with Kemper, "we made a barrel of money with *Paid in Full,* but the funny thing was that we really had a hard time with it in New York. The papers raved but we never got more than six thousand dollars on a week during the New York run. Sometimes we were down as low as fifteen hundred, but we were smart. Everybody thought we had a smash. Nobody knew those real figures. In New York *Paid in Full* was actually a financial flop, but we sent it on tour and we cleaned up. There were Emma Brookses all over the place. Helen Ware was one; Julia Dean was another. The stock companies went crazy over the play. We had seven companies on tour and sometimes they each played to figures like fifteen thousand and eighteen thousand dollars on the week. That was real money. That was ten thousand dollars a week profit per company. *Paid in Full* was more than a good play; it was just about the first intimate play."

The year of 1908 didn't belong entirely to Eugene Walter, but you might have thought so had you heard him holding forth in such meeting places as Rector's and the Knickerbocker following the opening of *Paid in Full*— bluster and self-satisfaction heightened no end by the presentation in the same year of his melodrama of virtue *versus* villainy in the Canadian wilds, a piece entitled *The Wolf,* put on by the steadily expanding Shuberts at the Bijou.

There was considerably critical uproar regarding the element of virility, introduced in the writings of ex-sergeant Walter, as there had been when Paul Armstrong began to assert himself. It was also the time of James Forbes and his engaging comedy, *The Traveling Salesman;* of Harrison Rhodes and Thomas A. Wise and their *Gentleman from Mississippi* ("It's a corker!" screamed the billboards, quoting Theodore Roosevelt); of Charles Rann Kennedy and *The Servant in the House,* brought over from

England by the Brooklyn-born Irishman, Walter Hampden. And it was the time, too, of Booth Tarkington and Harry Leon Wilson and *The Man From Home*, the enormously popular fable of the Indiana lawyer who went all the way to Sorrento to save his pretty ward from marriage to an impoverished, title-holding fortune hunter.

Tarkington and Wilson wrote the role of Daniel Vorhees Pike—the man from Kokomo—with Nat Goodwin in mind, but Goodwin declined the play and it went to the tall, lanky William Hodge, born in up-State New York, who had done a little of everything in the theater. His performance as the drawling, easygoing, sense-making Hoosier, not at all awed by earls or grand dukes, contributed greatly to the popularity of *The Man From Home*, and as he went on playing the role, year after year, he became more and more identified with the town of Kokomo and found himself continually called upon to answer questions about the folks back in central Indiana. Hodge was a man with red hair and a terrific temper and was not popular with his fellow players. During the Chicago engagement that excellent actor, Eben Plympton, who had appeared with Booth and Barrett and Mary Anderson, played the Grand Duke and received applause after nearly every exit, with the result that Hodge didn't speak to him during the entire Chicago run. Plympton, preferring peace of mind to work in a hit, quit before the play was brought to New York. George C. Tyler always insisted that Hodge's characterization was quality acting unsurpassed in any of the productions of his lifetime, but he and Hodge didn't speak either —not for four years. "To be with William Hodge," observed Hassard Short recently, "was to have one row after another—but it was fun."

And this was also the time of Edward Sheldon, graduated from Harvard in 1907, who came somewhat spectacularly into the theatrical scene at the age of twenty-two with the sale of his first play, *Salvation Nell*, a study of the New York slums, to Mrs. Fiske. Sheldon wrote nearly twenty plays and remained an inspirational force in the theater for years after he had been stricken with blindness and paralysis. His drama, *The Nigger*, well ahead of its time, was a controversial play of a Southern governor, with Negro blood in his veins, who had been elected on a white-supremacy platform. His *Romance* was a sentimental play that lasted Doris Keane for a full five years in America and for an additional engagement in London. His *The Boss* was an entertaining account of the ruthless politician, one Michael

Regan, played fiercely and with enormous skill by Holbrook Blinn and produced by William A. Brady.

"Hell," said Brady, in discussing that play years later, "I was a low-brow. I got *The Boss* because I started Blinn in the theater at twenty-five dollars a week and he brought it to me. It was one of the happiest productions of my life. It was on Sheldon's advice that Grace George revived *The Circle.*"

Through the years of Sheldon's invalidism, almost up to the very hour of his death, distinguished men and women of the New York theater went to him for his advice, his wisdom, his humor, his understanding—and to be guided by his judgment. He was never lacking in conversational brilliance as he lay upon his back with a satin mask over his sightless eyes. Robert E. Sherwood read to Sheldon the first script of *Abe Lincoln in Illinois.* Ruth Gordon went to his bedside to give her first performance in *A Doll's House.* Helen Hayes sought his approval of her impending marriage to Charles MacArthur—should she or shouldn't she? "Go to it," Sheldon advised, and she did. Elizabeth B. Ginty, for years the faithful secretary to David Belasco, began writing about Jesse James under the title of *Missouri Legend* and she took her unfinished play to Sheldon. He liked it, but had some suggestions. He wanted to include a bank-robbing scene. Miss Ginty, on the verge of tears, said she couldn't do it—simply couldn't. But she went home, sat down over her play again—and robbed a bank. *Missouri Legend* might never have reached the stage had not Guthrie McClintic come upon the manuscript while dining at Sheldon's. He began reading it and acting it out. The next day he bought it. And during Sheldon's earlier years, when he was living with John Barrymore, his proddings brought Barrymore to turn from his light-comedy ways, to quit the theater that was represented by such pieces as *The Fortune Hunter* and *Kick In* and *The Yellow Ticket,* and give his limitless talents to *Justice* and *Redemption.* Sheldon then predicted that Barrymore would be a great Hamlet. And for years he tried to talk Helen Hayes into playing Lady Macbeth. She's still thinking about it.

Harrison Grey Fiske brought *Salvation Nell* into the Hackett Theater with Mrs. Fiske in the title role and with that fine actor, Holbrook Blinn, playing the brawling Jim Platt, who is sent to prison for ten years. Harrison Grey Fiske's production started Sheldon on a career that was to be all too short for the theater's general welfare. *Salvation Nell* was quite the most impressive play submitted to New York that fall, a fall that yielded *A Gentleman from Mississippi,* William Hurlbut's *The Fighting Hope,* Somerset

Maugham's *Jack Straw*, Henri Bernstein's *Samson* (with William Gillette), Clyde Fitch's *The Blue Mouse*, and *Pierre of the Plains*, written by the handsome and popular actor-playwright, Edgar Selwyn. *Pierre of the Plains*, with Elsie Ferguson as its leading woman, caused only a minor stir at the Hudson, but the story of the brothers Selwyn must not go unrecorded.

The Selwyns, Edgar and Arch—Edgar was polite, polished and handsome; Arch was sly, caustic, outspoken, and enormously likable—were the sons of a Polish Jew named Simon, who wandered from New York to Cincinnati to Alabama to Canada. Edgar came to New York first, got work as a necktie salesman, and was ushering at night at the Herald Square Theater and living in a two-dollar-a-week furnished room when the younger Arch, in 1897, made his bedraggled appearance in the great city, coming via the Erie station in Jersey City. Arch, his knees sagging and his face begrimed and tear-streaked, trudged into the lobby of the Herald Square, wailed that he had a brother working there, and then sat down and sobbed. Edgar fed the hungry Arch, took him in surreptitiously as a roommate (the landlady, eying Edgar suspiciously, later remarked that every time she saw him he looked different), and got him a job ushering at the theater.

The Selwyns went on to become, in the from-rags-to-riches fashion of Broadway heroes, successful play agents and wealthy producers, but those early years were filled with uncertainty. Arch didn't have leading-man looks and was without acting ambition; the lithe Edgar had the physique but he was not planning a stage career for himself until he and Winchell Smith, also doing a part-time job of ushering at the Herald Square, went into an imitation of Richard Mansfield in *Beau Brummel*—and it was done just as Mansfield, unseen, stood ten feet away. He told the startled young men to call upon him the next morning, and they thought they would be fired. Instead, Mansfield told them that he was convinced that they should take up acting—and they did. Smith was given his start by William Gillette in *Secret Service* and Edgar Selwyn turned up in Augustus Thomas's *Arizona* in the role of Tony. When *Arizona*, with its players including Eleanor Robson, Vincent Serrano, and Theodore Roberts, reached the Herald Square on a September evening in 1900, Arch was still an employee of the theater, and as Brother Edgar made his first appearance Arch, in

86

accordance with a carefully laid plan, led his fellow ushers in a violent outburst of applause. Arch then felt a gentle hand upon his shoulder, and these words were whispered into his ear: "Very gratifying, young man, but by no means conclusive." He turned quickly and was looking into the reproving eyes of Augustus Thomas.

Edgar Selwyn became an actor of considerable skill, appearing with Ethel Barrymore and Maude Adams, before turning to his own *Pierre of the Plains,* and continued with his playwriting, following *Pierre* with *The Country Boy,* a hearty hit, and *The Arab,* his story of the love of the son of a Bedouin sheik for an American girl. It was during the run of *The Arab* at the Lyceum that Selwyn decided that he had had enough. He had created the title role, and the notices given him for his performance were better than he received as a dramatist. But as he was removing his make-up after a matinee he stared at himself in his dressing room mirror and spoke two words: "How silly!" That night he told Henry B. Harris that he was through. He put up notice, closed the play, and never appeared on the stage again.

Selwyn's renunciation of the trade of acting came along at a time when many of his contemporaries were getting into the headlines, news pages as well as amusement pages, for a variety of reasons, mostly matrimonial. . . . Mary Mannering became the bride of Frederick E. Wadsworth, wealthy boatbuilder of Detroit; and James K. Hackett, her former husband, went into bankruptcy (not an infrequent occurrence with celebrated stage folk in the days gone by) for $126,427, and Arnold Daly (second time) for $34,000. Margaret Anglin was married at St. Patrick's Cathedral to Howard Hull, a writer on the staff of "Everybody's Magazine." Ethel Barrymore announced her engagement to Russell Griswold Colt of the arms manufacturing family. Nat C. Goodwin obtained a Reno divorce from Maxine Elliott, and the unperturbed Miss Elliott, as an actress manager, opened her beautiful playhouse in 39th Street, the first New York theater since the time of Laura Keene to take its name from an actress. Even in that day the rumor went forth, as it was to do in succeeding decades, that the theater was a gift to Miss Elliott from J. P. Morgan, a trifling token of his friendship and esteem—a rumor tartly denied by her on more than one occasion. "Lee Shubert and I borrowed money for this venture from an insurance company," she said, "and we are paying five per cent. If it is a success I suppose I shall be known as a very wise woman; if it is not I'm sure that I shall be called otherwise."

This was a time, too, when the new favorite, Billie Burke, who had charmed New York in *My Wife*, was playing *Love Watches;* when an old favorite, Lillian Russell, was engaged with the race track play, *Wildfire;* when Walter Hampden, was finding a public with Charles Rann Kennedy's *The Servant in the House;* when the humdrum life of a Brooklyn trolley car motorman was brightened by the receipt of a fifty-dollar check from Maude Adams for having stopped to give her a lift in the middle of Williamsburg bridge after her car had broken down. And when the glittery new Knickerbocker Hotel, built of terra cotta and limestone and finished in French Renaissance style, rising fifteen stories at Broadway and 42d Street, was one of the show places of New York.

The Knickerbocker, with its famous Maxfield Parrish painting, "Old King Cole," with its fine grill and its celebrated guests (Caruso among them) was flashy, it was popular, it was tremendously successful—and it was in existence for only thirteen years. Certainly there was no one to foresee, during the Knickerbocker's exciting reign—it was known as the "42d Street Country Club" by the boulevardiers of the town—that it would shut its doors in 1920 to be converted into an office building. This was a transition that saddened many New Yorkers, who attributed the passing not so much to the demands of voracious commerce on the island of Manhattan but more to the general blight brought upon the metropolis by the coming of prohibition.

The luncheon table of the members of the Theatrical Syndicate and sycophantic outsiders was in the rear of Rector's restaurant. At twelve-fifteen every day seats were taken by such formidable men of the theater as A. L. Erlanger, Marc Klaw, Al Hayman, and William Harris. Charles Frohman didn't bother—too busy. An occasional guest was James Buchanan (Diamond Jim) Brady, dealer in railroad supplies, Broadway habitué, first-nighter, prodigious eater, and lavish entertainer. It was at one of these sessions that Erlanger turned to William Harris, father of Henry B. and William, Jr., and told him that he had a play by Charles Klein called *The Third Degree* that he liked very much, but that his partners were against it.

"How much have you paid down on it?" asked Harris.

"We gave Klein twenty-five hundred dollars when the contract was signed."

88

"I'll take the play," said Harris, "and will give you your twenty-five hundred and a five-hundred-dollar bonus."

"Don't you even want to know what it's about?" cried Erlanger.

"I don't care," said Harris. "Henry and I made a million dollars out of Klein's *The Lion and the Mouse* and we can surely afford to gamble three thousand dollars on him. Since *The Lion and the Mouse* he has had two failures, *The Stepsister* and *The Daughters of Men*. It's his time to have a success. We'll take the chance."

The deal was concluded. The pudgy, friendly, aggressive Henry B. Harris read *The Third Degree* immediately, liked it, engaged Edmund Breese, the emotional Helen Ware, and the young and increasingly popular Wallace Eddinger for leading roles, and brought it into the Hudson. Klein's melodramatic tale of the results of a confession of murder wrung from an innocent young man by brutal police methods was received by the press as a forceful drama; it earned several hundred thousand dollars for Henry B. Harris and his associates.

Eugene Walter's *The Easiest Way* was a harsh, convention-shattering drama, the story of Laura Murdock, a Wall Street man's luxury-loving mistress, who made a futile struggle for reformation and an honest love. *The Easiest Way* (it was banned in Boston; a kiss was not allowed in Norfolk) was written by Walter on the beach at Southhold, Long Island, during six hard-drinking months. It was taken by his friend and play agent, Arch Selwyn, to David Belasco. The Governor, as some of his associates called him—to others of the worshiping he was "Mr. Dave" and "Mr. B." —accepted the play instantly, but wanted to make some changes. Walter refused to permit alteration of a sentence. Belasco decided to go on with it, but not with Charlotte Walker, for whom the play had been written, in the role of Laura Murdock. This decision angered the easily infuriated Walter but he did not want to withdraw his manuscript: it had been his notion, since he began writing, that Belasco was the man to produce it. Belasco went about the casting of the six-character drama with extraordinary care and patience. Joseph Kilgour, a smooth technician, was engaged for the role of the wealthy and possessive broker who used all his wiles to win back the weak-willed Laura after she had pledged herself to the handsome but penniless Westerner, John Madison. Laura Nelson Hall was given the part of the flashy Elfie St. Clair, an ex-show girl, handsomely kept; and

William Sampson, the finest character actor of his time, was engaged for the part of a broken-down theatrical press agent, and Emma Dunn for that of the predatory Negro maid.

Many weeks were spent in quest of an actor to play the high-minded Westerner. Belasco saw scores of players, he sent forth calls to the stock companies, and finally his gaze fell upon a young man, Edward H. Robins, who had never played in New York. Robins, handsome and stalwart, stood upon the stage of the Republic Theater in 42d Street in the glare of a pilot light; Belasco fumbled with his forelock, circled Robins several times, and mumbled words of satisfaction. He later told his stage manager to rehearse Robins in the part created by Robert Hilliard in *The Girl of the Golden West,* and after several days of work Robins was called upon to give a performance, with the stage manager reading all the other parts and with Belasco and some fifty others looking on. Robins finished and walked off in great relief; win or lose, the ordeal was over. He was called back to the center of the stage; there stood Belasco, smiling quizzically, and still stroking that forelock.

"Young man," he said, "you did very well. You are too big across the rear and your hair is too long. You are to join the Y.M.C.A. and use the gymnasium and tomorrow you will be taken to my barber. Then Mr. Benjamin Roeder will give you a three-year contract." The cast for *The Easiest Way* was complete.

The part of Laura Murdock belonged to Frances Starr from the very instant that Belasco began reading the script. Miss Starr had received valuable training with Henry V. Donnelly's Murray Hill stock company after coming to New York from Albany. Belasco saw her in a minor comedy called *Gallops* and later engaged her for *The Rose of the Rancho.* Then came *The Easiest Way.*

"Laura Murdock," Frances Starr once told me, "has plagued me all my life. *The Easiest Way* is a play people remember. People still tell me about the things I did as Laura—brushing the snow off the milk bottle, sewing a glove, sitting on the trunk at the close of the play, crying out, 'I'm going to Rector's to make a hit and to hell with the rest.' . . . I didn't want to play Laura Murdock any more than Dorothy McGuire wanted to play Claudia. I knew Belasco was going to do *The Easiest Way,* but having just graduated from *The Rose of the Rancho* and having become the Cinderella ingénue —the theater's best bet for mothers to take their innocent children to see—

90

I naturally did not want to get my white dress and blue sash all mussed up by any problem child like Laura Murdock, no matter what! Nor did Eugene Walter want me any more than I wanted him. He was kept out of the theater during rehearsals and I don't know that he ever came to it all the time the play was running. But the wise Belasco knew that a frail young ingénue was what the play needed for Laura, and how right he was! . . . I have always been grateful for *The Easiest Way* but, in a way, I have also resented it, for it came too early in my career. It was difficult to find a play to top it and to stop that endless chorus, 'I shall never forget you in *The Easiest Way*.' That was always especially discouraging after the opening performance in a new play."

The sheer power and boldness of *The Easiest Way* was readily acknowledged by the majority of the New York critics when the play opened at the Belasco-Stuyvesant in mid-January of 1909; there was unanimous acclaim for the performance of Frances Starr as the tragic Laura. The late Channing Pollock, one of the busiest men of his generation, whose activities during a useful lifetime included playwriting, article-writing, lecturing, play-reviewing, and the maintenance of an enormous personal correspondence, recorded his impressions in the then famous "Green Book," the illustrated theatrical monthly. He wrote:

The Easiest Way is a remarkable piece of writing. Miss Starr reveals to us a new type of livery lady; a courtesan with all modern improvements, as it were. Our Camilles, our Saphos and our Zazas have been large women with a strong inclination toward gasps, gurgles, eye-rolling and scene-chewing. Miss Starr's Laura is simple, natural, unaffected, exerting a wonderful appeal and making a strong, if unreasonable requisition upon our sympathies.

And Charles Darnton, writing in the "Evening World," asserted that *The Easiest Way* provided "an evening of good acting and bad morals."

Al Woods turned up on Broadway about this time with the risqué farce, *The Girl from Rector's*, taken by Paul M. Potter from the French, and began his uptown operations in a year that brought forth theatrical fare in considerable variety—Thompson Buchanan's *A Woman's Way*, starring Grace George; *The House Next Door*, the Hartley Manners play that starred J. E. Dodson, and Johnston Forbes-Robertson arrived in *The Passing of the Third Floor Back*. Elsie Ferguson, New York–born, emerged in *Such a Little Queen*. Walker Whiteside gave the best performance of his career as the transplanted young Jew, in love with an Americanized Russian girl, in Israel Zangwill's preachy but effective *Melting Pot;* Mary Roberts Rinehart and Avery Hopwood contributed a merry farce hit in *Seven Days*. *The Chocolate Soldier* came along with its enduring Oscar Straus score. The Booth Tarkington–Harry Leon Wilson team continued its collaborating in *Springtime* for Mabel Taliaferro. Nance O'Neil, authoritative and powerful, gave a stirring performance in Belasco's production of *The Lily*. Lew Fields introduced a child actress by the name of Helen Hayes in his musical piece, *Old Dutch*. And Joe Weber brought into Weber's Theater, as a matinee attraction, a remarkable four-character play, *The Climax*, written by Edward Locke, who had been a singer and an actor.

The Climax was put on with vast doubts as to its value, but it became immediately popular. It was moved into Daly's for a season's run, and was later done by several touring companies. Playwright Locke moved from dingy Ninth Avenue quarters into a handsome Park Avenue apartment and collected royalties for twenty years. Effingham Pinto (Don Effingham Amore De Cordova Pinto), a Yale man of Latin appearance and with tremendous talent as a pianist, created the role of Pietro Golfanti, the young Italian composer who adored the beautiful singer, Adelina, and he made something of a career of the part and the play. Whenever some management decided that it was time to revive *The Climax*, the first step was to call the Lambs Club and engage Pinto to play Pietro. *The Climax* made and held a place for itself in the theater; the role of Adelina was played by many singing actresses, including Leona Watson, Anne Swinburne, Eleanor Painter, Norma Terris. The earnings of *The Climax* ran into big figures, but the author died in the Actors' Fund home.

The Climax surprised and delighted New York some months before the Gaiety Theater, a playhouse of long runs, drew the popular comedy, *The Fortune Hunter*, produced by Cohan & Harris with John Barrymore playing Nat Duncan, the dejected young man who was talked out of throwing himself into the East River, and who took a sudden and new interest in life when told by a more successful friend how he might earn a million dollars—merely by taking himself off to a small town and following the rules. And the rules, as glibly outlined by the farseeing Henry Kellogg, would result in Duncan's marriage to the richest girl in town.

There is a lesson in thrift (one which might possibly be recommended to all young and striving playwrights) in Winchell Smith's experience with *The Fortune Hunter*. It was his first play done without collaboration. It was rejected by Dillingham and by Frohman (the great man, you see, said "no" to many good ones), and finally Smith cornered George M. Cohan in a Buffalo hotel lobby. "All right, kid," said Cohan. "Sounds pretty good. Let's go right upstairs and you can read it to me." Smith, expert in his reading, finished the first act and paused. Cohan rose and said, "That's enough. We'll do it. That's the best act I ever heard. Go ahead and get a cast."

Smith rushed back to New York, got his cast together—Hale Hamilton was engaged for the rule-making friend and Mary Ryan for the heroine's role—and *The Fortune Hunter* came into the Gaiety. For two or three weeks the response of playgoers, notwithstanding the exultant press, was negligible. Then, all of a sudden, *The Fortune Hunter* caught on. And it was then that Mrs. Winchell Smith made this suggestion: "Let's try something. Let's not touch one cent of the royalties from this play. We'll put all the money in the bank and spend the money from the next." "All right," said Billy Smith. Within two or three years *The Fortune Hunter*, as successful on tour as it was in New York, had piled up a fortune for the Smiths.

The year of 1909 was also the year of that gigantic failure, the New Theater; of William Winter's abrupt resignation from the "Tribune" after forty-four years of service as its dramatic critic; of Clyde Fitch's death, and the presentation of his last play, *The City*.

The New Theater, which sought to establish itself as a sustaining art theater, its purpose being to give playgoers better plays than were possible when commercial considerations were supreme, started bravely. It had the good will, along with the doubts, of press and public. Winthrop Ames was its director and Lee Shubert its business manager, choices that met with widespread approval. Ames, a tall, spare, thin-faced New Englander, a Harvard graduate and a man with a cultivated voice and a contagious smile, was thirty-nine when he accepted the job of directing the operations of the magnificently equipped playhouse, impressive in appearance, that occupied a block frontage—62d to 63d Street—in New York's Central Park West. The gentleman from North Easton, Massachusetts, had enormous charm, but he was also quick to sarcasm and he had a temper.

It was seldom, if ever, displayed to his working associate, Lee Shubert. "I happen to like Lee," Ames said, "and I can get along with him. I believe he's honest."

Ames's New England family was somewhat horrified when he went into the theater, via the Castle Square in Boston, instead of following a career as an architect, for which he had been trained. But even those who had been the most vigorous in their opposition had to concede, however grudgingly, that the post of director of the New Theater was one to be respected. John Corbin, who had given years to dramatic criticism, was appointed literary director of the new organization, and the company engaged included some of the leading players of the New York stage—Ferdinand Gottschalk, Louis Calvert, Henry Stanford, Beverly Sitgreaves, A. E. Anson, Pedro De Cordoba, Lee Baker, Annie Russell, Edith Wynne Matthison, Howard Kyle, Harriet Otis Dellenbaugh, Reginald Barlow, Albert Bruning, Jessie Busley, Olive Wyndham, Rowland Buckstone, Beatrice Forbes-Robertson, Guy Bates Post.

The plays selected were Galsworthy's sociological, capital versus labor drama, Strife; Edward Knoblock's fanciful Cottage in the Air, Edward Sheldon's significant and provocative drama, The Nigger, and that charming allegory, The Blue Bird, a play of spiritual beauty, written by Maurice Maeterlinck, the Belgian poet-dramatist, and somewhat similar in treatment to Barrie's Peter Pan. Shakespeare's Antony and Cleopatra was chosen—an unfortunate choice it was—for the opening bill on November 6, 1909, with the distinguished romantic actor E. H. Sothern as Antony, and Julia Marlowe, in Shakespearean partnership with Sothern for several years, in the role of Cleopatra. They were far from impressive in their first-night performance. A distinguished audience sat attentively through the long, wearying stretches of the tragedy and remained, in a state approximating exhaustion, until the last curtain finally fell at eleven-forty on the death of Cleopatra, to give the stars and the company an ovation. The event drew front-page coverage in the New York press; thousands upon thousands of words were written in tribute to a project designed for permanence. But from the very beginning there were misgivings—the acoustics were defective and the theater was much too big—and these were misgivings that were shared by the founders who occupied the royal boxes at the première and by humble purchasers of the low-priced seats who

94

were drawn into Central Park West that night by the urge of curiosity, or expectation of pleasure, or by a sense of duty to the drama.

For two seasons the New Theater struggled to fulfill the hopes of its art-patron supporters. But at the end of those two seasons the organization faced a deficit of $400,000. The realistic J. P. Morgan, one of the original backers, heard of this deficit when he dropped in at a directors' meeting. He snapped his own decision in three words: "Let's close it." So it was voted. Winthrop Ames was given notice, and the company was out of business within a few days. At the time, and during the years that followed the collapse of the New Theater, numerous reasons were offered as to why the high-minded undertaking had not succeeded. For one thing—and there was general agreement on this point—the theater was too far up-town. For another, the great majority of playgoers have always regarded repertory as something of an inconvenience; it has never been a financial success in New York in this century. And there was the fact that the beauti-ful temple of the drama in Central Park West had been designed for operatic rather than theatrical presentations. Julia Marlowe, in speaking of the spaciousness of the playhouse, once said, "I used to come on the stage from 62d Street and Mr. Sothern from 63d."

The house was leased to George C. Tyler and Liebler & Company. They later brought in a popular attraction, *The Garden of Allah,* a claptrap drama, done with real desert sand, real camels, and real Arabs, and for which the beautiful Mary Mannering (born Florence Friend) was brought back to the theater from blissful and luxurious retirement. She played her sandstorm scene in a hard-finished, tailormade frock and impeccable, patent leather pumps, and the disillusioned founders of the dream theater began to look about for a site for the erection of something of less im-mensity in the way of a playhouse. A site was found in 44th Street, but the millionaires—the original founders included John Jacob Astor, J. P. Mor-gan, August Belmont, Harry Payne Whitney, William K. Vanderbilt Cornelius Vanderbilt, George J. Gould, and Otto Kahn—were losing their enthusiasm, and the project was soon abandoned.

It was then that Winthrop Ames, deciding to go in for production on his own—and it was always entirely his own money in his projects—built in 44th Street the Little Theater (299 seats at the time of its opening) from his own designs, set up his own organization, which included Guthrie Mc-

95

Clintic and, later, Johnson Briscoe, who had been official prompter for the New Theater, and took his place as one of the leaders of the theater of his time. Such productions as Galsworthy's *The Pigeon*, Schnitzler's *The Affairs of Anatol*, the Laurence Housman–Granville Barker *Prunella* and the revival of Clyde Fitch's *The Truth* were indicative of Ames's skill as a showman and his feeling for the finer things of the stage. Briscoe, a reformed actor and a stage historian of boundless enthusiasm and knowledge, and the able McClintic were Ames employees who regarded him with something approximating worship. McClintic got his early New York training in the Ames workshop and began his career as a director-producer with the blessings of "the Master," plus his financial assistance.

"How did you and Guthrie get together in the first place?" Ames was asked after McClintic had scored an emphatic first success with *The Dover Road*.

"I really don't know," smiled the showman from Massachusetts. "I looked up one day during rehearsals of Arnold Bennett's *The Great Adventure* and there Guthrie was."

The theater's sensation in the final month of 1909 was Clyde Fitch's last play, *The City*. Fitch died in France, at Châlons-sur-Marne, in early September; in late December *The City* was produced by the Shuberts at the Lyric Theater. It was Fitch's conviction, when he finished *The City*, that he had done the best work of his short but crowded life, that in the telling of his sins-of-the-fathers story of the rise and fall of George Rand, Jr., and in his expounding of virtues of the city versus the country, he had effectively answered the charge that he could not write a man's play. His confidence in his final work was reflected in his exciting reading of it, the first reading, to a group of friends in his gray and yellow study in the Other House at Katonah, New York, finishing at 2 A.M. He went about the casting of the play with great care. Walter Hampden, Mary Nash, Eva Vincent, and Lucile Watson, necessary to all Fitch plays, were immediate choices. Fitch wanted Tully Marshall for the role of the dope fiend and blackmailer, George Frederick Hannock, and invited Marshall to talk it over at the house in 40th Street. But the actor declined, and did so firmly. When the playwright sailed on his annual trip to the Continent he expressed his disappointment in having been unable to engage Marshall; he was elated

with his casting for the other parts, but his play was still without a Hannock, the man who was to scream out "goddam" for the first time in a play
in New York. (The oath was in the original script and was used at every
rehearsal and at all performances save for those in Boston prior to the New
York opening.)

It was after the news reached New York of Fitch's death that Tully
Marshall relented and decided to play in *The City*. He never regretted it.
The role of Hannock was later relished by many players in stock and road
productions—certainly by an actor named Geoffrey C. Stein who was in
it when *The City* toured the South. The second-act "goddam liar,"
shouted by Stein when told that he had married his own sister, so shocked
a member of the board of stewards of the Methodist Church in a Georgia
city that he instantly left the theater, dragging along his reluctant female
companion. It was this same Geoffrey Stein who later came into the headlines in New York in a damage suit filed against critic Heywood Broun.
The sapient Broun, in reviewing a play called *The Awakening of Spring*,
produced under the auspices of the "Medical Review of Reviews," in
which Stein appeared, made the observation that the actor gave the worst
performance he had ever seen on any stage. The play had a run of one
performance. Stein asked for damages of $10,000. The trial was pending
as Stein appeared in another play, also reviewed by Broun, who asserted
that the actor was up to his usual standard. Stein's suit reached the courtroom and Broun, on the witness stand, denied that his written opinion
had been actuated by any malice. A verdict was returned in favor of
Broun and the "New York Tribune," the court holding that Broun, in his
capacity as a critic sitting in judgment on a performance, was within his
rights in expressing his displeasure as he did.

The New York opening of *The City*—December 21, 1909—stays in the
memory of playgoers who were present; it belongs with the theater's
legendary first nights, a category that includes, of course, the *première*
performance of J. M. Synge's *The Playboy of the Western World*, which
brought on a riot. When the curtain fell on the second act of *The City*
men and women stood and screamed, waving arms and hats and handkerchiefs. Lawrence Reamer, reviewing the play for the "New York Sun,"
applauded, fainted, and applauded again, and he was still applauding as
he rushed off at the end of the third act to write his notice. The pande-

monium kept the players in *The City* jumpy all evening; they were under great tension but got through the performance without faltering. Cast-member Lucile Watson recalls all details of the backstage story.

"*The City*," she relates, "was the play in which Fitch took greater pride than in anything he had ever written and the fact that he had died three months before the opening was known to nearly everybody in the theater that night. We could feel the tension from the audience—Tully Marshall, Walter Hampden, Mary Nash, and all of us. When Tully yelled 'goddam liar' it was a terrific shock to the audience. We could all feel that shock backstage. There were curtain calls—oh, so many of them. I've always thought I counted nineteen. We all took them but for one call, suddenly, the stage was bare. No member of the cast walked out. Here was a bare stage and an audience screaming. Finally somebody went out; I guess we all did. . . . Several times, days and weeks, later, persons who were in that hysterical first night crowd told me that they had seen, through their tears, Clyde Fitch walk to the footlights and take a bow. . . . Clyde Fitch had a magnificent sense of the theater; he would have written great plays and he was at the beginning of an entirely new career when he wrote *The City*. The day I got the news of his death—it was from a newspaper head-line—there also lay at my door a card from him in Germany. I suppose I was a pet of his. I stood in great awe of him. And I also adored him."

The dramatized novel lost its vogue as the twentieth century's first decade passed; the parlor comedies of W. Somerset Maugham came into favor. New dramatists, such as William Vaughn Moody, whose *The Great Divide* was a drama of solidity and poetic beauty; Langdon Mitchell, who combined social satire with high comedy in *The New York Idea*, and Josephine Preston Peabody, who came along with verse drama in *The Piper*, were among those who brought new stimulation into the professional theater. It was also the era of the well-made play. Such dramatists as Augustus Thomas, George Broadhurst, Charles Klein, and Eugene Walter were not inspired writers but they knew their jobs. They delivered the sort of plays that the theater of the time was heartily accepting, and they wrote them swiftly. Every established dramatist was more or less expected to deliver a new play every season, and two-in-a-season productivity brought forth no surprise.

The vast earlier success of the popular novel, the sentimental and historical novel, in play form can be attributed to the fact that the America of the closing years of the nineteenth century—the era of hammocks and broad verandas, livery stables and blacksmiths, harness stores and tandem bicycles—was eager to receive, in the flesh, legendary characters from the bookshelves. There was a rush upon the playhouses to see just how this or that fictional or historical character would appear when brought to life in a play. I shall certainly never forget the gnawing impatience with which I awaited the coming of a Southern road company in George Barr McCutcheon's *Graustark* and how I picked cotton all day in the scorching south-Georgia sun to get the price of admission and the round-trip railroad fare to the city of Savannah from the drowsy hamlet called Guyton. It was labor cheerfully undertaken for the privilege of gazing upon Princess Yetive and Grenfall Lorry in a behind-the-footlights incarnation. The dramatized-novel vogue was heightened by the theatrical success of such popular works as *Trilby* and *The Prisoner of Zenda*, and it was a craze that swept on relentlessly for eight or ten years. It declined toward the end of the first decade of the new century as playgoers became sharper, somewhat wiser, less susceptible to artificiality. And an important factor in the disappearance of the trend, in the opinion of William Lyon Phelps, was the American sense of humor.

The theater was on its way toward maturity during the 1900–1910 decade. The New Theater, although it failed dismally, gave the stage brilliant ensemble acting and several notable productions. There was a great deal of Shakespearean activity, more and more of George Bernard Shaw, and more and more of Ibsen, who had a profound effect upon playwriting and upon the conditioning of audiences for sounder and stronger fare in its playhouses, for the realism that was to come. Ibsen contributed enormously to the rising revolt against artificiality; he stirred playgoers with his power, and he had to be taken seriously or not at all. During these years that Ibsen was being discovered by the American theater he was never "box office" to the extent that Shaw was getting to be, or that Shakespeare was —and always will be—on so many occasions, but leading actresses were beginning to relish the roles of the tortured women written into his brooding Scandinavian tragedies. Mrs. Fiske liked her Tess and her Becky Sharp, but she would never have been content without her Nora and her Hedda. Ethel Barrymore's success as Nora gave her the needed confidence to accept another serious role, that of Mrs. Jones, the charwoman, in Galsworthy's first play, *The Silver Box,* a serious social study. When Charles Frohman offered her the part, he didn't believe for an instant that she would consider playing a role of such bleakness. Miss Barrymore won critical applause for the performance, but her public didn't want her in such a dreary play, and *The Silver Box* quickly expired.

The decade brought increased prestige to Florenz Ziegfeld for the introduction of the new revue form; to Victor Herbert, as a master in the light opera field; to George M. Cohan, as a many-sided genius—song writer, dancer, actor, director, producer, and high-speed dramatist—and it gave indications, here and there, of the new styles in plays that were on the way. The farcical melodrama, well-populated with crooks and gunmen, the play combining comedy with thrills, was soon to be submitted to the Broadway market. And so was the success-story comedy of the young man faced with seemingly insurmountable problems, having difficulty in love, and who, by the time of the final curtain, would be rich, would have won his girl, and would be wearing a dress suit. Credit George M. Cohan and Winchell Smith and Harry James Smith for the creation and the popularization of that pattern. It was a formula that was worth a million to Cohan and to Winchell Smith before they wore it out.

CHAPTER VII

Luana, Peg, and Mary Turner

WHEN THE CHIMES of Old Trinity brought in the year
of 1910 there was unbroken peace throughout the world; life in America
flowed along placidly. William Howard Taft was going his then untroubled
way as the nation's Chief Executive. Charles Evans Hughes was Governor
of New York. William Jay Gaynor was the great city's Mayor and Charles
Whitman its new District Attorney, having succeeded the stormy and brilliant William Travers Jerome. New Yorkers were playing bridge, golf, and
the horses. They were riding in the wonderful new motorcars of the day—
the Benz and the Cadillac and the Buick, the Hudson and the Lozier and
the Isotta, the Bearcat Stutz and the Locomobile and the Ford and the
Marmon and the Maxwell ($600 up). They were taking round-the-world
tours, and trips to the West Indies and to the Orient and to Boston via
the Joy Line. And, on the morning of January 1, 1910, they were nursing
headaches brought on by New Year's Eve merriment at Martin's and the
Café des Beaux Arts, at the Little Hungary in Houston Street and the
Café Boulevard in Second Avenue, at Rector's and Shanley's and Delmonico's, at the Knickerbocker and the Holland House and the Astor.

New Yorkers, in the early months of 1910, flocked to such plays as *Seven
Days* and *The Fortune Hunter*; to see Otis Skinner in *Your Humble Serv-
ant* and H. B. Warner in *Alias Jimmy Valentine*, Cyril Scott in *The Lottery
Man* and Guy Bates Post in Sheldon's *The Nigger*, Raymond Hitchcock in
Cohan's *The Man Who Owns Broadway* and Nance O'Neil in *The Lily*,
and to Charles Dillingham's new theater, the Globe, to enjoy the antics of
Montgomery & Stone in George Ade's *The Old Town*. New Yorkers were
reading the play reviews of Acton Davies in the "Evening Sun," Adolph
Klauber in the "Times," Ashton Stevens in the "Journal," Louis V. De Foe
in the "World," and Arthur Warren in the "Tribune." They were going to

101

Schulte's (thirty stores) for their cigars, Jaeckel's for their furs, Knox's for their hats, Goodrich's for their tires, and to Cavanagh's for their shellfish dinners. They were hearing about a remarkable young song writer named Irving Berlin, who had moved uptown from Mike Salter's in Chinatown and Jimmy Kelly's in 14th Street and who was soon to enchant the town with "Alexander's Ragtime Band," and they were paying their money, and eagerly, to see the Johnson-Ketchel fight pictures and to watch such vaudeville headliners as Maggie Cline, Bert Levy, Valeska Suratt, Fannie Ward, and a young "mountebank" known as Al Jolson, but who was born Asa Yoelson, of Washington, D.C.

In 1910 resident stock companies, such as the famous Crescent in Brooklyn (the bill for any week was likely to be *St. Elmo* or *Alice of Old Vincennes*), were spreading. Touring companies totaled more than three hundred, and the popular-priced theater, as represented by the Stair & Havlin Wheel (E. D. Stair, J. H. Havlin, and George H. Nicolai), a circuit extending all the way to Kansas City, and by such specimens of villain-pursues-the-working-girl melodrama as Theodore Kremer's *Bertha, the Sewing Machine Girl* and Owen Davis's *Nellie, the Beautiful Cloak Model,* was on its way into oblivion. The bustling firm of Sullivan, Harris & Woods, purveyors of the 10-20-30-cent thrillers, was dissolved when Al Woods got the notion that he wanted to go out on his own. Woods, done with the downtown phase of his career, had now come to Broadway. So had Sam H. Harris, and the amazing Owen Davis, who had then written more than 200 plays, Bowery-style, and was determined to better himself.

"I saw it coming," Owen Davis told me, in talking for this book, "and I decided to get out. I went to Woods and told him and he was of the same mind. We both realized that the popular-priced circuit of some thirty-six houses had killed itself by going in for big shows, by trying to do them too expensively, and all that resulted in diminishing profits. And then the motion pictures were coming on and I knew we were doomed. Those Stair and Havlin plays were written according to formula; one would be a Western, next would come a fast-life city story, and then another would be a sentimental play. I wrote so many I had to begin using another name on a lot of them. I made a barrel of money and Woods must have made ten times as much.

"Al Woods was a curious man, a great showman for a long time. Al began as an advance agent; his real name was Herman and his brothers were

102

In Diamond Jim Brady's Day

*Legends of some of the celebrated restaurants—eating, drinking and some
with dancing, too—in the New York of another generation.*

Martin and I.C., a gentle little fellow who made a lot of money manufacturing handkerchiefs. Al was a curious guy. He never had stocks or bonds. He kept his money in cash, a lot of it in thousand-dollar bills. Interesting fellow in lots of ways. He'd give you his shirt. Go to dinner with him and he'd always want to pay but he'd order six plates of ice cream and nothing else. . . . Theodore Kremer? He was a serious-minded German who thought, honest to God, that he was an inspired writer." And these were the words of a Harvard man, Owen Davis, who earned a fortune with *Edna, the Pretty Typewriter, Convict 999,* and *Gambler of the West,* before moving uptown and changing his ways.

The exuberant Woods, who grew up on New York's lower East Side, was born in Budapest, coming to this country at the age of three. The Bowery was his dream street, the Great White Way of his early years. He worked for a time as a shipping clerk in a cloak-and-suit house and as advance agent for a road flop called *The American Gaiety Girl.* He operated a nickelodeon on the Bowery, and as he prowled that thoroughfare by day and by night he got the notion that there was a play in it and he went to his friend Walter Moore of the Miner Lithograph Company, and got him to print up some gaudy posters, depicting scenes of terror, madness, violence, and demoniacal villainy that were supposed to be contained in a melodrama known as *The Bowery After Dark.* Woods took his posters, went with them to Theodore Kremer, and told him to write a play around them. Kremer did so. Woods then hurried to P. H. (Paddy) Sullivan for financial aid, the play was put on at the Star Theater Christmas night in 1899, and the foundation for Woods's reputation as a king of melodrama was thereby laid. The partnership of Sullivan, Harris & Woods was formed, Sam H. Harris then being as stage-struck as Woods was, and the firm flourished.

Woods later told his partners that he wanted to operate independently. Harris joined George M. Cohan, and Woods went on to do such pieces as *Queen of the High Binders, Queen of the White Slavers,* and *Confessions of a Wife.* He had had experience with popular-priced musical plays and in the operation of theaters when he got ambitious and decided that he was ready for Broadway, whether Broadway liked it or not. *The Girl from Rector's,* with Violet Dale in the title role, started him on his uptown career. He never again went below 23d Street except for dinner at Luchow's. Within three years after *The Girl from Rector's* Al was calling everybody

104

"Sweetheart," he was smoking better cigars, taking impromptu trips to Europe, winning the confidence and affection of some of the leading players, and opening his own theater, the Eltinge.

Playwrights in the news and in Broadway's house-board billing during the 1910–1911–1912 period in the New York theater included Arthur Wing Pinero, Eugene Walter, Margaret Mayo, Edgar Selwyn (to whom Miss Mayo was married), James Forbes, Charles Klein, Thompson Buchanan, George Broadhurst, Rachel Crothers, Edward Sheldon, Somerset Maugham, George M. Cohan, Philip Bartholomae, Edward Knoblauch, Charles Kenyon, Bayard Veiller, Hartley Manners, and the spectacular Paul Armstrong whose *Alias Jimmy Valentine* was an enormously popular piece of the day.

Armstrong was a man who could turn out a full-length play with greater speed than any other dramatist of his time. Consider the case of *Jimmy Valentine*. He had submitted to Liebler & Company a play they didn't want, and it was suggested that he read a book of O. Henry stories, to which the firm had the dramatic rights. Armstrong read the stories overnight and told the office that he thought there was a hell of a play in *A Retrieved Reformation*, the tale of a former convict who, as a trusted bank employee, turns to his old trade of safecracking to save the heroine's young sister, who has been accidentally locked in the big vault. Armstrong took the story with him to the Algonquin, the fabulous inn at which Frank Case, who later owned it, found employment as a clerk in 1902. Armstrong sat down before a typewriter in the Algonquin's suite 711 on a Friday morning; the following Monday afternoon he rushed to the Liebler offices with the completed manuscript of *Alias Jimmy Valentine*. Theodore Liebler, Jr., sent the play to George Tyler in Chicago. Tyler read it in two hours, liked it, began casting immediately, and two weeks later the Chicago critics were called forth to attend the opening—a time elapse of only twenty days since Armstrong read the O. Henry story!

"Armstrong," Liebler told me, "was a stubborn man. An interesting man with a fine dramatic instinct, but I never liked him. Anyway, he was stubborn. But so was George Tyler. We later went to Chicago with *The Deep Purple*, written by Armstrong and Wilson Mizner. Paul wanted to build up a certain part, one played by a beautiful young actress. Tyler positively refused. The play was a success just as it was. Paul then wired Mizner in exactly these words: 'I'm taking *Deep Purple* away from Liebler. Are you with me.' Mizner wired back, 'I'm with you if you win.'"

There were some extraordinary skillful performances by women of the New York stage during the Armstrong–Mizner–Liebler & Company era. Laurette Taylor, once of such overwrought and lachrymose drama as *From Rags to Riches,* was hired by the Lieblers at $200 a week, and she played charmingly as the heroine in *Alias Jimmy Valentine.* Ethel Barrymore, who went from Ibsen to Barrie to Galsworthy after achieving stardom as Mme. Trentoni in *Captain Jinks,* distinguished herself with her playing as Zoe Blundell in *Mid-Channel,* Pinero's study of a turbulent marriage. Mary Mannering, an actress never too fortunate in her choice of plays and seldom seen in one worth her talents, found a well-written drama in *A Man's World,* Rachel Crothers's consideration of the double standard. Dorothy Donnelly shed her tears convincingly as the desolated Madame X, defended by her own son (unaware of her identity) at her trial for the murder of a scoundrel—a play that had been rejected by Margaret Anglin. Emily Stevens, New York–born and trained by her illustrious cousin, Mrs. Fiske, appeared with distinction in *The Boss,* Edward Sheldon's play of the reform and domestication of a political roughneck (magnificently played by Holbrook Blinn).

Margaret Illington gave a thoroughly moving characterization as the pathetic Maggie Schultz in Charles Kenyon's worthy but short-lived *Kindling,* a drama of the misery of the slums. Hazel Dawn, pride of Ogden, Utah, delighted New York with her blond beauty, her singing and violin playing in *The Pink Lady,* and Christie MacDonald came forth as the charming prima donna of *The Spring Maid,* which gave Charles Dillingham serious doubts as to his own perspicacity. Dillingham had an option on *The Spring Maid* but he did not renew it. The firm of Werba & Leuscher took over the rights and put it into rehearsal, with George Marion directing. During the rehearsal period Dillingham met Marion at the Lambs and asked him what he was doing.

"I'm directing *The Spring Maid* for Christie MacDonald," said Marion.

"Oh, my God!" cried Dillingham. "I love that little girl and hate to see her get such a lemon for her first starring vehicle."

"You're wrong, Charlie," said Marion. *"The Spring Maid* is likely to be as big a success as *The Merry Widow."*

106

"George," murmured the immaculate Dillingham, "you're crazy—completely crazy."

Dillingham was ill and in a hospital when *The Spring Maid* came into New York and was received as a lively and melodious hit. On his first night out of the hospital, Dillingham, with seats purchased from a speculator, went to the Liberty Theater and knocked upon Miss MacDonald's dressing room door. He was kneeling as she opened it. "I was wrong," he said. "My congratulations!"

As for Hazel Dawn, she was brought back from London after Ivan Caryll, the composer, had seen her in *The Dollar Princess*, and went through the frightening ordeal of singing before an audition committee of A. L. Erlanger, Marc Klaw, and Florenz Ziegfeld. When she finished, the smiling Erlanger walked up to her, pinched her gently on the cheek, and said, "Talk about apple blossoms—just a pink lady!" And then, with sudden delight, he cried: "That's the title for the new show—*The Pink Lady!*" Miss Dawn was engaged at $100 a week, with Klaw and Ziegfeld in vast approval, but Julian Mitchell, the director, disliked her instantly and heartily. Later, during the rehearsal of a dance number, as a thunderstorm raged, the stone-deaf Mitchell, with his eyes upon Miss Dawn, screamed, "Stop! Someone is scraping their feet!" They told him about the thunder, and the dancing was resumed. There was no cessation in his hostility toward Miss Dawn until Erlanger went to him and said, "Now lay off that girl. She's with the show, she's staying in the show." And Hazel Dawn was the Pink Lady when the production opened in New York.

The jolly comedienne, May Irwin—she was also a hardheaded and cantankerous business woman and later made half a million in New York realty transactions—set Broadway to laughing in *Getting a Polish*, written for her by the obliging Booth Tarkington and Harry Leon Wilson. The dainty Marguerite Clark appeared in the farce hit, *Baby Mine;* the youthful Ruth Chatterton brought her charm and freshness to *The Rainbow*, written by that excellent technician, A. E. Thomas, and Laura Nelson Hall contributed a resolute performance to Henry W. Savage's production of Walter Browne's morality play, *Everywoman*.

The colorful Savage gave New York three hits during 1911—*Excuse Me*, Rupert Hughes's Pullman farce; *The Million*, a farce from the French, and *Everywoman*, which became an extraordinary theatrical property. Most of the *Everywoman* rehearsals, which began in January, were held in the

Lyric Theater, unheated during the day, and Walter Browne, the author, got a chill and came down with a severe cold. When the company left for Hartford for the final dress rehearsal he was not on the train, and the company was told that his cold had developed into pneumonia. The opening at Hartford's Parsons Theater took place on schedule, and the usual morning-after rehearsal was called to check on Savage's notes. The producer assembled the company on stage at 11 A.M. and stood before the cast. Then, in a quiet voice, he shocked his players with the announcement that Walter Browne had died the evening before, and at just about the time the curtain was rising on the first performance of his play. Savage spoke feelingly, apparently with great sincerity, and somewhat tremblingly as he paid the late playwright a touching tribute. There were tears in the eyes of the *Everywoman* players; some of the women sobbed softly. But as the producer finished his eulogy his manner changed. He became abrupt and businesslike and turned to James Shesgren, his press agent, and said, in his usual, clipped, hard New England voice: "Did you get all that down for the papers, Jim?"

Everywoman opened at the Herald Square Theater in late February, 1911, giving Broadway such bright young players as Patricia Collinge, Wilda Bennett, and Juliette Day, a trio to be heard from as the seasons went by. The reviews were tough. Alan Dale, resisting the youthful appeal of Miss Collinge, called her "pathetically treacle-voiced." The company was somewhat subdued at the morning-after rehearsal call, but Savage was brisk and confident. "Don't worry about those notices, children," he said. "We're in the theater for a long run. The company is dismissed." His prediction was correct. *Everywoman* had a profitable New York engagement and was a money-making road attraction for several years.

But Savage held his grievance against the press and when called upon to speak before the National Press Club in Washington, at the time *Everywoman* was touring the land, he delivered his tirade: "We have a set of critics in New York who write largely, if not entirely, from the point of view of self-exploitation. . . . The public becomes discouraged with the so-called trained and expert opinion. . . . We producers gamble $40,000 on a production and we are treated as one who is being prosecuted by the district attorney. . . . I have seen, with my own eyes, a critic signal across a crowded auditorium to a confrere by holding his nose, thus giving his opinion of the play."

Taylor Holmes, who created the role of Shaw's Marchbanks in Chicago several years before Arnold Daly did *Candida* in New York, was engaged by Savage for a leading role in *The Million,* adapted by Leo Ditrichstein, and told to be prepared to inject funny lines into the play at rehearsals. On the first day Holmes tried his first interpolation. Ditrichstein leaped from his chair and screamed, "If you can act, which I doubt, that will be all that will be required of you." The next morning, and to the considerable amusement of the company—Eugene O'Brien, Irene Fenwick, John A. Butler, Jane Peyton—Holmes made another substitution, and now Ditrichstein was fairly wild.

"If you ever again dare to change one word of my script," he roared, "I'll have you thrown out of the theater." At lunchtime Holmes sought the counsel of Savage, who said, "Stick to Leo's script until tomorrow morning. Think up your best quip and spring it after ten-thirty. I'll be in the theater by that time and will take over." Holmes followed directions carefully, waiting until ten-thirty-five to introduce a witticism of his own, and then Ditrichstein exploded. He was moving across the stage toward Holmes with fists clenched when, out of the darkness at the rear of the orchestra floor, came Savage, drawling, "Wait a minute there, Leo. That line sounded sort of funny to me. Let the boy keep it in, and if it doesn't go before an audience we can always cut it out. Let him put them in as fast as he can think of them—we can't lose anything."

The Million opened in Trenton. The farce wilted and died in its first performance. Erlanger's scouts turned in a report of such condemnation he canceled the play's booking for the Gaiety. This action infuriated Savage and he instantly canceled all of his Klaw & Erlanger bookings and went into the Shubert camp with fourteen productions. Ditrichstein, controlling himself with great difficulty, went to Savage after the first disastrous Trenton performance and said that Holmes had ruined his play. "Would you care to sell your interest, Leo?" asked Savage quietly. "Thank God, and yes!" cried the actor-dramatist. "And for one dollar!" Savage wrote an agreement on the back of an envelope, got Ditrichstein to sign it, and handed him a $500 bill. Taylor Holmes rewrote the play, it reopened in four weeks, and was an immediate hit on the night of its *première* at the 39th Street Theater. "Well," said Savage to Holmes when the final curtain fell, "we licked Erlanger. He's only had one hit in his life and that was *Ben Hur.* He's still touring it."

The public gets few of the accurate details of the theater's inside stories; it hears actually little of the behind-the-scenes feuds, jealousies, scandals, rages, and romances, of the practical jokes and general horseplay, of backstage accidents and near tragedies. There was the realism in *Kismet*, the notable spectacle-play that came along at the time of *The Million*, that almost cost Hamilton Revelle his life. Otis Skinner, a romantic actor of robustness and gusto, who had received his thorough and intensive early training under the management of Augustin Daly, found his most colorful role in that of the beggar, Hajj. Hamilton Revelle played the evil Wazir Mansur, and in the final act he was thrown into a large pool by Hajj and drowned. It was in Revelle's contract that the water temperature was never to be below 65 degrees Fahrenheit and not above 75, but some nights the water was icy cold and on others it was sickeningly hot. During the second season of *Kismet*, when it was playing at Ford's in Baltimore, the two girls who disported themselves in the tank at the beginning of the final act came off blue with cold and said, "Mr. Revelle, you can't go in tonight; the water is freezing." Revelle, during the scene in which he was stabbed by Skinner, tried to whisper to the star not to push him into the pool. Skinner didn't catch the words, couldn't understand why Revelle was resisting so strongly, and finally, and rather angrily, used all his strength to hurl Revelle into the water. Revelle suffered a chill, had a doctor for the rest of the week, left the cast the next week with a high fever, and for two weeks his condition was critical. Klaw & Erlanger, fearing a damage suit, sent Revelle a note wishing him a speedy recovery and tactfully enclosed a check for $500.

And it was during the run of *The Return of Peter Grimm*, Belasco's play of the supernatural, that David Warfield kept all members of his fine cast constantly on edge with his tricks and his pranks. On one occasion he spread limburger cheese inside the petals of a bowl of tulips and when Janet Dunbar, who had the leading feminine role, went to bury her face in the tulip bowl during Peter's long farewell speech she almost became ill on stage. In the first act of the play Joseph Brennan, playing the doctor, had a scene in which waffles and coffee were served, and as it was a Belasco production, freshly made waffles and hot coffee were before Brennan at every performance. But one evening the prankful Warfield, carrying whimsy to quite an extreme, substituted castor oil for the maple syrup. Percy Helton, then a boy actor playing Willem—and he played the role tremulously and beautifully—told me in later years that Brennan's face, after he had scooped up a mouthful of castor oil, was something not to be forgotten in a lifetime. So life went at the Belasco when one Dave was the star and another owned the shop.

New theaters were being erected in the New York of 1911–1912. Winthrop Ames opened his exquisite bandbox, the Little. William A. Brady put time and money into his trim Playhouse, which was a gift to Grace George. The Shuberts, aware of the gradual northward march of the drama, negotiated a deal with William K. Vanderbilt which gave them the Broadway–50th Street site, occupied by the American Horse Exchange, a horse show ring, and upon the site they erected the fabulous Winter Garden. Broadway's hits of the period were whopping hits; runs were getting longer. Such productions as *The Pink Lady, Bunty Pulls the Strings, Bought and Paid For, Around the World* (a Hippodrome spectacle), *Within the Law,* and *Peg O' My Heart* played remarkable engagements. The tough-talking Brady was moving along. He was making many errors of judgment, as when he let that million-dollar property, *Within the Law,* slip from his hands. He wasted his time on such nonsense as *Sauce for the Goose* and Owen Davis's *Making Good,* but over a period of three weeks he brought forth two of the most successful plays of the decade—*Bunty Pulls the Strings* and *Bought and Paid For. Bunty,* a placid Scotch comedy by Graham Moffat, was refused by Grace George because she thought it should be done with an all-Scotch cast. It wasn't too sturdy as a touring attraction, but in New York it packed the Comedy Theater for a run of nearly four hundred performances.

George Broadhurst's *Bought and Paid For* was a story of a millionaire who marries a telephone girl and reminds her of the difference in their stations when he takes too much to drink. The play was written as a serious drama, and much of it was played seriously, but it succeeded because of its good comedy, because of the abundant entertainment supplied by the character of Jimmy Gilley, a brassy shipping clerk. Broadhurst was a-prowl in the theater district one evening when he looked in on a scene of William Hurlbut's play, *New York,* just in time to hear an obscure young actor deliver a "goddam you" speech to Beverly Sitgreaves. He went backstage when the curtain fell and engaged Frank Craven for the role of the flip Gilley. Some months prior to the New York opening Brady tested the play in Middletown, New York, with Henry E. Dixey and Ida Conquest in the

111

leading roles. He then closed it, dismissed Dixey and Miss Conquest, and engaged Charles Richman and Julia Dean in the belief that they would give greater strength to the serious side of the play. But it was still Jimmy Gilley's play when *Bought and Paid For* came into the Playhouse in the fall; it was Craven's performance as the heroine's glib and parasitical brother-in-law that turned Broadhurst's drama into a hit.

Craven, a child actor in *The Silver King,* and once employed in a tack factory, had had a dreary stage career up to the time of *Bought and Paid For,* but with that he achieved solvency. And prestige. His job-hunting days were over. There was now to be time for his golf and for playwriting on his own account. And as Craven kept playgoers roaring with laughter, and as the play sold out night after night, Bill Brady, his black hat pulled down low over his eyes and his black cigar clamped in his mouth, would stand at the 48th Street curb, presenting a study of a satisfied showman, watching all New York surge into his new Playhouse. This same Brady found himself in the news columns, unpleasantly enough, two days before Christmas when Wright Lorimer, who had been the star of *The Shepherd King* (his real name was Walker M. S. Lowell, and he had filed suit against Brady for $148,400 for alleged violation of contract), killed himself by thrusting his head into the oven of a gas stove.

There was little theatrical small talk that fall that failed to include smiling mention of the brazen Jimmy Gilley; playgoers developed an affection for the upstart, just as they were to do in seasons to come for Winchell Smith's Lightnin' Bill Jones and George Kelly's braggart, Aubrey Piper. And if tavern talk in Shanley's, at the Knickerbocker grill, or in Jack's, over scrambled eggs and Jack Dunstan's famous Irish bacon, overlooked Craven's characterization of Gilley, it certainly got around to Mlle. Gaby Deslys (pronounced *gah-bee deh-liss*) and to George Arliss's performance as the crafty and brilliant Prime Minister in Louis N. Parker's *Disraeli* at Wallack's.

Arliss was a thin-faced, smallish man, inclined to sinister roles, a creative and intellectual actor who invariably gave a lesson in acting to fellow members of his trade, whether he was playing the wily Devil in Molnar's *The Devil,* or a superior Shylock in Winthrop Ames's production of *The Merchant of Venice,* or the evil Rajah of Ruhk in *The Green Goddess* or the brilliant Jew of Parker's historical play, *Disraeli.* Arliss, seldom without his monocle, started at London's Elephant and Castle Theater in 1887 in the melodrama *Saved From the Sea,* and after a generally discouraging career came to America with Mrs. Pat Campbell for a stay of four months, and remained for the greater part of a lifetime. It was Arliss's extraordinary character delineation of Disraeli at the time (the play was staged by that skillful workman, Hugh Ford, and presented with a cast including Dudley Digges, Marguerite St. John, Herbert Standing, and the inevitable and indispensable Margaret Dale) that brought this tribute to the Britainborn actor from the observant and theater-wise Walter Prichard Eaton, writing in "The American Magazine": *

He holds the attention just as the striking personality of Disraeli would in life; he brings the spectator under the spell of his eyes and his voice. Disraeli was, with it all, a good bit of a bluff, and knew he was, and a good bit of a humorist, with a warm corner in his heart for his elderly wife; and a good bit of a dreamer, too, who saw an imperial England with an Oriental's eyes. It is easy to find the suggestion of all these contradictory traits clearly made in Mr. Arliss's portrait, and yet fused into unity, as in the man himself. . . . He represents for us acting in its best estate, an art at once broad and subtle, vivid as life, and truly creative. To miss seeing him is to miss one of the finest pleasures of our contemporary theater.

Mademoiselle Gaby Deslys, of the Gaby Glide, had a round, pretty, doll-like face and big gray eyes. Her reputation as a charmer, prior to her arrival in New York in the fall of 1911, was founded upon a monstrous fabrication, that she had upset the throne of Portugal, and she just never took occasion to deny that gifts had been lavished upon her by the boy monarch, King Manuel. When she set foot upon the soil of the United States after walking down the gangplank of the liner *La Lorraine* she was met by a swarm of reporters, including women representatives of the sob squad, and dozens of photographers. It was a greeting that might have been expected by a Bernhardt. Gaby was news on her first day in America, and the Shubert press department, as represented by the relentless A. Toxen Worm, taking over when the City Desks were done with the story, kept pounding away in behalf of the fair Parisian.

She was a considerable disappointment—certainly her dancing was— in her first Winter Garden appearance, but she was a striking figure when she came forth in a long green and gold opera coat, a toque of brilliants, and a towering black feather. And when she appeared two months later in

* Eaton, Walter Prichard, "George Arliss," *The American Magazine,* January, 1912.
113

Vera Violetta her English had improved, she was much more vivacious, she danced with more spirit, and the Shuberts were then glad that they had brought her over. "Gaby," says Lee Shubert—and his eyes light up when he speaks of her—"was a wonderful woman and a good actress. She would never leave the theater; she was a grand person, an artist, and not a party girl. We paid Gaby four thousand dollars a week in town and five thousand on tour. That was more than we ever gave anybody in any show until *Wonder Bar* came along. Then Al Jolson got six thousand a week."

On the less sensational side, Mrs. Fiske, of the darting comedy and the finger-at-the-forehead style of playing, found an amusing comedy in Harry James Smith's *Mrs. Bumpstead-Leigh*. John Drew turned again to the suavity of Hubert Henry Davies for his written-to-order *Single Man*. Augustus Thomas contributed a thoughtful play, his best play, in writing about the double standard of morality in *As a Man Thinks*, in which John Mason gave his finest performance as the liberal-minded Dr. Seelig. E. H. Sothern and Julia Marlowe did a series of Shakespearean performances at the Broadway Theater, went to England and got married, and returned for more of Shakespeare at the Manhattan Opera House. There was no lack of Shakespeare during the year, as it was also given by John E. Kellerd and the redoubtable Robert B. Mantell.

The Irish Players of Dublin, brought over by Liebler & Company, opened Synge's *The Playboy of the Western World* to a night of wild hostility, to boos and jeers and vegetable throwing, a reception similar to that the play had received in Dublin. And it was on the opening night of the Armstrong-Mizner *The Deep Purple* that George M. Cohan went up to Paul Armstrong and said, "It's great, kid. You ought to thank George Tyler for that cast."

"Not speaking to him," said Armstrong.

"Well," said Cohan, "you should thank Hugh Ford for his direction."

"Not speaking to him, either," said Armstrong.

Later, when Cohan met a crony at the Gilsey House bar, he was asked why Armstrong hadn't made a speech. "Oh," grinned Cohan. "He's not speaking to the audience."

Armstrong and Mizner knew the trick of melodrama writing. They also had a certain affection for the sordid characters who peopled their plays; they mingled with many of the types in their after-dark, about-Manhattan prowlings. Their *Deep Purple* was a hearty success, and they followed it with a seagoing melodrama, *The Greyhound*, snapped up by Wagenhals &

Danilo and "The Widow"

Donald Brian and Ethel Jackson in a blissful moment from Franz Lehar's *The Merry Widow*, the rage of 1907 (Culver Service Collection—Photo by White).

The Castles

Vernon and Irene Castle as a dancing team that thrilled New Yorkers in *Watch Your Step* in 1914 (Hill Studio).

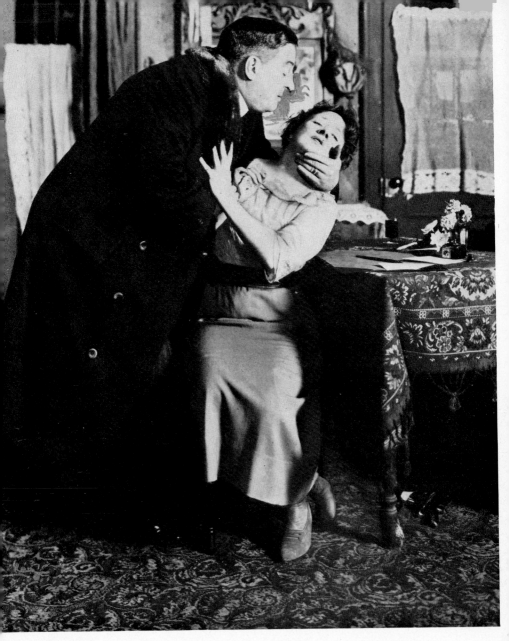

The Easiest Way

Joseph Kilgour, as the wealthy and predatory Wall Street man, and Frances Starr, as the irresolute and tragic Laura Murdock, in a second-act scene from Eugene Walter's powerful drama—Stuyvesant Belasco Theater, 1909 (White Studio).

Kemper the instant it was off the typewriter. *"The Greyhound,"* Douglas Wood now recalls—he was in the original cast—"was certainly no great shakes as dramatic literature, though it was a gripping and effective melodrama. However, the authors, Armstrong and Mizner, a couple of characters, took their brainchild very seriously. Every now and then at rehearsal they would decide that the dialogue needed careful rephrasing. All action would be halted, and the very large company would remain frozen in suspended animation while Mizner, with his perpetual brown derby angled at the side of his head, and Armstrong, with a black sweater and rough cap, strode back and forth across the stage, arm in arm, in whispered consultation. Finally they would halt. The new line had been decided, and was to be inserted in the manuscript. It would turn out to be something like this: 'She ain't never done nothin' like that nohow.' "

The Armstrong-Mizner following, which was considerable, turned out at the Astor Theater in late February of 1912 to watch the aboard-ship underworld at work—Henry Kolker as a polished villain, who thought his pretty wife had swallowed poison; Elita Proctor Otis, as a flamboyant adventuress, Deep Sea Kitty; Jay Wilson as a dumb crook. And there was Robert McWade as McSherry, the sharp-eyed detective, who gave the gang a hell of a time. *The Greyhound* boomed along to enormous trade, packing the Astor as *Seven Days* had done, and then, in mid-April, there was hardly any business at all. For on the evening of Sunday, April 14, at eleven-forty o'clock, the White Star liner *Titanic*, largest steamship afloat, New York–bound on her maiden voyage, collided with an iceberg 800 miles off Newfoundland and some 1,284 miles east of Sandy Hook. At 2:30 A.M. the *Titanic* upended and sank with the loss of 1,513 of the 2,206 aboard. The New York producer, Henry B. Harris, was among the 1,513 who perished. The catastrophe served to reduce sharply the attendance in the New York playhouses for several nights and caused playgoers to shun *The Greyhound* for nearly a week. The make-believe ship scenes upon the Astor stage brought to mind, all too vividly, the proud liner that had plunged to the bottom of the Atlantic.

Paul Armstrong continued his playwriting right up to the time of his death in 1915, but the restless Mizner, a man of many trades, quit as a playwright with *The Greyhound.*

I met him years later when we were both working on the Warner Brothers lot in Burbank, California. Tall, gaunt, and outspoken, hearty, lewd,

115

and crude, he liked to talk of the Klondike and of the Broadway of Lillian Russell and Diamond Jim Brady; he didn't belong in that strange Hollywood world of stucco and tiled roofs, Jap butlers and cocktail parties, lemon groves and polo ponies.

"You're right," he said. "What the hell am I doing out here? I'm a fish out of water. But I'm working. They're paying me goddam well. And there's one way to look at it. Being in this screwy business is the shortest cut between here and the grave."

Enter Oliver Morosco upon the Broadway scene. He was a Californian, a one-time acrobat, who came into the theater with a shoestring of forty dollars and ran it into fifteen million. He had money, prestige, theaters, and swarms of actors working for him; he operated the old Burbank Theater in Los Angeles as a West Coast producing center and built the beautiful playhouse in New York that bears his name. But throughout his career he was plagued by lawsuits; in the mid-twenties he went into bankruptcy with debts of a million and assets of two hundred dollars; and he was a disillusioned and embittered showman, with eight cents in his pocket, when, some years later, he was killed by a Los Angeles streetcar.

Morosco brought numerous plays to Broadway from his California laboratory, and his success average with these productions was unusually high. In one year, 1912, he presented two pieces, *The Bird of Paradise* and *Peg O' My Heart,* both of which have become legendary. *The Bird of Paradise,* an idyll of Hawaiian life, was all about the love of Luana, beautiful native princess, for an American scientist who was in the Hawaiian island seeking to isolate the germ of leprosy. The American, upon meeting Luana, renounced his American sweetheart and gave himself over to the languors of the islands. When he finally got tired of her she hurled herself into the crater of a volcano. The play was written by Richard Walton Tully, graduate of the University of California, ranch owner and breeder of pedigreed Arabian horses—an authorship challenged by Mrs. Grace Fendler, an erstwhile schoolteacher, who charged that the play was plagiarized from her own *In Hawaii,* and whose bitter litigation was in the courts for eighteen years. She won a verdict of $608,000, but this award was later reversed by the New York Court of Appeals, which ordered Mrs. Fendler to pay a judgment of $2,338 to the author and Oliver Morosco.

The Bird of Paradise got a cast that deserved better material. Laurette

116

Taylor, New York–born and of Irish-American parentage, who had been billed as La Belle Laurette in her early vaudeville days, was engaged for the role of the tragic Luana; her co-players included that able actor, Lewis S. Stone, who later gave up the theater for a career in pictures. *The Bird of Paradise* took something of a blasting from the New York press, but it did well enough on Broadway and became a prodigious money-maker as a road show and as a stock-company play. The countryside swarmed with Luanas—Lenore Ulrich (she later dropped the "h") and Bessie Barriscale were among those who toured in the part—and Laurette Taylor could have played Tully's heroine in thirty states, but she lost all interest in Luana when she found herself suddenly taken with a sentimental comedy called *Peg O' My Heart.*

Written by J. Hartley Manners, this was a tale of a gauche, redheaded, untutored little Irish girl who comes to live, by the terms of an uncle's will, in the frigid household of a family of aristocratic English relatives. The comedy was unceremoniously rejected by George M. Cohan, but it was taken by Morosco after he had read the first act. There came the time for the first New York rehearsal, called for the stage of the old Weber & Fields Music Hall on a morning in the late fall of 1912. H. Reeves-Smith, Hassard Short, Christine Norman, Reginald Mason, and others of the company arrived at 11 A.M. and waited until one-thirty, but Miss Taylor did not appear. The stage manager suggested that everybody leave and return at two-thirty. The players were back at that time and waited until five-thirty. No Miss Taylor, no Mr. Manners. The same thing happened on the following day and again on the third day. On the fourth day the company, quite out of patience and ready to drop the play, was prepared for a walk-out when star and author appeared. They had an excuse: they had been married after the successful coast tryout of *Peg O' My Heart* and just did not want to interrupt their honeymoon. Manners went around speaking to everybody, but Miss Taylor ignored her cast, and by the time the reading of the play began everyone was fairly furious. But the instant she spoke her first line—and I have this on the eye-witness testimony of Hassard Short—the entire atmosphere changed. "That alluring smile and those hazel blue eyes and that brogue," relates Mr. Short, "were just too much for all of us and we suddenly found ourselves adoring Laurette as much as her audiences did for years."

During the long, long run of *Peg O' My Heart* at the Cort, Laurette Tay-

lor and her players were asked to give a special performance, a performance to begin at 11 A.M. for an audience of exactly one person, a distinguished visitor then appearing at the Palace Theater. All members of the
company excitedly agreed and a souvenir program was printed. It read
thus:

Mardi le vingt-sept mai 1913
REPRÉSENTATION   SPÉCIALE
en honneur de la grande
SARAH BERNHARDT
Hommages respectueux de ses confrères Américains
LAURETTE TAYLOR
dans une comédie de jeunesse en trois actes
Peg de mon coeur
Par J. Hartley Manners

"The Divine Sarah" sat completely alone, far down front, in a special
chair and with a footstool for her bad leg. She was a responsive audience,
laughing and applauding at the right times. Miss Taylor made a little curtain speech, taking Michael, her dog, out with her. Bernhardt thanked the
American actress; the Americans, she observed, were a hospitable people
and seemed to be getting more so as the years went by. Perhaps sometime
Miss Taylor would be in Paris? If so, she would be invited to see *Camille*
under the same conditions.

Peg O' My Heart played for more than six hundred times at the Cort and
could have stayed three years, but Laurette Taylor was tired of the role.
She didn't care about touring in it, either. Not even to Chicago. But there
were many actresses clamoring for it, and Morosco sent out six companies.
Miss Taylor went to London to do "Peg," and about a decade later she
revived the comedy in New York, but then it failed as emphatically as it
had succeeded.

The year of Morosco's invasion of the East was one of considerable novelty, experimentation, and managerial daring in the Broadway area. Winthrop Ames brought over Max Reinhardt's production of *Sumurun*, a word-
less play out of the spirit of the Arabian Nights, a play of humor and fancy
and love and tragedy, beautifully done. Ames also opened his tiny Little
Theater with Galsworthy's *The Pigeon*, a thoughtfully written comedy that
brought forth human and delightful characterizations from Frank Reicher

and Russ Whytal. And later, within the confines of his charming and cozy playhouse, Ames offered Arthur Schnitzler's *The Affairs of Anatol,* a comedy that was witty and wise, and entirely Continental in flavor. John Barrymore was a beguiling Anatol; his five leading women, appearing in as many episodes, were Marguerite Clark, Doris Keane, Isabelle Lee, Gail Kane, and Katherine Emmet. Perhaps the most unforgettable of Anatol's affairs was that with Mimi, an actress, who had agreed with Anatol that "when the time comes we'll each go our own way without any fuss." The time did come when the lighthearted Anatol wanted to go his own way, and he found it an ordeal to tell Mimi of his decision. But before he could break the news to her he found himself overcome with fury upon being told by Mimi that she was madly in love with someone else. That episode was called "The Farewell Supper," and Doris Keane was an excellent Mimi.

And then there were such pieces as the widely discussed *Hindle Wakes,* Stanley Houghton's drama, which won high critical approval but scant attention from the public; *The Yellow Jacket,* Chinese fantasy done in the Chinese manner; the all-star revival of *Oliver Twist,* and Charles Frohman's presentation of *The Attack,* written by Henri Bernstein, author of *The Thief.*

Houghton's *Hindle Wakes,* considered daring at the time, was a study of life in Lancashire, telling its story of the seduction of a mill girl by the wealthy millowner's son during a week end spent together at Blackpool, and of the girl's rejection of an offer of marriage. "You say he's behaved like a blackguard to me," she says. "Will it make an honest woman of me to marry me to a blackguard?" This sex-problem drama was dominated by the performance of a tall, lank, slightly stoop-shouldered young actor from England named Herbert Lomas, in the role of the old fanatical and Puritanical millowner. It remained for Percy Hammond, then writing for the "Chicago Tribune," to make the unqualified statement that Lomas's acting was the best he had ever seen.

This was the same Hammond who observed, after he had shifted his operations to New York, that if gin and senility didn't get him, the Shuberts would. Hammond had always believed that the day would come when he would be barred from all the Shubert playhouses. Such exclusion was in store for Alexander Woollcott and for other and less spectacular practitioners of the trade of dramatic criticism, and the brilliant Hammond, whose seemingly effortless reviews gave no indication of the agonies that

119

went into the composition of every notice, kept wondering as to when it would be his turn to take his place on the Shubert blacklist.

"Oliver Twist," one of the first of the Dickens novels to be dramatized, was impressively produced by Liebler & Company, with Constance Collier as Nancy, Lyn Harding as Bill Sikes, Marie Doro as Oliver, and Nat Goodwin as Fagin, the arch criminal. There was considerable tumult about Goodwin's performance, and critic Channing Pollock, with time to think it over, conceded that it was a good characterization but by no means a great one.

John Mason contributed strong acting, as usual, to Bernstein's *The Attack*, but the principal service given by that drama was the introduction to New York of a young Swedish actress, Martha Hedman. Charles Frohman received her at London's Savoy during one of his many stays in England and was instantly pleased with her voice, poise, and beauty. He had been having difficulty finding an actress for his New York production. The play was then being done in Paris by Lucian Guitry. Could Miss Hedman go to Paris the next day and see the play? She could. Would she come to him immediately upon her return and tell him if she could play it. She would. She went to Paris, returned to London, and called again upon Frohman. There was a long, awkward silence after she had exchanged greetings with him. He kept his eyes upon her and finally he spoke abruptly.

"Can you, or can you not, play that girl's part?"

"I can."

"That's fine. I'll give you a contract. Three months' guarantee and your fare back and forth across the ocean. I shall see you in New York in the beginning of August." So Miss Hedman, who studied for the stage in Helsingfors, Finland, under the tutelage of Madame Siri von Essen Strindberg, first wife of the dramatist, came to New York. She was an immediate success in *The Attack* and she charmed the town three seasons later in *The Boomerang*. Then she married and neglected her career. Many actresses have been known to do it.

There were other developments of the time that must not be overlooked in this chronicle. Three plays dramatized from best-selling novels—"The Trail of the Lonesome Pine," by John Fox, Jr.; "The Grain of Dust," by David Graham Phillips, and "Freckles," by Gene Stratton Porter—were quick failures, and not because the fad was disappearing but because they were completely lacking in vitality as pieces for the theater. William Faversham gave an eloquent performance as Antony in his own production of *Julius Caesar*. The farce *Officer 666*, written by Augustin MacHugh and expertly rewritten by Winchell Smith, became a surprise success for Cohan & Harris. Effie Shannon and the accomplished Bruce McRae gave distinction to *Years of Discretion*, written by the Hattons, Frederic and Fanny Locke; and Douglas Fairbanks strengthened his hold upon the affections of our playgoers with his energetic performances, which included wall-scaling, in an inconsequential comedy labeled *Hawthorne of the U.S.A.* This one told how a young American soldier of fortune came to the rescue of a Balkan monarch, put the monarchy on a paying basis, turned it into a democracy, and won a royal bride after winning half a million at Monte Carlo.

When Effie Shannon, who had begun her stage career at the age of ten in *Uncle Tom's Cabin*, signed her contract to play in *Years of Discretion*, an allowance of $500 for gowns seemed adequate, but in further reading of the play she came to realize how well the part of Ellie Howard would have to be dressed and she found herself in acute distress. She kept a clothes-buying appointment with Belasco at Bendel's at 10:30 A.M. and they were in the shop all day, with the mannequins in an endless parade before her. She selected, among other things, a rose brocade evening gown, a rose velvet evening wrap trimmed in sable, two lace negligees, a handsome velvet street dress, and several wonderful hats, one of them with the most beautiful aigrettes she had ever seen. And then she spent a restless night worrying. Why, those aigrettes alone would take all of the $500 that had been allotted her. In the morning she made a decision. She would give up the part in *Years of Discretion*. She well knew that she couldn't afford all of that Bendel finery, and she called immediately, and almost tearfully, upon Tunis Dean, Belasco's general manager. Belasco appeared as she was talking to Dean and telling him that they would have to get another actress. Belasco listened. Then he smiled. Then he murmured, "Effie Shannon, you didn't really think I was going to let you in for all those rags, did you? I don't want you to pay for them. All I want you to do is to shine in them."

Plays of crime and criminals—"underworld drama" was the category into which they were grouped by the press—came along in a steady procession. *The Man Inside,* a melodrama by Roland B. Molineaux, the only former inmate of a death house to become a Broadway playwright in the history of America—he had spent twenty months at Sing Sing following his conviction in 1901 for the murder by poison of Mrs. Katherine L. Adams, and won acquittal in a second trial—was a mildly effective piece, given a good production by Belasco, but the theater's most exciting night in that year of 1912 was brought about with the opening of the melodrama, *Within the Law.* It earned $980,000 with its Broadway run and numerous road companies.

The story of the strange case of *Within the Law,* Bayard Veiller's melodrama of the shopgirl unjustly accused of theft and sent to prison, who avenges herself by the device of marrying the handsome son of her erstwhile employer, has been recited many times but it is dramatic enough to be worth another, and an accurate, retelling. Veiller, who had learned the ways of cops and robbers in his days as a New York police reporter, wrote *Within the Law* in three months. It was sent to, and firmly rejected by, George M. Cohan, George Tyler, Wagenhals & Kemper, and Charles Frohman—another million that C.F. missed by a wrong decision. Cohan liked the melodrama but he didn't believe any play with a crook for a heroine had a chance. Finally, William A. Brady read *Within the Law* and bought it. Grace George declined the part of Mary Turner, and Emily Stevens was engaged for it. In the meantime, Veiller was having financial difficulties. He needed $3,000 to save his house, and for that ridiculously paltry sum—his royalties within another year or so would have exceeded $3,000 weekly had he held his play—he sold *Within the Law* outright to Selwyn & Company, his agents, Arch Selwyn doing a lot of scurrying to get the cash.

Brady took the play to Chicago. Emily Stevens was utterly miscast as the tearful and beautiful Mary, controlling the operations of a group of crooks, and the melodrama seemed a doubtful property. Arch Selwyn, however, didn't think so, and he kept after Brady, trying to buy him out. Brady, annoyed, finally agreed to sell his interest for $10,000, but he imposed a condition. The time was then three o'clock in the afternoon. Selwyn would have to bring in the money by six o'clock on the same day—and in cash. "I'll be back in three hours," said Selwyn, and hurried out. He went instantly to Elizabeth Marbury, who was a partner in his play agency. Selwyn mortgaged his and brother Edgar's interest in the business—Edgar was then in Egypt with his bride, Margaret Mayo—and Arch had to forge his signature—and at exactly six o'clock he was again in the presence of Brady and Lee Shubert. He put ten one-thousand-dollar bills on the desk. A slow smile spread over the broad, Irish face of Brady, who had not expected Selwyn to get the money. He turned to the grinning Selwyn and said, "Young man, I wish you luck."

Selwyn took Jane Cowl to see the final performance of *Within the Law* in Chicago, and she agreed to play Mary Turner. He engaged Holbrook Blinn to restage the play, sold Al Woods an interest in the production, and *Within the Law* opened the Eltinge Theater, just built by the oncoming Woods. The melodrama sold out the second night and almost every night for the next two years. Eight companies were sent on tour. Money rolled in for everybody except poor Veiller. He didn't own a dime of the play, and the suddenly rich and somewhat contrite Selwyns began paying him $100 per week per company. When Arch Selwyn met Brady soon after *Within the Law* became Broadway's sensation, Selwyn, in his peculiarly sadistic fashion, asked the older showman if he had any more plays to sell.

San Francisco Bill glared at him, bit into his cigar stub, and said slowly, "Young man, it will give me a great deal of pleasure if you will get the hell out of my sight."

CHAPTER VIII

The Stock Company Craze

GEORGE M. COHAN was, by now, a man of new importance in the theatrical scene; he was being taken seriously as a playwright. He deserted the song-and-dance field with his writing of the popular *Get-Rich-Quick Wallingford* from the stories of George Randolph Chester and he later came along with the nonmusical, *Broadway Jones*. And now, in 1913, he contributed *Seven Keys to Baldpate*, dramatized from the novel of Earl Derr Biggers. "Baldpate," a farce comedy with a trick finish, was the best playwriting job of Cohan's career. It brought a widespread, if somewhat reluctant, appreciation of his skill as a dramatist. He followed "Baldpate" with *The Miracle Man*, and its failure was tremendously disappointing to him. But "Baldpate" was enough of a success to satisfy a playwright for a decade. Stock companies did it for ten years; amateur organizations turned to it zestfully; The Players of New York's Gramercy Park selected it for a spring revival. In one way and another, it earned money for Cohan throughout his life. Except for sheer luck, he would never have seen the play on any stage. As he was driving to Hartford for the tryout at Parsons Theater, one of his favorite road stands, his car overturned as it was approaching the city. His daughter Georgette suffered a fractured skull; Cohan and Wallace Eddinger, his leading man, received cuts and bruises. Eddinger was unable to appear at the opening performances, and Hartford saw Cohan in the role of the writer, William Hallowell Magee, who took himself off to the desolate Baldpate Inn in the dead of winter to get the desired peace and quiet for the writing of a book. Eddinger, a thoroughly engaging actor, who had been something of a boy wonder in the role of Little Lord Fauntleroy, recovered in time for the tumultuous *première* at New York's Astor Theater. He gave a smooth, expert, tongue-in-cheek performance as the harassed Magee.

124

"It's a hell of a hit, kid," said Sam Harris to Cohan as the curtain fell on the first of the two acts of "Baldpate." "That Eddinger," said Cohan. "He's showing me how that part should be played."

Arthur Hopkins, a short, thick-set, laconic Ohioan, strolled down to Eighth Avenue and 23d Street in 1905, rented a musty storeroom, started a nickelodeon, and thereby entered the amusement world of the metropolis. He tried playwriting in a tentative fashion, went in for producing vaudeville acts, and in 1912 the manuscript of a fantasy by Eleanor Gates called *The Poor Little Rich Girl*—all about the adventures of little Gwendolyn, who was rich in everything save the companionship of her parents—came his way. He liked it, and he was a man who was to make a career of backing his own judgments, producing plays because he liked them.

It was entirely characteristic of Hopkins, as he went about his preparations for *The Poor Little Rich Girl*, to be completely unawed by the fact that the far better known David Belasco was just then engaged with plans for a fantasy of his own, *A Good Little Devil*, and for which he had engaged such talented young people as Mary Pickford, Wilda Bennett, Lillian Gish, Regina Wallace, and Ernest Truex. The role of the good little devil, a poor little Scotch lad, who had a monstrous aunt, a vile old hag given to brewing witches' broth in caldrons, was assigned to Truex, who was then in his early twenties and married, although he didn't look more than seventeen. And Mary Pickford, already coming into fame on the screen, played Juliet, who loved the good little devil.

The competitive productions reached Broadway during the same month, and Hopkins won out. His *Poor Little Rich Girl* got a far better reception from the press; it fared better at the box office. He had a commercial and an artistic success in his first try. His name got into the papers and into the theater talk of the time.

It was very much in the consciousness of a young law clerk named Elmer L. Reizenstein (later changed to Rice) who, some months later, completed his first play, something he called *According to the Evidence*, and in which, by resorting to the flashback, he had written a melodrama backwards, violating all of the conventions of playwriting. Rice was aware of the imaginative showmanship put into the production of *The Poor Little Rich Girl* and he decided that Hopkins was the man for one of the two copies of his play; the other copy was for Selwyn & Company, a firm fairly bursting with

125

success since *Within the Law*. He delivered his two scripts and two days later he received a letter from each office. Would he care to drop in and talk about his play? He called first at the Selwyn office, but Crosby Gaige, who had written the letter for the Selwyns, was out at lunch. Rice decided not to wait. He went around to the Putnam Building to see Hopkins. And there, in a conversation of something less than fifty words, a deal was made. Rice rewrote portions of the play, following his producer's valuable suggestions, and Hopkins took the new script to Cohan & Harris. They bought it without hesitation, and Hopkins retained an interest as associate producer.

Rice's play, under the title of *On Trial*, was taken to Stamford for a two-day tryout. When the curtain fell on the second act at the opening-night performance Cohan walked up to Rice in the lobby and said, "Kid, I'll tell you what I'll do. I'll give you thirty thousand dollars right now for all your rights in this show. Right now—a check for thirty thousand. That's on the square."

The dazed young author, somewhat numbed, just looked at Cohan. Here was a twenty-one-year-old playwright, having his first experience in the theater and with theatrical people, who had been working for six years in a law office and had finally attained a salary of $15 weekly and who had thought he could get it up to $25 in another five years. And here was the great Cohan offering him $30,000! If Cohan had said $2,500 Rice would have quickly accepted it, but $30,000 was more money than there was in all the world. So he smiled weakly, tried to achieve a sophisticated attitude, and said he guessed he wouldn't sell. "I guess you're a pretty smart kid," said Cohan, giving him a nudge, and then he walked away.

Rice was being a shrewd businessman without knowing it. His royalties from the Broadway run of *On Trial*, which became a tremendous hit, and from the road company returns and stock company rights, totaled about $100,000, and that was in a day before Hollywood was paying its fantastic prices for stage hits. *On Trial* prowled America as *Peg O' My Heart* and *Within the Law* and *Seven Days* and *Paid in Full* and *The Man from Home* had done, and as *Fair and Warmer* and *Turn to the Right* and *The Man Who Came Back* and *The Bat* and *Abie's Irish Rose* were to do in seasons to come. Mary Ryan played the role of the harassed heroine of *On Trial* during the New York engagement. When a number three company was being organized Hopkins selected a young actress named Pauline Lord for the part. "Polly," he remarked later, "had actually retired at the age of

126

Perhaps You Saw These Hits?

eighteen or nineteen after her success in *The Talker.*" He sent her into the South, doing one-nighters. The Hopkins-Lord association continued for a decade.

Playgoers of New York in those months before war struck the European continent were entertained by John Barrymore in the Harvard Prize play, *Believe Me, Xantippe,* a farcical melodrama written by Frederick Ballard, a one-time cowpuncher; they were thrilled by some large-scale melo-dramatic rubbish called *The Whip;* they were charmed by the Laurence Housman–Granville Barker *Prunella;* jolted by *The Lure* and Richard Bennett's *Damaged Goods,* a clinical study of the results of hereditary syphilis, and completely fascinated by the Grand Guignol plays put on by Holbrook Blinn at the Princess.

The Lure, which brought the New York police galloping to the defense of decency and public morals, was written by a thirty-eight-year-old Texan, George Scarborough, born in Waco, the son of a lawyer. He had no interest in a career in law, but he definitely had in playwriting and he wrote nu-merous pieces (unsold, unproduced) during his days as a newspaper re-porter and as a Federal secret-service agent. It was while he was working for the government that he investigated a white-slave case and decided that it offered the material for a play. Result: *The Lure,* written in five days. Scarborough took his play to the Shubert office, and returned the same day and got an acceptance, a contract, and an advance payment. *The Lure,* telling its story of a girl rescued just as the madam was trying to talk her into becoming an inmate of a palatial brothel, brought protests from a squeamish press, the "Herald's" critic deploring it and asserting that "it treats of subjects not often discussed on the stage or mentioned in polite society." And later the police called and shut the play down. It reopened and continued to a moderately successful run. Scarborough stayed in the Broadway scene for some years. He wrote a good melodrama in *At Bay* and he was soon working for Belasco, completely surrounded by realism.

The Princess Players, offering horror plays in the Grand Guignol tradi-tion at the new and tiny theater in 39th Street, were in vogue for two years and contributed evenings of shocks and shivers as they operated under Blinn's astute direction. They did such short plays as Stanley Houghton's *Fancy Free,* William Hurlbut's *The Bride,* George Jean Nathan's *The Eter-nal Mystery,* Edward Goodman's *En Deshabille,* and Edward Ellis's study of a streetwalker, *Any Night,* grimly played by Ellis and Wilette Kershaw, who had created the part of the flashy showgirl in Edgar Selwyn's *The Country Boy.* Miss Kershaw copied her make-up for *Any Night,* she will tell you today, from that of a woman who used to be a habitué of the Haymarket (30th Street and Sixth Avenue)—black velvet suit, black wig, very white face, red lips, and a big black hat with a big feather.

The thrillers, Blinn discovered, were better than the comedies as box-office pieces. Perhaps the most popular of the chill and shudder plays was that ghastly playlet, *The Black Mask,* written by F. Tennyson Jesse and H. M. Harwood, London dramatists. It was acted by Blinn and Emelie Polini with all the artistry of professionals who knew how to get the utmost from every syllable, and it told its story of the Glassons, James and his wife Vashti. Glasson, a North-of-England miner, has been disfigured by an explosion in a mine and always wears a mask to cover his hideousness. He leaves one day for treatment and his wife's lover, Willie Strick, appears. Glasson returns unexpectedly. Willie attacks him and believes that he has killed him. Willie and Vashti decide to throw the body down a nearby mine shaft. She goes out of the room for a minute. Glasson regains consciousness and murders Willie and covers the body. He has on the mask when Vashti reappears, it having been agreed that Willie must wear it and pass as the husband until they can get to America. But now Vashti, in the belief that she is talking to her lover, tells him to take the dreadful thing off. They go into her bedroom. Her shriek of horror brings the play to its end.

"Those Princess thrillers never paid off," says Willette Kershaw, "because there were too many managers—Blinn, Brady, the Selwyns, Shubert, Comstock, and Gest." And from Brady there is this comment: "They didn't pay off because the theater was too small. We didn't lose much, but there was no profit. But one-act plays have never been a box-office success in New York except when Noel Coward and Gertrude Lawrence tried them. That was the only time."

Emily Stevens, who gave over the greater part of her brilliant and comparatively short career to the playing of neurotic and disagreeable women, came along at the time of the Princess Players to win further distinction in *Today,* a drama of a luxury-loving woman discovered in a house of assignation by her own husband. Doris Keane found her play of a lifetime in

Edward Sheldon's sentimental *Romance.* Elsie Ferguson won additional prestige in *The Strange Woman,* William Hurlbut's story of a woman of the world whose ideas shocked Delphi, Iowa. Maude Adams turned again to Barrie for *The Legend of Leonora,* in which the heroine pushed a cranky man off a moving train because he insisted upon keeping a window open, thoughtless indeed of him inasmuch as Leonora's daughter was suffering from a sniffy little cold. Billie Burke tried a serious play, Somerset Maugham's *The Land of Promise,* and Florence Reed revealed unsuspected dramatic power—not unsuspected, perhaps, by Al Woods—in the role of the hounded Marya Varenka, forced to wear a badge of shame in Michael Morton's melodrama, *The Yellow Ticket.* And it was when she was appearing in this play that she had the curtain rung down on John Barrymore. The incident is now to be recorded in its exact details.

The impetuous Woods (the success of *Within the Law* at his theater, the Eltinge, and the popularity of his own production of *Potash and Perlmutter* had put him to bidding for most of the plays being written and for the services of just about all the actors in New York) was no man to be discouraged once he decided that he needed a certain actress for a certain part. Florence Reed, daughter of a showman (Roland Reed, the actor-manager) and one-time leading woman of Proctor's Fifth Avenue Stock Company, was at the German Dispensary (renamed Lenox Hill Hospital after we went to war with Germany), recovering from a serious operation, when her door opened slowly one evening around nine o'clock and Woods poked in his head; he had sent flowers and champagne some hours before. The startled Miss Reed did not fail to observe that a manuscript bulged in his pocket as he came toward her.

"Becky," he said—he always called her Becky—"you've got to get well in a hurry. I've got the greatest play you ever heard of. I can't imagine anybody saying a wonderful nine-minute speech that begins, 'I am a Jewess,' but you. You've had a tough time, haven't you, sweetheart?" And then, abruptly, as he pulled the script from his pocket, "How long will it take you to get the hell out of here?" Woods's play was *The Yellow Ticket.*

Several days later Woods returned with the author and Hugh Ford, the director, and Barrymore, who was to have the leading role, and rehearsals actually began at Miss Reed's bedside. It was a visitation so fascinating to the floor nurses that a man in the adjoining room, whose light had gone unanswered, came very near choking to death. Florence Reed eventually

Distinguished American Dramatic Critics

1. James Huneker 2. Lawrence Reamer 3. Alexander Woollcott 4. Percy Hammond 5. William Winter 6. George Jean Nathan 7. Louis V. De Foe 8. Heywood Broun 9. Alan Dale

Within the Law

The tearful Mary Turner (Jane Cowl), shopgirl unjustly accused of theft, under arrest in the first act of Bayard Veiller's *Within the Law*, the melodramatic hit of the American theater in 1912–1913 (Culver Service Collection—Photo by White).

got out of the hospital with a half-paralyzed left leg, went to New Haven with the company, sat behind scenes during the first and second acts as an understudy played Marya Varenka, and then went on herself for Act Three, limping and hobbling through it. She received an ovation that shook the playhouse.

The Yellow Ticket moved into New York's Eltinge, became a hit, and went along for months, with Barrymore creating backstage tension every night by not appearing at the theater until a few minutes before his cue to go on. There came the evening during the last week of the run when he arrived in no shape for a performance. He was still in his dressing room when his cue came. The players on stage did what they could to cover his delay, and finally Barrymore, decidedly unsteady, made his entrance, went to Florence Reed and spoke words that were not in the script: "It's all right, little woman; it's all right, little woman." Miss Reed raced to the side of the stage and called out, "Ring down the curtain." Down came the curtain. Al Woods came thundering backstage, and John Mason, who played the evil Baron, went before the curtain and told the audience that an understudy would continue in the role of Julian Rolfe, that Mr. Barrymore was ill. It was an announcement greeted with a roar of sardonic laughter. They then began *The Yellow Ticket* all over again. John Barrymore never returned to the cast. His role was played on tour by Sydney Booth.

The tour of *The Yellow Ticket* was not without incident, either. There was a scene in the play in which the heroine, locked in a room by the predatory and lustful Baron, flung herself with all her strength against double doors in an effort to escape. Two stagehands were assigned each night to brace themselves against these doors as Florence Reed crashed into them at high speed. During a Pittsburgh matinee Miss Reed fled as usual from the pursuing Baron and hurled herself, as usual, against the scenery. This time the door yielded, Miss Reed hurtled through the opening, and John Mason had to run after her and bring her back. The two Pittsburgh stagehands who were supposed to block Marya Varenka's charge had gone out to get a beer. They never came back to the theater.

The swarthy, skinny, Russian-born Irving Berlin (once Izzy Baline, son of a rabbi), a former troubadour from the sidewalks of Manhattan, had by this time established himself as a big-time uptown composer. "Alexander's Ragtime Band" had made a song-writing hero of Nigger Mike's former singing waiter; and the facts in the case of Berlin's notable song hit are now duly presented. Henry B. Harris and Jesse Lasky built the Folies Bergère, the first cabaret-theater in America, and engaged Ethel Levey for the three-part opening bill. Lasky asked Berlin to write a song for her. Berlin responded with "I Beg Your Pardon, Dear Old Broadway." ("By the way," Berlin says today, "it was a very bad song and never got anywhere, although Levey sang it beautifully.") Berlin was sitting in at rehearsals when Lasky went to him again and said they needed a spot-in-one for Ethel Levey. Did he have another song? Yes, Berlin did have a new song, one he'd just finished and that nobody had ever heard. He then sang the chorus of "Alexander's Ragtime Band." "Yes," nodded Lasky, "that *is* a good song, but it's certainly not for Levey. She's a contralto and needs a song that can be sung much slower." "Alexander" was whistled by Otis Harlan for one performance only, the opening night of the Folies Bergère. It was sung for the first time by Emma Carus, who introduced it in Chicago, and was later put into the Friars' Frolic of 1911 and sung by Berlin, on the insistence of George M. Cohan.

The Folies Bergère experiment was an awful failure. When the theater, later named the Fulton, was completed it was discovered that there was insufficient space for the musicians and that there was no dressing room for chorus girls. The frantic management leased the cellar of a nearby house, and a tunnel to permit passage of performers from one place to the other was hastily constructed. The house from which below-ground space had been obtained turned out to be a brothel, but this revelation left the members of the Folies Bergère company seemingly undisturbed. It was sometime later that the brothel's madam went to Henry B. Harris to protest vigorously, on behalf of her inmates, about the language used by the showgirls!

The collapse of the Folies Bergère had been forgotten, Henry B. Harris had gone to his death aboard the *Titanic,* and "Alexander's Ragtime Band" had been sung throughout the world when C. B. Dillingham, then in the days of his greatest prestige, called upon Berlin to do the music and lyrics for a big new show, *Watch Your Step,* to be presented at the New Amsterdam. The librettist was, of course, Harry B. Smith, a man of amazing productivity, who wrote the books for a hundred musical shows in the course of a long career. Smith's books were generally riddled by the critics, and when *Watch Your Step* opened, the program bore this credit line: "Book (if any) by Harry B. Smith." Berlin's songs and his lyrics delighted both Smith and Dillingham. *Watch Your Step* had its Syracuse opening late in 1914 with its high-priced talent including Vernon and Irene Castle and a juggler by the name of W. C. Fields.

Vernon Castle, an Englishman, became the foremost dancer of the period, a success puzzling to American observers because the English never quite mastered the intricacies of America's ragtime dances. Vernon and Irene did the tango and the turkey trot in *Watch Your Step* and they created the delightful Castle Walk to a song Berlin wrote called "The Syncopated Walk." There were ovations for their dancing and for the clowning and juggling of W. C. Fields on the opening night in Syracuse. Fields was such a hit that nothing could follow him, and he threw the whole production out of key. Dillingham then had to choose between *Watch Your Step* and this Australian juggler. Fields was taken out of the show—he went on to fame via the *Ziegfeld Follies*—and *Watch Your Step*, now coordinated, was the success everybody thought it would be.

New York came under the spell of the Castles, it yielded to the madness of the new dances, and it gave its homage to Irving Berlin. He startled the song-writing world with his unending procession of hits—"Everybody's Doin' It" (not written to glorify any particular dance but rather the dance craze of the period), "Ragtime Violin," "I Want to Be in Dixie," "When the Midnight Choo Choo Leaves for Alabam'," "The International Rag," "Somebody's Coming to My House." "Irving Berlin," the "Theater Magazine" remarked, "has outdone Berlin in the writing of music and lyrics. . . . Berlin is now a part of America."

Stock companies were booming throughout America at the time World War I descended upon the continent of Europe. Road companies swarmed over the land, from ocean to ocean. Motion pictures were getting stronger, but the on-from-Broadway touring attractions and the resident stock organizations scattered over forty states were quite oblivious of threats to their existence from the industry of the screen.

The urban stock companies, operating in cities with populations from 20,000 to half a million, multiplied. They opened, they closed, they reopened. Some went along for two years, three years, without a week's layoff; they were integrated into the community life of their localities. And they were all over. Sylvester Poli, a stock pioneer, had companies in New

Haven and Bridgeport and Waterbury and Worcester and Scranton. The Lucille La Verne Players were in Atlanta, the Hazele Burgess Players in Jacksonville, the E. A. Schiller Players in Savannah, the Edward H. Robins Players in Toronto, the Albee Players in Providence, and the Bijou Players in Fall River. There was stock in Denver (Elitch's), in Boston (the Castle Square), in Brooklyn (the Crescent), in Manhattan (B. F. Keith's Harlem Opera House), in Portland, Oregon (the Baker Players), in Baltimore (the Auditorium Players), in Elmira (the Mozart Players), in Tacoma (the Wilkes Company), in Detroit (Jessie Bonstelle), and in Pittsburgh (Harry Davis), in San Francisco (the Alcazar), in Cleveland (Vaughan Glaser).

Stock stars had devoted followings. Priscilla Knowles drew money into a stock theater box office; so did Izetta Jewel, Evelyn Vaughan, Beulah Poynter, Bert Lytell, Norman Hackett, Emma Bunting, Evelyn Varden, Warda Howard, Eda von Luke, Leah Winslow, George Alison, Robert Gleckler, and Richard Buhler. Irene Timmons created stage-door stampedes on matinee days; so did Henrietta Browne, Thurlow Bergen, Theodore Friebus, Rodney Ranous, Lowell Sherman, Alfred Swenson, and Paul McAllister. The dark-haired and good-looking Clara Joel held stock audiences in her spell. Winifred St. Claire billed herself as "the best dressed leading woman in stock." Cecil Spooner, never a Broadway actress but always a stock favorite, wrote plays, managed her companies, ran a farm at New Canaan, Connecticut, and was once arrested for putting on a white-slave drama, *The House of Bondage*. John Craig, who presided over the famous Castle Square Theater in Boston, gave numerous plays long runs; he once reported that a family of four came to see one of his plays thirty-five times.

The stock company admission prices, ranging from 10 to 75 cents, were within the reach of all purses; managements didn't expect to get rich—and never did—and were content with a reasonable weekly profit. The cost of operating a stock company in the 1912–1915 period of the stock industry ran to $1,200 weekly—and up. Take Pittsfield, Massachusetts, one of the famous stock towns. William Parke, running a company there in 1912, estimated that his costs came to $1,300 a week, with actors' salaries consuming $700 of this, and that a week's intake of $3,000 was possible if capacity prevailed at all performances—but it never did. He made the point, somewhat ruefully, that the operating cost for the competitive motion-picture show was only $100 a week. Parke's plays were the popular bills of the time

—Mrs. Temple's Telegram, The House of a Thousand Candles, Alias Jimmy Valentine, The Man of the Hour; his patrons were his friends, his players were town favorites, and his theater brought the living theater to a stock-era city of 30,000.

When the stock company craze was at its peak more than four hundred companies were operating in the United States and in Canada. The royalty charges on plays ran from $150 to $400 weekly, but $600 was frequently paid for a late release. The leading women of stock were paid from $150 to $500 weekly, and some of the more illustrious ones received a percentage of the gross. Leading men drew from $150 to $300—some got more—and a competent director generally got $150 a week. Ingénues and juveniles received from $60 to $75, comedians were hired at $75 and up, and character players were paid from $75 to $100 in the better companies. Stock players with numerous companies, and for several years, were called upon to play an incredible total of twelve performances weekly; the eight-performance week was in effect generally as operating prices went up and conditions changed.

Actors and actresses had to supply their own clothes for ordinary roles, and a leading woman with an extensive wardrobe, and who had good looks and the ability to play a variety of parts, could find work fifty-two weeks in a year if she wanted it. Priscilla Knowles, who was a tremendous favorite with the devoted patrons of New York's Academy of Music, played at that house for more than two thousand performances. Many stock players, such as the dark, vigorous Miss Knowles, were known to the trade as "quick studies." There was a handsome leading man by the name of Rodney Ranous, who had a remarkable photographic memory. He always was letter-perfect by the time of the second or third rehearsal. His director was astounded one Monday evening, just before the curtain rose on the first performance of The Prisoner of Zenda, in which he had a long and tricky part, to find him studying in the wings as he waited to go on. It was so unusual that the director—he was James W. Doyle, one of the foremost men in the field—asked Ranous about it. Oh, smiled Ranous, there was nothing the matter. He was merely breaking in his part for the *next* week before giving his first performance of "Zenda."

Living theater reached the byways of America via the road show, which spread its tentacles to the far corners of the land. Many towns that did not have stock companies were served by traveling companies, all of them not necessarily engaged with Broadway-tested plays. *The Shepherd of the Hills* never got to the New York stage, but it was done in the one-night stands by four companies. *The Common Law* was never seen on Broadway, but three companies took it to the midlands. *The Rosary* had an insignifi-cant metropolitan run, but seven companies were necessary to show it to its enormous cross-country public. *Fine Feathers,* always considered by Eugene Walter to be his best play, gave up in New York in less than three months, but it got fifty-two weeks of road travel. *Fine Feathers* was played in New York by the handsome, forceful Robert Edeson, who came into the theatrical business via the box office of Colonel Sinn's Park Theater in Brooklyn. During the engagement of Cora Tanner in *Fascination* a member of the company was suddenly taken ill, and a performance might have been canceled except for Edeson's willingness to learn the part, and play it, in the emergency. He won a wager of one hundred dollars from Colonel Sinn and he never went back to his job as treasurer. He made numerous Broadway appearances, and he achieved definite matinee-idol status in his playing of the title role, that of a full-blooded North American Indian, in the college play, *Strongheart,* which William C. De Mille wrote and sold to Henry B. Harris three hours after he had completed it.

Such plays as *Fine Feathers*—*Strongheart* came along eight years earlier —took the living theater, imperiled by the rise of the motion picture and later given reason to fight for its very existence by the popularity of the talkies, to the great cities and to the towns and cities with populations of 5,000 and 10,000 and 20,000 and 50,000. They took it to East St. Louis and to Goshen, Indiana, to Boise, Idaho, and Waterloo, Iowa, to Hannibal, Missouri, and to Bath, Maine, and to Wichita Falls, Texas, and Logan, Utah, and Janesville, Wisconsin, and on up into Saskatoon, Saskatchewan. In January of 1913 more than two hundred touring companies were prowling the land. There were four companies out in *Bought and Paid For,* four in *Get-Rich-Quick Wallingford,* and three in *Baby Mine* and three in *Officer 666.* And in that Broadway flop, *The Rosary?* The total was six!

The menace that the movies held for the living theater, a menace heightened by the fact that such highly solvent and enterprising companies as Famous Players, Essanay, Biograph, Pathé, Kalem, Universal, Lubin, and Thanhouser were now engaged in fiercely competitive operations, was

136

stressed in a display advertisement inserted by the General Film Company of New York in the "Dramatic Mirror" in 1916. It read:

MANAGERS, ANSWER!

Is business poor in your house—poorer
even than last year?
Do you have to divide the patronage that
used to be all yours?
LISTEN——

Moving Pictures have saved the life of many a manager in your position.

There is no doubt about the movies—they will keep your house filled all the time. No human element to worry you, no quarrels and kicks. Every dressing room becomes a STAR room —your actors are always there on the moment. Your scenery is always perfect—your acts are the best that money and judgment can secure from the four corners of the world. Your program is excellently balanced with great multiple headliners—your companies are the best by selection and long experience.

But your public can no longer be fooled by low-grade pictures. The fans have been educated. They know and demand GOOD pictures. The General Film Service takes care of all that for you.

The mass migration of Broadway professionals to the West had not then begun, and the country's supply of actors—good actors, well-trained actors, for both stage and screen—then seemed inexhaustible. But the screen was being definitely successful in obtaining the services of such stage players as Dustin and William Farnum, John Barrymore, Marguerite Clark, Marie Doro, Tully Marshall, Cyril Scott, Digby Bell, Burr McIntosh, and Thomas W. Ross. They brought their theater training to a medium which owed a great deal of its popularity to the magic of Mary Pickford, to the debonair ways of Francis X. Bushman, to the intensity of Norma Talmadge, and to the heroics of Broncho Billy Anderson. And there was no American showman to dispute the claim of David Wark Griffith's *The Birth of a Nation*, based upon Thomas Dixon's *The Clansman*, to being the greatest road attraction of its time.

The high-speed farce comedies of the 1912–1915 era, plays for which the dynamic George M. Cohan set the style, were in particular demand as road and stock company attractions—such plays as *Officer 666* and *Never*

Say Die, Stop Thief and *Nearly Married, A Pair of Sixes* and *It Pays to Advertise, The Show Shop* and *The Rule of Three*. They were all expertly put together, well played and directed, but not one of them was the equal of Cohan's *Seven Keys to Baldpate* in mad, rollicking nonsense and sheer ingenuity. William Collier, a gifted, quiet-spoken, deadpan, underplaying comedian, was an actor who specialized in farces—*On the Quiet, Caught in the Rain, The Dictator, Nothing but the Truth*, and such. He got a good New York run out of *Never Say Die* and he decided, upon taking the play on the road, that he would break away from the conventional ballyhoo. So when he got to Chicago he passed around a circular that read thus:

We have not run a year on Broadway. We have run 163 performances, which, considering the conditions of the current season, is rather nifty. *Never Say Die* is not the greatest play in the world. It is a good comedy and you will like it. I am not the world's greatest actor, but my role fits me and every once in a while somebody in the audience laughs.

Margaret Mayo's farce, *Twin Beds,* seemed hopeless in its first New York week, and desperate means were necessary to keep it alive. The wily Arch Selwyn engaged a press agent named Pinky Hayes, a one-time circus man, and told him to do all he could for the piece at the Fulton. Hayes did. He hired four hay wagons and arranged for the simultaneous breakdown of each, on the stroke of noon, in four of the busiest blocks of mid-town Manhattan. Traffic jams ensued, gaping crowds gathered, and the wagon drivers were arrested for obstructing traffic and heavily fined. But Pinky Hayes's stunt had worked. Thousands had seen the *Twin Beds* banners atop the hay wagons, and the story of the tie-up appeared in all the papers. *Twin Beds* was selling out by the end of its second week.

A Pair of Sixes, written by Edward Peple, had all the appearances of a flop when it opened during a snowstorm in Hartford to $147 and it seemed even worse when it tried again in Newark—so weak that George Cohan went to Edgar MacGregor, who had staged it for H. H. Frazee, and said, "Listen, kid, you'll never get away with it." But the stubborn MacGregor liked his play and his cast—Hale Hamilton, Ann Murdock, Maude Eburne, Ivy Troutman, George Parsons—and he reopened after closing a second time and came into New York's Longacre Theater on an early spring evening in 1914.

"Before the run was over," remarked MacGregor many years later, "I turned in eighty thousand dollars to Harry Frazee and he never put in a nickel. That hit gave Harry big ideas. He went into baseball and before long he was selling Babe Ruth to the Yankees."

Cohan missed on *A Pair of Sixes,* as he had done on *Peg O' My Heart,* but his judgment was sharp enough when Roi Cooper Megrue and Walter Hackett came along with the racy *It Pays to Advertise,* and he gave his opinion to his partner, Sam H. Harris, in four words: "Sam, let's buy it."

It Pays to Advertise, with Ruth Shepley as its heroine and Grant Mitchell engagingly playing a rich soapmaker's son, who goes into business as a competitor and eventually sells out to the old man at a wonderful price, kept New York laughing for more than a year. Incidentally, Rodney Martin, Jr., besides making a million, got his girl. In those farces they always did.

Theatrical projects in considerable variety were submitted to New York in that first year of the grim, jolting headlines of the devastation of a continent in the grip of war. Mrs. Patrick Campbell, a headstrong woman and a vigorous actress, who had created the role of Pinero's Paula Tanqueray in the long ago, was brought over by George Tyler and the Lieblers to familiarize Americans with the adventures of Eliza Doolittle, a flower girl out of London's gutters, and her professor of phonetics in George Bernard Shaw's *Pygmalion.* The same Mrs. Pat, of course, who had shrieked in protest, during an early-century rehearsal, against the everlasting clop-clop-clop of passing hoofbeats in 42d Street, and for whom tanbark was spread across the thoroughfare—the literal-minded A. Toxen Worm, an earnest young press agent of prodigious build, taking George C. Tyler at his word when told to run down to City Hall and get from Mayor McClellan a tanbark permit. Mrs. Pat made her American debut on that visit of 1902, with George Arliss in her company, and offering a repertoire that included *The Second Mrs. Tanqueray* and Henry Arthur Jones's *The Notorious Mrs. Ebbsmith.* And she was now, in 1914, somewhat mature for the role of Eliza but she gave a spirited and enormously amusing performance.

The deft playwriting team of Harvey J. O'Higgins and Harriet Ford supplied an engaging comedy of kidnapers and detectives in *The Dummy,* a piece that was helped along mightily by delightful performances from Ernest Truex as the boy detective and little Joyce Fair, of the golden curls and pretty bows, who went on to playwriting fame—and to Congress—as Clare Boothe Luce. A trick melodrama of smuggled pearls called *Under Cover,* the work of Roi Cooper Megrue, erstwhile playreader, and cast with considerable magic by the Selwyns, brought excitement into the New York theater. William A. Brady put most of the scenery in his storehouse to good use in another melodrama, Thompson Buchanan's massive *Life,* done at the Manhattan Opera House, and done, as Walter Hampden later recalled, "with boat races, galloping horses, shootings, murders, heroism, and with my being hissed as the villain." And that was not so long after Hampden had been very saintly and sacred in *The Servant in the House.*

And it was during this year that Clyde Fitch's *The Truth,* gracefully revived by Winthrop Ames with Grace George as Becky Warder, again failed to bring playgoers stampeding to the theater; that David Belasco presented Leo Ditrichstein in Ferenc Molnar's delicate and well-acted *Phantom Rival;* that John Barrymore returned to A. H. Woods's management in Willard Mack's taut melodrama, *Kick In,* and that Jack Lait, from out of the City Room, wrote a glib and topical play of the perils of stenographers in *Help Wanted.*

There was also, and definitely on the side of art and the side of beauty, the romantic spectacle play of the Orient known as *A Thousand Years Ago,* the work of Percy MacKaye, son of Steele MacKaye, who turned to the writing of drama in verse when he came out of Harvard and who gave the theater *Jeanne d'Arc* and *Sappho and Phaon.* His *The Scarecrow* (in prose) delighted the critics even though practically nobody went to see it when it was first done at the Garrick Theater in 1911. It later won far greater appreciation in the foreign theater. MacKaye, the poet, student, and crusader, was more poetic than he was dramatic. He rendered conspicuous service in the writing of masques and chronicle plays and pageants, but he was too visionary for a theater that was frankly commercial.

News of Rita Jolivet's appearing in *A Thousand Years Ago,* of Conway Tearle and Ferdinand Gottschalk and Zelda Sears joining Grace George in *The Truth,* and of a very pleasant young leading woman named Lily Cahill, from out of Texas, coming forth in *Under Cover,* belonged to the province of the amusement pages. But the news pages in that year of 1914 carried items relating to folk of the theater that had elements of surprise. There was Adolph Klauber's resignation as dramatic critic of "The New

York Times" to become a member of the firm of Selwyn & Company, for whom his beautiful wife, Jane Cowl, had worked in *Within the Law*. There was the crush of filmgoers to see Annette Kellermann, of the Form Divine, in her first picture, *Neptune's Daughter*. There was the teaming of Evelyn Nesbit Thaw, seldom out of print since 1906, with Jack Clifford for dancing at the Jardin de Danse. There was the marriage in Hoboken, at the Lutheran Church, of Billie Burke and Florenz Ziegfeld. They had been introduced at a dance of the Sixty Club at the Hotel Astor, and it was during the run of *Jerry* at the Lyceum Theater that she left the theater after a Saturday matinee, picked up Ziegfeld at Sherry's, and she was Mrs. Ziegfeld when she returned from New Jersey for her evening performance. And there was the shocking announcement of the bankruptcy, in December of that year, of the high-powered producing firm of Liebler & Company. Its prodigal productions had been a drain upon its resources; it was overwhelmed by the immensity of its own large-scale operations. And the war in Europe, which was to flood the New York stage with hastily written war-theme plays during the next four years, had shut off many of the Lieblers' foreign markets.

The overambitious Lieblers (plus George C. Tyler) gave New York its first glimpse of Bernard Shaw's *Pygmalion*, just as Arnold Daly and Robert Loraine, with *Man and Superman*, had been early-century pioneers for G.B.S. It remained for the imaginative Granville Barker, the London actor-director-playwright, to submit *Androcles and the Lion* and *The Doctor's Dilemma*, and in so doing, and by bringing Anatole France's *The Man Who Married a Dumb Wife* into his bill, he introduced a genius in stage design, Robert Edmond Jones. Before the advent of Jones, scenery was just built, and with no great ceremony. It was painted, and usually by such men as Physioc, Ernest Thor, or Gates & Morange. Jones, in creating the scenery, properties, costumes, and color for the Anatole France satire on the garrulity of womankind, brought fame to himself and opened up a new department of the theater, a field that was soon to be overrun and overcrowded by less inspired practitioners.

Granville Barker was an advocate of unconventional stagecraft, a champion of new art forms and experimentation in stage design. He was content to use footlights and conventional interiors in his production of *The Doctor's Dilemma*, played with a fine English cast that included O. P. Heggie and Ernest Cossart. When he turned, however, to A *Midsummer Night's Dream,* footlights were omitted, old Merrie England folk songs were introduced, the fairies were gilded from head to toe, and the "curious settings suggested rather than portrayed the actual scenes of the play." The poetry was read swiftly, the text was uncut, and the production provided a generally exhilarating evening in the theater. But Barker's principal service to the New York stage, in the minds of many, was his introduction of Robert Edmond Jones. In later years, in writing of the decorative art of the theater, Jones made the assertion that he was more satisfied with the first-act design for the modern comedy, *Good Gracious Annabelle,* than with any other piece of work he had ever done. And he also observed that "America does not have to go to Europe for plays, nor for producers and artists. . . . I am heart and soul for Broadway and I believe that Broadway is worthy of a far better reputation than is accorded her."

In the pre-Jones years in the theater playgoers became accustomed to scenery that consisted of shaky wood wings and wrinkled ceilings, or no ceilings at all, and rumpled, unsteady backdrops. The scenery man always seemed to be someone who had engaged to do a hasty job just before the dress rehearsal. But with the introduction of the art of scenic design into the theater the new specialists came into a production before a cast was engaged; they worked to catch the feeling and atmosphere and mood projected by the dramatist and to make the scenery as much a part of a play as the writing and the acting, but never to make the play subservient to their backgrounds. Jones, with his stunning settings for *The Man Who Married a Dumb Wife,* led the way, and along came such masters of design and of stage lighting as Joseph Urban, Lee Simonson, Cleon Throckmorton, Norman Bel Geddes, Livingston Platt, Woodman Thompson, Ben Ali Haggin, Jo Mielziner, Raymond Sovey, Donald Oenslager, Stewart Chaney. Simonson, a designer of boundless imagination, made prodigious contributions to the productions of the Theater Guild. Urban, an American born in Vienna, who began his career in the office of a Viennese architect, designed castles and villas on the Continent and the Czar's Bridge over the Neva at Petrograd. He began his American career with the Boston Opera Company and was soon bringing pictorial loveliness to the *Ziegfeld Follies.* There was one occasion when Urban's lush and beautiful scenery was so elaborate, so expensive, and so unwieldy that it helped to kill off Edward Sheldon's *The Garden of Paradise,* the biggest Liebler failure.

There were several unexpected developments in New York's world of the theater—a small, tumultuous, congested, and self-obsessed world, bounded, as of early 1915, on the south by the Garrick Theater, the north by the Century, on the west by the Frazee, and the east by the Belasco—at the time Barker was being acclaimed and Jones was being discovered. *Sinners*, a moderately honest drama by the patient and plodding Owen Davis, was presented by the Playhouse by William A. Brady and became an enormous success, and *Children of Earth*, Winthrop Ames's ten-thousand-dollar prize play, written by New Hampshire's Alice Brown and selected by Ames, Adolph Klauber, and Augustus Thomas from 1,646 manuscripts, failed utterly at the Booth. The continuance of Davis's non-prize *Sinners* and the early closing of the fifty-seven-year-old Miss Brown's *Children of Earth* brought forth comment and head wagging on the subject of Broadway's unpredictability, but nothing like the consternation created by the discharge of one dramatic critic and the banishment (from Shubert theaters) of another.

Samuel Hoffenstein, the keen, dour, brilliant introvert who covered plays for the "Evening Sun," was fired for his review of Edward Knob-lock's *Marie-Odile* after David Belasco had made an in-person call on the managing editor. Hoffenstein, in considering the plight of the incredibly innocent nun, Marie-Odile, suddenly come down with child after a supposedly harmless meeting with a German corporal, made the observation that the play was "lacking in cumulative force, in human appeal, in every essential of dramatic quality"—criticism that would have been hardly noticeable in the considerably harsher New York reviews of a decade later.

Alexander Woollcott, given to emotional and sputtering prose in his enthusiasms and to hysterical abuse in his dissents, was blacklisted by the Shuberts for his review of a minor comedy, *Taking Chances*. He had served as critic for "The New York Times" for only a year at that time. Woollcott brought upon himself the damnation of the Shuberts for deciding that *Taking Chances*, a piece adapted from the French, was not "vastly amusing." The Shuberts asked the "Times," with a politeness hardly to be expected under the circumstances, that some reviewer other than Woollcott be assigned henceforth to cover its openings. The "Times," bristled, threw out the Shubert advertising—and a big daily chunk it was—went to court, and got a temporary injunction restraining the Shuberts from barring

Woollcott. The jubilant Woollcott, under this court order, went on attending the Shubert plays. The temporary injunction was vacated, but in a later decision a Supreme Court justice ruled that the producers had no legal right to keep the "Times's" critic out of their playhouses and directed that he be readmitted, pending an appeal.

The Shuberts fought the case to the highest tribunal of the state, the New York Court of Appeals, which eventually reversed the lower court. Its decision was that a theater manager may exclude any person from his playhouse save for reasons of race, creed, and color, holding that a theater, unlike a hotel or a restaurant, is not a public place. And Woollcott, for whom the ruction had been enormously advantageous, resulting in a by-line, more money at the office, and fairly worshipful attention from people of the theater, was again denied entrance to the Shubert houses. The brothers, Lee and J.J., and their tireless attorney, William Klein, won out legally, but as the months went by it became apparent that the Shuberts needed the "Times," and its circulation, far more than the "Times" needed the Shuberts. The brothers gave in. What was all the fuss about anyway? Why, of course Woollcott could come back to their theaters—welcome any time. He was a very decent fellow, and hadn't Mr. Lee often said that he was a very clever writer? So Woollcott smugly resumed his down-front seat and his kingly marches up and down the Shuberts's enchanted aisles, and the Shuberts's advertising was again accepted by "The New York Times."

Trans-Atlantic travel in the spring of 1915 was not an experience sought by timid souls. The Atlantic was infested with German submarines. But Charles Frohman, now fifty-five, foremost figure in the American theater since the mid-nineties, and a man of many crossings, was not one to be deterred by the German menace. He was by no means scornful of the danger but he did not share the apprehension of his friends, and there was business, important business, that awaited him in London. He wanted to get there on a fast boat and he was aboard the Cunard liner *Lusitania* (as was Charles Klein, the dramatist) when it steamed out of New York harbor, England-bound, on May 2, 1915, with 1,917 persons aboard. On May 7, while passing Kinsale Head, Ireland, about ten miles off shore, the mighty liner was torpedoed without warning by a German submarine. It sank in twenty minutes with a death total of 1,153. During the last terrible minutes, just before the *Lusitania* went down, Frohman stood beside Rita Jolivet, the actress, and her mother-in-law and then, in a voice of great calm, he said, "Why fear death? It is the most beautiful adventure in life." Confirmation of this message as Frohman's last quiet and exact words was given to me only a few months ago by Rita Jolivet in a letter from her home in Monte Carlo.

Survivors and recovered bodies were taken in lifeboats and small vessels to Queenstown, Ireland, where scenes of indescribable horror were unfolded. Survivors shrieked in their misery; they went insane; they died. A New York reporter at the scene (Wilbur Forrest, of the "Tribune") who had been called upon to identify the body believed to be that of Frohman, wrote:

There on the floor of the improvised morgue containing bodies of indiscriminate warfare's innocent victims, most of them with all the agonizing emotions stamped and frozen upon faces still in death, lay the remains of the New York producer. Save for a small bruise on one cheekbone the body appeared quite normal. A serene expression was on his face, in strange comparison with the distorted countenances of others about him.

Charles Frohman's death stunned people of the theater. Daniel Frohman was in his Lyceum studio, reading a new play, when the news reached him. C. B. Dillingham sank into a chair in his office at the Globe and broke into tears. Maude Adams was told upon reaching the Grand Theater in Kansas City for her matinee of *Quality Street*. She collapsed. Preparations were made to cancel the performance, but Miss Adams told the management that she would go on. She did go on, with her eyes puffed and tear-stained, and her voice broke frequently in her opening scenes, but she got through. Her road manager received the Kansas City press, which suddenly besieged the theater, and spoke for her. No, Miss Adams could not be seen. Yes, she would give her evening performance. Yes, she would continue her Western tour, for the time being. No—and the newsmen had withheld this question to the end—Miss Adams had not married Mr. Frohman. "He was not her husband," said that road manager, and his own voice was now breaking, "but he was the greatest friend of her life."

CHAPTER IX

The Theater and World War 1

A YOUNG KENTUCKIAN named Cleves Kinkead, who had been a lawyer, reporter, and a member of the House of Representatives of his state, got to know about the theater via the road plays that the New York booking offices condescended to send to Louisville. He decided that he'd like to try writing a few of his own and he went to Harvard to take the 47 Workshop course of George Pierce Baker, who gave valiant service to the theater and whose teachings helped to bring some plays of ideas and distinction to the commercial stage. Edward Sheldon studied playwriting under Professor Baker; so did Frederick Ballard, Edward Knoblock, Josephine Preston Peabody, Philip Barry, and Eugene O'Neill.

Kinkead began working on a drama called *Common Clay*, the story of a pretty housemaid who is seduced by a rich man's son. John Craig, operating the fabulous Castle Square Theater in Boston, was then offering $500 and a guarantee of a Boston production for the best play written by a Harvard man, and in the fall of 1914 the award went to Kinkead for *Common Clay*, an artificial and manufactured theater piece, but effective in performance. It was produced by Craig, with its cast including a tall, eager, and obscure young actor from Wisconsin named Alfred Lunt. *Common Clay* attracted a great deal of attention; it ran on and on. It was seen by numerous men of the theater from New York. Kinkead began getting offers, and he soon found himself commuting between New York and Boston. He was in a state of tormenting indecision until the day Al Woods walked into his room and said, "Hello, sweetheart," and put a contract and a check for one thousand dollars on the table. Woods was like that. He got *Common Clay*.

Things then happened fast. Life began moving dizzily for Cleves Kinkead, accustomed to Louisville's easygoing ways. Woods engaged Jane

146

Matinee Idols and Ziegfeld Beauties, 1910–1930

1. Gladys Feldman   2. Henry Woodruff   3. Marion Davies   4. Charles Cherry   5. Richard Bennett   6. Gladys Glad   7. Dustin Farnum   8. William Faversham   9. Justine Johnston   10. William Courtenay   11. Douglas Fairbanks   12. Marilyn Miller   13. Doris Vinton

Famous Players in Famous Roles, 1912–1940

1. Raymond Massey, as Lincoln in Robert E. Sherwood's *Abe Lincoln in Illinois* 2. Jane Cowl, as Mary Turner in Bayard Veiller's *Within the Law* 3. Lionel Barrymore, as Milt Shanks in Augustus Thomas's *The Copperhead* 4. Jeanne Eagels, as Sadie Thompson in *Rain* 5. Henry Hull, as Jeeter Lester in *Tobacco Road* 6. George Arliss, as the Rajah of Rukh in William Archer's *The Green Goddess* 7. Laurette Taylor, as Peg in J. Hartley Manners's famous *Peg O' My Heart*

Cowl for the role of Ellen Neal—the Miss Cowl for whom Belasco had prophesied no future at all at the time she was working for him in *The Easiest Way*, playing an invisible role, and whose *Within the Law* performance had put her into the big-money category. Woods engaged John Mason for the Judge, who turns out to be the disturbing Ellen Neal's father, and *Common Clay* was put on at the Republic Theater, where it stayed for a year. It was played on tour by four companies, sold to stock, and within two years the beautiful Ellen was being seduced from the Dakotas to the Gulf of Mexico. The play had its screen life, of course, being done by the movies that talked and those that didn't, and it remained a source of income for its author for more than a quarter of a century. Kinkead vanished from the Broadway scene just as suddenly as he had appeared upon it. Did he ever bother to write another play? Yes, one or two, but his career as a dramatist actually began and ended with *Common Clay*. He went back to Louisville, found a big chair at the Pendennis Club, and from that comfortable vantage point he sat back and watched the world whirl by.

The bustling, both-feet-on-his-desk Albert Herman Woods, the overrich Selwyns, and the ever-expanding Shuberts were busy showmen at the time of the arrival (and the departure) of Kentucky's Cleves Kinkead. So were Cohan & Harris and the fiery William A. Brady, who was just then planning, with Grace George, an ambitious season of repertoire with the notion of giving due attention to the supposedly uncommercial drama. But before Miss George got her plays selected and her company organized an extraordinarily interesting modern-trend group known as the Washington Square Players, devoting its energies and talents to plays of a type that were scorned by the Broadway theater of that time, began its New York operations.

The Washington Square Players—the founders included Edward Goodman, Robert Edmond Jones, Helen Westley, Lawrence Langner, Albert and Charles Boni, Philip Moeller, Ida Rauh, and Florence Enright—had been offered space, rent free, behind a small modern art gallery in Washington Square South, and began making announcements and soliciting subscriptions. The response was encouraging, the subscriptions began coming in, and it was then that the art dealer changed his mind; he would have to be paid for the use of his quarters. The Players decided to look elsewhere for an auditorium, and finally it was Florence Enright who found the tiny

147

theater in East 57th Street called the Bandbox. The house was rented, in the beginning, for Friday and Saturday nights, and there, on a mid-February evening in 1915, the Washington Square Players—the name was retained, geography notwithstanding—gave their first performance to a capacity audience, the house having been sold out previously by subscription. Only two seats had been sold for the second performance, and Edward Goodman, elected executive head of the organization, was wondering what they were going to do about it. But on the morning after the opening "The New York Times" carried an exciting review of the performance, a notice written by Brock Pemberton, and there was another sellout the second night.

The plays in the first batch included pieces by Philip Moeller, John Reed, Edward Goodman, Maurice Maeterlinck, Murdock Pemberton, and Rose Pastor Stokes. The Players turned later to Chekhov's *The Sea Gull* and to such short plays as *The Clod*, written by Lewis Beach and called by Walter Prichard Eaton the best one-act play he had ever seen; Takeda Izumo's tragedy, *Bushido*, the most successful piece to be done by the group; *The Red Clock*, by Josephine A. Meyer and Lawrence Langner, and *The Antick*, by Percy MacKaye. And later to Susan Glaspell's *Trifles*, Goodman's *Eugenically Speaking*, and Edward Massey's *Plots and Playwrights*, the locale of which was a dingy lodging house in which an inebriated dramatist encountered a short-story writer who insisted that there must be a play on every floor. Those who saw *Plots and Playwrights* gazed upon a slim, dark girl with a lovely voice, not long out of Mrs. Merrill's school for girls at Mamaroneck. She also appeared in *Bushido* as an old Japanese woman. In this play she spoke just one line: "My son, my son!" Her name was Katharine Cornell.

The Washington Square Players stayed for two seasons at the Bandbox before moving into the Comedy Theater. The organization continued its operations until the spring of 1918, and then, with the government taking its players for the Army, it went into a convenient and voluntary bankruptcy, Edward Goodman giving the war as the cause. Many of the Washington Square offerings were not deserving of production on any stage, but several of the group's short plays, such as *The Clod* and *Bushido*, were pieces with genuine distinction. In the intense and tragic *Bushido* a once powerful ruler, Suguwara, hides his son in a boy's school to protect him, but Suguwara's relentless enemies discover the boy and demand his head.

Suguwara's faithful Matsuo knows but one way to prevent the slaughter of the boy, and that is by sacrificing his own son. Heroically, he goes through with the plan, identifying the head of his child as that of Suguwara's.

Grace George, an actress plagued throughout her career with inferior plays—such utter rubbish as *Sauce for the Goose, The Marriage of William Ashe, Under Southern Skies,* the dreadful *Billy Draws a Horse,* and *Clothes,* the Hopwood-Pollock crazy quilt—gained immeasurably in stature when she launched her repertory season as an actress-manager at her husband's Playhouse in the fall of 1915. William A. Brady had no illusions about himself as an intellectual; he had no inclinations toward artiness. He merely desired to put on some plays that would show Mrs. Brady to the best advantage. So his smallish Playhouse became something of a 48th Street art center, five stimulating productions being offered at a $2 top from September to mid-April, and the fact that the season was played at a loss meant nothing to the producer. It was important to him to have Grace George engaged with theater that was worth her time and his money, and he was a prouder showman during that season than he ever was when *Bought and Paid For* and *The Man Who Came Back* were selling out every night.

Miss George's most successful offering was her production of Shaw's *Major Barbara,* which she introduced to America, and in which she gave an earnest, honest, and thoroughly delightful performance as the religion-minded daughter of Andrew Undershaft, the munitions manufacturer, one of Shaw's most invigorating characters. She played Lady Cicely, a role cherished by Ellen Terry, in *Captain Brassbound's Conversion,* and Robert Warwick, unaccountably enough, was excellent as the half-savage and bombastic Brassbound, ruling over his gang of British outcasts and cut-throats. When the dress rehearsal of "Brassbound" was held Warwick did not have his silk hat, morning coat, striped trousers, or spats, and throughout the rehearsal he wore the rough garb that had been his costume for the first part of the play. But he made his entrance on the opening night, with his face bronzed by the African sun and in all his sartorial splendor. Miss George was facing upstage. She turned and gave a little gasp. "What does he look like?" she whispered to Rexford Kendrick, who was playing Osman. "'The King of Dahomey,'" muttered Kendrick. "No," responded Miss George in another quick whisper, "Chauncey Olcott in blackface!"

Three other plays—Langdon Mitchell's *The New York Idea,* Henry

149

Arthur Jones's *The Liars,* and James Bernard Fagan's *The Earth*—found their way into Miss George's repertory program. Her company gave employment to such able players as Louis Calvert, Mary Nash, Ernest Lawford, and Conway Tearle. John Cromwell, who learned his trade as an actor-director in the Broadway field and went on to Hollywood to become one of its outstanding director-producers, was in Miss George's organization as an actor and director. Recently, in mellowing reminiscence, he made this observation: "Miss George's repertory theater went the way of all repertoire in this country—too much publicity and too many stars."

Guthrie McClintic, then grimly determined to be an actor, was also around the Playhouse, and it was during Miss George's battle with repertoire that another young actor, who was also to make his way as a producer, went to the Bradys in quest of a job. He was Vinton Freedley, Philadelphia gentleman and former Harvard quarterback, who had proudly taken the beautiful Hazel Dawn driving about Boston in his Stutz Bearcat during his undergraduate days. Freedley decided against a career as a lawyer after having been admitted to the bar, and when he went to present himself to Miss George he brought along some impressive letters. But he waited from 10 A.M. to 5 P.M. and was leaving, in complete dejection, when he met her on the elevator. She looked him over, read a letter or two, and engaged him for *L'Elevation,* which she was doing with Holbrook Blinn.

A short time later, however, a stagehand interrupted one of Miss George's most dramatic speeches with coughs and sneezes, Freedley was named as the culprit, and was fired. He worked for Brady again when that showman did *The World We Live In,* playing the male cricket, and made quite a hit, but was given notice the day after the opening; Brady explained that he had to cut expenses. Miss George has often remarked that Freedley had the best manners, the best real manners, of all the young actors of his time. She told him so, too, and he remembered her words. He also remembered the words, and the glacial glances, of Rachel Crothers, to whom he went for a part in her play, *Nice People.* "I'm sorry," she said, "but you won't do. You wear your dinner coat too much like a gentleman to be one."

During the time Grace George was giving playgoers a course in Shavian wit, wisdom, and nonsense, a one-time Shakespearean actor, Charles Hopkins, a Yale man with a sound appreciation of the finer things of the theater, delighted the town with a presentation of a dramatization of Stevenson's "Treasure Island" at his 299-seat playhouse, the Punch and Judy. A frightened young actress named Ruth Gordon made her first-time-on-Broadway appearance with Maude Adams as Nibs in the Empire revival of *Peter Pan* (December, 1915). A confident Ethel Barrymore found substantial success with *Our Mrs. McChesney*, written by Edna Ferber from her short stories and introducing to the theater that new phenomenon, a woman in business. A terrified fat man, Irvin S. Cobb, made a curtain speech at the opening of *Back Home* in which he asserted that "all my stuff that Bayard Veiller has used is a semicolon, a period, two commas, and a damn." A nervous, jerky, and fascinating Mrs. Fiske entertained frequently at the Murray Hill Hotel as she went on with her playing in *Erstwhile Susan,* and her cousin, Emily Stevens, exerted a spell over her audiences as the harsh, predatory Caroline Knollys of Louis K. Anspacher's *The Unchastened Woman,* a comedy that was then considered very bold, very modern, and very clever. John Barrymore came to see the play faithfully every week, sitting in the gallery.

Emily Stevens was an actress with a sense of humor, somewhat on the cruel side, that frequently got her into difficulties, on stage as well as off. Mrs. Fiske was in the audience one evening, and Miss Stevens urged her co-players to do their very best for Cousin Minnie. During the second act Hassard Short had some business with an alarm clock, which was to go off during the love scene, and which he was supposed to take into the bedroom and put under the mattress. The property man wasn't about when Short went off stage, and he hurled the clock to the floor to stop it. It did stop— for a few seconds. When he got back on stage the alarm started again, Miss Stevens began laughing, and the scene broke up in hysteria, all to Mrs. Fiske's considerable distress. There came the night during the road tour of *The Unchastened Woman*—it was the first performance in Salt Lake City—when Hassard Short, as he made his entrance, saw seven gray-haired Mormon women sitting in the stage box. He whispered to Emily Stevens that they all looked like H. Reeves-Smith's wife. She gave way to a shriek of laughter and couldn't speak for the rest of the act. Oliver Morosco got a report of the performance, wired his star and Short that they had behaved disgracefully, and that he would close the play in San Francisco. He did.

John Golden, an energetic, cyclonic, and bombastic showman, gave up one trade, song writing, to become a producer. He began his career with a million-dollar hit, *Turn to the Right,* done in partnership with the extraordinarily sagacious Winchell Smith. Here was a homely comedy of peach jam, mortgage-lifting, and the regeneration of likable crooks, originally written by John E. Hazzard, an actor. Winchell Smith, the theater's emergency man, completely rewrote Hazzard's crude script, and he and Golden formed a managerial partnership. But they discovered that their enthusiasm for the play was by no means contagious. The usually gracious C. B. Dillingham, offered a small percentage, read the script and said bluntly, "It's no good." Al Woods and Edgar Selwyn, given an opportunity to buy a half interest, saw a run-through rehearsal, thanked Golden, wished him luck, and hurried out of the theater. *Turn to the Right* came into the Gaiety, and Burns Mantle, writing in the "Evening Mail," proclaimed that it would be right there for a year or two. It was.

The tall, lank, and frequently caustic William Harris, Jr., who merely insisted, somewhat to the astonishment of many of his fellow showmen, upon liking a play before he produced it, had a prewar success in Bayard Veiller's well-written mystery melodrama, *The Thirteenth Chair,* a play of suspense and surprise. It came to Broadway via Poughkeepsie, and it was there that the second act started twice. In Veiller's play a murder was committed at the end of the first act as thirteen people, sitting in a circle and holding hands, were locked in a room. The elderly medium, who was conducting a séance, had requested that the doors be locked so as to make certain that she was not bringing in any assistants. The first act curtain fell with a group of twelve awaiting the arrival of the police—twelve and the body of the murder victim. The curtain of the second act, supposedly starting ten minutes later, rises on the picture of the twelve and the body.

On the opening night in Poughkeepsie the players were so pleased with the way the first-act séance had gone that, instead of hurrying to their dressing rooms, they sat talking on stage. The stage manager joined them and, at the proper time, said cheerfully, "All right, let's get on with it." Margaret Wycherly, playing the medium, Rosalie La Grange, got back into her chair, the others took their places, and the curtain went up. It was then that Miss Wycherly, watching, and with no lines at the moment, realized that two of the actors necessary to the scene were missing. She whispered, "Ring down the curtain," the whisper was relayed across stage, and just as Harrison Hunter, playing the Inspector, made his brusque entrance with the line, "What is all this?" down came the curtain in his face. And at that exact instant, through the great fireplace calmly walked the two missing players. The harassed stage manager now took charge, and the second act started all over again.

War plays were coming to the stages, war plays that had been written hurriedly for production while they were timely; plays written to capitalize on patriotism, and plays written on the supposition that America, even after the sinking of the *Lusitania,* was observing a blind and inert neutrality. Consider the program note inserted by the Selwyns in the playbill for Roi Cooper Megrue's *Under Fire:*

This play deals with certain phases of the Great War and it attempts to be neutral, although its characters, being English, Belgian, French and German, are naturally partisan. The management earnestly requests, therefore, that no member of the audience will indulge in any unpleasant demonstrations which might be offensive either to others in the audience or to those on the stage.

This was Broadway tact carried to a ridiculous extreme.

War plays, some of them plays with a mission, were turned out by experienced dramatists and by those new to the trade. They were manufactured by playwrights who learned about the war from the headlines, who never got any closer to the firing line than the lobby of the Astor. They were dashed off by noncombatants who got their plots at the Knickerbocker bar. They were written by such zealous patriots as Samuel Shipman and Aaron Hoffman, who took a whole week in the fighting zone along Atlantic City's Boardwalk to finish *Friendly Enemies,* the biggest hit of them all; by such battle-scarred veterans of the 42d Street sector as Channing Pollock and Edgar Selwyn, by Jane Cowl and Jane Murfin amid the cannonading in New York's luxurious Hotel Belmont.

The Cowl-Murfin play was the wartime romance, *Lilac Time.* Miss Cowl had told the story to Henry Miller, who was so touched by it he began to cry; he could always cry very easily. He asked when he might read the play. "Why," said Miss Cowl, hesitating for an instant, "you can have it Saturday." On Wednesday she and Miss Murfin began writing in a suite at the Belmont, and they wrote for four days without raising the shades. At four-thirty Saturday afternoon they finished their manuscript and telephoned Miller, who was living in the hotel. He read the play immediately and said he would produce it, but by Monday he had changed his mind. Miss Cowl, exasperated but still confident, telephoned Arch Selwyn, told him about the play, and mentioned the players she and Miss Murfin wanted. "Let's go ahead," he said. The Selwyns produced *Lilac Time.*

Earl Derr Biggers's *Inside the Lines* was the first of the war plays to be offered, and the procession was unending for three years—*Moloch* and *Stolen Orders, Arms and the Girl* and *Doing Our Bit, Seven Days Leave, Three Faces East* and *Where Poppies Bloom, The Big Chance* and *The Long Dash, Allegiance* and *Getting Together. Allegiance,* written by Prince and Princess Troubetzkoy (Amelie Rives), was about the conversion of German-Americans in this country to intense pro-Americanism, and *Getting Together,* done with a big cast, including soldiers from the British Army, had the songs of Lieutenant Gitz Rice, a valiant war worker, and Blanche Bates and Holbrook Blinn as its stars. There was the poignant drama, *Under Orders,* with its four characters magnificently played by Effie Shannon and Shelley Hull. There was the hollow, synthetic, written-to-order *Out There,* done over a week end or two by J. Hartley Manners, presented in New York and later taken on tour, with a spectacular cast, as a fund-raising spectacle for the Red Cross. There was the vastly entertaining *Yip, Yip, Yaphank,* the work of Sergeant Irving Berlin, and there was, to the delight of practically everybody, *The Better 'Ole,* a humorous play which gave a faithful picture of life at the front from the British soldier's point of view, and which was worth a dozen of the spy melodramas that cluttered the Broadway stage.

Most of the war-theme plays presented during the period of the emergency were utterly meretricious. They were pieces that were quickly forgotten, but they packed theaters, brought in money for wartime contributions, and served to stimulate recruiting and patriotism. *Arms and the Girl,* because of the charming performance of Fay Bainter, and *The Better 'Ole,* because of the truthful writing in it and the rollicking performance of Charles Coburn in the role of Old Bill, of the walrus mustache, are pieces that stay vividly in the memory of playgoers of the time. *The Better 'Ole,* the work of Captain Bruce Bairnsfather and Captain Arthur Elliott, with music by Herman Darewski and Percival Knight, won the affection and respect of soldiers and civilians alike during its long New York run. Such notable plays as *What Price Glory* and *Journey's End* were still some years away.

Liberty Theaters, huge, sprawling wooden structures, hastily erected, sprang up in the coast-to-coast cantonments after America entered the war. These theaters were served by touring professional companies, and the youth of the country, in rigorous military training, saw the Liberty

Theater plays with coupons from Smileage Books that sold for $1 and $5 and that were bought by the public and sent, by the hundred thousand, to the camps of the nation—to Camp Gordon, to Camp Jackson, to Camp Custer, to Camp Pike, to Camp Meade, to Camp Lewis, in the far North-west. Popular plays of the time, including *Turn to the Right, Here Comes the Bride, Cheating Cheaters,* and *Kick In,* went from theater to theater.

The theatrical profession gave a magnificent account of itself during those war years. People of the stage and screen worked tirelessly in enter-taining troops at home and abroad; they were unremitting in their labors for the Liberty Loan and the Red Cross and the Naval recruiting cam-paigns. Julia Marlowe recited *The Road to France* from the steps of New York's Public Library. Elsie Ferguson sold $85,000 in Liberty Bonds in less than half an hour. Geraldine Farrar opened a loan campaign on the steps of the Treasury in Washington. Irving Berlin, in his thin, squeaky voice, sang his own and immortal "Oh, How I Hate to Get Up in the Morning" from flag-draped platforms. James T. Powers, Fred Stone, George M. Co-han, Jane Cowl, Ethel Barrymore, Annette Kellermann, Nora Bayes, Fran-ces Starr, Grace George joined in the speechmaking, the flag waving, and the bond selling. And beyond and above them all, there was Elsie Janis, the official sweetheart of the AEF, who sang, danced, talked, and did imita-tions and handsprings as she toured the front, her black velvet tam pushed back on her tossing hair. Alexander Woollcott wrote in "The New York Times," after seeing her perform in a French trainshed packed to suffoca-tion:

When she leads a leather-lunged regiment in the strains of "God Save Kaiser Bill," the future of that uneasy monarch really seems more insecure than it did, and it is not fanciful to say that more than one company has marched off to its first night in the trenches with brighter eyes, squarer shoulders and a more gallant swing because, at the very threshold of safety, this lanky and lovely lady from Columbus, Ohio, waved and sang and cheered them on their way. That is why, when the history of this great expedition comes to be written, there should be a chapter devoted to the play-girl of the western front, the star of the AEF, the forerunner of those players who are now being booked in the greatest circuit of them all, the Y.M.C.A. huts of France.

And it remained for an actor-playwright to give the war its greatest song. On the morning of April 6, 1917, the day of our tardy declaration of

155

war against Germany, George M. Cohan, then living in Great Neck, found a stub pencil, seated himself on his porch, and wrote the chorus of a song on a scrap of paper. During his drive into the city to the Cohan & Harris offices, he finished the verse and told Sam Harris that he thought he had written a pretty good martial tune. He had completed it in less than two hours. A title? Oh, yes. He had decided to call it "Over There."

There were, incredibly enough, some nonwar plays that found their way to Broadway's stages after that fateful April of 1917—such pieces as Eugene Walter's *The Knife*, Harry James Smith's *A Tailor-Made Man*, the George Middleton–Guy Bolton *Polly With a Past* (Ina Claire), Willard Mack's *Tiger Rose* and the *Passing Show* of the Shuberts and the *Follies* of Ziegfeld, all duly covered by such gentlemen of the press as Heywood Broun of the "Tribune," Louis Sherwin of the "Globe," Lawrence Reamer of the "Sun," and Robert Gilbert Welch of the "Evening Telegram," the only dramatic critic in all history to give his life in an effort to save somebody from drowning.

During the delirium of the war years several extraordinarily interesting figures turned up in the theater of New York. The dark, volatile Lenore Ulric, born in New Ulm, Minnesota, whose education ended in the third grade, came forth as a young actress of uncommon force and vitality in Willard Mack's melodrama of the Canadian wilds and the Mounted Police which was called *Tiger Rose*, and which was Belasco-staged. John D. Williams, who produced Augustus Thomas's *The Copperhead*, revealed himself as a showman of taste, intelligence, and an awareness of the best that the theater had to offer. Clare Kummer, discovered by Arthur Hopkins, brought a genuine talent for light comedy writing to *Good Gracious, Annabelle, Be Calm, Camilla*, and *A Successful Calamity*, in which William Gillette, as a weary multimillionaire, pretends to be ruined in order to bring his self-centered and reckless family into line. Jesse Lynch Williams contributed an amusing and incisive study of the state of matrimony in his *Why Marry?* to which Nat Goodwin brought the finesse and authority and brilliance of a lifetime in the theater. And there was that spectacular showman, Morris Gest, of the slouch hat and the inevitable Windsor tie, who presented (in partnership with F. Ray Comstock and William Elliott) the spectacle play, *Chu Chin Chow*, and who was on his stage-struck way to some bold and exciting adventures.

156

The trim, dapper Comstock, who came to New York from Buffalo—he sang in a choir and worked in a bank up-State—and the Russian-born Gest, who earned a tidy sum soon after his arrival in this country by painting sparrows yellow and selling them as canaries—got together after the Shuberts had taken over the Hippodrome. Comstock had been put in charge of the Hippodrome's vexating concessions, such as publishing the programs, and Gest wandered in one day with a proposition.

"You're too busy for all these details," he said. "Take me in with you and I'll do all the work."

That notion appealed to Comstock tremendously—he liked his relaxing hours on the sands of Palm Beach as much as any producer ever did—and he told Gest to go ahead. That was the beginning of a partnership that lasted for fifteen years and that gave to the theater the Princess Theater plays of Bolton, Wodehouse & Kern—such unforgettable pieces as *Very Good Eddie, Oh, Boy!* and *Oh, Lady! Lady!! Oh, Boy!* was the kind of a hit that never played to a vacant seat, and the popularity of *Very Good Eddie* was such that two companies played it in New York simultaneously, and in the same block in 39th Street!

This was also the time when an actor, John Barrymore, and a playwright, Eugene O'Neill, were emerging into greatness. Edward Sheldon had successfully talked and taunted Barrymore into dropping the *Kick Ins* and the *Yellow Tickets,* the *Anatols* and the *Fortune Hunters,* and going in for valid drama, for plays that would give him his place as the finest actor in the American theater. Barrymore listened to Sheldon, and to hardly anybody else. So it was a Barrymore in an entirely new guise that playgoers beheld when, under John D. Williams's guidance, he came forth in *Justice,* Galsworthy's protest against the rigidity and the lack of humanity in England's penal laws. The light comedian of other years gave a repressed, moving, and completely unforgettable performance as Falder, the humble clerk of good intentions, who raised a check to provide funds to relieve the suffering of a persecuted married woman with whom he was in love. Falder is subjected to the torture of solitary confinement, hounded by the law after his release, and eventually commits suicide.

Barrymore, heartened by the reception accorded *Justice,* turned next to *Peter Ibbetson,* the dramatization of the Du Maurier novel. Here, again, he was guided by Sheldon, and he took over the title role, with a remarkable cast including Lionel Barrymore, Constance Collier, and Laura Hope Crews. It was while he was appearing in *Peter Ibbetson* under the management of the Shuberts that he heard Arthur Hopkins was planning to bring forth Tolstoy's "The Living Corpse" under the title of *Redemption.* He went instantly to Hopkins and said he'd like to do the play. He didn't need to say much more; he was just the actor the producer had in mind for it.

"I told him the play was his," said Hopkins, in talking with me years later of Barrymore's visit, "and I also told him I wanted to keep him in the Plymouth Theater for three years, doing two more plays, and all of this actually came about. Jack was a great actor—the greatest of our time. He could have been the greatest of all time, but he had a way of losing interest after the opening night."

So Barrymore, beginning an association that was to be a memorable one, and one that contributed enormously to the theater's vitality in that period, went under the management of the taciturn showman from Cleveland. In *Redemption,* in which Tolstoy inquired into Russian marriage laws and expounded his theories on the stupidity and oppression of certain phases of constituted authority, Barrymore played a self-sacrificing weakling who feigns suicide to leave his wife free to marry another. A blackmailer, who discovers the truth, comes into the scene; the authorities intrude upon the happiness of the wife's second marriage; and the despairing Fedor Vasilyevich Protosova, played by Barrymore, finally finds the courage to take his own life. In *Redemption* John Barrymore made another step forward; he gave the theater his strongest performance up to that time.

It was as Barrymore was coming into an acting province rightfully belonging to him by heritage and histrionic ability that the unheeding Broadway managers, Ames and Hopkins and Williams included, were hearing more and more of Eugene O'Neill by way of Provincetown and a reconverted stable in New York's Macdougal Street, and by way of the Washington Square Players' presentation of the gripping *In the Zone.* The brooding son of a romantic actor of another era of the theater was then being represented by his vivid short plays of the sea—*Bound East for Cardiff, Moon of the Caribbees, The Long Voyage Home.* The ardor and zeal for discovery of George Jean Nathan had brought O'Neill's writings into print, upon the pages of the alert and impudent "Smart Set" magazine, and when these same plays were put upon the stage, any stage, they were even more effective in the playing than they had been in the reading. O'Neill had

158

made his beginning, a beginning that gave prophecy of startling deeds to come. I shall return to him in this chronicle as he moves into the theater of Broadway, and into the theater of all the world.

The year of 1918 yielded three plays that took their places as exciting contributions to the New York stage. They were Barrie's *Dear Brutus,* *Lightnin'*, written by Winchell Smith and Frank Bacon, and *The Copperhead*, a drama by Augustus Thomas. Each brought forth a performance of rare artistry. Playgoers had to go back to memories of Maude Adams's magic in *Peter Pan,* to the ineffable qualities of Ruth Chatterton's playing in *The Rainbow,* to find an enchantment comparable to that which young Helen Hayes, then a seasoned trouper despite her years, exerted in Barrie's fantasy, *Dear Brutus.* She was merely a member of a cast supporting a distinguished star, William Gillette, but the play was hers on the opening night, and so it remained throughout the long engagement at the Empire.

Helen Hayes was actually at the threshold of her career when she did *Dear Brutus,* but the years were closing on Frank Bacon; he had had a long and arduous career as a character actor when the New York stage was suddenly reminded of his existence. Bacon was running a prune farm on a hill overlooking California's Santa Clara Valley at the time of the San Francisco earthquake, and that catastrophe, he always insisted, blew him out of the state. He took to barnstorming, he played in the stock companies, he had engagements in such hits as *The Fortune Hunter* and *Stop Thief* and *The Cinderella Man,* but he was still an undiscovered actor (and an old man) at the time of *Lightnin'*.

He stepped upon the stage of the Gaiety Theater and brought the qualities of Joe Jefferson into his warm and authentic characterization of Lightnin' Bill Jones, the village loafer and liar, who once drove a swarm of bees across the desert in the dead of winter and never lost a bee. Playgoers responded to that performance and to the homely, beguiling, Winchell Smith–fixed play so heartily that *Lightnin'* broke all of the then existing long-run records in the history of the theater, achieving a Broadway run of 1,291 performances. Such a total then appeared incredible, but who was there to foresee a time when the *Lightnin'* engagement would seem, in retrospect, as a mere season or two? *Lightnin'* was, for Frank Bacon, glory enough. He often remarked that the play would outlive him, and it did. He was playing old Bill in Chicago when he died.

159

Lionel Barrymore was also an actor little known to playgoing New York when John D. Williams persuaded him to play the role of Milt Shanks in *The Copperhead,* Augustus Thomas's only worth-while play since *As a Man Thinks.* Shanks is a border-state copperhead, a martyr to his faith at the outbreak of the Civil War, who lets himself be branded and ostracized as a traitor because, under such circumstances, he can give greatest service to his government. Many years later, when his supposed sins are about to come down upon the head of his granddaughter, the long-silent Shanks produces a letter from Abraham Lincoln which justifies his actions of the sixties and completely clears him of infamy.

Barrymore played his early scenes with skill and restraint, "but it was in the recital of his long suffering under misunderstanding and slander," the "New York Sun" wrote, "that he gave such an exhibition of feeling and technical finish as the contemporary stage rarely witnesses. The effect of his acting was to arouse the audience to the highest pitch of enthusiasm. He was repeatedly recalled and his personal triumph was the impressive incident of the evening." It was Lionel Barrymore's great night in a lifetime given to acting. His triumph was witnessed by his brother John. The evening's New Haven performance of *Peter Ibbetson* had been canceled to make John's presence possible.

There were some lesser, but also satisfying, evenings in the showshops during that year. Al Jolson, now as highly paid as anybody in the profession, still working for the Shuberts and singing the songs of Sigmund Romberg, came into the big and hospitable Winter Garden in *Sinbad.* Roi Cooper Megrue supplied an urbane and genuinely witty comedy in *Tea for Three.* A. H. Woods put Hazel Dawn and Enid Markey into negligee and into a harum-scarum farce, *Up in Mabel's Room,* written by an Ohio drugstore clerk, Wilson Collison (and rewritten to some extent by Otto Harbach)— and then pulled up his chair outside the Eltinge Theater and watched it pay off.

Henry Miller opened his trim and tasteful new theater in 43d Street, a playhouse bearing his name, with an indifferent comedy, *The Fountain of Youth.* Arthur Hopkins presented Nazimova in *The Wild Duck* and a few weeks later in *Hedda Gabler* and wasn't at all surprised that neither lasted more than a month. He wanted to see Nazimova as Hedvig and as Hedda and he did, practically every night. Violet Heming, of the unchanging

160

beauty, came forth as a highly dramatic heroine of Anthony Paul Kelly's *Three Faces East,* subjected to considerable tinkering by George M. Cohan. Jeanne Eagels, from out of the chorus of *Jumping Jupiter* of some seasons back, brought playgoers sharply to attention with her playing in a money-making trifle called *Daddies.*

The stormy, headstrong, and genuinely gifted actor, Richard Bennett, who never achieved the standing that his abundant talents should have given him, provided some exciting moments in the tricky and melo-dramatic *Unknown Purple,* right out of the Theodore Kremer school of long ago. The theater-wise John D. Williams unfolded a funny farce in *Sleeping Partners,* with H. B. Warner and Irene Bordoni. Frances Starr, now in the hire of Belasco for thirteen years, was again a vibrant player in Edward Knoblock's *Tiger! Tiger!* Samuel Shipman and John B. Hymer got away with a "velly lotten play," as described by Heywood Broun, in William Harris's production of *East Is West.*

Harris, in talking later of that big hit, said that he had persuaded Shipman and Hymer to change the ending of the play because they had actually written *Madame Butterfly* and that he didn't want to produce *Madame Butterfly.* "All right," said Shipman promptly, "we can fix. We'll have our Chinese heroine turn out to be white." And so they did.

And then there was the wonderful night, during that final year of the war, when Irving Berlin's *Yip, Yip, Yaphank* took over the stage of the Century. Berlin had gone into the Army as a private and he had risen, by sheer application to duty and tact hardly to be expected from a millionaire composer, to the rank of Sergeant. As he held such rank he wrote the words and music for a camp show, an amateur company was assembled and re-hearsed, and *Yip, Yip, Yaphank* opened in the playhouse that had been the graveyard of the New Theater, and to an audience that included the great and near great of the profession. The big moment came when Berlin, half asleep, was aroused in his tent and began singing, in his plaintive voice, of his love of bed and his loathing for all buglers.

Did *Yip, Yip, Yaphank* succeed? Was it worth all the trouble? Well, take the testimony of a man who should know, Berlin himself. "We made ex-actly eighty-two thousand dollars," he said some months ago in talking of the Yaphank days. "The money belonged to the camp fund. And whatever became of all that dough I don't happen to know—not even to this day."

161

By now, vaudeville, after being in operation for a quarter of a century, had spread throughout the land, and New York's Palace Theater, its main store and most celebrated showcase, was a flourishing institution, the goal of all performers who gave over their time to the profession of the two-a-day. A pause for a passing consideration of vaudeville, which became a new factor in the amusement business of the nation under the ministrations of Benjamin Franklin Keith in Boston in the early 1880s, now seems in order.

Keith, born on a New Hampshire farm, began his activities in a vacant candy store adjoining the old Adams House in Boston's Washington Street, in 1883. He first called his place the Gaiety Museum. He wanted women and children for his patrons, he was careful to avoid all vulgarity in his presentations, and he was soon calling his business "vaudeville." He was successful from the beginning. In 1885 he took young Edward F. Albee, a boy with ambitions to be a circus owner, into his organization, and their association was to continue through the years. They shared the belief that a high standard of acts had to be maintained, that "refined vaudeville" was to be their policy, and that comfort must be provided in their theaters. Keith began extending his operations after Albee joined him. He acquired a theater in Boston, an old opera house in Providence, and built a theater in Philadelphia. Such was the nucleus of what was to be a great chain.

In 1893 Keith took the step that was inevitable—he invaded New York. He set himself up in the vaudeville field at the old Union Square Theater, and it was then that this New Englander, of French and Scotch parentage, was called "the continuous man from Boston." He found formidable competition from the actor-manager, Tony Pastor, who had been a performer at Barnum's Museum—P. T. Barnum went in for a bit of experimentation with vaudeville in the Sixties—and from F. F. Proctor, both of whom were taking pride in bills designed for family trade, with the realization that when women and children were won over as patrons vaudeville would be on its way. It was such competition that later resulted in bringing name players from the legitimate theater into the new and fascinating world of the two-a-day.

Tony Pastor, the ballad singer, was born in New York's downtown Greenwich Street in 1835 and made his first public appearance at a temperance revival when he was six years old. He was an infant prodigy at Barnum's Museum by the time he was eight and at twelve he was doing a bareback

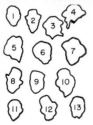

They Made Us Laugh—From Weber & Fields to Bobby Clark

1. Eddie Cantor 2. Ed Wynn 3. Weber
4. Fields 5. Bobby Clark 6. Paul McCullough
7. Will Rogers 8. James T. Powers 9. Fred Stone
10. Leon Errol 11. Raymond Hitchcock
12. W. C. Fields 13. Al Jolson

Celebrated Ladies—and Lightnin' Bill

1. Jeanne Eagels   2. Gertrude Lawrence   3. Pauline Lord   4. Emily Stevens   5. Frank Bacon
6. Tallulah Bankhead   7. Margalo Gillmore
8. Alice Brady   9. Lenore Ulric   10. Billie Burke

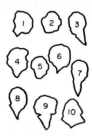

singing act with a circus. He became a clown and a ringmaster; he served as end man in a minstrel show, and became a singer in a variety show at 444 Broadway. From his earliest years, he had ambitions to do his own managing and he got his start in Paterson, New Jersey, in 1865. But his thoughts were upon New York and he soon turned up on the Bowery as a variety manager and with a new policy—women were admitted to his performances.

Tony was a showman of imagination, resourcefulness, and foresight; he was among those of the eighties and nineties who realized that the theatrical district of New York would gradually be moving northward. He gave up his Bowery quarters to open at 585 Broadway, where he introduced the exquisite Lillian Russell to the city's playgoers in a burlesque of *H.M.S. Pinafore*, and when 1881 came around he had invaded East 14th Street. There he made his stand. There he presented Nat C. Goodwin, Weber & Fields, Gus Williams, and Maggie Cline, and Eddie Foy in soft-shoe dances. The Four Cohans appeared under his guidance; so did Denman Thompson, Jennie Hill, Amelia Summerville, Annie Yeamans, Chuck Connors, and Fritz Williams, who had played a violin in the orchestra pit. Tony Pastor gave many obscure performers the opportunity to show their wares beneath his hospitable roof, and the holdover policy was in effect at his playhouse. Whenever an act definitely pleased his clientele it was always invited to remain beyond the time of the original booking. And all performers of the era knew that a good engagement at Pastor's was a guarantee of "time" elsewhere. Tony Pastor had a sense of graciousness; he was also very smart.

The celebrated performers of the variety stages of New York in the years when vaudeville was establishing itself included Tony Pastor himself and the Four Cohans, Ethel Levey, Maggie Cline, Weber & Fields, Charles T. Aldrich, and James and Bonnie Thornton; David Warfield, Hap Ward, Victor Moore, and the then-renowned Maurice Barrymore. Also Vesta Tilley and Vesta Victoria; Montgomery & Stone and the Four Mortons; McIntyre & Heath and Nat M. Wills, the happy tramp. The desertion of variety performers to the legitimate theater of Broadway began about the time the Four Cohans gave up variety to take up musical comedy, but from its early years vaudeville drew upon the ranks of the legitimate for the services of famous stars, and it was upon the stage of the renowned Palace, in 1918, that the great Bernhardt, minus a leg, made her final appearance in

163

America. Olga Nethersole tried vaudeville and enjoyed it; so did Fritzi Scheff, Clara Morris, John Mason, Nazimova, William H. Crane, and Robert Edeson, the virile stage star.

Oscar Hammerstein, with Hammerstein's Victoria, became a factor in the vaudeville field of New York. Percy G. Williams, John J. Murdock, and Alex Pantages were other competitors. In 1905 the Keith and F. F. Proctor interests were merged, and the United Booking Office established. In 1912 Percy G. Williams, whose will created a home for actors at East Islip, Long Island, sold his circuit of vaudeville and stock theaters to the Keith circuit, and at the same time the Keith interests closed a deal uniting Keith's Eastern theaters with those of the Orpheum circuit, which operated west of Chicago. This was a merger of great magnitude, one involving two hundred theaters in a chain that reached from ocean to ocean, and with Martin Beck remaining in charge of the Orpheum operations. Beck, born in Czechoslovakia, came to New York with a German stock company, went to St. Louis and to Chicago, and in the mid-eighties to San Francisco to run the Orpheum Theater, which became the nucleus of the Orpheum circuit. Prior to the Keith-Orpheum consolidation, he built the beautiful Palace Theater in New York because he wanted Broadway representation—when it opened in 1913 it was under joint control—and he introduced Sarah Bernhardt to vaudeville in Chicago in 1912 by going to Paris to get her. He had tea with her and engaged her at her own price—$7,000 weekly.

Vaudeville flourished throughout the land following the Keith-Orpheum merger; the Palace took its place as the foremost variety house in the nation. The great favorites of the two-a-day during the Palace days, during World War I, and the immediate postwar period included the Castles, Vernon and Irene; Jack Norworth and Nora Bayes, Irene Franklin, Grace La Rue, Fanny Brice, Blossom Seeley and Rube Marquard, Eva Tanguay, Belle Baker, Annette Kellermann, Eugenie Blair, Joan Sawyer, Emma Carus, Adeline Genee, Isabelle D'Armond, Sophie Tucker, Lou Holtz, William Gaxton, George Jessel, the Duncan Sisters, Jimmy Savo, Jack Benny, Harry Richman, Kate Smith, Eddie Cantor, Clark & McCullough, Joe Cook and Ed Wynn. Will M. Cressy and Blanche Dayne had a vast vaudeville following; one of Cressy's favorite characterizations was that of a crusty old storekeeper in a small-town general store. Belle Baker was "the Bernhardt of Song," Ray Samuels was "the Blue Streak of Vaudeville," Gus Van and Joe Schenck formed "the Pennant-Winning Battery of Songland,"

164

Frank Fogarty was "the Dublin Minstrel," Douglas Fairbanks, borrowed from the legitimate, was a breezy performer in the sketch *A Regular Business Man*. Nazimova found a provocative short play in the serious *War Brides*. Alan Dinehart came upon an enduring vehicle in the well-written sketch, *The Meanest Man in the World*, which was turned into a full-length play under the guidance of George M. Cohan. Frank Keenan did a playlet called *Conscience*, and Harrison Brockbank appeared as Napoleon in *The Drummer of the Seventy-sixth*.

Established dramatists found relaxation, plus profit, in writing for vaudeville. James M. Barrie wrote a three-scene playlet, *Half An Hour*, in which Blanche Bates appeared. Rupert Hughes, Paul Armstrong, and Jack Lait contributed to the variety stage. Edgar Allan Woolf was the Owen Davis of vaudeville; he wrote more sketches than he could ever count. And Channing Pollock, Rennold Wolf, and Clifton Crawford collaborated on *A Regular Army Man*, which Victor Morley played with enormous success.

Kitty Gordon was her dazzling self upon the vaudeville stages in Jack Lait's sketch, *Alma's Return*. Gertrude Coghlan appeared in William C. De Mille's *Food*, and Robert T. Haines in William Hurlbut's *The Man in the Dark*. The great Bernhardt played repeat engagements at the Palace; Ethel Barrymore graced its stage, and so did Amelia Bingham, Irving Berlin, and Elsie Janis. Lillian Lorraine came along with her songs and fascinating gowns. Julian Eltinge offered his female impersonations. Cecil Lean and Cleo Mayfield were standard favorites. Mitzi Hajos tried a tabloid version of *Her Little Highness*. Elizabeth Brice and Charles King were teamed together in a delightful dancing act; and the variety offering, running for an hour and more, and introduced by Gertrude Hoffman, came into considerable popularity. Gus Edwards had a revue that ran for fifty minutes. Blanche Ring did a forty-five-minute adaptation of her musical comedy, *When Claudia Smiles*. Langdon McCormick gave vaudeville an elaborate sketch, *The Forest Fire*, which became the basis of a successful play, *The Storm*. And Sylvester Schaffer, a one-man show, offered eight distinct acts. A wonder man, that Schaffer, who went in for violin solos, coin tricks, juggling, and sharpshooting.

And there were also, of course, such popular performers in the two-a-day as Chip & Marble, Ruth Budd, "the Girl With the Smile"; Joe Jackson and his trick bicycle, Pat Rooney and Marion Bent, Eddie Leonard, Paul Whiteman, Claire Rochester, Roshanara and her classic dances, Bernard Granville, Hermine Shone, Marion Murray, Belle Story, Hazel Cox, W. C. Fields, Stella Mayhew, Cissie Loftus, and Loney Haskell's talking dog.

The two-a-day, in its era of vast prosperity, also claimed the services of such famous teams as Adelaide & Hughes, Smith & Dale (Dr. Kronkhite), Olsen & Johnson, Clifton Webb and Mary Hay, Burns & Allen, Kennedy & Berle (Milton Berle), and of such individuals as Will Mahoney, Joe Laurie, Jr., Phil Baker, Bob Hope, Jimmy Durante, John Dooley, Gilda Gray, and the extraordinary Ina Claire. Olga Petrova appeared; so did Louise Dresser, Ray Dooley, May Naudain, and Winona Winter. Fred and Adele Astaire brought their dancing magic to the leading houses, and Walter Huston was well known to vaudeville followers before Broadway had ever heard of him.

Bert Williams was another popular headliner. Jack Benny was in a violin and piano act under the name of Benny & Woods. Doyle & Dixon were delightful in a dancing act. Walter C. Kelly was a famous storyteller. Herman the Great was one of the best of the magicians. Houdini always packed a house. Corse Payton, the stock company star, tried his dramatics on the two-a-day. Lew Dockstader was a popular performer; so was Frank Fay. Joe E. Howard sang popular songs, and such people as Trixie Friganza, Ruth Roye, Joseph Santley, Charles Grapewin, Anna Chandler, Wellington Cross & Lois Josephine, and Ralph Herz were always welcomed in the variety theaters. And then, in earlier years, there was the matter—and the problem—of the Cherry Sisters, Addie and Effie, from Iowa. They were considered to be atrociously bad, and to such an extent that they became tremendously successful. The Cherrys were known as "the vegetable twins" because of the garden missiles that were being continually thrown at them.

Those were vaudeville's great days. Vaudeville's prosperity and popularity continued on into the twenties and through the decade. But before the crash of 1929 motion pictures and the Broadway theater had begun taking away the foremost performers of the variety stage, and the audiences were diminishing. The branch of the American amusement business that had been thought up and built up by Benjamin Franklin Keith was doomed to an untimely death.

CHAPTER X

The Postwar Scene

STROLLERS in the vicinity of New York's Knickerbocker Theater, Broadway and 38th Street, in the early fall of 1918 seemed to walk just a little faster when they came alongside that playhouse; hardly any of them stopped to buy seats for the melodramatic comedy called *Someone in the House* or even paused to read the tidings upon the house boards. But it was this play, produced with no elation at all by George C. Tyler and shunned by a preoccupied public, that marked the beginning of the playwriting career of George S. Kaufman, a tall, dark, dour, and sharp-witted young man from Pittsburgh. He came to be of the theater via play-reviewing in Washington and his labors in the dramatic department of "The New York Times."

Someone in the House was first written by Larry Evans and Walter Percival. Evans became seriously ill, and Percival, in the words of a close friend, "was a hell of a nice fellow but not a writer." The fretful Tyler, even then beginning to sour on the theater and to resent its ever-changing trends, called upon Kaufman for a rewrite job. At ten o'clock on the evening before rehearsals started, the showman from Chillicothe telephoned Kaufman, saying that he had engaged Lynn Fontanne for a small part and wanted the part built up by ten o'clock the next morning. Miss Fontanne was the young actress from London toward whom the American theater had been definitely acquisitive since she came over to play *The Harp of Life* with Laurette Taylor's company.

Kaufman listened to Tyler's plaint, said he'd do his best, and hung up. Then he paced the floor. Along about two o'clock in the morning he borrowed the Dulcinea character from the column of Franklin P. Adams and was up writing for the rest of the night. He got the job done. Tyler was vastly pleased and Lynn Fontanne thanked Kaufman profusely. And it was

167

two years later that she suggested writing a play around the character, and *Dulcy* came into existence.

Someone in the House played fifteen tryout weeks and four weeks in New York, and after it closed, Kaufman, as he has remarked since, dug thirty-five separate acts from his desk drawer at the "Times." During the bleak run of the play at the Knickerbocker the waggish young dramatist prepared copy for ads which, he thought, should get into the papers. One read, "AVOID CROWDS! See SOMEONE IN THE HOUSE at the KNICKERBOCKER THEATER." And another read, "DO YOU WANT TO BE ALONE WITH YOUR GIRL? See SOMEONE IN THE HOUSE at the KNICKERBOCKER." Tyler smiled—and said no. It was later that Kaufman was introduced to Marc Connelly, not long out of McKeesport, Pennsylvania, in the lobby of the Hippodrome. They began collaborating and did eight plays together in four years. Four hits, four flops.

On an afternoon in December of 1918 a group of three—Helen Westley, Philip Moeller, and Lawrence Langner, who had brought along a revolutionary idea—sat around a marble-topped table at the Hotel Brevoort and talked with gradually increasing excitement. When they rose, after nearly two hours, they had a purpose and a plan. The Theater Guild, which was Langner's notion, had been born. All that now remained to be done was to find the play with which to make an impressive beginning and to find the money to produce it and the actors to play it.

The Theater Guild, it was decided in that session at the Brevoort, would break away from the conventions and restrictions of the commercial theater; it would do plays that had been ignored and neglected by Broadway but that would have—that must have—audience appeal. That first-meeting trio readily conceded that an art theater, however daring, could not exist unless it paid off at the box office. So the first-play decision wasn't an easy one for the Theater Guild's five founders—Langner, Moeller, Miss Westley, Lee Simonson, and Maurice Wertheim. The alert, practical, New York–born Theresa Helburn of the gray-blue hair did not join the group until some months after the beginning. Lee Simonson observed twenty years later in his "Part of a Lifetime:" *

* Reprinted by permission of the Publishers, Duell, Sloan and Pearce, Inc. Copyright, 1943, by Lee Simonson.

168

A more illogically assorted group could hardly have been chosen to become for a decade at least a major force in the regeneration of the American stage—an actress of no great reputation or experience [Westley], an author with a single one-act play to his credit [Moeller], a successful patent attorney [Langner], an unsuccessful painter and interior decorator who had designed a few posterlike settings [Simonson], an investment banker [Wertheim] and a graduate of Bryn Mawr [Helburn]. . . . Basically, we were amateurs and were considered presumptuous outsiders by Broadway and by sonorous Thespians who had been born, if not in the wings of the theater, at least next door and could point to a very distinguished theatrical ancestry.

The play finally selected for the Guild's very first production was Jacinto Benavente's *The Bonds of Interest*. Money for the Guild's start—and the subscription plan was to be put into operation immediately—came in slowly, but by April the Guild had its modest capital and its cast. On the evening of April 19, 1919, the Theater Guild, which was to achieve permanence in the American theater, made its tremulous start in West 35th Street, putting on *The Bonds of Interest* at a hoodoo house, the musty and long-forgotten Garrick, which had been in neglect and disuse for years, a playhouse that had had its glamorous and its riotous days during the regime of Ned Harrigan. Such players as Dudley Digges, Rollo Peters, Augustin Duncan, and Edna St. Vincent Millay were in the Guild's first cast; they were all in sympathy with the general idea and were working, in a pioneering spirit, for meager wages. The critical response to *Bonds of Interest* was enormously encouraging, but the public showed scant interest in exploration in 35th Street, and the Benavente play failed completely, being taken off after a month's engagement. St. John Ervine's *John Ferguson* had been chosen as the second play, and the life of the new organization was now actually at stake. It was down to pennies. The new play *had* to go—and it did. *John Ferguson* won an exultant press. There were cheers for the acting of Augustin Duncan as the old Irishman and the playing of Dudley Digges in the role of the oily, craven, sniveling Jimmy Caesar, and theatergoers began surging into 35th Street. *John Ferguson*, put on for less than one thousand dollars, earned nearly fifty thousand. The Theater Guild was now on its way.

"There came times," says Theresa Helburn, in talking of those early years, "when things looked bad. Why, we once were down to two hundred

169

dollars in the bank—and what saved us? It was Tolstoy's tragedy, *The Power of Darkness*."

New York's postwar theater brought in a welcome deluge of comedies, the procession of spy plays having finally, and mercifully, come to a halt. Some of the new comedies provided engaging stage material. Certainly Laurence Eyre's *Mis' Nelly of N'Orleans* did, with Mrs. Fiske as blithe and as skimming and as expert as ever. George M. Cohan's *A Prince There Was* found him being entirely believable as an actor if not as a dramatist. Peter B. Kyne and Edward E. Rose put together a likable comedy in *Cappy Ricks*, skillfully played by William Courtenay and Thomas A. Wise, and Rachel Crothers, in a somewhat startling outbreak of industry, and not content with the success of *A Little Journey*, came through with the diverting *39 East*.

Stage fare of an entirely different sort was submitted with dramatic suddenness when Arthur Hopkins, going along with the clan of Barrymore, brought in *The Jest*, Sem Benelli's drama of violence and fratricide, a colorful tale of Florence in the days of Lorenzo the Magnificent. John Barrymore's great friend, Edward Sheldon, made the translation, but would not accept a cent for his services, telling Hopkins to divert to Barrymore any royalties that might be coming to him for putting Benelli's Italian text into a tight, ready-to-act, English version. Hopkins was well aware of the box-office strength of his co-starring Barrymore brothers at the time of *The Jest* and when the play was established as a success he took no chances on their being dissatisfied with their weekly intake. Lionel was then compensated on a straight-salary basis, receiving $1,750 a week, and John was given $1,000 salary and half of the weekly profits, which were considerable.

"None of that," Hopkins asserted later, "represented generosity on my part. I merely wanted to make things so that motion pictures wouldn't be a temptation to Jack. But they were, anyway."

Rumors of impending strife between Broadway's actors and producers —the basic dispute was the matter of recognition of the Actors' Equity Association as the representative of the actors, recognition which had been denied by the newly formed Producing Managers' Association—were spreading as New York's sidewalks began to sizzle under the summer's heat of 1919. But only the more radical spokesmen of the opposing forces expected a situation that could not be, that would not be, adjusted over the conference table. Certainly no one foresaw a Broadway shutdown for that summer. In the early days of August, however, it became apparent that a strike of the actors, unprecedented in the annals of the American theater, was not to be avoided.

On the evening of August 7 the strike was called, and the city of New York was afforded a great free show, a truly extraordinary and continuously entertaining spectacle, until it ended, on September 6. Twelve plays closed when the walkout began; twenty-three were affected before hostilities were over. The Gaiety Theater, housing *Lightnin'*, the town's biggest hit, went dark immediately. Its star and co-author, Frank Bacon, was on the side of his own people, the actors. Owen Davis's melodrama, *At 9:45,* played through the strike without missing a performance. It was a one-set production and its stagehands were not called out because it could have continued without them. The Hippodrome gave up when 412 stagehands failed to appear for an evening's performance of *Happy Days.*

There were parades and speeches, street fights and street arrests, suits and countersuits, committee meetings and mass meetings as the actors and managers denounced one another; as the stagehands and musicians and chorus girls joined the actors, and as the public enjoyed it all enormously. Playgoers in general were with the actors; so were such stars as Ethel Barrymore, John Drew, Al Jolson, Marie Dressler, and Raymond Hitchcock. But George M. Cohan, around whom the strike seemed to revolve, went along with the wrong team—wrong for him, anyhow. The Actors' Fidelity League was hastily organized, with Cohan as its leading spirit. Fidelity took the side of the managers and its members, which, including some of the theater's outstanding stars, came to be scornfully known as "Fidos."

Cohan, at the time of the strike's beginning, was a man idolized by his profession. He *was* the theater, he *was* Broadway, to thousands; he was an actor himself, and one who had come up the hard way. He had won, by reason of his performances and his plays, by his writing of "Over There" and by many acts of generosity in behalf of unfortunate and indigent players, the respect and the affection of a multitude. And had he given a little more thought to the situation in early August, before taking and making his stand, he might well have thrown his lot with his fellow actors. And had he done so he might have emerged as the biggest man in the theater. But Cohan antagonized many of his old friends; he picked the losing team,

171

and that didn't go well with him. He had been a man who had played winners all his life.

Cohan did many things during that turbulent month, and most of them, in the judgment of the striking Equity members, were the wrong ones. He lost his temper, and childishly. He announced that he would never produce another play, that he would run an elevator before he did. He spurned actors with whom he had been associated since boyhood. He resigned from the Lambs and the Friars and resisted the tearful pleas of fellow Friars who had come to him in a body, in an unforgettable demonstration. He was stubborn and defiant, and he went down to an overwhelming defeat, one that gave him a bitterness that was to endure for the rest of his life. His feelings about the strike, and about Equity, were as strong in 1929 as they had been in 1919. And to many in the membership of the Lambs and the Friars, when peace between actors and managers was brought about on September 6, Cohan's violent personal participation on the side of the managers had caused more pertinent issues to be overlooked. To some who had been stunned by the attitude and actions of the Yankee Doodle Boy, the story of the strike could be summed up in four words: Equity wins, Cohan loses.

The Equity victory was a complete one. The managers signed an agreement recognizing the association and giving it full power to represent its individual members and to arbitrate for them. Scarcely less important was the establishment of the fact that actors could and would submerge personal and professional differences and would stick together under extreme pressure. And there were other gains from the strike—the eight-performance week, limitation of free rehearsal time, and wardrobe and baggage concessions. New York's actors went jubilantly back to work. Equity was established as a potent force in the theater; its authority as the official representative of its membership was never again challenged.

The fall of 1919, which brought zero and subzero temperatures to New York, along with the postwar delirium, was one of vast excitement theatrically. The city was jammed with visitors, including hordes of veterans of the AEF, late in getting back from overseas; they were roaming Broadway, seeing the plays as well as the sights, and they were spending money crazily. Such celebrated showmen as Belasco, Savage, Ziegfeld, Dillingham, Woods, Cohan & Harris, Wagenhals & Kemper, Erlanger, and the Shuberts, now controlling nearly half of the New York playhouses, were enjoying the boom, and were predicting great times to come. Old theaters were soon to vanish; new ones were coming up. The good old legitimate theater was asserting itself.

Ethel Barrymore was regally starred in the serviceable *Déclassée*, written by Zoe Akins, who was revealing a lively and vigorous playwriting talent. A hitherto obscure actor named Frank McGlynn came along to give an extraordinarily impressive performance in John Drinkwater's sound historical drama, *Abraham Lincoln*. Channing Pollock, not yet turned evangelical, quite outdid himself in the writing of a sharp melodrama, *The Sign on the Door*, excitingly played by Lowell Sherman, Mary Ryan, and Lee Baker. Hassard Short, recurrent in Broadway casts since the early century, gave up in complete disgust with the closing of the inept *First Is Last*, and went in for a new career, stage direction. Ina Claire, once of vaudeville, and who made a *Ziegfeld Follies* all her very own with her devastating imitations of Jane Cowl, Irene Castle, and Geraldine Farrar, turned up as a comedienne of rare skill in David Belasco's high-powered production of an Avery Hopwood farce, *The Gold Diggers*. Edith Day had a hit in *Irene*, for which a delightful score was written by Harry Tierney. Ruth Chatterton, who failed to sustain her early and enormous promise, found a pleasantly sentimental comedy in George Scarborough's *Moonlight and Honeysuckle*.

That fall of 1919 brought a sudden, and undoubtedly startling, fame to two players new to the Broadway scene—the young and lovely Margalo Gillmore and the tall, rangy, and fascinating Alfred Lunt. James Forbes sold his play, *The Famous Mrs. Fair*, to Henry Miller, who was nearing the close of his long and successful career, and Miller engaged Blanche Bates for the title role and Margalo Gillmore for the part of the ingénue. Miss Gillmore's father, Frank Gillmore, had organized the strike of the actors and, as the fighting executive secretary of Equity, he had directed Equity's battle. Miller had allied himself with the Fidelity League, and there was considerable speculation as to how he would treat Gillmore's daughter; the bitterness that had existed between the Fidos and Equity had by no means disappeared. But Miller gave orders that there was to be no political discussion at rehearsals, and Miss Gillmore made the observation in later years that she had never worked for a more considerate manager.

The part of Sylvia Fair was the first important one of her life, and she spent a sleepless night before the day of the first rehearsal. So did her mother and grandmother, who sat up all night making the dress that she was to wear. She was nervous when she reached the theater, and the warm, generous, and understanding Blanche Bates knew it. She went quickly to Margalo, put her arms about her, turned to Miller, and cried, "Henry, I love my daughter."

Henry Miller worked carefully and patiently with the young Miss Gillmore. Early in the rehearsals she came to a scene in which she tried tears. It was then that Miller broke in with a sharp correction: "No, no, Margalo. You don't want to be a Fall River Camille." The tears stopped. And later, in correcting Blanche Bates, he said, "Don't be stage polite. It's a bore."

Alfred Lunt, the man from Waukesha, Wisconsin, got his training, his valuable early training, at Boston's theatrical laboratory that was known as the Castle Square Theater. He played many minor roles, but they had variety. He was an exuberant collegian in *Strongheart,* a Balkan soldier in *Graustark,* a gray-sweatered bum in Channing Pollock's *In the Bishop's Carriage,* a walk-on in *If I Were King,* and a red, red Indian, given to many grunts, in *The Girl of the Golden West.* He was playing in a touring company of Booth Tarkington's *The Country Cousin* when Tarkington, on his way to Kennebunkport, stopped over in Boston to see a performance. The novelist-dramatist was greatly impressed by young Lunt's expert acting and went backstage and introduced himself.

"I'd like to write a play for you," Tarkington said, and he did—almost immediately. It was *Clarence.*

Tarkington, by that time, had become discouraged with himself as a playwright. His *Mister Antonio,* written for Otis Skinner, was a failure in New York; other writers had made plays of his *Seventeen* and his *Penrod,* and whenever his friends got to talking theater with him they always went back excitedly to *The Man From Home,* a triumph of many years before, and were rather tactfully vague about everything else. He now suggested to George C. Tyler that the authorship of his new comedy be credited to some nonexistent dramatist.

But George Tyler overruled him. "You have a great comedy," Tyler reiterated. "It will be the biggest hit of your life. Just wait and see."

Tarkington waited—and he saw. *Clarence* delighted its first audience, at the Hudson on a September evening in 1919. Tarkington won acclaim that had been long denied him. And Alfred Lunt was Broadway's new hero. There was jubilation in the Wisconsin hamlet known as Genesee Depot, which was glad to spread the news that it had become the actor's home town.

Ed Wynn (Edwin Leopold, son of a Philadelphia millinery manufacturer) was a musical comedy mountebank, one of the superior clowns of his time, given to lisps, chuckles, and nervous giggles, and always with his acrobatic eyebrows in full play. George White, a dark, slender, hard-jawed ex-hoofer, started his *Scandals* revues and in one or two of his productions he outdid Ziegfeld. Margaret Lawrence gave a brilliant performance in *Wedding Bells*, took her place as an accomplished comedienne, and lost it because of her irresponsibility; her life ended when an insane actor fired a bullet into her brain, and then killed himself. Maxine Elliott bade her farewell, and rather forlornly, to the stage in a negligible drama by William Hurlbut called *Trimmed in Scarlet*. John Drew engaged himself with an easy trifle, Rupert Hughes's *The Cat-Bird*. Margaret Wycherly gave an affecting performance in St. John Ervine's *Jane Clegg*. Theda Bara, temptress of the silent screen, turned to the stage, and regretted it, in *The Blue Flame*, one of the worst plays ever written. Al Woods, before becoming "Green Hat" conscious, was in the bedroom-farce phase of his career, buying expensive negligees for beautiful actresses, and was finding that it paid off. Grace George, true to her play-picking form, came forth in some utter nonsense called *The "Ruined" Lady*. Olive Tell brought her surpassing beauty to Thompson Buchanan's fairly entertaining *Civilian Clothes*. The buoyant Elsie Janis arrived with her gang, and the pretty and chubby Louise Groody and the lank Hal Skelly danced captivatingly in a good musical show, *The Night Boat*. . . . All of these were people of the Broadway scene at the time George M. Cohan and Sam Harris made the final production of their partnership.

George and Sam—they were George and Sam to the people of their Broadway world, just as they had been back in 1904–1905—brought in *The Acquittal*, a taut and well-acted melodrama, written by Rita Weiman and rewritten in part by Cohan, and then they quit. They quit suddenly. Their sixteen-year firm was dissolved; they were through. They were now to go their separate ways. Broadway was stunned by the news of the break; it

175

was disturbed and puzzled, and speculation as to the exact cause of it went on for years. Sentimentalists deplored it, and among them was Arthur Hopkins.

"It was a foolish split," he said years later, "and it never should have happened. They both got to be very sorry that it did happen. They were closer than ever during the last years of their lives."

Eugene O'Neill moved in upon Broadway in February of 1920, and he came when he was needed; the presentation of his first full-length play, *Beyond the Horizon*, at the Morosco Theater was an event of tremendous importance to the American stage. He came along when the theater was prosperous, when censorship was almost nonexistent, when the press and public were less squeamish about permissible stage subjects, and when playwriting was in rather a bad way. The theater fairly shrieked for a playwriting leader, for a dramatist who would assert himself—and O'Neill did. Augustus Thomas was through, and his *Palmy Days* proved it. Fitch was a memory. Eugene Walter was finished and so was George Broadhurst. Edward Sheldon's fine years were behind him; Elmer Rice's best work was still to come. William Vaughn Moody had been dead for years. Tarkington was an infrequent, and an almost casual, contributor to the stage. O'Neill moved in, took hold, and opened the way.

Suppose we take stock, as of 1920. Consider, in retrospect, the decade of 1910–1920. Three producers—Winthrop Ames, Arthur Hopkins, and John D. Williams—towered above the field; they brought to the New York stage productions of taste, imagination, and discrimination. There were some, but not many, plays of distinction. George A. Birmingham's *General John Regan* was a satirical comedy of lasting values. There had been quality in such pieces as K. G. Sowerby's *Rutherford and Son*, Eugene Walter's *The Easiest Way*, Louis N. Parker's *Disraeli*, Augustus Thomas's *The Copperhead* and *As A Man Thinks*, and Molnar's *The Phantom Rival*. Cohan's *Seven Keys to Baldpate* provided an unforgettable evening, as did Charles Kenyon's *Kindling*, Sem Benelli's *The Jest*, Galsworthy's *The Pigeon*, and *The Better 'Ole* by Bairnsfather and Elliott and *The Boomerang* of Winchell Smith and Victor Mapes. And playgoers had found abundant entertainment and excitement in St. John Ervine's *John Ferguson*, Edward Sheldon's *Romance*, and Jesse Lynch Williams's *Why Marry?*.

The decade of 1910–1920 yielded some memorable individual performances—Lionel Barrymore in *The Copperhead,* John Barrymore in *Redemption* and *Justice,* Helen Hayes in *Dear Brutus,* Marjorie Rambeau in *The Eyes of Youth,* Laurette Taylor in *Peg O' My Heart,* Chrystal Herne in *Our Betters,* Dudley Digges in *John Ferguson,* Emily Stevens in *The Unchastened Woman,* Ruth Chatterton in *The Rainbow,* Nat Goodwin in *Oliver Twist.* It had revealed enormous talent in such young players as Jeanne Eagels, Ina Claire, Margalo Gillmore, Shelley Hull, Alice Brady, Lynn Fontanne, and Fay Bainter, and had brought forth exciting personalities in Gaby Deslys, Nazimova, Vernon and Irene Castle, Douglas Fairbanks, Will Rogers, the cowboy philosopher, Marilyn Miller, Patricia Collinge, and Bert Savoy, a very funny and entirely new type of female impersonator, a comedian who was to die by a stroke of lightning at a time of his greatest popularity.

During the 1910–1920 decade, as in the decade that preceded it, the theater-is-going-to-hell note was sounded by eminent authorities. Early in the century William Winter deplored conditions generally, asserting that the baneful star system stunted the actor's artistic growth and that the theater was in "the control of a coterie of businessmen who avowedly have little sympathy with the drama save as a source of money-making." Henry W. Savage turned upon the critics in a speech of considerable violence at the time *Everywoman,* which they had derided, was touring the country to huge profits.

The usually even-tempered and laconic Arthur Hopkins blasted his friends of the press for the reception accorded his production of *Evangeline,* saying sharply, "Even Longfellow has no standing with the critics. The tragedy of it all! When will it end? When will newspaper owners decide that the theater is a great influence that deserves their help? When will they awaken to the fact that the American theater is years behind the theater of Europe? When will they realize that the theater's greatest handicap is silly-witted, venomous and cringing dramatic criticism?" . . . And so it has gone through the years, and so it will ever be.

Now, in 1920, New York was becoming more and more the theatrical center of the nation. It had once served merely as a showcase for plays that had comparatively brief metropolitan engagements and that were rushed by eager managements into the highly remunerative and seemingly limitless territory offered by the road. Now the road was slowly declining. This condition was brought on by numerous factors—the increasing popularity

177

of motion pictures, the conversion of many legitimate theaters into film houses, the disaffection of many old friends of the theater in cross-country cities—a revolt created by dissatisfaction with the quality of the road companies—and the increase in railroad rates. The spectacle of an America with only fifty-one attractions playing cities outside of New York, Chicago, Philadelphia, and Boston had been presented in January of 1918 when the government, as a wartime measure, drastically curtailed theatrical travel out of New York. And it was in the wartime period that many country-wide theater operators, realizing the hopelessness of trying to keep their houses open with the road shows, began making plans—and some of the more sentimental showmen doing so with great reluctance—for the showing of pictures. There were definite indications that the road was beginning to fall apart. Fewer plays were being sent to El Paso, to Atlanta, to Moose Jaw, to Wichita and to Denver and to Fargo. The shrinkage was to come on gradually within a decade.

In New York City, the theater's citadel, the drama thrived. There was money for new plays, new producing companies, new playhouses. Numerous managements were financially sound. That bold, new organization, the Theater Guild, was well established; it achieved its second popular success with *Jane Clegg*, and it was determined to avoid some of the mistakes— and the collapse—of its predecessor, the New Theater. Costs in play production had not yet taken to their skyrocketing ways. It was still possible to pay off stagehands and musicians without using up most of the money in the till; still possible to do a one-set play for less than ten thousand dollars, and it was still the day of the "moderate success." The time had not yet come when a play had to be a smash hit—or nothing. Small-cast plays could go along to weekly grosses of from $7,000 to $8,000—and in some cases to intakes of $5,000 and less—and make a little money. The New York theater had good actors, several able and important producers— Ames, Hopkins, and Williams were still contributing distinguished productions—but it was lacking in inspirational playwriting.

Into such a scene came Eugene Gladstone O'Neill, born in New York's Cadillac Hotel, and an able seaman, a reporter, and gold prospector before he turned to playwriting. O'Neill soared, and the theater went right along with him. His advent brought on a general and genuine awakening of the American drama. He was now to exert an enormous influence on playwrights and playwriting as he gave vigor, poetry, mysticism, experimenta-

178

tion, and power to his work. He became a terrific force, and with his emergence the stage came suddenly and dramatically to life, acquiring maturity and vitality. The New York and the American theater, as of 1920, was on the threshold of big things. A new and an exciting decade lay ahead.

CHAPTER XI

The Drama's Revolt—and O'Neill

THERE WAS considerable variety in the theater's plays of the early twenties; also, imagination and daring as O'Neill led the way. John Drinkwater's *Abraham Lincoln* was a dignified and impressive chronicle play, and Frank Craven delivered an extraordinarily true-to-life comedy in *The First Year*. St. John Ervine's *Jane Clegg* was ably produced by the Theater Guild. Galsworthy contributed his provocative and symbolical drama, *The Skin Game*. William Archer, the English critic, wrote a colorful melodrama, *The Green Goddess*. Ferenc Molnar, recurrent in the Broadway scene ever since *The Devil*, came along with the tender and affecting fantasy, *Liliom*, done by a fine Guild cast, with Eva Le Gallienne appearing as Julie, Joseph Schildkraut as Liliom, Dudley Digges as the evil Sparrow, and Helen Westley as the amorous and violent Mrs. Muskat. Porter Emerson Browne's best play, *The Bad Man*, revealed how delightfully human the Mexican bandit chief could be when played by Holbrook Blinn. George M. Cohan, now shorn of the shrewd and theater-wise Sam H. Harris and going it alone, made an uproarious travesty of the play called *The Tavern*. Gilda Varesi and Dolly Byrne collaborated in the writing of a popular comedy, *Enter Madame*, and Mary Roberts Rinehart and Avery Hopwood gave Broadway a gigantic hit in the thriller, *The Bat*.

There are behind-the-scenes stories in connection with several of these plays that should not go unrecorded. Winthrop Ames, not a man for melodrama, was completely fascinated by *The Green Goddess* and decided that he would produce it if George Arliss could be induced to play the principal role, that of the cultured, sinister, barbaric Rajah of Rukh. Arliss agreed instantly. Ames wanted Olive Wyndham for the part of the tormented heroine and invited her to come to his office, but before she did so she had a dream that she couldn't forget: she had been made a prisoner in a marble palace and her jailer was a man of fantastic appearance, and at that time Miss Wyndham had not read a line of the Archer manuscript. It was later that William Archer told her that he had had a similar dream and that without it he would never have written *The Green Goddess.*

Frank Craven, upon the completion of his comedy of the early marital woes of the Tommy Tuckers, took the script of *The First Year* to John Golden, who had earned a fortune with *Turn to the Right* and *Lightnin'.* Golden's enthusiasm for *The First Year* was shared by Winchell Smith, and a unique production arrangement was agreed upon: a three-way split of the profits, with Golden as the producer, Smith as the director, and Craven as author-actor, each getting one third. *The First Year,* presented at the 450-seat Little Theater, won the unrestrained cheers of the reviewers, and seats at the tiny Little Theater during the first season of the run were prized like precious stones.

Brock Pemberton, a tall, quiet-spoken, and frequently sour-faced Kansan, born in Emporia, worked in the dramatic departments of the *World* and the *Times* before entering the employ of Arthur Hopkins. He was play-reading for Hopkins when Gilda Varesi, who was then in *The Jest,* told him that she had written a play and wanted to read it to him. Later, with Carlotta Monterey (Mrs. Eugene O'Neill) listening, she read two acts, and then had to rush downstairs to make her appearance in the final act of *The Jest.* Pemberton liked the Varesi play and recommended it to Hopkins, who read it and also liked it. But he never gave Miss Varesi a contract and nothing was done about going into production. It was about this time that Pemberton was fired when something he had been told to do by Hopkins didn't work out, and the young Kansan had to think up a quick explanation to give to his friends. It came easily. Why, yes. He had quit to go into production for himself. So then he took what money he had, got some from a Kansas cousin in the oil business, and put on *Enter Madame.* The comedy was enjoying a hearty run when Pemberton, now looking for all the plays in the world, came upon the manuscript of a play he had already read. It was called *The Choice of a Superman,* by Cora Dick Gantt. "It's the sort of play," Pemberton told himself, "that George M. Cohan might like." Cohan did and agreed to produce it if the author would give permission to rewrite it as he pleased. This consent, reluctantly granted, set Cohan to work. He got his cast together and rehearsals began, with the play being delivered to the players scene by scene. The final pages

181

were not finished until just before the opening, and it was then that Arnold Daly discovered, to his unconcealed consternation, that the romantic character of the Vagabond, in which he had been taking great relish, was nothing more than an escaped lunatic.

The New York theater enjoyed a great postwar boom as the Nineteen hundred and twenties came along. Fifty-odd plays were running simultaneously in the Broadway area. There was a stampede for seats to the established hits; many lesser plays survived with help from Joe Leblang's cut-rate bargain counter in a Times Square basement, the fabulous business which had been started by the Budapest-born Leblang in a bleak little cigar store at Sixth Avenue and 30th Street in 1897, Leblang then believing—and it was a conviction to which he clung throughout his years—that the cut-rate theater patron was the most satisfied playgoer in the world. The drama's New York prosperity spread to the farthest-north Manhattan-Island stand at 96th Street, and into the teeming borough of Brooklyn. Such near-to-New York towns as Atlantic City, Stamford, Long Branch, and Asbury Park were thriving tryout centers, and the Boardwalk at Atlantic City was a parade ground for celebrated folk of the theater.

The theatrical managers of the early postwar years were giants in their field—Belasco, Henry W. Savage, and C. B. Dillingham, A. H. Woods, Ziegfeld, and the brothers Selwyn, Tyler, Ames, and Wagenhals & Kemper, Brady, Golden, and Arthur Hopkins, Sam Harris, Cohan, Erlanger, and the Shuberts. Most of these men were rich and self-indulging. They had money and they spent it. They were forever taking trips—to Atlantic City, to French Lick, to Hot Springs, Arkansas, to California, to Florida, to London, to the Riviera.

Lee Shubert and his brother J. J. now controlled twenty-odd New York houses; Mr. Lee, as employees and many associates called him, stuck to his sun-lamp treatments and was getting browner and browner and richer and richer. Al Woods, a spectacular figure of the period—he had companies swarming all over the country and was one of the most active of the showmen—was buying plays, giving big advances, giving watches to his authors and making his impromptu Atlantic crossings. Ziegfeld was writing longer and longer telegrams, buying imported shirts and jade elephants, creating bigger and bigger *Follies,* and suggesting to his millionaire friends that a theater be built for him.

Belasco, still fingering his forelock and puttering, trancelike, about his cluttered workshop atop the theater bearing his name, went Chinese with George Scarborough's *The Son-Daughter* and was acquiring rare and costly objects for his long-dreamed-of production of *The Merchant of Venice*. His son-in-law, Morris Gest, talked only in terms of spectacle-plays, such as *Mecca* and *Chu-Chin-Chow* and *Aphrodite*, and murmured dreamily about bringing the Moscow Art Theater to our shores. George M. Cohan, still bitter about Equity and his personal defeat of 1919, rejoined the Friars, from which he had resigned at the time of the strike (he returned because his mother wanted him to do so); George M. and Helen F. were the only members of the Four Cohans who were left. And Sam H. Harris and Irving Berlin, with Lee Shubert as a third partner, opened the costly and exquisite Music Box Theater. On an evening in the early fall of 1921 Harris and Berlin engaged a suite on the northwest corner of the Hotel Astor and stood at a window watching well-dressed first-nighters file into their beautiful playhouse.

"It was a wonderful, wonderful sight," Berlin relates. "We had started a new kind of grandeur in the theater with that first *Music Box Revue*, but it was the second of the series that was the most expensive production the New York stage had had up to that time. The second revue had cost $250,-000 when we raised the curtain. We got our money back and made a little profit."

Theaters were going up, up, up as the twenties came in, bringing along the dire prohibition era and its attendant evils. Such institutions as Rector's and Churchill's and Reisenweber's vanished; speakeasies, ornate and dingy, palatial and low-down, took up operations throughout Greater New York, with a concentration of them in the mid-town Manhattan area. The fancier establishments began opening to the east of Broadway and the after-theater drift of diversion-seekers was eastward, but the drama, not yet threatened by that new monster, the talking picture, held its ground in the Broadway area. Forty-second Street remained the world's greatest theatrical thoroughfare; the building of playhouses continued, and New York's commercial theater (there has never been any other kind that amounted to anything) wallowed in a prosperity that was to endure until the Crash of 1929.

There was money in murder melodrama, as in *The Sign on the Door*. There was still money in bedroom farces. There was certainly money in

183

mystery thrillers, such as *The Cat and the Canary*. But there was little of it, or none at all, in revivals.

The revival craze, dormant at times, was then asserting itself, just as it has been doing in the American theater throughout the years. The percentage of failure in the revival field has always been ruinous, but some sentimental managers never appear to be convinced of it. Each showman who cherishes a fondness for an old hit always has the feeling that his production will be the exception, although it is statistically true that not five in fifty pay a profit. The famous *Florodora*, shown to skeptical playgoers of the twenties, failed to repeat its early-century success, but it was generally agreed by veteran playgoers who compared the two productions— and this was positive heresy—that the new Sextette girls were prettier than those of the original company! Eugene Walter's *The Easiest Way* was mild in a second incarnation. Laurette Taylor failed with *Peg O' My Heart*, as did Doris Keane with *Romance*, and Walter Hampden with *The Servant in the House*. The once sensational *Hindle Wakes*, under the title of *Fanny Hawthorn*, was no longer shocking and not even provocative. Galsworthy's *The Pigeon* played to vacant seats; so did such out-of-the-past drama as *The Squaw Man* and *Trilby*. And George Broadhurst's once popular *Bought and Paid For*, in which the wealthy and drunken husband smashed down his pretty wife's bedroom door, was now dated and a little silly.

The star system, which had been losing ground steadily, prevailed to a moderate degree upon the advent of the century's tumultuous third decade. John Drew, his eyesight failing, was closing out a brilliant half-century career; rehearsals for the Rupert Hughes play, *The Cat-Bird*, hadn't been easy on the nerves of Drew's co-players, for he was then approaching blindness, and Hughes, who was assisting in the direction, was very deaf. The indomitable Mrs. Fiske carried on, but Maude Adams remained resolutely in retirement. Maxine Elliott, still beautiful but now seriously doubting her resources as an actress, called it a career when William J. Hurlbut's *Trimmed in Scarlet* failed, and made immediate plans for spending the rest of her life abroad. Ruth Chatterton, who had charmed New York in *The Rainbow* and who was equally successful in *Daddy Long-Legs*, was now only moderately effective in Barrie's *Mary Rose*, which had been declined by Maude Adams. Lionel Barrymore was curiously ineffective as Macbeth. The beautiful, intelligent, and experienced Marjorie Rambeau, who had come out of the West to find a warm welcome on Broadway, failed utterly as Rosalind. Billie Burke, who had been having play-finding trouble ever since the passing of Charles Frohman, had a fairly pleasant time with Somerset Maugham's *Caesar's Wife*, in which she appeared as the youthful and emotional wife of a middle-aged and high-ranking diplomat in Cairo.

But there was undiminishing progress for some of the theater's established players. John Barrymore, following *The Jest* with *Richard III*, had taken his place as the theater's finest actor; he was still to do *Hamlet*. Holbrook Blinn, a steadying and inspirational influence on his fellow players for more than a decade, was now an actor of extraordinary finesse and charm; he had advanced in technical skill and understanding of his art since his early appearances with Mrs. Fiske and Eleanor Robson.

Emily Stevens had come into the fullness of her power; Alice Brady was giving the theater some fine performances; Alfred Lunt and the London-born Lynn Fontanne were accepted as two of New York's outstanding young players. There was considerable interest in Jeanne Eagels, and a certain moderate enthusiasm for two young actresses who found roles in the cast of Rachel Crothers's comedy, *Nice People*, which brought the flapper into the American theater.

Francine Larrimore, a skillful actress, recurrent since her *Fair and Warmer* days, was the star of *Nice People*. The cast included two obscure young women, Tallulah Bankhead and Katharine Cornell. Rachel Crothers, when given to reflection in later years, always found herself amused and amazed in thinking back on the players she had hired for *Nice People*. Tallulah Bankhead, born in Huntsville, Alabama, had been sent to Miss Crothers the year before with the request that she be given a chance, and in she had walked—eighteen years old, very pale, very direct, with flopping ash blond hair. Miss Crothers, quite dubious, handed her a copy of her comedy, *39 East*, which was then running. The young actress stood before the fire and read, quite fearlessly, the leading role as Miss Crothers listened in complete astonishment—it was a reading, the dramatist recalls, that revealed "an unmistakable gift for acting, as naturally as a bird sings." Tallulah was promptly engaged to understudy Constance Binney in *39 East* and she was later given her role in *Nice People*, that of a sophisticated young creature, which she played with the abandon and the poise of a true professional.

The flamboyant Miss Bankhead became discouraged with her New York

185

progress after an artificial play, *The Exciters,* failed, and she borrowed $1,000 to go to England to continue her career. She bloomed in London; the stall-holders loved her. The Gallery Gods queued up for a block for a glimpse of her after seeing her as Camille. She returned to America as a star, and then there was a general clamor for her services.

I talked with her in her charming Farm Street house during her London years and again when we met in Hollywood. "Hollywood?" she said. "What am *I* doing out here? Christ, I love the place. They're paying me. Why shouldn't I?"

Katharine Cornell, dark and lithe, with high cheekbones, an expressive, full-lipped mouth, and widely separated dark brown eyes—she was not, and is not, a beautiful woman but she gives the illusion of beauty from the stage—was born in Berlin, where her father, Peter Cortelyou Cornell, was studying surgery. He later gave up medicine and took to theater managing in Buffalo and there the spirited, athletic, tomboyish Katharine appeared in her first school plays and got her first yearnings for the stage. She also wrote school plays while attending the Merrill School at Mamaroneck, New York. Edward Goodman went to Mamaroneck to direct a commencement play, became greatly impressed with Miss Cornell's talent, and told her to come to see him if she ever cared to take up the theater professionally.

Several years later she went to Goodman, and he got her started with the Washington Square Players. But there was hard work ahead. She played with Jessie Bonstelle's fine company in Detroit, toured for William A. Brady in one of his several *Man Who Came Back* companies, and went to London for an engagement in *Little Women.* It was there that she was seen by the actor, Allan Pollock, who was stirred by the quality of her voice. Later, when Pollock was in New York casting for C. B. Dillingham's production of Clemence Dane's *A Bill of Divorcement,* and in frantic search for a young actress to create the role of the flapper—the wise, gentle, knowing, high-spirited Sydney Fairfield—his thoughts went back to the American girl in London.

"She'd be wonderful," he told Miss Dane and Dillingham.

"Let's get her," responded Dillingham.

They got her. And on an October evening in 1921 Clemence Dane's poignant drama of the return of a shell-shocked war veteran opened in New York. The role of the daughter, in whom the father found understanding and companionship, was played with feeling and insight by young

Katharine Cornell. New York's first-string reviewers had passed up *A Bill of Divorcement*, going that night to see Helen Hayes in a minor comedy by Booth Tarkington called *The Wren*. But word of Miss Cornell's exciting performance got around quickly, the regular critics began rushing to the Cohan Theater, and a play that was struggling to survive was turned into a hit. Katharine Cornell, who had just become the bride of Guthrie McClintic, was acclaimed as a future star.

A great surge of new playwriting talent was bringing new vitality to the theater. Dramatists of the prewar era were on their way out, but Rachel Crothers and Owen Davis continued their labors valiantly. Davis followed the writing of his best play, *The Detour*, with a study of New England life in a drama called *Icebound*. He took his manuscript to the typing service offices, later called for his six neat copies, and distributed five copies to Broadway managements. He went for lunch at the Knickerbocker grill, and Max Gordon, then making his start as a legitimate producer, came to his table.

"What's that?" asked Gordon, peering at the blue-covered manuscript in Davis's pocket.

"My new play," said Davis.

Gordon reached for it and walked out with it.

That was just after noon, on a Saturday. The next morning, about breakfast time, he appeared at the Davis apartment and said, "We're going to produce your play." And he put one thousand dollars in currency on the table.

Well, they did produce it—Gordon and Al Lewis and Sam H. Harris. In the spring of 1923 Owen Davis got a telephone call from Al Woods, his erstwhile partner in blood-and-thunder melodrama. "Sweetheart," bellowed Woods, "do you want to know who just won the Pulitzer Prize?"

"Who did?" asked Davis.

"Why, you big sap!" roared Woods. "You did!"

Gilbert Emery, an actor, joined the ranks of the postwar dramatists, now engaged so forcefully in the projection of the theater's new naturalism and realism, with the writing of a bitterly ironical piece called *The Hero*—a play about a war hero back from France, who reveals himself to be a blackguard, a seducer, and a thief when he moves into the humdrum home of his insurance-clerk brother. Zona Gale turned her best-selling novel, *Miss Lulu*

187

Bett, into a touching and affecting family-life play. The playwriting team of Kaufman & Connelly went on from *Dulcy* to *To the Ladies* and *Merton of the Movies.* Lula Vollmer, born in North Carolina, was working as a box-office treasurer when her play, *Sun-Up,* telling its tale of the mountain woman, the Widow Cagle, who loses her son in the war, was accepted as a drama of great simplicity and honesty, and it brought forth a genuinely moving performance from the former stock star, Lucille La Verne. Arthur Richman revealed perception and freshness as a dramatist with his grim play of middle-class life, *Ambush.* George Kelly emerged from vaudeville with his devastating satire on the Little Theater movement called *The Torchbearers.* But convention-shattering Eugene O'Neill towered above the field, just as he was to do for the next fifteen years.

O'Neill had been acclaimed for the power of his one-act plays—*Moon of the Caribbees, The Long Voyage Home, Bound East for Cardiff*—and had come to be accepted by readers of "Smart Set" (Mencken & Nathan) as a writer of enormous promise when his first full-length play, *Beyond the Horizon,* which had been taken to the progressive John D. Williams, was produced at New York's Morosco in 1920. *Beyond the Horizon* presented its tragic story of the poet and dreamer, Robert Mayo, who longs for the far places of the world. He is suddenly accepted by the girl he believed to be in love with his brother, the unimaginative Andrew. So it's Andrew who goes to sea, and the visionary Robert stays home to run the farm. He makes a ruin of the farm and of his life. *Beyond the Horizon* won the Pulitzer Prize; it gave O'Neill enough ready cash to permit him to forget financial cares, and it marked the arrival of a great new force in the American theater.

The excitement over *Beyond the Horizon* had by no means abated when another and finer play, *The Emperor Jones,* a harrowing dramatization of fear, told its enthralling story of the flight of Brutus Jones, ex-Pullman porter, with the beat of the tom-toms sounding ominously through the blackness of the impenetrable forest. Charles Gilpin, the Negro actor, gave a memorable performance as the Emperor—vivid and real and true—but an even stronger one was contributed later by Paul Robeson, who brought his great voice and all his primitive strength to the role.

O'Neill's plays were giving the theater a new richness and boldness; critics and playgoers alike came under the spell of the playwriting son of one of the theater's old-time romantic actors. O'Neill's *Diff'rent,* a sharp and uncompromising treatment of sex psychology, followed *The Emperor Jones,* and then there was *Gold,* a study of a sea captain's lust for treasure, which was a failure. But with *Anna Christie,* brought into the Vanderbilt Theater in the fall of 1921, O'Neill increased his prestige as a dramatist and also achieved a popular success.

Anna Christie, telling its tale of the old sea captain, his prostitute daughter, and the bellicose Irishman named Matt Burke who loved her deeply, had been tried out by George C. Tyler under the title of *Chris Christopherson.* Lynn Fontanne was in the principal role, but the play was withdrawn in Philadelphia. O'Neill revised it and sent it to George Jean Nathan, who had been his ardent and outspoken champion from the time his short plays began appearing in the pages of "Smart Set." Nathan, fairly overwhelmed by the vigor of the new script, sent it to his friend, the debonair Edgar Selwyn, then one of the most successful of the Broadway managers. Selwyn didn't like *Anna Christie* and said so with charming and characteristic frankness. Nathan, regarding him with some pity, but retaining his well-rehearsed poise, then had the manuscript put upon the desk of Arthur Hopkins, who accepted it instantly.

Anna Christie, with its opening scene in the waterfront dive that O'Neill knew when he was living at Jimmy the Priest's, became an overnight success and brought stardom to Pauline Lord, an actress who is so jerky, so halting, so gasping, so volatile, and so brilliant in her style of playing. Hopkins had unhesitatingly given Miss Lord the role of the wanton Anna, whose regeneration was brought about through the devotion of a simple Irishman.

"Yes," says Hopkins, "I loved *Anna Christie* when I read it, but I told O'Neill it was a half hour too long. He said, 'Well, you cut it.' He never saw the play until he came to the dress rehearsal."

Two of the theater's in-the-big-money dramatists at the time of O'Neill's spectacular ascent were journeymen playwrights—Anne Nichols and Channing Pollock. They won vast popular success because they believed in their plays—when nobody else did. Miss Nichols, a minor actress—she had once played a walk-on in *The Shepherd King*—was born a Methodist in a Georgia hamlet and brought up on the outskirts of Philadelphia. She had an unshaken conviction that her comedy, *Abie's Irish Rose,* was a play of great mass appeal, and that if it could be kept running long enough it would find a public—it would create a public. Channing Pollock, hypnotic speaker and crusader, a kindly man and also an egotist, was unwilling to

189

believe that all of humanity could not be brought to sharing his enthusiasm for the play he called *The Fool*.

Abie's Irish Rose came first. "Abie," an American phenomenon, was rejected by every New York manager to whom it was shown and when it did get into New York, and into the Fulton Theater—at a time of the year when the season was considered officially over by almost everybody, critics included—it arrived under its author's sponsorship. She had been made to realize that it could never get a New York hearing in any other way.

Miss Nichols had had an affection for her "Abie" ever since the evening in Buffalo when she was sitting in a restaurant with her husband, Henry Duffy. A Jewish boy named Berg entered. He was in tears—positively frantic. As he sobbed he told Miss Nichols of his plight. He had just become a bridegroom but he had lied to his stern father, telling him that the girl was Jewish. But his bride was Irish!

"There," observed Miss Nichols after young Berg had departed, "is a situation for a wonderful farce comedy. I shall write it."

She did, within three months, and then she began trying to sell it in New York. A. H. Woods was among those who declined it heartily; he told her that it would bring forth protests from both Jews and Catholics.

"Sweetheart," he said, "don't produce that play. They'll kill you."

Miss Nichols ignored his warning, put the manuscript of *Marriage in Triplicate* into her bag, went West, and got a production from Oliver Morosco. When the play opened in Los Angeles, in which it achieved a remarkable run of thirty weeks, it was known as *Abie's Irish Rose*. Miss Nichols, then determined to have a New York showing, took the production to New York. And on the evening of May 23, 1922, the comedy that cost five thousand dollars and that earned six million, had its historic *première*. The names of its original players must go into the record: Mathilde Cottrelly, Bernard Gorcey, Howard Lang, Alfred Wiseman, Robert B. Williams, Marie Carroll, John Cope, Harry Bradley, Dorothy Grau. And the name of Laurence Marston appeared upon the playbill as the director.

It's one of the theater's legends—and so very many of them are false in every detail—that *Abie's Irish Rose* was condemned by the first-night press. No such thing. The majority of the reviews were gentle. William B. Chase, writing for "The New York Times," gave the play its most cordial notice. Percy Hammond, who had come on to the "New York Tribune" after valiant service in the Chicago field, didn't like the play but he foresaw a Broadway success. Alan Dale, in the "American," conceded it to be diverting. Leo Marsh was friendly in the "Morning Telegraph" and so was Kelcey Allen in "Women's Wear." Heywood Broun, writing in the "World," was savage in his abuse; so was George Jean Nathan. Robert Benchley was enormously amusing in his derisive, week-to-week capsule comment, published throughout the long years in the old "Life," and he admitted as the seasons went by that he had a simply terrible time thinking up a new descriptive blasting every seven days. It was during the trial of Miss Nichols's suit against Universal Pictures for piracy of "Abie" in the film series, *The Cohens and the Kellys*, that the plot was traced back to *Romeo and Juliet*. Miss Nichols denied, from the stand, that she had ever read Shakespeare or George Jean Nathan. She lost the case.

Abie's Irish Rose, owned outright by Anne Nichols, had a struggle to survive during its early weeks. There was not a winning week from May until October—and then the landslide. Miss Nichols became desperate early in the run; more money was needed to keep "Abie" alive. She and Henry Duffy went boldly one afternoon to Arnold Rothstein, the gambler, and asked for a loan of thirty thousand dollars.

"Do you believe in this play?" he asked quietly.

"Completely," said Miss Nichols.

He then told her she could have the money if she would agree to let him write all the insurance on the play, personal and otherwise, throughout its existence. Miss Nichols walked out with Rothstein's check for thirty thousand dollars.

Abie's Irish Rose fought its way through and became the sensation of show business; it became America's favorite play. Stay wide awake for a minute as I drone out the figures: a year in Chicago, 29 weeks in Cleveland, 28 in Pittsburgh, 14 in Washington, 12 in Baltimore, 17 in Toronto, 14 in Kansas City, 11 in Buffalo, 10 in Montreal, 32 in Boston, 8 in Rochester, 6 in Atlanta, and 4 in the astonishing city of Erie, Pennsylvania, which was known to all the booking managers as a one-night stand!

Ten companies, five years in New York, 2,327 Broadway performances—such was the achievement of the comedy that began its Broadway career as an openly derided, bargain-counter play and then, five months later, astounded the theater-wise of the town by breaking out of cut-rate society and selling out night after night, month after month, year after year, in 42d Street's Republic Theater, once known as the Belasco. It was after *Abie's*

191

Irish Rose had become an old, old settler of theater-town that Alexander Woollcott got around, condescendingly enough, to pay a call upon the extraordinary comedy. Woollcott wrote in the "Herald":

The whole comedy, as written and performed, makes no great appeal, of course, to the mature playgoer whose happier hours in the theater are spent with such salty and adult works as *The Show-Off* and *Fata Morgana*. But even such a one can derive a mild enjoyment from "Abie" and can wonder with frank bewilderment how his fellow scribes of the journals and the gazettes came to find it so distasteful a bore that they still use the play as a synonym of all that is cheap and ornery in the American theater, and as fresh proof that the average American theatergoer is no brighter than he looks.

"Abie" gave Anne Nichols her millions, but, in the opinion of Henry Duffy, since divorced, she might have developed into an important American playwright if she had never written it at all!

Channing Pollock's *The Fool*, like *Abie's Irish Rose*, was a flop in its early weeks. It was a play of a man of modern times who tries to live as Christ did. The press was not greatly impressed with *The Fool;* it was failing at the box office, and it was then that Pollock got mad. Letters and telegrams had poured in upon him from people in all walks of life who *had* liked the play, and they set him on fire. His crusade began. He attacked the press, he wrote his own advertisements, he delivered speeches at luncheons and dinners and at club meetings and from the lecture platform. He gave forth his tirades in strolling to and from the theater; he went from forum to forum, from city to city, and he turned *The Fool* into an enormous hit. He was still brooding about it, and was still explosive in his vehemence, many months after *The Fool* had been seen by playgoers in all parts of America.

"They still say," he intoned, "that I'm a press agent, and I say that that's a lie. I fought for *The Fool* because I had to. I made 1,064 speeches. It was common sense to do so. The critics didn't like it because I didn't lie down and play dead when my play got panned. I've had thirty-two productions and out of all of that I've only received eight good notices. But I've made a million and a half and I can tell anybody to go to hell, including the critics.

"The only other writers who have been panned as much as the critics panned me are Charles Dickens, Ibsen, and Anne Nichols. Forty New York producers would have cut their throats because of the success of

192

'Abie' if they had not been consoled by the fact that the critics had said it was no good. . . . Critics be damned! I'm probably the happiest man in the world. Why the hell shouldn't I be? I don't have to make a living. I've got more money than I can ever spend. . . . The Broadway of today is hideously provincial. The managers? The old crowd was just as dishonest, just as illiterate as the fellows doing the plays today, but those old-timers did love the theater. Broadway is now interested in but one thing and that's its sophistication. I've been trying for twenty years to find out just what the hell sophistication really is."

CHAPTER XII

"Rain" and "What Price Glory"

TWO FINE PLAYS that were *not* written by Eugene O'Neill, curiously enough, helped to enrich the American theater of the early twenties. One of them was *Rain;* the other was *What Price Glory.* Somerset Maugham's acrid tale of San Francisco's Sadie Thompson—persecuted in the South Seas by the fanatical Reverend Mr. Davidson, whose evangelical zeal eventually gave way to lust—was the basis for the harsh and poignant drama called *Rain,* expert in its construction and crowded with as much sheer theater as the stage of America has ever known.

Maugham's story, entitled "Miss Thompson," was turned down, somewhat unaccountably, by Ray Long, editor of "Cosmopolitan," which had been buying the Maugham wordage eagerly, and at fancy prices. The author's agent, somewhat stunned, began trying "Miss Thompson" on other magazines, but the unqualified boldness of the story resulted in numerous rejections. Finally, the manuscript reached the desk of George Jean Nathan at "Smart Set." He wasn't a man to be disturbed by the power of a fable recounting the conflict between a missionary and a harlot, and he bought the story instantly at "Smart Set's" price—two hundred dollars.

Sometime later, in Hollywood, Maugham casually gave the galley proofs to John Colton, and Colton, to the Englishman's considerable astonishment, decided that there was a fine play in the material. He was given authority to go ahead with it.

Colton, later described by John D. Williams as a "dark-haired, life-loving, deep-voiced acrobat in English, magician in the theater," returned to the East and went to work with his dramatization, taking in Clemence Randolph as a collaborator. When they were done with half of the first act, written in pencil on sheets of yellow paper, they took it to Williams, who gave them a production contract with enormous enthusiasm. The play was

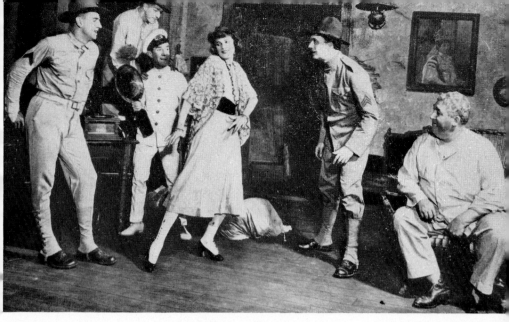

Life in Pago Pago

This is a scene depicting one of the merrier moments in that fine play called *Rain*, a sensation of the New York season of 1922–1923. Jeanne Eagels, playing Sadie Thompson, is dancing to the strains of her squeaky phonograph as four adoring Marines and trader Joe Horn (Rapley Holmes) look on with great approval (Ward Morehouse Collection—Photo by White).

The Century's Greatest Hamlet

BELOW   John Barrymore, pointing out the Ghost to Gertrude in the closet scene of Arthur Hopkins's memorable production of the early twenties (Culver Service Collection).

A Great War Play: *What Price Glory*

First-act scene in the Maxwell Anderson–Laurence Stallings epic of World War I, with Captain Flagg (Louis Wolheim) looking on from the right and Sergeant Quirt (William Boyd) listening warily at the table as an excitable Frenchman asks marriage and damages for his daughter, who has been seduced by an American (Theater Collection, New York Public Library).

O'Neill's Prodigious Drama

BELOW   Glenn Anders, Lynn Fontanne, Tom Powers, and Earle Larimore in a scene from the convention-shattering nine-act play, *Strange Interlude*, which was a theatrical sensation during the season of 1927–1928 (Vandamm Studio).

finished, and the search for an actress for the role of the agonized Sadie began.

Williams talked with agents and actors and managers; he took his script to A. H. Woods, then in a mood to do all the plays by all the playwrights. Woods got excited about *Rain*, as the play was then called and was sure he had the actress for it—Marjorie Rambeau. Williams approved. Several days later the manuscript was returned to the Woods office, and Woods called Williams by telephone.

"Sweetheart," he said, "Marjorie's crazy. She doesn't want your play."

It was later learned that Miss Rambeau hadn't been so crazy; she hadn't even read the play. But her husband, Hugh Dillman, had read it, hadn't liked it, and had turned it down for her! In another week Jeanne Eagels, under contract to Sam H. Harris, was engaged to play Sadie, and Harris assumed charge of the production, with Williams serving as director and retaining a 25 per cent interest.

There was a great deal of friction and near physical violence in connection with *Rain* prior to the New York opening. Sam H. Harris, a showman not easily unsettled, began to have doubts about Williams's direction and called in Sam Forrest before the production went to Philadelphia for its tryout. *Rain* opened at Philadelphia's Garrick in early October of 1922 and drew noncommittal reviews from second-string critics, the regulars having decided that *The Czarina*, starring Doris Keane, was a piece of greater importance.

The first-night performance of *Rain* was ragged. An after-performance conference became fairly hysterical, with only Harris holding himself in control. Eugene Walter was summoned to do some hasty rewriting, and during the next few days everybody, including the stagehands, had suggestions for changes. Walter wanted to put in a seduction scene, showing the Reverend Mr. Davidson and Sadie together after he had charged into her room, but he was finally overruled. Notwithstanding all the uproar and ruction, there was actually little revision made during the Philadelphia engagement. Most of Walter's time was spent in blasting Colton, whom he called a half-wit, and to whom he applied short, obscene words steadily for twenty-four hours. But Colton wasn't around to hear the vituperation of the author of *The Easiest Way*. The weary and discouraged Colton had stayed alone in his hotel room for most of the Philadelphia engagement.

Rain came into the Maxine Elliott Theater on a November evening in

1922, and the opening brought forth an emotional demonstration never exceeded in the theater of this country and century. First-nighters stood and screamed when the curtain fell upon Sadie's denunciation of Davidson at the close of the second act; they were as wild as spectators at a football game.

I occupied a seat in the rear of the balcony on that opening night and experienced one of the most genuinely stirring moments in all my theater-going years in the final scene of the third act when Sadie's long-silent phonograph broke into the haunting strains of "Wabash Blues," her gesture of complete disgust with all mankind. She had learned only too bitterly that the Reverend Mr. Davidson, the foe of all evil, who had finally convinced her that she must return to San Francisco and repent her sins, was an idol with feet of clay. Jeanne Eagels had her great night and she was acclaimed, and so was the play, the next day by the enthusiastic critics— Hammond, Broun, Mantle, Woollcott. Miss Eagels achieved a stardom that had been honestly earned and she went on to play the role of Sadie for 174 weeks.

During the long run of the play in New York no one had greater appreciation for the sheer artistry of Eagels than Kathryn Kennedy, her understudy, who fled to New Mexico in the mid-twenties in a last-chance effort to save herself from dying of tuberculosis. She lived. She decided that the Southwest was to be her home for the rest of her days and started a theater of her own, the Albuquerque Little Theater. And during the year of 1948 Miss Kennedy wrote me thus of the original Sadie Thompson:

I sincerely doubt if Jeanne Eagels really knew, in spite of her pretensions, that she was a great actress. She was. . . . Many times backstage I'd be sitting alongside of Rapley Holmes (Joe Horn, the storekeeper of Pago Pago) waiting for my entrance cue and suddenly Jeanne would start to build a scene, and Rap and I would look up from our books at once. Some damn thing—some power, something—would take hold of your heart, your senses, as you listened to her, and you'd thrill to the sound of her. . . . Jeanne was scared and unsure of herself before *Rain* opened. At one of the dress rehearsals she was told John Barrymore was out front with some friends. She stood it for awhile and then she became rattled and couldn't remember her lines, and she walked off the stage and said she wouldn't continue until Barrymore left. They got rid of him, and she went on. . . . Jeanne's surprise at her big hit was actually childlike, but that didn't last long. She began to yell for top billing and a hundred other things. One

196

night about a month after the opening, when she was really the hit of the town, her mother came backstage and said she couldn't get a seat. Jeanne told the stage manager to get her the seat. "I'm the star of this thing, by God!" she yelled, and then she looked quickly at several of us as if she expected us to deny it. Eagels had a fiery temper, and she was a long time fighting loudly for everything that she got, but beneath it all she was a lovable person. We'd all get mad as hell at her, but we had great affection for her.

Rain was still bringing its Pago Pago cloudbursts and its vehemence to the playgoers of America when Maxwell Anderson and Laurence Stallings came along with the lusty and magnificent *What Price Glory.* Anderson, born in Atlantic, Pennsylvania, son of a Baptist minister, was an editorial writer on the old "Morning World," and Laurence Stallings was on the copy desk, when they began talking together about the theater, and about the war. It was Anderson who did most of the listening as the Georgia-born Stallings, fascinatingly garrulous, told of his combat experiences in France with the United States Marines.

Anderson had come to the "World" after editorial-writing service in Grand Forks, North Dakota, San Francisco, and with the "New Republic" and the old "New York Globe." He had contributed an impressive play to Broadway in *White Desert*, which failed quickly, and was quite determined to quit newspaper work the instant he felt that he could afford the luxury of being a full-time playwright.

Stallings, a graduate of Wake Forest College, North Carolina, entered journalism via the "Atlanta Journal," one of the finest training schools for newspapermen that this country has ever known. When he joined the staff in 1916 (as I have good reason to know, because I was also on the "Journal" at the time) he was gay, voluble, irrepressible, and undoubtedly the best-read man in the City Room. He talked better than he wrote, but he was a young man of enormous confidence in his ability and in his future, and he was already then planning a New York career, probably as editor of "The New York Times."

Stallings was earning $12.50 weekly as a "Journal" cub when he walked up to City Editor John Paschall one afternoon and said, "Boss, you're losing a good man. I've joined the Marines."

Shortly before Stallings made that momentous announcement, he and I had been assigned to the midnight leg-work of getting pictures of the dead

197

and injured in a skating rink catastrophe—the roof had collapsed at a time when the place was jammed. Our chase led us to a dingy side-street hotel and to the bedroom of a pretty young woman who was among the injured. She was in bed, bruised and shaken. There was an excellent photograph of her upon the dresser, just the sort of picture the office wanted. I made a grab for it, as Stallings stood in the doorway. At that instant the girl's burly boy friend rushed past Stallings, caught me by the neck, and proceeded to beat hell out of me. I yelled to Stallings for aid but he remained in the doorway, shouting instructions to me, and convulsed in laughter. I took my beating, got back to the office with the photograph, and with the conviction that Stallings was a physical coward. But before another year had passed I reversed myself in that judgment. Stallings rose to the rank of First Lieutenant with the Marines; was sent overseas for combat duty, saw fierce action at Belleau Wood, had a leg torn apart by machine-gun fire, and was decorated for heroism.

In 1923, shorn of a leg, and reading copy at the "World," he told Maxwell Anderson of those Marines. Result: Anderson made the quick, rough draft of a play. Stallings took the manuscript, worked on it, put in the lingo of the Marines as he had known it and heard it. When the play was completed Stallings, with all of his enormous exuberance, talked to Alexander Woollcott about it as they dined together at the Hotel Brevoort. There was only one man in the theater, Stallings asserted, who had the taste and intelligence to bring forth such a play, and this man was Arthur Hopkins, for whom Woollcott had tremendous admiration.

On that very night Hopkins was also dining at the Brevoort. Woollcott, taking over the Mr. Fixit role with great relish, bustled over to the Hopkins table and said, "I'm with a friend who has a great play. You'd better meet him."

Stallings was presented to Hopkins, who read the vivid and antiwar *What Price Glory* the next day and bought it immediately. On September 3, 1924, the Anderson-Stallings chronicle of the feuding between Captain Flagg and Sergeant Quirt, against a background of realistic war, had its tumultuous opening at the Plymouth. Louis Wolheim played the foul but heroic Flagg; William Boyd was the swaggering sergeant; and Leyla Georgie created the role of Charmaine, the French slut, over whom they brawled. *What Price Glory*, put on for a mere ten thousand dollars, became a Broadway sensation. Maxwell Anderson bought a cane and quit his job

198

at the "World"; Stallings, by then the paper's Literary Editor, remained in newspaper work until he realized that there was fabulous money for him in motion pictures.

The Rain–What Price Glory period also brought forth The Show-Off, one of the finest of native comedies—a human, wise, indigenous play, written by that meticulous workman in the theater, George Kelly, former actor and writer for the vaudeville stage, Biblical student and raconteur. Kelly had revealed an instinct for characterization in his first full-length play, The Torchbearers, but he brought forth his masterpiece when he turned to writing of middle-class life in North Philadelphia and to presenting the case of Aubrey Piper, the likable liar and braggart, the glib, brassy, impish, and generally monstrous young man who condescended to accept employment as a clerk for the Pennsylvania Railroad. Kelly, besides being a playwright, was an able director, and his attributes included one of the most remarkably retentive memories known to man. He memorized every line of a play before he put it into rehearsal; he knew every detail of what is known in the theater as "business," and whenever an actor seemed defeated by a line or an inflection or a gesture Kelly was always ready to step in and show him how to read it, how to play it. Guthrie McClintic is another producer-director with such facility.

The Show-Off, expanded from a vaudeville sketch, had an odd, pre-Broadway history. It was presented in Atlantic City, then the most desirable tryout town in America, by Rosalie Stewart and Bert French. During the engagement at the shore Miss Stewart persuaded the reluctant Kelly to make a change in an important line, the curtain speech of the final act, which, as changed, made the triumph of the upstart Aubrey over his mother-in-law all the more complete. No other line in the script was altered at Atlantic City, and the company moved jubilantly to Stamford. There, just prior to the New York opening, Bert French was taken ill and died. Not until Stamford did Miss Stewart become convinced that Louis John Bartels was the actor for the role of Piper. Walter Catlett had been sought for the part, but Ziegfeld would not release him. George Kelly was fairly desperate when he was suddenly jolted at a rehearsal by the piercing and infectious laugh of Bartels, who had been engaged for a minor role. Bartels was immediately put into the part of Piper. His salary was doubled the day the New York notices appeared.

199

George Kelly missed getting the Pulitzer Prize with *The Show-Off* because of a somewhat amazing action taken by the advisory board of the School of Journalism of Columbia University. *The Show-Off* had been selected by the jury of award and recommended for the Pulitzer Prize; the jury's members included Dr. William Lyon Phelps, professor of English at Yale. But the jury's recommendation was overruled and disregarded by the University, which diverted the award to Hatcher Hughes's play, *Hell-Bent fer Heaven*. Later, for the season of 1925–1926, Kelly won the Pulitzer Prize with *Craig's Wife,* far inferior to his masterpiece.

Players of this period, along with the playwrights, were coming in for the theater's lively appreciation. Mrs. Leslie Carter, now of the forgotten-star status, returned in regal splendor to appear with John Drew and a fairly dazzling cast in Somerset Maugham's *The Circle.* The soaring John Barrymore took his place with the theater's immortals in giving his fervent and electric performance as Hamlet. James K. Hackett, of the legends of *The Prisoner of Zenda* and a survivor of the declamatory and posturing school of acting, came along as a surprisingly creditable Macbeth, in contrast with the monotonous characterization of Lionel Barrymore in the same role. Jane Cowl, who had given over her beauty and talents to melodrama and inconsequential comedy for many years, embarked boldly upon Shakespearean adventures. She was a radiant Juliet, with freshness and spirit and delightful stamina. If she was less successful in her projection of Cleopatra, it was a failing that had been common to all American actresses who had, up to that time, accepted the challenge presented by the arduous, jerky, and strangely unsatisfying role that Shakespeare wrote for his Queen of the Nile. Ethel Barrymore, in a Walter Hampden production of *The Merchant of Venice,* drew approval and disapproval, but Gilbert W. Gabriel, the "New York Sun's" aisle-seat representative at the time, was captivated and responded thus:

The first glimpse of her [Miss Barrymore] in green and gold, a later memory of her coming into the courtroom in a gown of unbridled scarlet, the honeyed contemptuousness of her talk to and about her suitors, the sprightliness she brought for once to that usually most apologetic of all Shakespearean anti-climaxes, the last act . . . these were holiday gifts for fair. . . . Her phrasings held warmly to their clear, deft meanings, and the manner in which she transformed that tattered old Christmas card about the unrestrained quality of mercy into a throbbing, living plea was proof of the art of finest readings. . . . She can now add to the Isolde-like loveliness of her Ophelia the wit and gracious mischief, fortitude and regal manners of the famous young hostess of Belmont.

And then there was, on a just-before-Christmas evening in the year of 1922, the coming forth of David Warfield in the long-desired role of Shylock and in the production for which David Belasco had been planning and talking—talking dreamily, with fully-closed eyes—for many years. Planning it as a production of such lushness and richness and splendor that it would bring to an end, and for all time, murmurings of all other productions of *The Merchant of Venice* given upon the stages of the world for the preceding two hundred years.

The New York press, accepting the Belasco-Warfield presentation as one of the decade's events in the world of the theater, gave unlimited space to its coverage of the premiere. Nearly four columns of solidly packed type appeared in "The New York Times"; the "Times'" critic, John Corbin, in a review of a column and three-quarters, contended that Warfield's voice lacked "range and volume" and that "neither in stature nor in physical vitality is he equal to Shylock's volcanic outbursts." But it was Woollcott's decision in the "Herald" that Warfield was "a good Shylock, one that wastes and scatters itself a little by too much vehemence, one that does not attain and may not have tried to attain heroic stature, but one that is authentic, believable, human and interesting." For all of that, for all of the stampeding of ticket-buyers during the early weeks, the production on which Belasco had squandered time, thought, energy, and money, was a gigantic failure.

Take the words of Warfield himself, given to me only last year, in telling why he had gone into what seemed a premature retirement: "I had done what I wanted to do, and that was Shylock, so I quit. What was the use of continuing? I didn't need any more money and I saw no sense in trying to make more. I had my allotment. I had ambitions to do other Shakespearean roles but I didn't want to go on. I had always wanted to play Shylock, and Belasco did it for me. The production cost $250,000 and Belasco never got the money back. When I quit 'The Merchant' on tour I knew it was my swan song. I didn't want any farewells. I'd had more than forty years of the theater and I just sneaked out of it as I had gone into it."

Warm and affectionate tribute was paid John Drew on his golden jubilee anniversary, a testimonial dinner marking the passing of fifty years since he made his first appearance on the stage of the Arch Street Theater in Philadelphia. . . . Lynn Fontanne became the bride of Alfred Lunt and they later began their joyous play-acting partnership in Molnar's comedy, *The Guardsman*. . . . Elsie Janis romped back to town and gave a remarkable impersonation of John Barrymore as Hamlet. . . . Emily Stevens, via Ernest Vajda's *Fata Morgana,* again asserted herself as an actress of enormous resourcefulness. . . . George Middleton's *The Road Together* was withdrawn after a bewildering one-performance engagement: its star, Marjorie Rambeau, was by no means herself for that opening night.

And word came from Paris of the passing, at seventy-nine, of Sarah Bernhardt. A crowd was at her theater to see her play *L'Aiglon.* Fifteen minutes before the scheduled curtain time the curtain unexpectedly rose. A member of the company stepped forward and said quietly, "Our great Sarah has just died. The theater will be darkened in mourning. Your money will be refunded." Then the curtain fell. . . . Of such was the drama during the first half of the incredible twenties.

The bold and imaginative Morris Gest reached back to his native Russia to bring over Constantin Stanislavsky and the Moscow Art Theater for a Russian-language season and in a formidable repertoire that included Gorki's *The Lower Depths,* Chekhov's *The Cherry Orchard* and *The Three Sisters,* and Dostoevski's *The Brothers Karamazov.* Notwithstanding the strangeness of the language, the visitors fascinated our playgoers with their magnificent teamwork and the richness of their characterizations. They caught the imagination of the public, and some of the company members—Stanislavsky, Madame Olga Knipper-Chekkova (the widow of Chekhov), Ivan Moskvin, Maria Ouspenskaya, and Olga Tarasova left impressions that were unforgettable. Morris Gest also sponsored the bland, moon-faced Nikita Balieff and his Russian vaudeville, the merry *Chauve-Souris,* whose most engaging number was the "Parade of the Wooden Soldiers"; and it was Gest, working in partnership with the less flamboyant F. Ray Comstock, who brought over Max Reinhardt's *The Miracle.* This spectacle-production cost $500,000—Norman Bel Geddes transformed the Century Theater into a cathedral—and a lot of it was borrowed on a note from Otto Kahn, to whom everybody in the theater automatically turned when the need of funds became urgent. *The Miracle* was taken across America, playing highly publicized engagements in auditoriums in important cities, and it earned back its production cost, the highest in the theater's history, and finished playing with a profit of about $300,000.

Ethel Barrymore brought her years of training and her thrilling voice to Pinero's *The Second Mrs. Tanqueray,* somewhat rheumatic by now but still effective theater; and Katharine Cornell, who had risen to an honestly earned stardom, tried and failed utterly with *Tiger Cats* for David Belasco, admitting later that "he didn't understand me and I didn't understand him."

The tall, stately, theater-wise Walter Hampden, who had played everything from the hero in *The City* to the villain in the spectacle-melodrama called *Life,* came through with a magnificent performance in that gallant and enduring play, Rostand's *Cyrano de Bergerac.* Hampden had done Shakespeare and Ibsen; he had gone through his solemn period in *The Servant in the House;* he had had his pleasant whirl in the light comedy of Clare Kummer; he had lived in the theater and for the theater since the days of his schooling at the Brooklyn Polytechnic Institute, but in the character of Rostand's rueful, long-nosed, heroic lover and duellist he found his greatest role. He played the part for more than a thousand times.

Years later, as he talked quietly with me of his career, he made this reflective comment: "Cyrano was really one of the tough ones, but the part that always took the most out of me was Macbeth. The tremendous power of it, all those changes, and that combat at the end! Hamlet is a long part but never so trying as Macbeth or Cyrano. Shylock is a good part and a short one. The actors used to say that Shylock was the only decent person in the play. I always greatly enjoyed playing Macbeth but there's no reward in the part; everything goes to Lady Macbeth. Funny, but *Macbeth* is probably the most popular play Shakespeare ever wrote."

Native dramatists were bringing imagination, observation, and interpretation into their writings; they were meeting the challenge of the British and Continental authors. O'Neill's symbolical *The Hairy Ape,* his study of Yank, the stoker on an ocean liner, and the futility of brute strength when matched against modern society, was a stimulating play. It brought him increased prestige, as did his gloomy and masterful *Desire Under the Elms*, forcefully presenting the tragedy of Ephraim Cabot and his brood against a stark New England background of the 1850s, and in which Walter Huston distinguished himself as the fanatical Cabot, who based his life on his belief that "God is hard." Elmer Rice went in for expressionism with his *The Adding Machine*, coolly received by the press, but which lived on as a play to be done by theaters in all parts of the world. There was a dress rehearsal of *The Adding Machine* that lasted until daybreak, and about 3 A.M. Philip Moeller, who was staging the play for the Theater Guild, sent for the stage manager after there had been a vexing delay of nearly an hour. The stage manager was ready with an explanation. The play's final scene called for a gigantic adding machine that just about filled the stage, and it brought on a protracted dispute as to whether it was props or scenery. Was the moving of it a job for the grips or the clearers? A solution was somehow reached before the union heads were called out of bed.

Vincent Lawrence revealed a talent for pungent dialogue and amusing characterizations in several comedies, but also an inability to write last acts. Sidney Howard brought the Napa Valley of California and some human, substantial characters into the theater with his fond and touching story of the marriage of a San Francisco waitress to an aging Italian grape-grower in a winning comedy, *They Knew What They Wanted*. Zoe Akins, an alert and in-and-out dramatist, and one of the most industrious of them all, wrote a swarm of plays after becoming moderately wealthy with *Déclassée*, but she never fulfilled the promise of her earlier *Papa*. Lewis Beach, who contributed a sound and honest play in *A Square Peg*, which failed, found success with a lesser play, *The Goose Hangs High*.

Columnist Don Marquis, under the bland guidance of Arthur Hopkins, turned to playwriting with the popular *Old Soak*, and George S. Kaufman and Marc Connelly gave the theater their sharpest, wisest satire, the best play of their collaborative labors, in the cartoon on big business called *Beggar on Horseback*. The authors presented, in a fanciful and expression-istic play, a young composer's dream, which foretold what might befall him if he married the daughter of a millionaire. The principal role was artfully and charmingly played by Roland Young in Winthrop Ames's production.

Ames, Arthur Hopkins, and the Theater Guild were serving as forces in making the decade theatrically memorable. The Guild, unsubsidized but with money in the bank and retaining its status as an art theater, was continuing its exciting experimentation with the plays of advanced British and Continental playwrights, and was bringing upon itself much critical abuse for its apparent disinterest in native authors, for ignoring such a dramatist as Eugene O'Neill. The self-supporting Guild believed that concentration on the foreign market was then necessary to maintain its high standard and it was astonishing the experienced and skeptical Broadway showmen as it succeeded in selling to the supposedly uncultured and conventional-minded audiences of New York the plays of Shaw and St. John Ervine, of Tolstoy and Molnar, of Andreyev and Werfel and Kaiser. And the Guild, in so doing, helped to destroy the theory that brazen, blatant, frenzied New York has no claim to being a cultural center. St. John Ervine's *John Ferguson* was a lively success in the Broadway area; it failed dismally in Boston and elsewhere.

When the Guild was done with Ervine's *Jane Clegg* and Molnar's *Liliom* and Tolstoy's *The Power of Darkness,* it brought forth richly satisfying productions of Bernard Shaw's *Heartbreak House* and his *St. Joan.* It also provided its surprisingly receptive clientele with Leonid Andreyev's *He Who Gets Slapped,* the imaginative *R.U.R.* of Karel Čapek, and Georg Kaiser's expressionistic *From Morn to Midnight.* The Theater Guild's Acting Company, along at the time of Werfel's *Goat Song* and his *Juarez and Maximilian,* was the finest that the theater of this country had known since the collapse of the New Theater in 1911, but the Guild experimented only halfheartedly with repertory, it did not hold its impressive personnel together for an extended period, and it went on with its policy of engaging new players for specific productions. There were fine players in that Guild organization of the twenties—Alfred Lunt and Lynn Fontanne, Helen Westley, Clare Eames, Dudley Digges, Earle Larimore, Henry Travers, Morris Carnovsky, Margalo Gillmore. And the brilliant Edward G. Robinson. Here was an actor, skilled in characterization and a master of dialect, who could have gone on to a definite and enduring stardom in the theater, but he quit. He preferred the easier life of California, and the Hollywood millions, to a career in the living theater. He loved the stage, but he walked out for screen fame and an art collection. There are undoubtedly those who will say that his choice was a wise one.

CHAPTER XIII

Frenzy of the Twenties

THE VOGUE of Michael Arlen and his *The Green Hat* seized New York's world of the theater just as it was being charmed by the wit and sparkle of the comedies by Frederick Lonsdale; as it was being jolted and fascinated by the playing of Noel Coward in his own probing treatment of decadence in the play called *The Vortex,* and as two brothers from Brooklyn decided that the island of Manhatten needed more playhouses. So they built them.

Al Woods gave the theater *The Green Hat.* Woods had never read a line of the novel but there must have been a few book-readers in the swarm of callers at his fabulous quarters in the Eltinge Theater building, because he was aware of its popularity, and he wasn't one to be scornful of any literary work that might offer him a play. The day came when a friend cabled him from London that Arlen was making a dramatization of the best-selling *The Green Hat.* Did Al want it? Immediate action was necessary.

The New York showman took his feet off his desk, threw his cigar to the floor, and composed a characteristic cablegram, one with a "Hello, sweetheart" salutation that included love and kisses and an advance royalty offer of $2,500. Arlen, pleased by the money and puzzled by the "love and kisses," had never heard of Woods, and he began asking questions. He received varying replies—"nice chap," "hard-boiled old boy," "a real tough one," "a wonderful fellow who's never read a book in his life."

More cablegrams came. More love and kisses, and Arlen yielded. He finished his damatization of *The Green Hat* and cabled Woods his acceptance. And then the Armenian novelist-dramatist, born Dikran Koujoumdjian in Roustchouk, Bulgaria, decided to make his first crossing of the Atlantic and have a look at those astonishing Americans. On his first

206

day in New York, Woods called upon him at the Ritz-Carlton and presented him with a case of whisky; on the second day Woods sent over a welcome-to-New York gift, a platinum wrist watch encircled with diamonds. "I'm going to like America," Arlen said that evening to Katharine Cornell and Guthrie McClintic. "I'm going to like it very much."

Arlen's green-hatted Iris March and Noel Coward's neurotic Nicky Lancaster were two of the talked-about characters of the New York stage when theaters designed and built by the short, dapper Chanin brothers, Irwin S. and Henry I., began springing up all over mid-town Manhattan.

The Chanins believed that the audience-comfort that was to be found in the motion-picture palaces spreading across the land was lacking in many of the existing legitimate houses, and they sought to catch up with the times. They adopted the stadium or amphitheater style of design for two of their largest houses; they provided large and beautiful foyers and spacious and elaborate smoking rooms; and when they finally decided that they'd done enough they took an account of their operations: five theaters built in three years. Perhaps someone else would now take over.

But when the Chanins ceased their theater-building operations, construction in the Broadway area came to a halt; the din of the riveters and the steam shovels suddenly ceased. Boom times were still on, and New York was getting more plays than it had theaters to house them—the year of 1926 was the peak year in New York's theatrical history, the year of the most plays, the most producers, the most theaters, and the greatest theater-ticket sales—but those who were inclined toward investments in new and greater playhouses were somehow restrained by a strange foresight, by a foreboding of leaner and darker times for Broadway, for New York, for all of America.

Two of the Chanin-built houses were admirably suited to the needs of the theater's song-and-dance department, which was then enjoying immense popularity and prosperity. There was an unending procession of revues and musical comedies; the field was fiercely competitive. Ziegfeld, continuing his *Follies,* was being challenged by George White with his year-to-year *Scandals* and by the *Vanities* of the tall, gangling, soft-spoken Earl Carroll, who wore creamy silk shirts and was given to suavity, fitful indignations, brief ministerial tirades, and many acts of unpublicized generosity. The typical revue consisted of comedy sketches and blackouts, songs and dance numbers, girls and nudity. It was a type of entertainment

207

that had been borrowed by Ziegfeld from Paris in devising his 1907 *Follies* and perfected by him in his season-to-season editions.

The firm of Jones & Green, deciding to imitate the form, came along with the *Greenwich Village Follies* after George White had already presented his first *Scandals*. The Shuberts, who had been doing the *Passing Shows* for some years, now introduced the revue, *Artists and Models,* and with the notion of putting on a new edition annually; they gave up on the series after a few seasons. A modest and beguiling revue entitled *Garrick Gaieties,* crowded with fresh and youthful talent, brought into Broadway's consciousness the composer-lyricist team of Richard Rodgers and Lorenz Hart.

As the competition increased the producers began employing famous composers to write hit numbers, and established authors, such as William Anthony McGuire and Ring Lardner, to contribute blackout material. They also stole famous show girls from one another, and such ladies of the ensemble as Martha Mansfield, Olive Thomas, Dorothy Knapp, Billie Dove, and Gladys Glad were exploited so diligently and so resourcefully and so continually that there was no great amount of time or newsprint left for attention to the stars of the era—Will Rogers, Marilyn Miller, Eddie Cantor, W. C. Fields, Ray Dooley, Ann Pennington, Lou Holtz, Eddie Dowling, Fannie Brice, Joe Cook, Sophie Tucker.

Two or three of George White's *Scandals* were the equal, in all-around showmanship, of the best productions of Ziegfeld. Carroll's *Vanities* swarmed with beautiful girls but they generally offered inferior music and mediocre sketches. The *Greenwich Village Follies* productions were pictorially exquisite and brought forth revolutionary staging from John Murray Anderson, but the series was short-lived. The magnificent *Music Box Revues* were too costly to continue; so was Hassard Short's *Ritz Revue.* Playgoers went fairly wild over Beatrice Lillie and Gertrude Lawrence when they were brought over in the *Charlot Revue* and these same playgoers swarmed down to lower Manhattan's Neighborhood Playhouse for the wit and topical nonsense to be found in the *Grand Street Follies.*

The American musical comedy—I'm now considering the "book" show as distinguished from the revue—is, at its best, a production vastly rewarding to eye and ear. The musical comedy flourished in the theater of the early 1900s; it gained enormous popularity with the coming of *The*

208

Merry Widow and such pieces as *The Chocolate Soldier* and *The Pink Lady;* and its prestige was increased immeasurably when the firm of Bolton, Wodehouse & Kern—Guy Bolton, P. G. Wodehouse, and Jerome Kern —turned to the writing of their delightful musical plays for the tiny Princess Theater. The early twenties gave the theater such popular song-and-dance exhibits as *Rose-Marie* and *Sunny* and *Sally, Good Morning, Dearie* and *No, No, Nanette.* They brought along the brilliance of George Gershwin in *Lady, Be Good.* And the decade's first half developed such specialists in musical comedy composition as the Gershwins, George and Ira, Vincent Youmans, Lewis E. Gensler, Rudolf Friml, Herbert Stothart, Cole Porter, Kern and Hammerstein—they all showed extraordinary facility in writing the scores for successful musical plays. And there was the young, dark, swarthy, good-looking Richard Rodgers, then giving to wondering about his capabilities and to worrying about his place in the New York theater. He could have saved himself the bother.

Broadway awoke one morning to discover that a young and smart express agent named Jed Harris, badly in need of a shave, had come challengingly into its busy midst. Harris was—and is—a dark, lean, sardonic, brilliant, and often childish man of the theater who was born in Vienna under the name of Horowitz and who has never tried to endear himself to anybody if he could possibly help it. He went to Yale for a time and he worked on the theatrical paper known as the "New York Clipper." He was working as a press agent in Detroit, representing a William Hodge comedy, when Philip Dunning, then an actor and stage manager, talked to him of a melodrama he had written, a play which had been known as *Bright Lights* and *The Roaring Forties.* It had been rejected by George Cohan and by Al Woods and it was now the property of William A. Brady, who had made unsuccessful efforts to induce Texas Guinan to play the role of a night club hostess. Jed Harris never thought of the play again until Dunning, manuscript in hand, called upon him in New York.

"Here's that play," he said. "Brady's option expired this morning."

Even then, in its far-from-polished form, the play that was to be known around the world as *Broadway,* seemed to dramatize effectively the general madness of the twenties and the prohibition period, that delirious era of gangs and gangsters, bootlegging and bootleggers, peepholes and door-smashing and glass-smashing, murder and vice and frenzied spending—a strange, vicious, headlong decade. Harris got increasingly excited as he turned Dunning's pages.

In less than two hours he had Dunning on the telephone. "I want it," he said.

George Abbott was brought in as collaborator and director, some revision was done, and tryout bookings were made for Long Branch and Asbury Park. In these engagements *Broadway,* a swift, garish melodrama which told its story of a shot-in-the-back murder in the Paradise night club, and which carried along the romance of Roy Lane, the exuberant hoofer (excitingly played by Lee Tracy) and his pretty sweetheart, looked like a million dollars. It still had that look when it opened in New York. Jed Harris read the notices the next day, went to the barber's, and began making plans for taking over the American theater.

The trend was toward entertainment in the mid-twenties. The trend was toward comedy, and the New York theater had the people who could write it. George S. Kaufman, still holding his job on the drama desk of the "Times"—it was his theory that a dramatist had just so much to give to a playwriting career and that by holding back a bit he could last longer—wrote, in his first solo effort, an amusing piece about a young hick who invests in show business, and he called it *The Butter and Egg Man.*

On the very second night of the play's engagement Kaufman covered the opening of a frisky musical comedy, *Merry Merry,* and when the curtain fell I walked with him from 48th Street to Times Square. "That show seemed very good," he said. "But I suppose any show would be all right with me tonight. *The Butter and Egg Man* sold out at the Longacre."

Marc Connelly, also now operating on his own, gave the theater a charming comedy-fantasy, *The Wisdom Tooth.* Anita Loos and John Emerson transformed Miss Loos's book, *Gentlemen Prefer Blondes,* into a broad, funny, and best-selling comedy. That suave Londoner, Frederick Lonsdale, with the aid of Winchell Smith's directorial expertness, achieved huge success with *The Last of Mrs. Cheyney,* brilliantly played by Ina Claire and Roland Young; and that master of revue direction, Hassard Short, dug up a comedy by two new writers, Russell Medcraft and Norma Mitchell, that kept Broadway laughing for months. Short read the manuscript of *Cradle Snatchers* one evening, telephoned his acceptance the next morning, and went quickly to the Sam Harris office. He told Harris

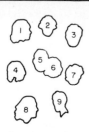

Some Important Players of Our Stage Today

1. Helen Hayes 2. Margaret Webster 3. Ina Claire 4. Judith Anderson 5. Alfred Lunt 6. Lynn Fontanne 7. Ruth Gordon 8. Katharine Cornell 9. Eva Le Gallienne

Masters of the Art of Acting

1. Walter Huston 2. Dudley Digges 3. Holbrook
Blinn 4. Walter Hampden 5. Leslie Howard
6. Philip Merivale

that the production would cost $30,000 ($80,000, under the conditions of 1949), and that he would put up $15,000. Would Harris come in for the other half?

"If you say it's that good," said Harris, "let's go ahead."

And there were Maxwell Anderson's sagacious *Saturday's Children*, skillfully staged by Guthrie McClintic and played by Ruth Gordon, and Molnar's *The Play's the Thing*, which gave the matured, polished Holbrook Blinn an actor's holiday.

On the serious side, George C. Tyler introduced a twenty-four-year-old playwright in John Van Druten, then teaching in a Welsh university. His *Young Woodley*, a play of love and sex and adolescent frustration, was put on with the changing of only a few lines of the original manuscript. The play was banned in London by the Lord Chamberlain on the ground that it represented an attack on the English public-school system and would be painful to teachers and parents alike. Tyler acquired the rights for American presentation, but America seemed very far away to young Van Druten and he went on with his teaching, trying to forget his disappointment in not having a London showing. On the night that *Young Woodley* opened in Boston, with Glenn Hunter and Helen Gahagan as its leading players, there came an extraordinary coincidence—the motion picture of *Merton of the Movies*, with Hunter in the title role, was offered in Aberystwyth, Wales, the town in which Van Druten was teaching, and Van Druten was in the film theater to receive it. America then seemed a great deal nearer. The London-born Van Druten soon began receiving the notices, and the royalty checks—and packing his bag for his first trip to New York.

Also on the serious side, and very much so, was William Hurlbut's *Bride of the Lamb*, which combined sex, psychology, and evangelism with dramatic results (and which brought a thrilling performance from Alice Brady), and that disturbing drama of Negro life, *In Abraham's Bosom*, the work of the social-minded, liberal-thinking Paul Green, North Carolina-born teacher and author. His *In Abraham's Bosom* presents, with overwhelming power and sensitivity, the tragedy of an educated Negro, whose father was white and who is mistrusted by the white race and despised by his own. Green found the genesis of this play, which won the Pulitzer Prize for the season of 1926–1927, in an unforgettable incident out of his childhood, and he has written to me of it with such poignance that I must now give you his own words as they come to me from Chapel Hill:

211

It was many, many years ago. I was a little boy come to the neighboring town of Angier on a bright day to get a load of fertilizer for our farm. I wanted to see the train come in. I stood by the little shack of a station waiting along with several others, among them an old Confederate soldier leaning on his walking stick, for the train to put in its appearance. Soon it showed its round black moon of a locomotive end around the bend. It puffed and wheezed along toward us and finally drew in with a rusty squealing of its brakes. It was an old wood-burner, and the climb into town had been tough. The engineer piled out of the cab, grease-marked outside and full of spleen and frustration inside. He began to work on the old locomotive, squirting grease here and there into its aged joints. I looked down the track and spilling out of the Jim Crow car—there were only four in all, a white car, a Negro car, a freight car and a caboose—spilling out was a swarm of little Negro school girls all dressed in their pink and white and blue picnic garments and with ribbons in their hair. Also there was a sprinkling of young Negro boys all ironed and pressed and scrubbed clean by their mamas for this great day. At the head of them was a tall yellow Negro man wearing gold-rimmed glasses and with a wide expanse of white slick-ironed shirt front and wing collar, and big black bolster tie. The little Negro children twittered and chirped in the sunny air, looking about them, happy as only children can be happy. They were on their way to Durham, North Carolina, on what was called in springy parlance of those days a "skursion." The big yellow man was the teacher and he was taking the children on this jaunt as a wind up for his year's school teaching. He came strolling forward toward us and toward the irate and working engineer. He felt good. He was expansive. The world was sitting to his hand.

"Good mawning, gentlemen," he said graciously to us. The old Confederate soldier blinked up at him, continued leaning on his stick, said nothing. I, a little boy, naturally said nothing. But I was already in my heart admiring this gracious, this genial, this successful and respectable representative of the Negro race.

"What time do the train get to Durhams, sur?" the Negro teacher asked of the engineer.

"None of your damned business," called the engineer behind him, still bent over one of the drivers with his oil can. Then he looked around. He straightened spasmodically up and glared at the colored man.

The Negro already had taken a shocked and rebuffed step backward.

"Sorry, suh, sorry," he said, and he was beginning to bob his head up and down a bit, bending his body at the waist.

"Take off your hat," the engineer suddenly squealed. Off it came in the culprit's hand. The little children down at the other end of the train began to see something was wrong, and in the blink of my eye I saw them begin to huddle together a little closer as if some fearful threat were beginning to be felt in the air.

"Take off your specs," the engineer snapped.

"But I ain't done nothing, white folks, ain't done nothing," said the colored man, and he backed away a couple of more steps.

"Don't white-folks me!" the engineer shouted. He flung the oil can behind him, snatched the walking stick from under the old Confederate soldier's resting hand and quick as lightning struck the Negro teacher a terrific wham across the face. Before the engineer pulled the stick away the blood had already rushed out and stained its splintered wood.

A little babble of shrieks and moanings rose from the school children, and like a gang of pursued goats they bounded up the steps of the Jim Crow car and inside to safety. The old Confederate soldier had almost fallen on his face when his support was jerked away. He righted himself with spread-out legs; the engineer handed his walking stick back to him. The old soldier took it and resumed his resting without a word. I couldn't look at the dreadful stick. I couldn't look at the colored man. I shivered as if some bitter freezing chill had overspread the world. A low whimpering moaning sound came from the Negro school teacher. And what did he say? What was his accusation there for a moment in time and space? He simply said, "Lawd, white folks, you done ruined my shirt."

"All aboard!" yelled the engineer. He climbed hastily into his cab, pulled the whistle cord a couple of times. The Negro school teacher turned, still holding his big white handkerchief, now dyeing itself all over crimson, against his face. . . .

Yes, that was a sort of anecdote. Years later when trying to speak a word for the Negro people, the scene haunted me and I sat down and wrote the story of a school teacher who tried desperately to help his people and failed. It wasn't a Confederate veteran's walking stick that laid my hero low. It was something

213

more up-to-date and final—a shotgun. The school teacher of that spring morning long ago still lives—now a very old man. A bad scar still shows on his face, running from his forehead down across his chin. And there must be a scar in his heart too. There is in mine, and always will be.

Eva Le Gallienne had yearned for some years to do the classics in a playhouse of her own; notions of a Gilbert & Sullivan cycle had never left the keen mind of Winthrop Ames. Both well knew the risks of repertory in America; both went relentlessly ahead, and more or less simultaneously. Miss Le Gallienne, high-strung daughter of the poet, Richard Le Gallienne, was born in London, educated in Paris, and made her somewhat terrified stage debut in London's West End in *Monna Vanna* in 1914. She played numerous roles in the New York theater, giving distinctive performances in *Liliom* and *The Swan*. But she continued planning to work for herself.

Finally, and doggedly, in the fall of 1926, she obtained the Fourteenth Street Theater, a playhouse with a leaky roof and an illustrious past. It was here that she would make her stand, presenting the works of Shakespeare, Ibsen, Chekhov, and Barrie at a popular-price scale—35 cents to $1.50—and doing these plays with her own permanent and carefully selected company. She was of the conviction then, and still is, that a great mass audience could be found for fine plays and that the location of the theater didn't matter and never had. She also decided that there'd be no such nonsense as playing downtown and living uptown so she set up housekeeping on the theater's top floor, and, with Otto Kahn and Mrs. Edward Bok (later Mrs. Efrem Zimbalist) among her backers—her principal backer has always insisted upon remaining anonymous—she began her long-planned experiment on a late October evening with Benavente's *Saturday Night*. It was a disastrous opening and the project seemed doomed on the very first night but Chekhov's *Three Sisters*, which followed, was impressively presented, and the Civic Repertory Theater was on its way.

Nearly forty plays, including representation for Schnitzler, Goldoni, and Hauptmann, were presented during Miss Le Gallienne's downtown regime. Her permanent company included such players as Alla Nazimova, Joseph Schildkraut, Jacob Ben-Ami, and Beatrice Terry, and they were guaranteed minimum seasons of twenty weeks. The audiences consisted largely of workers, students, and teachers—there was always a large foreign element in attendance at each play—and the Civic's devoted followers took relish in such offerings as *The Cherry Orchard, Romeo and Juliet, Camille, Peter Pan, Hedda Gabler,* and *Alice in Wonderland.* Miss Le Gallienne staged many of the productions and appeared in the majority of them. She played everything from Sister Joanna in *The Cradle Song* to Varya in *The Cherry Orchard,* and when she did Juliet she wrung from Brooks Atkinson, writing in the "Times," this tribute:

During the last two or three years the superstition has grown up that Miss Le Gallienne is a better director than actress . . . but her Juliet reveals her as an actress, not merely of intelligence, which she has always been, but of scope and resilience, which she has become this season.

Miss Le Gallienne operated her theater for five seasons, closed it for a sabbatical year, and then played for three more seasons. Did the experiment finish with a deficit? Yes, and definitely. A considerable deficit. But it was planned as a subsidized theater, and its founder could see no reason —and she still can't—why a classical repertory theater operating at popular prices and offering the finest plays to be had from the library shelves should not be subsidized along with opera, symphony orchestras, art museums, and such.

Even with the subsidy lacking, the Civic Repertory made a brave fight of it. During the final two seasons it was generally playing to 97 per cent of the capacity, and indefinite continuance might have been possible had the Actors' Equity Association yielded to Miss Le Gallienne's earnest pleas for permission for Sunday performances. She made the point, almost tearfully, that the fate of her entire experiment might well depend upon its decision. But Equity was adamant in its ruling. When the ban on Sunday performances was eventually lifted it was too late to do Eva Le Gallienne any good. She had gone out of business, and the 14th Street Theater had become, once more, the city's forgotten playhouse.

"We learned a great deal at the Civic," Miss Le Gallienne now asserts, "and I suppose we were ten years ahead of our time. I made a great many mistakes that I would not now repeat. We drew people who really loved the theater to those Fourteenth Street plays—and there are ever so many such people in New York today, and all over America. We had audiences such as those you might find waiting for hours to get into Carnegie Hall or into the Met, but we never had enough capacity at the Civic. And it's also true that many people stayed away because Fourteenth Street seemed as

215

far as Oshkosh. . . . *Peter Pan* and *Romeo and Juliet* went wonderfully, but *The Cherry Orchard* was probably our best."

Winthrop Ames, never quite satisfied with the way he had seen Gilbert & Sullivan done and still apparently unconvinced, notwithstanding his New Theater experience, that repertoire couldn't be sold to playgoing New York, summoned his casting director, Johnson Briscoe, one morning and said, "Why don't we do *Iolanthe?*"

"Sounds fine," said Briscoe.

"Do you think we can cast it?" Ames asked.

"We can certainly try," said Briscoe.

It was to be a production of freshness and novelty, and they went about the casting with this thought in mind.

When Ernest Lawford, the Frohman-trained dramatic actor, was invited to play the role of the Lord Chancellor he was mildly stunned. "But I can't sing!" he protested.

"Wonderful," said Ames. "Just talk your songs. Gilbert's lyrics are always better that way."

So Ames, the producer who introduced the pleasures of A. A. Milne to American playgoers via the comedy, *The Truth About Blayds*—that comedy of the patriarchal poet who confessed, upon reaching the age of ninety, that he was a complete fraud—gave New York the most distinguished production of *Iolanthe* it had seen in a quarter of a century. It was a production that set the critics to cheering, and it was Gilbert W. Gabriel, in a later review of *The Mikado*, who voted Ames the decoration of the Rising Sun.

Iolanthe took its place as an instantaneous hit in the crowded, highly competitive Broadway field. Here was Gilbert & Sullivan packing a New York theater with an English dramatic actor in a highly important role and with a cast that included redheaded Lois Bennett and an unforgettable sprite named Paula Langlen, young players nobody had ever heard of. Perhaps Ames should have stopped right there, but his staff couldn't restrain him. He went on to do—and to do beautifully—*The Pirates of Penzance* and *The Mikado*, and before Briscoe could say "Pooh-Bah" he had them playing in repertoire, along with *Iolanthe*. The every-night or every-other-night change of bill confused playgoers, just as it did during the New Theater's reign, during Miss Le Gallienne's gallant years in 14th Street, and just as it will do for as long as the drama persists

216

on the face of this earth. Winthrop Ames got his soul-satisfaction, and if he lost money on his cycle, the money was his own. There used to be producers who had never heard of backers.

It was to this same Ames, gentleman-showman, that Eleanor Robson and Harriet Ford went with their tidy thriller which was successfully produced under the title of *In the Next Room.* Miss Robson, who had never set foot upon the stage since she left it to become the bride of August Belmont in 1910, was visiting at Amy Lowell's in Brookline, Massachusetts, and in seeking a bedtime mystery novel she reached to the bookshelf saying, "I'll take the red one." What she got was "The Boule Cabinet," by Burton Stevenson. She read it with steadily increasing excitement and as soon as she returned to New York she talked to Harriet Ford about it. Was there a play in it? They agreed that there was, and they went to work. Miss Ford had had Broadway productions but it was Miss Robson's first playwriting try. When the script was finished they decided that their friend, Winthrop Ames, would be the producer; there was not an instant's thought of anybody else. Eleanor Robson read the play to him. He then said, with all the charm that he had brought from North Easton into the strange world of the theater, that he liked both the reading and the writing and that he would give his decision within twenty-four hours.

"It might be fun," he said. "I've never done anything like it. Might be fun and certainly very different."

Two days later he told his staff that he was producing *In the Next Room.*

The erudite, earthy Robert E. Sherwood—six feet six, and the tallest playwright in captivity—now comes forcefully into the American theater and into the pages of this chronicle. Once the editor of the "Harvard Lampoon," Sherwood was editing the old and lesser "Life" magazine when he sold *The Road to Rome*—which showed the great Carthaginian hero, Hannibal, being turned back at the very gates of Rome by a wise and beautiful woman—to Dwight Deere Wiman, of Moline (Illinois) plow millions, and William A. Brady, Jr., the truculent son of the famous showman. Jane Cowl accepted the play instantly; she had been seeking just such a role as that of the shrewd and delightful Amytis.

Wiman, in his dealings with Miss Cowl, was all tact and charm, but the younger Brady took her very casually. There came the night of the dress rehearsal in Washington. She was in her dressing room, two hours late but with countless reasons as to why she was delayed. Wiman was there with her, pleading with her to start the rehearsal, when Brady suddenly appeared at the door, hat cocked sidewise. He listened to his star for a minute and then he muttered, "Beautiful but dumb."

Miss Cowl turned upon him, banged her dressing room table with her fist, and cried, "I have never had any claims to beauty, but dumb I am not!" Four minutes later she was on the stage.

The Road to Rome became a New York hit and Sherwood gave up his job at "Life."

It was about this time that the discerning Arthur Hopkins did some rewriting on a crude script, the work of George Manker Watters, a new man, and then he engaged a young actress he had never seen upon any stage for the heroine's role in the play to be called *Burlesque*. He liked the sound of her voice; her name was Barbara Stanwyck. Hopkins also paid a handsome young actor named Clark Gable $75 weekly for playing a small but picturesque role in *Machinal*. He put the redheaded, gangling, and fascinating Katharine Hepburn into a school-life play, *These Days,* and listened with smiling satisfaction as she instantly caught and held the attention of an audience with the few lines she had to speak. A pale, gawky, and uncertain ingénue named Bette Davis was put into the leading role of Martin Flavin's comedy, *Broken Dishes,* and given the part, as Flavin asserted with vehemence, "Over my dead body." Mae West was jailed for ten days after her play, *Sex,* had been raided by the police. George M. Cohan gave members of his profession an acting lesson with his expert underplaying and his extraordinary sense of timing in his loosely written melodrama, *Gambling.* And Henry Miller closed out a distinguished career in a minor play, Lee Wilson Dodd's *Angel in the House,* in Baltimore. Miller caught cold at the Hotel Belvedere during the Baltimore engagement, and the cold developed into pneumonia. He was taken to New York and to the hospital. There, as he was dying, he beckoned to his son Gilbert to move closer. Then, in a barely audible whisper, Henry Miller spoke his last words. Just two words. They were these: "Poor Dodd."

New York's play-producing factory, which had been operating full-time throughout all these postwar years, delivered the incredible total of seventeen plays to Broadway's doorstep during Christmas week of 1927. On the evening of December 26, 1927—this was a historic night for the theater—

eleven plays opened. Yes, eleven! Ship news reporters, court reporters, City Hall reporters, and assistant music critics were drafted for service as dramatic critics.

The majority of the eleven plays were rubbish. Nine failed utterly. George Kelly's *Behold the Bridegroom*, in which he turned serious and told gropingly, and never convincingly, his story of a spoiled, willful, idiotic girl who had made a wreck of her life and who came too late upon the man who might have redeemed her, was given respectful attention and it had a moderate run. A fair-to-middling comedy of theater folk, *Excess Baggage*, written by Jack McGowan, survived for some months, but the others vanished quickly. Their titles must go into the record: *Bless You Sister*, by John Meehan and Robert Riskin; *Venus*, by Rachel Crothers; *Celebrity*, by Willard Keefe; *Paradise*, by William Hurlbut; *It Is to Laugh*, by Fannie Hurst; *L'Aiglon*, by Rostand; *Magnolia*, by Conrad Westervelt; *Restless Women*, by Sydney Stone, and *White Eagle*, a musical version of Edwin Royle's *The Squaw Man*, with music by Rudolf Friml.

On the following evening, with the smoke of battle cleared, the theater returned to normal and took on stature. Philip Barry's glib comedy of New York high life, *Paris Bound*, was brought in by Arthur Hopkins, and the immortal *Show Boat*, with its incomparable score written by Jerome Kern and its enduring lyrics contributed by Oscar Hammerstein II, had its historic *première*. Percy Hammond, the "Herald Tribune's" critic, decided that evening to cover *Paris Bound*, there being some sort of mystifying tradition in critical circles that always gave dramatic plays priority over musical pieces. Richard Watts, Jr., was assigned to review *Show Boat*, and it turned out to be one of the memorable evenings of his playgoing career. It was during the intermission that the Southern-born managing editor of the "Herald Tribune," one of several transients to hold the managing-editorship over a brief period, walked up to Watts and gave his own extraordinary review of *Show Boat* in exactly three words: "Too many niggers."

Some weeks before the New York opening of *Show Boat* Florenz Ziegfeld was standing at the rear of the New Amsterdam Theater with Dr. Jerome Wagner and he suggested that they take a stroll to the 44th Street Theater; there was a girl by the name of Norma Terris playing at the 44th in a revue with Phil Baker and Ted Healy. When they reached the theater, Ziegfeld asked Dr. Wagner to go up to the box office and buy the tickets;

219

he did not want Lee Shubert to know that he was entering a Shubert theater. Ziegfeld and the doctor went inside and remained for about an hour. In returning to the New Amsterdam Ziegfeld suddenly remarked that Norma Terris was to be his Magnolia in *Show Boat*.

"But," protested Dr. Wagner, "you already have a girl under contract."

"Can't help that," said Ziegfeld. "Miss Terris will play Magnolia." And Miss Terris played Magnolia. Later development: Miss Terris became the bride of Dr. Wagner.

The legend of infallibility that had now come to surround the theater's new wonder man, Jed Harris—he had put Helen Hayes into a serious role in the beautifully produced *Coquette*—was bolstered by the success of *The Royal Family*, which was written by Kaufman & Ferber, and he continued on his thundering way. Winthrop Ames contributed a tidy production of *The Merchant of Venice*, with George Arliss as a thoughtful, mocking, and somewhat patrician Shylock—Peggy Wood was an eye-filling Portia and the character of Launcelot Gobbo was actually funny in the playing of Romney Brent—and melodrama continued to assert itself. Willard Mack, a dramatist with whom the new theater had completely caught up, turned out a courtroom play called *A Free Soul*, and mention of it would be omitted here except for the fact that William A. Brady, its producer, turned back the years, put on make-up, and came forth as an actor once more. He took over the role of the attorney for the defense and, without ever bothering to memorize his lines, gave a vigorous, old-style performance, and sipped iced champagne in his dressing room before, during, and after every performance.

The cause of melodrama was also served with the return of *The Shanghai Gesture* for a brief engagement. Here was John Colton's gaudy tale of the fanatical and powerful Mother Goddam, once a Manchu princess, who was betrayed by her English lover, sold to the junkmen, and who waited twenty long years to get her revenge. But in getting it, she makes the bitter discovery that a wildly dissolute girl, a dope fiend, drunkard, and nymphomaniac who comes to her brothel, is the daughter she bore to the faithless Sir Guy Charteris. The only course left to her is to murder the wretched Poppy, whom she despises and also loves. A. H. Woods became fairly wild with excitement when he read the Colton manuscript and decided that the role of the vicious and hellish Mother Goddam was one

220

that only the Du Barry of the theater's yesterdays could play—and Mrs. Leslie Carter was engaged.

The play went into rehearsal under the direction of the canny Guthrie McClintic, four settings of extraordinarily elaborate design were built, and Woods took his star and his enormous production to Newark for a tryout. Mrs. Carter fumbled her way through the opening night performance—her farewell to the theater was completely disastrous. It had been apparent, throughout rehearsals, that she was having great difficulty remembering her lines, and at the close of the first performance the most celebrated player of the old Belasco regime was given her notice. Woods couldn't tell her; he was actually too soft-hearted. He sent Lowell Sherman backstage to give Mrs. Carter the news that the play would be closed after the Newark engagement. And Sherman, stammeringly and not too tactfully, let Mrs. Carter know that her manager considered her too old for the role. Mrs. Carter didn't speak as she turned from him. She went to the mirror and stared at herself for a full minute. Then quietly, and as if speaking a line from a well-rehearsed scene, and gazing steadily into the mirror, she murmured two words: "Too old."

Florence Reed was engaged for the role of Mother Goddam; the play reopened and became one of Woods's super-hits, regardless of the critical derision piled upon it. Miss Reed's recitation of the "I survived" speech, in which she told of pebbles being sewn into the soles of her feet and of the other tortures she had received at the hands of the junkmen, remains one of the most vivid tirades ever to be delivered in the history of melodrama.

Eugene O'Neill's gigantic nine-act drama, *Strange Interlude,* came along early in 1928; the entire world-theater was shaken by the impact of it. This psychological drama of the passions, the frustrations, the bitterness in the life of its principal character, Nina Leeds, was written by O'Neill in Bermuda and in Maine.

The Theater Guild had rejected his muddled recital of the adventures of Juan Ponce de León in search of the fountain of youth in *The Fountain* but it had accepted his *Marco Millions,* and Lawrence Langner went to Bermuda with a cold and a hunch—he thought there might be a new play to be had from O'Neill. He went by horse and buggy to O'Neill's house and found him working on *Strange Interlude,* with six acts completed.

When Langner departed he had the six acts under his arm and he read them in enthrallment that night as a thunderstorm howled at his window.

The next day—very early the next day—he telephoned O'Neill and told him that *Strange Interlude* was the greatest play he had ever read. Could he have it for the Theater Guild? Well, it seems that O'Neill had promised the play to an important actress (she later turned it down), but Langner clung to the six acts and excitedly presented them to his colleagues at the Guild. The Guild's board was difficult to convince on *Strange Interlude*. There was a great deal of discussion and much turmoil. Langner, fairly frantic, and feeling that he would not be able to express himself adequately at the meeting at which the final decision was to be made, wrote out an impassioned plea in behalf of the play, setting forth the view that O'Neill, now honored across the world, could no longer be ignored by the Theater Guild, and that it would bring distinction upon itself by producing *Strange Interlude*. The meeting was held. Langner, Theresa Helburn, and Maurice Wertheim voted for the play. The ayes won.

Strange Interlude, making use of the aside or soliloquy out of the old-time and time-honored theater and lengthening the playing time for a drama from two to four hours, was done in two sessions: the first half starting at 5:15 P.M. and the second at 8:30, with six performances a week. The rush upon the John Golden Theater, in a seemingly out-of-the-way location in 58th Street, began the instant seats were placed on sale, and within a week after *Strange Interlude* opened, and to Broadway's complete astonishment, it had become a rage, a craze, a sensation. There were some ecstatic reviews, but there was also some sharp dissent. Prior to the New York opening Alexander Woollcott attacked the play in an article in "Vanity Fair," with the result that he was not permitted by Herbert Bayard Swope of the "World" to cover the *première*. And even after the nine-act wonder had been awarded the Pulitzer Prize the scrupulous and fair-minded Brooks Atkinson commented thus in the "Times:"

The characters are automata; the plot is restricted in scope. Although the play is in nine acts Mr. O'Neill has no time in which to develop his characters in the round and to show us the subordinate qualities which have made them people of standing in the world. Their boring propensity to talk, exclusively about themselves, implies a personal importance they do not have.

Strange Interlude, the saga of the introspective Nina Leeds and her five men, played on to solid capacity, with dining places springing up impulsively all over the neighborhood. Opportunistic restaurateurs knew there was big money in "Interlude's" dinner-hour business and they somehow foresaw indefinite continuance for O'Neill's mightiest work. It played right on through New York's sizzling summer. A company was sent on tour, and the story was the same everywhere—sellouts in Detroit, Indianapolis, St. Louis, Denver, Seattle, San Francisco. The New York engagement lasted for the remarkable run of 414 performances, and the role of Nina Leeds, created by Lynn Fontanne—created so magnificently—was later played by Judith Anderson, Pauline Lord, and Gale Sondergaard. How those earnest, hard-schooled leading women of the stock company era in the American theater, actresses who grew up on the roles of Peg and Luana and Mary Turner and Camille, would have relished a go at the nine acts of Nina Leeds!

CHAPTER XIV

Close of a Decade

THE VITALITY of the New York theater—and the New York theater means the American theater until the entire procedure of play production on this continent undergoes revolutionary decentralization— was increased immeasurably by *Strange Interlude* and by Elmer Rice's large-scale, and relentlessly observant, *Street Scene*. And just at a time when the stage was being challenged, and threatened, by that new and all-devouring menace, the talking picture.

Rice, a dramatist who is more effective when he is being topical than when groping for deeper meanings, had given the theater a richly imaginative play in the curiously ignored *Adding Machine*, and had emerged unbowed from a gallant collaboration with Dorothy Parker—the critics liked their *Close Harmony* but nobody else did—when he turned to the writing of a grimly realistic treatment of New York tenement life. He finished *Street Scene* in a rush of excitement, confident that he had done the best work of his career, but it was coldly rejected by the leading managements —the Theater Guild, Belasco, Arthur Hopkins, Jed Harris, Sam Harris, and Winthrop Ames, who had never read the manuscript but whose playreader had presumptuously decided that it was not the kind of play Mr. Ames wanted to do.

And it is now that the battling old-timer, William A. Brady, at the age of sixty-six, again comes dramatically into this narrative. Brady hadn't been doing so well; the new upstarts in the business he loved so much, and to which he had given his life, were crowding him hard. He had begun to wonder if he were through, and members of his own family had hinted as much. He was no longer getting first-chance reading, or even third or fourth, on any of the new plays. And *Street Scene* was heartily unwanted

224

by nearly all of Broadway when the battered manuscript finally reached his desk at the Playhouse.

"If I had kneeled down and prayed to God," he said later, "I couldn't have found anything I needed more. I wasn't actually broke. But *Street Scene* gave me something to work with, something to take up my time."

There were difficulties to be overcome before *Street Scene* reached the stage. Brady stubbornly disregarded the objections of his family. He needed additional money to make the production and he went to Lee Shubert for it. Numerous actors declined roles in the play—it had been around the managerial offices for a year and was, by now, pretty familiar material—and the director, George Cukor, who had been engaged after a fairly desperate search, walked out after the third day. It was then that Elmer Rice took over. There was to be no pre-Broadway tour for *Street Scene*—only previews.

There were nineteen curtain calls at the close of the first preview performance, but an hour later Lee Shubert called Brady and said he had been told that the play didn't have a chance—a member of his organization had attended that first preview. Two nights later *Street Scene* opened to a wildly enthusiastic audience; the next day's reviews were all that any manager could want. But when the jubilant Elmer Rice called on Brady in the afternoon the producer was deep in dejection; he had been talking to the ticket brokers and they didn't want *Street Scene*. Never mind those notices, they didn't believe in the play. Well, *Street Scene* stayed for 600 times in New York; it trouped the country, it was a success in London, and it was awarded the Pulitzer Prize. It was later that Kelcey Allen, amiable critic of "Women's Wear" and one of the theater's first wits, made the observation that Elmer Rice had won the Pulitzer Prize on the north side of 48th Street with *Street Scene* and would lose it on the south side with *See Naples and Die*.

Playwrights, those who were established and those just beginning, were in the talk of the showshops. Two young dramatists, Laurence E. Johnson and Preston Sturges, had simultaneous jackpot success with *It's A Wise Child* and *Strictly Dishonorable*, respectively. Two of the older writers, Booth Tarkington and Winchell Smith, were saying good-by to the drama.

The distinguished Tarkington, graying and slightly stooped, came to New York from Kennebunkport via the *State of Maine Express* and agreed, with considerable reluctance, to stop over en route to Indianapolis for a look-in on rehearsals of the farce, *How's Your Health?*, which he and his old friend and collaborator, Harry Leon Wilson, had put together in odd moments. The New York that he saw during that brief visit was a phantasmagoric world that unnerved and bewildered him; the frenzy, the crowds, the headlong rush left him with a desire to do some hurrying on his own account to the train that would put him back in Indiana. He was taken to the theater in which his little play was rehearsing, but he showed scant interest in the goings on upon the stage. He confided that day that he had seen but few plays in ten years; he hadn't noticed the new long skirts; he had taken his last drink seventeen years before, and that one at ten o'clock in the morning. He was now dictating all of his stories and books and finding it easy. He would not return to New York for the opening of his play but he would read the notices out in Indianapolis. That is, unless he forgot.

And Winchell Smith? This Connecticut Yankee was bidding the theater farewell from his beautiful place at Farmington and he was saying it in these exact words: "I've quit. I'm through. I'll never write another play. Why? I'm on to myself. I'm too damned old-fashioned. The theater's gone on ahead of me. I'm still stage-struck and I always will be, but I'm out of date. I found that out when I put on Michael Arlen's play, *The Zoo*, in Washington. I thought it was grand; everybody else thought it was terrible, so we closed it, and I haven't touched a play since. . . . Funny, but I've had about thirty productions since *Brewster's Millions* but I've really written only one play. That play was *The Fortune Hunter* and I wrote it because I wanted to. The others, all the others, were written because somebody else wanted them written. They were jobs. This or that fellow had an idea and came to me with it. Or a manager asked me for a show, or something like that. . . . Yeah, I'm through, all right. You bet! How do I know it? I'll tell you. I went to see *Street Scene* and *Journey's End*—two big hits. Well, if those plays had been brought to me I would have said that they didn't have a chance in a million. So you can see that the old boy has lost his grip."

Playwrights Sturges and Johnson, neither of whom stayed in the theater more than briefly, were stormy young men as Broadway success came in upon them. The tall, dark, glowering, and extraordinarily capable Sturges wrote a play called *The Guinea Pig*, which was accepted by Oscar Serlin for production, but it was Sturges who raised the money to put it on. Three

226

days before the New York opening he got mad with Serlin and removed his name from the billing; when *The Guinea Pig* began its brief and unprofitable engagement at the tiny President Theater the house boards bore the billing, "Preston Sturges Presents——"

It was later that Sturges was urged by Georges Renavent, an actor and an old friend, to call upon Brock Pemberton in the hope of getting a job. Why, asked Sturges, with reasonable skepticism, should Pemberton give him a job? Well, argued Renavent, he'd written a play, hadn't he? *The Guinea Pig* was a play, wasn't it? Sturges said yes, he guessed it was a play. In that case, went on Renavent, there should be a job for him with Pemberton, for what a producer needed around him more than anything else was a playwright. So they started for the theater in which Pemberton had a play in rehearsal, and which was being staged by Antoinette Perry. It's here that Sturges takes up the report:

"We entered the dark auditorium of the theater and found Pemberton sitting dismally by himself in the third row, watching the jolly Miss Perry guiding a bicolored cast through the complexities of a jolly little play called *Goin' Home,* concerned with miscegenation, *heimweh,* and murder. 'This is Preston Sturges, the playwright,' said Georges. 'He has just returned from a brilliant success in the provinces and I wondered if there might be something for him with us here?'

" 'Something like *what?*' said Pemberton looking bitterly at the mop of black hair on the top of my head.

" 'Oh, something like . . . anything,' said Georges. 'Something like an assistant stage manager, maybe, or something like that.'

" 'I am certain that we don't need any more assistant stage managers,' said Pemberton, evading my eye, 'but I'll ask Tony.' With one slantwise sneer at my wrinkled suit, he wandered down to the footlights and said, 'Tony, do we need still one more assistant stage manager who is also, I am told, a great playwright?'

" 'My God,' said Miss Perry, overdoing it a good deal, 'I should say we do. Where in Heaven's name were you able to find one? That's *exactly* what we need. Hire him at once.'

"Pemberton then looked longingly at his shoes, and then balefully at me. Finally he turned slowly to Georges and contemplated him with the warmth of a rattlesnake gazing at a mongoose. 'I see,' he twanged through both nostrils, 'that you spoke to Tony first.' But he gave me the job."

It was about a year later that Sturges sent to Pemberton the manuscript of *Strictly Dishonorable*, an honest and charming comedy that he wrote in exactly ten days on his father's dining room table in Goethe Street, Chicago. Pemberton telegraphed his congratulations—a somewhat extravagant gesture on the part of a conservative showman who is a resolute advocate of use of the mail—and told Sturges that he had a perfect first act, two skimpy other acts, and that with some work it was a comedy that could become a valuable property. The independent-minded Sturges was pleased but not particularly overwhelmed by the response from New York —he had already written pages and pages on a new play that was to be called *Recapture*—and in due time he took a train for the East. It was after the first conference that Pemberton, still gazing at his shoes and still as laconic as he must have been when he was the youthful editor of the "Coffeyville (Kansas) Record," remarked to Antoinette Perry that perhaps the big boy with the mop of black hair was a great playwright after all.

Miss Perry wanted Muriel Kirkland for the role of Isabelle, the comedy's impressionable heroine, but Sturges, with quite a mind of his own, also had an actress of his own choosing. Pemberton and Perry also wanted some script changes. Sturges agreed to make them but not if the leading role went to Miss Kirkland. Pemberton then called the cast together and told the company that everybody would be given a week's pay and dismissed unless the author decided to be more cooperative. Sturges relented to some extent, Miss Kirkland went on rehearsing the role, but he didn't supply all the needed script material and he became enraged at the Jackson Heights opening when he realized that his producer and director had written some dialogue for him. A few evenings later, to Sturges's seeming disgust, *Strictly Dishonorable* opened in New York and was instantly accepted as a sensational hit.

The fiery Laurence E. Johnson ran into trouble with David Belasco during the Atlantic City tryout of the comedy, *It's A Wise Child*. A rehearsal was held after the comedy had opened on the Boardwalk, and Belasco made a contemptuous comment on Johnson's writing of a particular scene. Johnson resented the remark and made some sharp observations of his own to the effect that Belasco's ideas for the comedy were out of line and out of date. Belasco, enraged, then denounced his author, belittling him, and told him to get back to his hotel in a hurry and start rewriting the script changes as they should be written. Johnson went white. He glared at Belasco, trembling, and then started toward him. Several of the players swarmed around Johnson and their combined strength was needed to prevent him from annihilating his producer.

Belasco, Al Woods, and William A. Brady were then the showmen who believed in early-August openings. The legitimate theaters were not air-cooled in those days—air conditioning for the legitimate houses did not begin until the mid-thirties and was not installed in some houses until as late as 1941—but Belasco and Woods and Brady disregarded the heat as well as the calendar. They didn't even bother to pass around fans, as Ziegfeld frequently did. And *It's A Wise Child* was brought into New York on a scorching summertime evening, a night of such oppressive heat that the playgoers were put to using their programs as fans and their handkerchiefs as forehead and neck mops. Through it all Belasco smiled benignly. He took a chair in the wings and stayed in it throughout the three acts. He listened to the play with half-closed eyes, and when the final curtain fell, with the audience applauding, there was the usual well-rehearsed backstage bustle about getting Belasco to take his bow. The audience waited, not to be denied a glimpse of "the Master," and there was the usual delay in bringing him forth, so as to give the impression (without fooling anybody) that he was being literally dragged onto the stage. And when he began to speak—hesitantly, shyly, barely audibly—he gave the best performance of the evening, that of a fine old modest gentleman, over-come with gratitude and now enduring a great ordeal. He was so humble, so overwhelmed, so confused, so grateful. Then, pulling at his famous prop, his white silken forelock, he backed off the stage.

There was good writing, plus showmanship, in numerous plays of the late twenties. Galsworthy's *Escape,* in which he examined the will of man-kind to aid a fugitive from the law, was beautifully staged by Winthrop Ames and expertly played by that gracious actor, Leslie Howard. Bartlett Cormack, from out of a Chicago City Room, contributed a tough, driving melodrama of Chicago crime in *The Racket,* and John Wexley turned out a harrowing drama of a revolt in a prison death house and called it *The Last Mile.* Ben Hecht and Charles MacArthur wrote a rowdy, melodra-matic comedy, *The Front Page,* packed with good theater, which outran a gentler newspaper play, *Gentlemen of the Press,* 276 performances to 128.

229

Sophie Treadwell came along with an imaginative and significant play in *Machinal*. Rachel Crothers revealed that she had retained the success-touch with her deftly written and observant piece, *Let Us Be Gay*, which brought forth Francine Larrimore's best performance. An exciting play of the dire possibilities of atomic energy was written by Robert Nichols and Maurice Browne and entitled *Wings Over Europe;* it was admirably produced by the Theater Guild, with Alexander Kirkland contributing a stirring performance.

Sean O'Casey, born in Dublin in 1884, and a bricklayer in the years before he turned to literature, gave new distinction to the Irish drama with the writing of the rich and imaginative play of Irish slum life, *Juno and the Paycock,* and he later contributed *The Plough and the Stars*, which became a world-wide success. He was introduced to the playgoers of America in the mid-twenties with *Juno and the Paycock,* which was greeted by the critics with mingled acclaim and dissent.

There was delicacy and beauty in John Balderston's play of the supernatural, *Berkeley Square*. Philip Barry, a Yale man who took Professor Baker's playwriting course, came forward as a comedy-of-manners dramatist who combined a facility for glib and urbane dialogue with an excellent sense of play construction. He contributed sparkling talk to *Paris Bound* and to *Holiday,* first-rate comedies, but he was less successful in his elusive *In A Garden* and in his frequently delightful *White Wings*. Martin Flavin, businessman turned dramatist—there was a period in which he had three plays running simultaneously in New York—gave the theater a prison-life drama of considerable power in *The Criminal Code;* and an Englishman, R. C. Sherriff, stirred New York with *Journey's End,* a war play of dignity and restraint, a play of the gallantry of English gentlemen in the trenches before San Quentin. One of the most affecting scenes that the theater has produced in this century came when Lieutenant Osborne, a former schoolmaster, talked calmly of his rock garden to the frightened young Lieutenant Raleigh just before they set forth on a raid—and one from which Osborne never returned.

Helen Morgan, white-faced, thin-legged, and deep-voiced, sang from a piano as the decade of the twenties was ending, sang in a delightful and backward-glancing musical play, *Sweet Adeline,* that glorified the nineties and paid its tribute to the vanished era of the Hoffman House, the horse-car, and the hansom cab. William Gillette, at the age of seventy-four, thrilled a first audience in a revival of *Sherlock Holmes* and was accorded one of the ovations of the year as he stepped out upon the stage in his old role—tall, austere, impassive, soft-spoken, magnetic. Florenz Ziegfeld, still collecting tiny elephants, paraded them across his desk in his elaborate offices in the new, beautiful, gold-carpeted and Urban-decorated playhouse that had been built for him by William Randolph Hearst and Arthur Brisbane.

The ebullient and caustic Alexander Woollcott, who had now forsworn dramatic criticism, turned to playwriting with *The Channel Road*, done in collaboration with George S. Kaufman, and based on De Maupassant's "Boule de Suif." Charles Hopkins continued his tasteful and very special productions at his tiny theater in New York's 49th Street. Jed Harris brought forth a sensitively directed presentation of Chekhov's *Uncle Vanya*. Joe Cook, the comedian of the daffy inventions, found a hearty success in the musical play, *Rain or Shine*, into which he and his canny producers had packed everything worth while into a rousing and overlong first act. By the time the weak second act started it was eleven o'clock and the critics were racing for their typewriters. *Rain or Shine* got an enthusiastic reception.

By now the world of the theater had been jolted by the Wall Street crash, talking pictures had taken hold in the Broadway area, and the motion-picture companies, which had scrapped millions in silent-film equipment, were buying up the audible-screen rights to famous stage hits, and were raiding the ranks of the theater's actors, playwrights, and directors. The silent-picture industry had been in a fairly precarious state—its product was becoming steadily worse and its attendance was falling off, and there had been a deterioration and gradual disappearance of the hilarious slapstick comedies that were supplied by Charles Chaplin, Harold Lloyd, Ben Turpin, and Mack Sennett. And the legitimate stage was in a period of enormous prosperity—seventy-two playhouses available for stage productions and sixty to seventy plays running simultaneously—when the gala and significant world *première* of *The Jazz Singer*, introducing the Vitaphone, a synchronizing device, and starring Al Jolson, was given at the Warner Theater at a $5.50 top.

That started it. Jack L. Warner, with solemnity and astonishing foresight, then predicted the death of the silent films and the revolutionizing of the entire motion-picture business. Along came Fannie Brice in *My*

Man, Richard Barthelmess in *Weary River*, Al Jolson in *The Singing Fool*, and finally, in 1929, the Metro-Goldwyn-Mayer sensation, *The Broadway Melody*—all-talking, all-singing, all-dancing.

The talking pictures caused stampedes at the Broadway ticket windows; they swept America. They contributed to the disappearance of the scattered and floundering stock companies that had held on even though their era was past, and they brought about the transformation of many cross-country theaters, former stands of the legitimate, into gaudy motion-picture palaces. And the Broadway-to-Hollywood movement on the part of the actors became a gold-rush stampede. Most of the established stars of the silent screen looked upon the coming of the talkies with vast uneasiness; many of them went in immediately for voice culture. But to the stage actor, the new medium was merely the business of standing up and speaking his lines, something that he had mastered in his days of stage apprenticeship. The talking picture took him out of the $100-a-week category and put him in the $1,000 brackets; it took him across plain and hilltop and set him down in a paradise of stuccoed houses, lemon and orange groves, house-boys, swimming pools, week ends on the desert, polo ponies, tweeds and flannels, tennis and badminton. It gave him health and sunshine and gave him, in many cases, more money than he had ever believed there was in the world.

Winthrop Ames, who was finishing his brilliant career as a director-producer, saw, in the coming of the talkies, a threat to the theater's very existence. He went with several members of his staff to the first New York showing of *Bulldog Drummond* and when the picture was over he invited them back to his offices in the Little Theater for a drink. "Gentlemen," he said quietly, after a long silence, "I'm afraid that what we've seen tonight means the end. This is what they want. I'm afraid that the theater, as you and I know it, is doomed. It will become small and highly specialized. . . . Gentlemen"—he raised his glass—"to the theater."

And it was Al Woods, about the time that the $2 talkie was jamming the New York theaters, who gazed upon the photographs of former players that covered an entire wall of his Eltinge Theater office. There was an affectionately autographed picture of Ronald Colman, who had worked for him in *East of Suez* at $75 a week. There was Charlie Chaplin, who had been with him in *Chinatown Charlie*. There was Mary Pickford, for whom he had put on *The Fatal Wedding*, and there were the pleasant and smiling faces of Dustin Farnum, Douglas Fairbanks, and John Barrymore.

"Hell," he said wistfully, "I don't need any new actors. I just need the old ones, those suckers who used to work for me. What plays I could now do—what comedies, what melodrama. I wonder what it would now cost me to get Jack Barrymore back."

The Wall Street crash of 1929 struck the theater a severe blow; it brought on an immediate and sharp decline in play-production activity. The total of 225 productions in the Broadway area during the season of 1928–1929 was reduced by 100 by the time the drama year of 1934–1935 came around. The crash came near to throwing some of the theater's most prominent showmen into bankruptcy. Sam H. Harris lost a fortune; so did Florenz Ziegfeld and Max Gordon. Gilbert Miller and George S. Kaufman were among the heavy losers. Al Woods was reduced from the status of millionaire to virtual pauper, but not because of his own speculations. Woods had never owned stocks and bonds, and the uproar in the financial district, the hysteria that seized Wall Street in 1929, had left him undisturbed. He hadn't played the market; that was only for suckers. All of his money, his hard-earned money in the only game he knew, the theater, was in a safety deposit box, more than $800,000 of it, and all right there in crisp, negotiable currency. There came the afternoon when he decided to go to his box to take an account of his cash holdings. He called at the bank, opened the box—and found it empty. He stood in stunned silence for an instant; he well knew the truth. Wall Street had ruined him after all; it had claimed the $800,000 rushed downtown in a crisis by the holder of a duplicate key, a person to whom Woods was always willing to give his last quarter. Woods smiled, shrugged, went back to his office, put a match to an expensive cigar, put his feet upon his desk, and telephoned the home of his gentle brother, I. C. Herman, the handkerchief manufacturer. Herman's wife answered. "Hello, sweetheart," said Al. "I'm hungry. Looks like I'm going to be hungry for a long time. Why don't I come up to dinner tonight?"

The American theater soared during the 1920s, and it was a decade that belonged to the writers. The new playwrights had vital things to say and they said them with raciness, originality, and imagination. The theater

233

broke away from accepted and long-standing conventions. Plays of ideas, plays that were intellectually stimulating, came along and prospered. Playgoers were put to thinking—and began liking it—by the vitality to be found in the offerings that the commercial theater, given suddenly to a new boldness, paraded before them. During the decade the bedroom farce disappeared, the mystery play lost ground, the courtroom drama held on stubbornly, the big revues and musical comedies multiplied and many of them succeeded.

The twenties, which brought in a swarm of perceptive native dramatists—O'Neill and Sherwood and Anderson, Howard and Kelly and Rice, Kaufman and Connelly and Barry, Behrman and Du Bose Heyward and Paul Green—gave the theater new experimentation, new realism and new power. Expressionism, influenced by theories put into practice on the Continent, reached the Broadway stage. The Italian dramatist, Luigi Pirandello, was discovered via *Six Characters in Search of an Author*. There was a hearty and heartening response to the works of Shakespeare, Shaw, and Ibsen, and to the writings of Chekhov, Gorki, and Werfel. The sudden uprising in the ranks of the playwrights, the outburst of a new and vigorous school of American dramatists, had the effect of sharpening and improving the taste of the playgoing public and in creating a new appreciation for stage forms that were revolutionary and unhackneyed. *The Show-Off* packed a playhouse, but so did the *He Who Gets Slapped* of Andreyev, and the *R.U.R.* of Karel Čapek. A negligible comedy, *It's A Wise Child*, a triumph of production over script, ran for a year in New York but so did a play of such substance as *Strange Interlude*, accepted by the mass as an intellectual treat and a challenge. The fact that thousands of playgoers flocked to *Strange Interlude* in a spirit of sheer defiance, determined to prove to themselves that O'Neill's brooding introspection was by no means beyond them, contributed greatly to the play's extraordinary financial success.

The Theater Guild came through the twenties as a sound, courageous organization, as an art theater not unwilling to compromise upon occasion with commercialism. It was by no means immune to failure but it had numerous triumphs, and it gave the drama valiant service in bringing forth *Porgy*, the Du Bose–Dorothy Heyward folk play of Negro life in Charleston, excitingly staged by Mamoulian; Bernard Shaw's *St. Joan*, O'Neill's *Strange Interlude*, Sidney Howard's *They Knew What They Wanted* and

234

The Silver Cord, and Molnar's *The Guardsman.* Winthrop Ames and Arthur Hopkins and Gilbert Miller held their places as showmen of taste and discernment; so did Guthrie McClintic and Brock Pemberton; and the talented Jed Harris jolted the Broadway world. Imaginative and intelligent stage direction came from this same Harris, and from Hopkins, Ames, McClintic, George S. Kaufman, George Kelly, Antoinette Perry, Winchell Smith, and Philip Moeller and Rouben Mamoulian, born in Tiflis. Scenic designers of the period were functioning brilliantly, with Robert Edmond Jones, Lee Simonson, and Norman Bel Geddes among the leaders.

The decade brought numerous players to the verge of greatness—John Barrymore, Jeanne Eagels, Helen Hayes, Emily Stevens, Holbrook Blinn, Katharine Cornell, Alfred Lunt, Lynn Fontanne, Dudley Digges, Clare Eames, Alice Brady. Helen Westley asserted herself as the finest character actress in the land. Such players as Margalo Gillmore, Morris Carnovsky, Earle Larimore, and Henry Travers contributed notably to the ensemble effectiveness of the Theater Guild's acting company. Walter Huston won the theater's respect as a natural actor, with a true feeling for characterization. The erratic Richard Bennett, talking back to his audiences whenever he was in the mood, had the fire of a Booth in a performance of one evening and nothing at all the next. Louis Wolheim contributed an unforgettable performance as the filthy, war-weary, undisciplined, heroic Captain Flagg in *What Price Glory.* Jules Bledsoe thrilled multitudes with his "Ol' Man River" in *Show Boat.*

The twenties brought forth John Van Druten as a young playwright of enormous promise; Dwight Deere Wiman as a young producer with ideas and taste; Paul Green as a regional poet-dramatist with a natural and abundant talent for storytelling; and Walter Hampden and Eva Le Gallienne as two of the theater's patient workers who were continually striving to bring the classics to playgoers in the mass. John Galsworthy, an intellectual dramatist, won further distinction with his fine sociological play, *Loyalties,* with its revelation of anti-Semitism in upper-class British circles following a theft at a fashionable house party. Lula Vollmer put believable characters into her *Sun-Up* and Bayard Veiller proved, with *The Trial of Mary Dugan,* that playwrights can come back. And a New York columnist named Russel (Buck) Crouse made his not too overwhelming stage debut in the role of Bellflower in the newspaper play, *Gentlemen of the Press.* The real Bellflower, a hard-working and tireless reporter in the newsy city of At-

235

lanta, had some misgivings about *Gentlemen of the Press* when told that a character had been named for him. He didn't object to that, but he had been covering police for a long time and he had also taken up the practice of law, and he knew about libel. He didn't want to be libeled. He wasn't.

The twenties revealed a certain squeamishness and sensitivity on the part of those safeguarding New York's morals. Censorious officials undoubtedly rendered a service in shutting down such scurvy theatrical fare as *The Good Bad Woman, Pleasure Man,* and *Sex,* but *The Captive*—a well-written and powerful play, skillfully adapted by Arthur Hornblow, Jr., from the French of Edouard Bourdet—should have been permitted to go its way unmolested.

New York City remained in serene and supreme command as the nation's theatrical capital as the twenties vanished. The drama-hungry hordes of midland America were in the habit of coming to Broadway to see the new plays without waiting for a restricted road theater to bring the plays beyond the Alleghenies. It was still possible, however, in a land newly under the spell of the talking picture, to see, in widely separated communities, resident stock company productions of such indestructible plays as *The Old Homestead, Way Down East, The Two Orphans,* and *Charley's Aunt.*

The summer-theater industry, which was soon to turn unoffending barns and haylofts of the Eastern countryside into cramped hot-weather playhouses, was just now in its nervous, formative stage. Little Theaters, in no way associated with the professional summer theaters, were in operation throughout the country but without ever becoming a factor in the development of players, directors, or playwrights. The late and brilliant John Anderson, an extraordinarily sharp and outspoken commentator on the state of the drama, complained thus, and bitterly, in his book "The American Theatre": *

There would be no reproach if the larger theater had not, during those years of Little Theater smugness, done very nicely by regional plays which the Little Theaters should have originated. *Porgy* came out of the South and found production with Theater Guild. Percy MacKaye's *This Fine Pretty World,* a drama about the Kentucky mountaineers, whose complicated dialect left a good part of it unintelligible, was done at the world's farthest remove from Kentucky, to wit, the Neighborhood Playhouse in

* Dial Press, Inc., New York, 1938.

Grand Street. Lula Vollmer's *Sun-Up*, *The Shame Woman*, and *The Dunce Boy* had similar metropolitan outlet, as did Virgil Geddes's *The Earth Between*, Lynn Riggs's regional dramas, and Paul Green's *In Abraham's Bosom*.

So ends a ten-year period, dominated by Eugene O'Neill as a dramatist and the Theater Guild as a producing organization, in which the American theater was stanchless and tumultuous—crowded with experimentation and new significance, and overflowing with talent. A decade to be remembered—and to be cherished.

CHAPTER XV

Some New Playwrights

WHEN the fourth decade of an incredible century came along, accompanied by the nightmare that was known as the Depression, the most exciting play in America—and also the most poignant, the most important, and one of the most successful—was *The Green Pastures*, written by the touchy, petulant, moodish Marc Connelly, of McKeesport, Pennsylvania. Here was a practical man of the theater who found exalted material in Roark Bradford's stories, "Ol' Man Adam and His Chillun," material for which he had enormous respect. He peopled his play with such characters as De Lawd and the Angel Gabriel and Noah and the King of Babylon and Ol' King Pharaoh, and also brought in such lesser beings as the Stout Angel and the Thin Angel and the Custard Maker and the children of the Heavenly Fish Fry. When he completed his manuscript Connelly began giving immediate thought to a production, and to the theater's producers. He expected no difficulty at all in getting an immediate contract, and he wanted his play brought forth under distinguished auspices. But when he began trying to sell *The Green Pastures* his troubles began.

Arthur Hopkins was enthusiastic but he told Connelly, after reading it twice, that he had not been able to decide upon a method of staging it, so he turned it down. Jed Harris liked the play enormously but he insisted that every decision he would make would have to be final, and Connelly, feeling it would be impossible for him to go along under such conditions, took the script with him when he left Harris's office. Theresa Helburn and Lawrence Langner voted for the production of the play by the Theater Guild, but Philip Moeller and Helen Westley found it cheap and sacrilegious. Crosby Gaige said that he had laughed all the way through his reading, but . . .

So it went.

Connelly, with "the curious feeling that someone would come along sooner or later," tried to forget about it for a while—and then came a call from the office of Rowland Stebbins, a Wall Street man, who had decided to have a fling at the theater. Charles G. Stewart, a showman of long experience, was being paid a salary by Stebbins and was trying to find a play for him. He telephoned George S. Kaufman and asked if he knew of any available plays. Yes, Kaufman did know of a play. He had just read one called *The Green Pastures* and he was of the opinion that it would be either a sensation or a tremendous flop. Stewart went quickly to Connelly and Connelly read the first act for him. That was enough. Stewart immediately took the manuscript to Stebbins, and when Stebbins finished it he asked one question: "Can we get away with it?" They were told that they could by Bishop Herbert Shipman, the Suffragan Bishop of the Episcopal Diocese of New York. He also observed that the play would serve as one of the greatest sermons man could ever preach.

Casting began. It was done in a Negro actors' agency in Harlem, and most of the players were selected from the thousand-odd applicants seen in a week.

"But we were still waiting," Connelly told me later, "after all of those trying, day-long sessions, for someone who could play God. Then one afternoon in walked Richard B. Harrison, right out of the blue."

Harrison, then sixty-five, an itinerant lecturer and erstwhile Pullman porter, wanted to play De Lawd but he had certain misgivings. He didn't agree to do the part until he, too, had gone to Bishop Shipman and had received the Bishop's hearty approval.

So *The Green Pastures,* at a cost of $85,000 of Rowland Stebbins's money —a production expenditure that included the installation of a treadmill— opened at the Mansfield Theater on the evening of February 26, 1930. It was received by the critics as a play of magnificence and greatness. Richard B. Harrison—he was engaged at a salary of $250 weekly and he was eventually paid $650 weekly—became one of the heroes of his race, and he played the role at the Mansfield for eighty weeks and for four seasons on tour. De Lawd came to be to him what Monte Cristo had been to James O'Neill, what Joshua Whitcomb in *The Old Homestead* had been to Denman Thompson, what Lightnin' Bill Jones was to Frank Bacon. He played De Lawd, with tenderness and compassion and fierce dignity, in the East and in the Midwest, in the Far West and in the South, and he only ceased

239

his touring when ill health stopped him. And when he died the play died with him.

An oddity in connection with the New York engagement of *The Green Pastures*, an engagement that grossed two million dollars, was the review given the play by that theater-wise weekly, "Variety." It was "Variety's" decision that Marc Connelly's play would have only a limited appeal, Joe Bigelow (Bige)—usually an expert in such matters—telling the publication's readers that "a ten-week stay at the Mansfield should be sufficient." It was the management's somewhat sadistic pleasure, for many weeks following the opening, to mail to the "Variety" office the weekly box-office statement.

The Green Pastures, Vicki Baum's *Grand Hotel*, Rudolf Besier's *The Barretts of Wimpole Street*, Robert E. Sherwood's *Reunion in Vienna*, the George S. Kaufman–Morrie Ryskind *Of Thee I Sing*, Maxwell Anderson's *Both Your Houses*, and Eugene O'Neill's towering *Mourning Becomes Electra*—these were the theater's outstanding plays of the early thirties.

Grand Hotel, adapted by William A. Drake, told its story of love and bitterness and tragedy within the walls of a huge, strident, and luxurious hotel, a fascinating and panoramic play, produced with great finesse by Herman Shumlin, a sharp, observant, Colorado-born showman, and Harry Moses. Katharine Cornell, done with her Far East killings in *The Letter*, done with the playing of wenches in green hats, turned happily, and as her own manager, to the sentiment and the crinolines of *The Barretts of Wimpole Street*, a gentle and affecting play of the romance of Elizabeth Barrett and her ardent Robert Browning.

Robert E. Sherwood's *Reunion in Vienna* was a delightful, swaggering romp, bold, lusty, impudent, and tremendously entertaining, with Sherwood writing for Alfred Lunt the role of the Grand Duke Rudolph Maximilian von Hapsburg, who has been driving a taxi in Nice, and for Lynn Fontanne that of Elena, his sweetheart of other years, married for a decade to a psychoanalyst. Sherwood did the play after he had gone to Sacher's Hotel in Vienna in 1929 and had been told of the parties still being given for its formerly wealthy but then down-and-out aristocratic patrons. Obviously, he decided at the time, the notion for a good play. And so it turned out to be.

Of Thee I Sing, the first musical play to win the Pulitzer Prize, found the

240

Gershwins, George and Ira, and George S. Kaufman and Morrie Ryskind working in collaboration. They devised a song-and-dance masterpiece, which offered some of the liveliest of the Gershwin music and a wonderfully nonsensical plot, all about the election of that jaunty fellow, John P. Wintergreen, to the Presidency of the United States on the love platform.

Maxwell Anderson's *Both Your Houses* was a sharply satirical piece, commenting on politics and politicians and the Washington scene. In contrast, O'Neill's *Mourning Becomes Electra,* was an inexorable and withering play of love, hatred, murder, and remorse. Thus mighty drama combined three plays, *Homecoming, The Hunted,* and *The Haunted*—presenting the murder of General Mannon, back from the Civil War, by his wife Christine, and her lover, Brant; the vengeance of the daughter Lavinia, and the son Orin, who track down and kill Brant; the eventual suicide of Orin and, finally, Lavinia's withdrawal into the gloom of the Mannon mansion. It was played with unerring skill and insight by Alice Brady, Alla Nazimova, and Earle Larimore. O'Neill achieved, with this trilogy, the finest work that he had done for the theater. *Mourning Becomes Electra* was written in an isolated French château near the river Loire, far from the world's distractions.

O'Neill talked with me of it, and of his other plays, as I sat with him at the Château Plessis before a great open fire in the spring of 1930.

". . . This new play is the hardest thing I've ever tried. God knows it's the most ambitious. I've done the first draft. I'll do a second and then lay it aside for a while. Later I'll call a stenographer from Paris and mail it to the Theater Guild. . . . The play of mine for which I have the greatest affection is *The Great God Brown.* Next, *The Hairy Ape.* And then, I suppose, *Strange Interlude.* My favorite short play is *The Moon of the Caribbees,* and I think the best writing I ever did for the theater was in *Lazarus Laughed.* . . . Looking back to *Dynamo,* I did eighteen long plays in eleven years. That's too much. If I could go back I'd destroy some of those plays—say, four of them—*Gold* and *The First Man* and *The Fountain* and *Welded.* In my notebook I have ideas for thirty more plays—perhaps thirty-two. That's work for a lifetime, isn't it?"

The depression was tough on the theater, but the drama fought its way through. It went its way to darkened houses and to a falling off in attendance, to curtailed play production, to a slackening in industry from some of

241

its playwrights, and to the old familiar lamentations about the theater's dire state.

The Broadway season of from 250 to 275 plays was gone, perhaps never to return. Some of New York's most desirable legitimate houses were in the clutches of the rapacious talking pictures, but there were still more than fifty theaters available for stage plays, which were no longer coming in with the bewildering profusion of the twenties. The Shuberts and the Erlanger forces were at peace and were working together on road bookings, and with many important road playhouses gone over to the talkies, or replaced by parking lots or gaudy bowling alleys, the theater began turning to civic auditoriums for its touring plays.

There came the evening when the Zoe Akins play, *The Old Maid,* starring Judith Anderson and Helen Menken, reached the city of Little Rock. A shrill and bustling woman who seemed to be in charge of things was making the rules, and the two visiting stars, who later regretted that they ever came near the state of Arkansas, were more than mildly jolted to receive, upon their arrival at the auditorium, typed-out slips of instruction as to how to go about giving the evening's performance. I saw these slips, and the wording, as I recall it, was to this effect: "The auditorium is large. The acoustics are not good. The audience cannot enjoy the play unless they hear it. So will you please keep all this in mind and, in saying your lines, step well downstage to the footlights and speak VERY DISTINCTLY."

Famous figures in the ranks of the play producers were now passing. David Belasco was dead, the victim of a heart attack. He was murmuring about his new-season plans until a few minutes before the end. Lincoln A. Wagenhals and Henry W. Savage had passed on. Florenz Ziegfeld, in ill health, was through as a showman and he knew it. George C. Tyler was now bitter and penniless. Charles Dillingham, who had made and lost fortunes, was still jaunty in his dress and gracious in his poverty. A. H. Woods, broke but cheerful, was still script-hunting, but he knew in his heart that his day was done. Winthrop Ames, who saw the new order coming, announced his retirement with calm dignity and was living at his Massachusetts birthplace. I shall never forget my last meeting with Tyler, a few years before he died. He popped up from behind his battered, rolltop desk in the New Amsterdam Theater building, an aging, emaciated,

242

They Wrote the Scores of Musical Hits

1. Richard Rodgers 2. Emmerich Kalman 3. Jerome Kern 4. Victor Herbert 5. Rudolf Friml 6. Harry Tierney 7. George Gershwin 8. Irving Berlin

Street Scene, Hit of 1929

A moment from Elmer Rice's grim and realistic study of tenement life in New York, which won the Pulitzer Prize for the season of 1928–1929 (White Studio).

and self-pitying figure. "You've come to see me?" he said, incredulously. "Why in the world would anybody want to come to see me?" He moved from his desk to the 42d Street window. "Just come and look down there —look at that awful street. It was once so wonderful. Now it's cheap and tawdry and half dead, like I am. What has happened to the theater that I knew and loved? What has happened to all the world?"

George M. Cohan, tired, confused, and steadily losing interest, was going along as an actor, but he was only halfhearted in his playwriting and producing efforts. William Harris, Jr., was producing so infrequently he was practically on the retired list. The theater of New York now belonged to the Theater Guild and to Theresa Helburn and Lawrence Langner, to Gilbert Miller and George Abbott and Jed Harris and the Group Theater, to Herman Shumlin and Harry Moses and Dwight Deere Wiman, to Richard Aldrich and Alfred de Liagre, Jr., and to Brock Pemberton and to the few of the old school who were holding on stubbornly—Sam H. Harris, John Golden, Arthur Hopkins, Arch Selwyn, William A. Brady, and the Shuberts.

When I say "Shuberts" I'm referring to the tireless Lee Shubert, terse, brisk, and frequently affable, who now paid his respects, and his blazing disrespects, to the theater of the early thirties in these words:

"The Shuberts have thirty-five theaters in New York; we have to keep producing for these theaters. We can't stop; we've got to go on always. We have 1,700 actors working for us this season and next season we'll have that many more. A man who produces hits must also have failures. I expect 10 per cent of my productions to be successful, 20 per cent to be moderately successful, and the rest unsuccessful. That's the average from season to season. The taste of the theatergoing public is now changing everywhere. Now there's a demand for class; the sensational type of play doesn't go any more. My friend Woods is finding that out, and his judgment on the chances of a play has been wonderful through all these years. . . . The critics? The New York critics are tired men. They're well intentioned and, for the most part, intelligent, but they're damn weary. They see too many plays. . . . Everything's greatly changed since my brother Sam started us off in New York. Now, take the Theater Guild. The Guild started to do good things in the theater, big things, and not just make money. Well, when they got a couple of hits they became money-mad and now they're more commercial-minded than any management I know of. The Guild gets its actors cheaper than the rest of us do. They sell the actors the idea that it's an uncommercial organization. I can only repeat that the Guild is money-mad and it ought to admit it."

There were odd, unexpected, stimulating goings on and developments in the world of New York's changing theater. . . . A tall, dark, suave ex-office boy named Moss Hart, one of the brightest young men to strike Broadway in years, came along as co-author (with George S. Kaufman) of *Once in a Lifetime,* the satire of Hollywood in the grip of the talkies. A stocky, broad-faced ex-stenographer named Ethel Merman shouted her way into theatrical fame via the musical comedy, *Girl Crazy.* A chunky, undersized master clown named Dave Chasen, participating in Joe Cook's crackbrained *Fine and Dandy,* drew a taut hand slowly across his face to the accompaniment of an imbecilic grin—a gesture that was adopted by the town.

The testy, well-fed Alexander Woollcott took a whirl as an actor (with Francine Larrimore in *Brief Moment*) and got away with it. The dapper, five-foot Billy Rose, one-time shorthand speed king, emerged as the husband of Fanny Brice and as the sponsor of such items as *Sweet and Low* and *Crazy Quilt.* The hulking, tousled, brainy Heywood Broun turned up in his own revue, *Shoot the Works.* The droll, unctuous Nikita Balieff returned to the Broadway stage with the *Chauve-Souris,* and with the same complete surprise and astonishment in his eyes as he received the ovation that he expected. The wealthy, stage-sure Winchell Smith bade his official farewell to the theater with his staging of Paul Osborn's comedy, *The Vinegar Tree,* which gave Mary Boland one of her best parts.

The delightful Margaret Sullavan charmed playgoers in her debut in a trifling comedy, *A Modern Virgin.* Katharine Hepburn, lithe and swift and appealing, gave an impressive performance in *The Warrior's Husband.* An actor named Rex Weber thrilled a first audience with his singing of "Brother, Can You Spare a Dime?" from the revue, *Americana.* A new playwright, James Hagan, turned in an affecting and lovable play in *One Sunday Afternoon,* which was all about our yesterdays. An impish and impudent and devastating Noel Coward came along with one of his slickest jobs in *Design for Living,* played for all its worth—and a great deal more— by himself and the Lunts. The writing team of Ben Hecht and Gene Fowler failed with a travesty called *The Great Magoo,* put on by Billy Rose. Row-

244

land Stebbins, using only his own money, spent eighty thousand dollars of it on a weird and flimsy play, *Red Planet*, about two scientists trying to communicate with Mars.

There were other developments of the immediate period that must not go unmentioned. . . . Two fine revues—*The Band Wagon*, the work of George S. Kaufman, Howard Dietz, and Arthur Schwartz, and *As Thousands Cheer*, written by Irving Berlin and Moss Hart—brought new prestige to the song-and-dance stage, just as *Luana*, the musical version of the famous *Bird of Paradise* (the tragic Luana, of course, who leaped into a volcano's crater) threw it back a few years. Alfred Lunt and Lynn Fontanne contributed showy and extraordinarily effective performances to Maxwell Anderson's play of two noble exhibitionists, *Elizabeth the Queen*. Women dramatists pursued their labors to good effect—Susan Glaspell with *Alison's House*, Rachel Crothers with *As Husbands Go*, Zoe Akins with the utterly trashy but popular *The Greeks Had A Word For It*.

Lynn Riggs, the poet-dramatist out of Oklahoma, contributed the pleasant and uneventful folk play, *Green Grow the Lilacs*, which became the basis of the sensational *Oklahoma!* George Kelly, whose best plays were definitely behind him, gave the theater a mild and quite second-rate comedy, *Philip Goes Forth*. Al Woods, now groping in a theater world he no longer understood, brought forth a bottom-of-the-barrel piece called *The Stork Is Dead*. George M. Cohan, deciding that novelty was demanded, contributed a strange bit of vaudeville that was frequently fascinating and played for two hours, without an intermission, under the title of *Pigeons and People*.

A vigorous new playwriting talent was revealed in *Little Ol' Boy*, the work of Albert Bein, and superbly played by Burgess Meredith. S. N. Behrman, a press agent turned dramatist, revealed more of his talent for the writing of the American comedy of manners in his urbane *Biography*, captivatingly played by Ina Claire. The Theater Guild brought forth a beautifully written Irish drama, *The Moon in the Yellow River*, by Denis Johnston. Elmer Rice came through with *Counselor-at-Law*, a tumultuous play of the life of a lawyer, his best work since *Street Scene*. Norman Bel Geddes produced an exciting, fast-moving *Hamlet*, compressed into three acts, with Raymond Massey giving a fine performance as a gaunt, lank, febrile Prince. The summer-theater craze swept the East—a fad, a mania that was to go on for years, and with crude, and seemingly collapsible, hot-weather playhouses springing up over the countryside from the highlands of south-western Virginia to the coastline of Maine.

The League of New York Theaters came into being, with one of its objectives the control and the suppression of theater ticket speculation. The purpose was a noble one; racketeering in tickets has long been one of the theater's evils. But how can it ever be eliminated as long as a visitor from the midlands—a wealthy and high-pressure individual, say, from Des Moines or St. Paul or Denver—gets off a plane or train at six o'clock and wants to see the best show on Broadway at eight-thirty? Wants to see it and is willing to pay $20 per seat. Or more.

The early 1930s saw the passing of vaudeville, of vaudeville as New York had known it since the turn of the century. In July of 1932 the Palace Theater, the citadel of the two-a-day, which had had nineteen glorious years and whose stage had claimed the services of Bernhardt, Ethel Barrymore, and Mme. Calvé, gave up, and vaudeville throughout the nation seemed to die right along with it. The famous Palace, bowing to the change of the times, introduced a change in policy, adding films to its variety entertainment, and the city's thousands of vaudeville lovers knew that the end had come. In 1935 motion pictures took over exclusively at the Palace, and by that time those performers who had not gone to Hollywood, or given up, were getting employment in variety acts offered in connection with the film bills at the motion-picture palaces and were always trying, sometimes with scant success, to hold back their tears.

There was news, as of the early thirties, of two of the theater's great ladies—Maude Adams and Maxine Elliott, both of whom had been long absent from the stage. Miss Elliott returned from her home in the South of France for an American visit, and with the assertion that she had never actually cared about the theater—"I just happened to be in it." And Miss Adams, resuming her career after thirteen years of inactivity, was taking to the road, taking to it for a long and arduous tour through many states, in *The Merchant of Venice,* with Otis Skinner as her Shylock.

I went to Cleveland for the opening in October of 1931; the play had been booked into the spacious Ohio Theater. The first audience was an odd mingling of young, middle-aged, and aging. Those who had given out their hearts to her when she had delighted them as Lady Babbie, who treasured their memories of her as Peter Pan and Maggie Wylie and Phoebe

246

of the Ringlets, were certainly responsible for the murmur, a most audible murmur, that swept the house as she came upon the stage as Portia, the heiress of Belmont, played in other years by Ellen Terry and Ada Rehan and Julia Marlowe.

Portia is a woman of beauty and intellect, given to gentle mockery, but also a creature of emotion and warmth and definite character strength. Portia has often been made too formidable and mature because she has seldom been played by young actresses, and now Miss Adams, at fifty-eight, was trying the role, trying it as she wore a peach taffeta gown with a robe of peach and silver and a golden chain over her hair and caught beneath her chin. The Peter Pan of a quarter of a century before was only partially successful in projecting Portia's many and quickly varying moods —she was actually no more suited to the part than she would have been to that of Desdemona—but as she spoke the verse she brought back some of the magic of a bygone day. There was that same peculiar lilt in her voice, the same quaint toss of her head, the same clasping of her hands, the same incommunicable something that had made her the most beloved of all actresses for a generation. Miss Adams played out her Cleveland engagement—she was as elusive and as mysterious and as inaccessible there as she was everywhere else—and then she went on with her tour. Cities large and small. One-night stands and sleeper jumps.

She played in the East, she went into the deep South and on to the Far West. Richmond, Virginia, paid $7,697 to see her for a single performance, but the intake in Alexandria, Louisiana, was only $1,231 because there was a flood in the Red River and a run on two banks. She played in her native Salt Lake City and in Denver and in San Francisco; and in Missoula, Montana, there was a twelve-hour delay because there was no train to take the company out. Miss Adams and her players returned to the East and she came as near to Broadway as Newark, but she decided, and perhaps wisely, against bringing her play to New York. When her tour was done Miss Adams took an accounting: she had played twenty-three weeks at a salary of $1,500 a week and half the profits. The profits for the tour came to exactly $2,533. "I made less than Mr. Skinner did," Miss Adams said with a smile and a shrug. And then she went back into retirement.

The dramatists who had emerged so vigorously in the theater of the twenties continued their labors, and newcomers to their ranks now included Lillian Hellman, Clifford Odets, Rose Franken, Lynn Riggs, Sidney Kingsley, Robert Ardrey, and Irwin Shaw. Hellman and Odets were the outstanding playwrights brought forth in the new decade. Miss Hellman, blond, sententious, New Orleans–born, a writer with a capacity for sharp characterization and powerful situations, attended three universities, receiving her M.A. at Tufts. She served in New York as a publisher's manuscript reader, as a playreader, and as a theatrical press agent, before writing her first play in collaboration with Louis Kronenberger, critic and essayist, who brought along a lively sense of the theater and a literary background that was frightening in scope (certainly to his colleagues) when he began functioning in the field of dramatic criticism. That first play, *The Dear Queen,* caused something less than a stir in the managerial offices and has remained unproduced. Miss Hellman went on with the writing of a second, the study of a maladjusted, neurotic child and the effect of her viciousness upon the lives of many others. She finished the play in Florida, returned to New York, took it to the typist, and when she collected her bundle of tidy scripts she went instantly to the office of Herman Shumlin in the Selwyn Theater building. She gave Shumlin a copy, took another for herself, and they began reading.

"Each act of the play," Shumlin said later, "left me increasingly excited and impressed, and as soon as I finished I congratulated Lillian and told her that I wanted to produce it very much. We made a deal right there and we signed the contract the next day."

The powerful *Children's Hour,* installed in the beautiful playhouse that bore the name of Maxine Elliott, won the critics' cheers as a fine, sound, adult drama, and Miss Hellman was on her way. Herman Shumlin took it for granted that Miss Hellman's highly respected drama would win the Pulitzer Prize, and when he was told that the award went to Zoe Akins's *The Old Maid* he was the maddest man in New York, and justifiably so.

Lillian Hellman went on to write *Days to Come,* which failed, and followed it with *The Little Foxes,* her merciless drama of the avaricious Hubbards and the building of a fortune at the turn of the century. *The Little Foxes* remains, to my notion, the finest play that Miss Hellman has written, and it brought forth a vivid and fascinating performance from Tallulah Bankhead. There was then no love between actress and playwright; each was ready at any instant to express an opinion of the other, and quite willing to be quoted.

Quotes from Miss Hellman: "Tallulah is a good actress, a very good actress, but she is also the biggest bore God ever created."

Quotes from Miss Bankhead: "Lillian is an excellent playwright, but I despise her."

When I caught up with *The Little Foxes* at a Saturday matinee in New York the Kentucky sage, John Mason Brown, whose exhilarating lectures on the drama have given him a following from the Harlem Ship Canal to Puget Sound, was across the aisle and shared my enormous enthusiasm for the play and for the playing of Miss Bankhead as the inexorable Regina.

"She's wonderful," said Brown. "And wouldn't she be great as Hedda?"

Clifford Odets, born in Philadelphia in 1906, was reared in the Bronx, went to high school for two years, played more or less invisible parts in productions of the Theater Guild, and worked as an actor for the Group Theater before becoming that organization's most important playwright. He revealed a talent for pungent dialogue, vital and eruptive characters, scenes of searing conflict—and a leftist point of view. The Group gave expression to Odets with excellent productions of a series of his plays—*Waiting for Lefty, Awake and Sing, Rocket to the Moon, Paradise Lost,* and *Golden Boy,* which was a vehement play about Joe Bonaparte, prizefighter, who had dreams of being a violinist until he ruined his hands in the ring—the tale of a confused, frustrated man following a career for which he had a secret loathing. Odets made his spectacular emergence in the playwriting field with his best play, *Awake and Sing,* a searching and impulsive study of the wretched Berger family, living in the Bronx, a harsh and turbulent theater-piece written in the mood and manner of Chekhov. It was beautifully played, for all its humor and its unflinching reality, by the superb Group Theater cast that included Stella Adler, Art Smith, Jules Garfield, Phoebe Brand, Morris Carnovsky, Luther Adler, J. E. Bromberg, Roman Bohnen, and Sanford Meisner.

The case of Odets is puzzling to those of us who believe that the theater is the medium which offers the greatest reward to such an artist as Odets was—and probably is. He began to care about the theater early in his youth; it offered him the open forum for which he clamored, and once he got into it, via the Guild, he had an instant liking for its atmosphere and its people. In turning to writing he won the respect of directors, producers, fellow playwrights, and all members of the critical fraternity. He made a good living as a dramatist, he greatly enjoyed his work and his success, yet he walked out on the theater—for Hollywood. But early in 1949, to the great satisfaction of his friends in the theater, he returned with a new play, *The Big Knife*, which wasn't a good one. It was, actually, an overwrought and overwritten drama, a plotty and cumbersome hodgepodge, all about frustration and viciousness and dreadful goings on in Hollywood. It served, however, to bring Odets back to combat duty, and with it he gave notice that he's back in the field to which he intends giving his talents for the rest of his life.

"That guy," remarks the alert Elia Kazan, in talking of his erstwhile associate of their Group Theater years, "doesn't belong in Hollywood. He is a theater writer. He needs the theater; it's not that the theater needs him. The theater can go along without Odets. What he should do, for the good of his soul, is to write, and write his plays—for Broadway and say good-by to California forever. . . . The Group Theater? It didn't fail; it lived its life. And its influence is still being felt."

The Group Theater, founded with the purpose of creating a permanent company and producing plays that might influence the American scene, and founded in the hope of developing playwrights, directors, actors, and designers, was successful in all but one of its original objectives. "The one respect in which the Group failed," asserts Harold Clurman, "is that it did not succeed in creating a group of responsible patrons necessary for any permanent theater with a permanent company. The Group was always able to raise money for individual shows on the basis of the ordinary commercial backing. But such backing is not adequate to the needs of a permanent company with a consistent policy of play production. No company since the Group has been able to win the kind of patronage required. No company since the Group has been able to endure ten years and produce twenty-five plays with or without patronage."

In the early years of the twentieth century, when Broadway had the show-window status, plays that were accepted as hits did not necessarily remain for long New York runs. John Drew was always satisfied with an engagement of a hundred-odd performances. *Alias Jimmy Valentine* was played on Broadway for only 155 times before Liebler & Company sent it to the cities, towns, and whistle stops of the nation. *Paid in Full* was withdrawn after a 167-performance stay, and Otis Skinner gave only 184 showings of his famous *Kismet* before metropolitan audiences. Occasionally a play came along—some such play as *The Lion and the Mouse* or *Within the Law* or *Peg O' My Heart*—that created a ticket demand of such proportions that discontinuance of the Broadway engagement, during the sell-out period, was never considered. But until the arrival of *Lightnin'*, which opened late in the summer of 1918, not one production since the turn of the century achieved a 700-times run in New York.

Lightnin', with its engagement of 1,291 performances, established a precedent and started a trend, and the long-run fever became contagious. *The Bat*, that tricky and adroit murder melodrama by Mary Roberts Rinehart and Avery Hopwood, remained for nearly 900 performances, and so did the melodrama, *White Cargo*, which showed the effects of African jungle heat upon an Englishman's mind and body. And then *Abie's Irish Rose* made anything seem possible; showmen began predicting that the theater would see a play that would open and never close. Runs of from 500 to 700 times got to be normal. But was the record-breaking engagement in the Manhattan theater of nearly two hundred years to be expected from a sordid, unpleasant play that was attacked by the press at the time of its *première?* That play is, of course, *Tobacco Road*, the folk piece of the squalor, the filth, the lust, the poverty, the depravity, and the death that surrounded Jeeter Lester and his hovel in the Georgia back country. It was a play, as critic Richard Lockridge observed, "that achieves the repulsive and seldom falls below the faintly sickening."

Tobacco Road, which brought forth a memorable characterization from Henry Hull in the role of Jeeter Lester, something of a heroic individualist for all of his loathesomeness, was written by Jack Kirkland from the novel of Erskine Caldwell, and it was played for the astonishing total of 3,182 performances. *Tobacco Road*, staged by an actor-director named Anthony Brown, was put on at the Masque Theater with Jack Kirkland's $6,200 savings on the evening of December 4, 1933, and its sudden closing was expected almost nightly for the next three weeks. But with Henry Hull accepting the minimum Equity salary, the play struggled on. Business improved when it moved to another theater. The sale of cut-rate tickets helped and so did a favorable editorial from the "New York Daily News," and *Tobacco Road* soon settled down to a run that did not end until May 31, 1941.

The production made money in New York and was tremendously profitable on tour, playing in forty-three states. The states that displayed no in-

251

terest at all in Jeeter Lester and his awful brood were Rhode Island, Maine, Vermont, New Hampshire, and Florida. There were numerous Jeeter Lesters during the reign of *Tobacco Road*. Henry Hull forgot the fine notices he had received after a time and decided that he couldn't take Jeeter any longer. James Barton, the hoofer, succeeded him and played Jeeter for one thousand times. Then along came James Bell and then Eddie Garr, and when Garr became exhausted Will Geer took over the role and he was playing the night that brought an end to the Broadway engagement, and to the suffering of the patient Forrest Theater, whose name was later changed to the Coronet.

There were many cast replacements in the New York company and on tour. John Barton, uncle of James, saw America for seven consecutive seasons in the role of Jeeter. New players turned up frequently in the New York cast, and among them was the pretty, bright-eyed daughter of a well-known Kentucky editor. She came to Broadway fresh from school, determined to go on the stage. She got a room at the Rehearsal Club and for two years—it must have seemed like ten—she went wearily from elevator to elevator, office to office, agent to agent, drugstore stool to drugstore stool, without getting so much as a walk-on. Finally, and just after she had bought her ticket to return forlornly to Kentucky, she heard of a vacancy in the *Tobacco Road* cast. Ten minutes later she was in the management's office—and she got the part. Then, for two or three years, she was lost to the world. She eventually decided that she did not want to spend the rest of her life on Jeeter Lester's scraggly farm so she gave her notice, packed her things, said good-by to Broadway and to the theater, and went back to the Blue Grass and got married. . . . *Tobacco Road?* I never saw all three acts of it, and I know few New Yorkers who did.

CHAPTER XVI

Prewar Theater—and "Life With Father"

STIMULATING PLAYS from the theater's major play-wrights enlivened the American stage at a time when play production was slowing down perceptibly and many playhouses were clamoring for attractions. Robert E. Sherwood, in Reno in May of 1934, heard fascinating tales of Carson City and of Virginia City and of Mark Twain, and he began to get ideas for a play. He rented an office and a typewriter and, with a road map beside him, started writing dialogue without knowing just where he was going. Further examination of the map revealed some little criss-crosses and the words, "Petrified Forest." That was enough. He had his title and he knew what the play was to be about. He finished *The Petrified Forest* in exactly four weeks, mailed it to Arthur Hopkins, and then spent the final two weeks of a necessary Nevada stay playing roulette, keno, and the slot machines—and just about breaking even.

Thus came the enormously entertaining *Petrified Forest* into the theater. It is one of Sherwood's best plays. In telling his story of the wandering poet, Alan Squier, disturbed about the state of civilization, who dies, by his own request, from a gunman's bullet, Sherwood effectively mingled melodrama with philosophical comedy; he combined two-gun thriller stuff with theater of deeper meaning. And in *Idiot's Delight,* which also had popular success, he expressed his dread of war and his fear of its awful nearness as he projected his message in the form of an entertainment. Sherwood got his idea for *Idiot's Delight* during an Atlantic crossing from England, when an aboard-ship friend, who had been on a trip around the world, told him of the extraordinary mixture of nationalities found in the hotel in Harbin, Manchuria. It seemed that all the people of Harbin were continually looking up into the sky for the bombers that would herald the start of World War II.

253

Here was the substance of a play, but Sherwood didn't get it worked out until he visited the Club Arizona in Budapest in the summer of 1935. Some battered-looking American chorus girls were doing an act. He became curious, asked the proprietor where he had found them and received this casual reply: "Those kids? Why, they've been touring the Balkans for years."

Sherwood began writing dialogue the next day and moved the Harbin hotel to the Italian Alps, near the Swiss and Austrian borders. And when a delighted Broadway received *Idiot's Delight* the American hoofer, Harry Van, artfully played by Alfred Lunt, was trouping the countryside with a collection of blondes, asking searching questions as to why war had to be, and trying to solve a vexatious personal problem: Was the glamorous and beautiful Irene, now traveling with the munitions manufacturer, the woman with whom he spent the night in the Governor Bryan Hotel in the city of Omaha in the fall of 1925? Sherwood never forgot, for an instant, as he went on with his serious play of world disillusionment, that he was also writing a comedy.

Maxwell Anderson, bringing the influence of a poet into the theater, as Percy MacKaye and Josephine Preston Peabody and William Vaughn Moody had done in other years, put splendor into *Mary of Scotland*, another of his large-scale examinations of history, in which Helen Hayes gave an exquisite performance in the role of Mary Stuart, shown in bitter conflict with Elizabeth of England. He achieved a beauty of language in the McClintic-directed *Winterset*, a tale of love and death, which gave its tragic account of a boy's efforts to clear the name of his father, who had been executed for a crime in which he had no part, of the boy's meeting with the Judge who had tried the case and the gangster who had committed the murder, all told in the shadows of an East River bridge. And in *High Tor*, a charming and fanciful play, Maxwell Anderson protested, in behalf of nature's beauty, against the ravages and despoliation of industrialism.

Sidney Howard and Paul De Kruif contributed fervor and a vast amount of documentary detail into a badly organized play, *Yellow Jack*, which depicted the heroic fight of medical science to determine the cause of yellow fever—the locale was Cuba in 1900—and in *Alien Corn* Howard wrote with poignance, if not with sustained dramatic effect, of the plight of an imaginative music teacher caught up in the stifling academic environment

254

of a college for women in the Midwest. Playwright Howard, with this play, found himself in the position of an author with a debt of gratitude to an actress who brought to his drama more than he had written into it. The actress was Katharine Cornell. Her long, calm recital of the frustrations and the bleakness in the life of Elsa Brandt provided five minutes of stirring theater. All of her finesse as an actress, and all of her great beauty of voice, came into her reading of that speech. It was an interlude to be remembered from years of playgoing, and if I, as a professional playgoer, refrained from applauding on that occasion, I now offer these lines to Miss Cornell in complete apology.

During this mid-thirties surge and splurge of good theater, in which the scenic designers—Jo Mielziner, particularly—also distinguished themselves, Sidney Kingsley wrote an effective play, *Men in White*, filled with fascinating detail of behind-the-scenes life in a great hospital. In the same period S. N. Behrman put suavity and charm into *Biography*, his story of a famous woman painter and the men in her life, and adult and intelligent talk into *Rain From Heaven;* George S. Kaufman and Moss Hart broke away from the field of comedy in *Merrily We Roll Along*, a play that ran backward; Katharine Dayton and the same able Kaufman supplied a biting comedy of social and political Washington under the title of *First Lady*, and Philip Barry wrote sharply, but with considerable confusion, about love and marriage and lust in the generally unsatisfactory *Animal Kingdom*. And Eugene O'Neill, leaving aside his trilogies and heavy tragedies, gave the stage his sentimental, backward-glancing comedy, *Ah, Wilderness*. Here was a warm, human, affectionate family-life piece with its locale in a small Connecticut city in 1906. It was written in a month at Sea Island, off the coast of Georgia, and accepted by the delighted Theater Guild for immediate production. George M. Cohan now comes into the scene.

Cohan had been taking it easy since closing in his prankful *Pigeons and People*. His comedies of the past few years hadn't amounted to a great deal, and he well knew it. He was not engaged in any writing, but was having a pleasant time going to the ball games, taking trips to Atlantic City, and meeting cronies for late-afternoon drinks in the far corner of the Oak Room of the Plaza.

He was in his Fifth Avenue apartment, in the Eighties, when Theresa Helburn called him from the offices of the Theater Guild. She told him the Guild had a play by O'Neill, one they thought he would like. She hadn't forgotten that they had sent him other plays and that he had always returned them, but this new one was something very special. Perhaps he'd be interested in playing the role of Nat Miller, a small-town editor. She sent the script to 993 Fifth Avenue—and waited. Cohan liked the play and the part. Ever since his early flag-waving days he had been speaking only lines that he had written for himself, but here was a play by a dramatist he had long admired, and whose father was one of the great actors when the Four Cohans—Jeremiah John, the Dancing Philosopher; Helen F., of the clan of Costigan; beautiful Josephine, and the young and nimble George M.—were barnstorming the land. Cohan put on his hat and went to the offices of the Guild. Sure, he'd like to do *Ah, Wilderness* if they could get together on salary, percentage, billing, and bookings.

Well, they got together. The Guild agreed to star an actor for the first time in its career. Cohan opened in Pittsburgh in *Ah, Wilderness,* came on to New York and received fine notices. He played a successful engagement, went to Chicago and for a tour of numerous cities, and in the late fall of 1934, without make-up or props or scenery, he gave the play in the Town Hall at North Brookfield, Massachusetts, to which he had gone for the summers of his boyhood.

The hall was jammed; loudspeakers brought the play to a swarm of listeners who assembled in the street just outside. Two old-timers who had known Cohan when he was a young hellion in the nineties, when he belonged to the gang known as the "Coughlin Disturbers," were in that North Brookfield audience and they got to talking of the play at the sidewalk curb after the performance.

"When did Georgie write this play?" one asked. "Never heard of it before."

The other said: "Looks like one of his old ones, doesn't it? I guess he just fixed it up and took the dancin' out."

American dramatists were discovering, even in this era of naturalism and realism, that good theater was still available in some of the popular novels. Helen Jerome turned Jane Austen's "Pride and Prejudice" into a creditable and enjoyable play. Frank B. Elser and Marc Connelly found some sound and atmospheric material in Walter D. Edmonds's "Rome Haul." Sidney

256

Howard did a masterly job in making a play of Sinclair Lewis's "Dodsworth." Sam Dodsworth, the automobile manufacturer who sold his business so that he might devote himself to travel and seeing the world, became a real person on the stage—warm, natural, vital—and his wife Fran came forth as she had in the book—shallow, selfish, childish, and frequently pitiful. Zoe Akins's play, *The Old Maid*, based on Edith Wharton's novel, had considerable stage success, and Owen Davis and his son Donald effectively dramatized Mrs. Wharton's "Ethan Frome." Davis *père* made an engrossing play from "The Great Gatsby," the novel of F. Scott Fitzgerald, in twelve days.

"Twelve days? That wasn't so startling," Davis told me in talking of the feat. "Fitzgerald had written a good book. It was a book with an idea: a man loves a woman so much he dies for her, and just before he dies he learns that she was unworthy of his great love. . . . Twelve days? Why, I did *Her Marriage Vow* in three days and it played for four years!"

A. E. Thomas, the New Englander who had been applying himself intermittently to the drama since his writing of *The Rainbow* in 1912 (Henry Miller and Ruth Chatterton), now made a lively return with a witty comedy, *No More Ladies*. Sidney Kingsley followed his *Men in White* with an excellent study of juvenile gangsters in *Dead End*, with a startlingly real Norman Bel Geddes setting, a dead-end street at the eastern margin of Manhattan showing the city's hoodlums and the rich in juxtaposition. Clare Boothe, New York–born, who had been a pert child actress with lovely blond curls in the Broadway hit, *The Dummy* (1914), and who was successful as a magazine editor-executive before turning to playwriting, wrote a savage indictment of her sex in the all-female *The Women*. Richard Watts, Jr., then writing in the "Herald Tribune," admitted that he had no fondness for the play, but conceded that it was likely to make a million dollars—and it almost did.

The Brock Pemberton–Antoinette Perry producing and directing team found another hearty success in *Personal Appearance*, a comedy by a new playwright, Lawrence Riley, and having to do with the meeting of the tempestuous screen star, Carole Arden, and a country boy, a good-looking filling station attendant at an overnight cabin camp between Scranton and Wilkes-Barre. Samson Raphaelson, who had written *The Jazz Singer* (that's the one, of course, that started all of that talking-picture hullabaloo), put together a neat and popular comedy in *Accent on Youth,* which came to be played in nearly every summer theater that had a stage, some lights, a little scenery, and a few actors.

Vinton Freedley, needing some revision on a musical comedy for which he had a Cole Porter score, went to Howard Lindsay about it, and Lindsay was willing to take on the job if he could get a collaborator. The original book, written by Guy Bolton and P. G. Wodehouse, had to do with a shipwreck and seemed funny enough, but when disaster came to the Havana liner *Morro Castle* Freedley knew that a new book would have to be found. Hence his call to Lindsay.

"Who the hell can we get to work on it with you?" he asked, as he drummed his spotless desk top with a bill of a blue marlin, a trophy of big-game fishing off Bimini. It was just about then that the telephone rang; Neysa McMein was on the wire. Did she know of any bright young man who might want to make a million dollars writing a musical show? Why, yes, she certainly did. His name was Russel Crouse, he was then working as press representative for the Theater Guild, and if Freedley would just get up and go to his window he could probably see Crouse at his desk in the Guild building on the opposite side of 52d Street.

Freedley went to the window, yelled "Hey, Crouse!" and did some wig-wagging, and thus Mr. Lindsay met Mr. Crouse. They then began one of the theater's most productive partnerships with the writing of the revised book for the show to be known as *Anything Goes,* and they put together a gay and funny libretto, without ever suspecting that it was faintly reminiscent of George Broadhurst's old farce, *What Happened to Jones,* the story of a hymn-book salesman who, to escape the law, put on the garb of a bishop.

It was just about this time that Gilbert Miller, something of a New York–London commuter, took an enormous liking to Laurence Housman's touching and episodic play, *Victoria Regina,* when he saw it in London, but the Shuberts had an option on it. They offered it to Helen Hayes. She liked it but wanted to appear as Queen Victoria under Miller's management and told the Shuberts she couldn't do the play with them because of a contract with Miller. And what happened? Let's give the floor to Lee Shubert:

"Milton Shubert was in London. I'd told him to be sure to renew our option on *Victoria Regina.* The option expired on a Saturday. Milton went

258

Some of Our Play Producers, 1940–1950

1. Lee Shubert 2. Vinton Freedley 3. Alfred De Liagre, Jr. 4. J. J. Shubert 5. Theresa Helburn 6. Lawrence Langner 7. Brock Pemberton 8. Arthur Hopkins 9. Eddie Dowling 10. Leland Hayward 11. Gilbert Miller 12. Oscar Hammerstein II

The Day Family of Madison Avenue, New York

Howard Lindsay as Father and Dorothy Stickney as Vinnie, with their red-topped sons—a family group from the century's most successful nonmusical play, *Life With Father*, written by Lindsay and Russel Crouse, based on the writings of Clarence Day, Jr. (Vandamm Studio).

Victoria Regina

Helen Hayes, who triumphed in the role of England's Queen in New York and throughout America, is shown here as Her Majesty nears the end of her reign—and the end of her life (Vandamm Studio).

to Paris, thinking everything would be all right until Monday. But Miller had put up his check with the author and he got the play. And what a hit it was!"

Now, in the fear of giving the impression that just everything from every important playwright and producer came through as a huge success at this time, let it be recorded that Noel Coward had a dismal failure with his crude tropical melodrama, *Point Valaine*, and with the Lunts, too! Grace George, a fine actress throughout the years, could do nothing with, or for, *Kind Lady*, Edward Chodorov's well-written play of the genteel, elderly art patron who was kept a prisoner in her own home by a gang of thieves. And Tallulah Bankhead, who had had a yearning to play Sadie Thompson —I must accept a portion of the blame for urging Sam H. Harris to let her do it—discovered that there was no longer a public for the once glorious play called *Rain*. Tallulah was a hoarse and fiery Sadie, but the years had taken a great deal of the sting out of *Rain*. Sam Harris, a supreme gentleman in defeat as well as in victory, called backstage to see his star.

"I guess they don't want us, kid," he said. "What'll we do?"

"My God, darling," cried Tallulah, "there's only one thing we can do. We'll take it off." And they took it off.

The theater in New York in the second half of the thirties, had bounced back from the depression. There was an increase in the attendance at the playhouses; there was quality in many of the plays, and Broadway was now adjusting itself to a play-parade of less than one hundred per season. The trend was steadily downward. A variety of causes contributed to the sharp decline in production: the rise in all production costs, the shortage of play-backing money, the continued rush of playwrights and actors to Hollywood, and, in consequence, the cessation of theater activity on the part of playwrights who knew their trade.

Broadway—and Broadway is, of course, an all-inclusive area, a frenzied chunk of mid-town Manhattan bounded on the south by the Empire Theater, on the north by Columbus Circle, on the west by the Martin Beck Theater, and the east by the Ziegfeld Theater—was in a state of transition. The legitimate theaters totaled thirty-odd, as compared with sixty-odd ten years previously. A decade had passed without the building of a playhouse and more construction seemed unlikely for another ten years—or twenty.

There were now new faces in the Broadway scene—new producers, directors, critics, hoofers, house treasurers, ticket takers, stage doormen. The stage-door Johnny, a figure of a certain gallantry in the theater of other years, had vanished. Chorus girls of the new age had heard vaguely of the legends of flowers and carriages and champagne suppers, but most of them now went home alone, and via foot or subway or bus, and were content with a bedtime snack, such as ham-and-cheese on rye. There were now changes in custom and in personnel, but "Variety" still came out Wednesdays; David Warfield still reported at the Lambs for his daily pinochle; and the Shuberts still parked their shiny cars in their private street called Shubert Alley.

Forty-second Street had gone Coney Island, a raucous and raging midway. The flea circus had moved in, so had the Minskys and burlesque, and the thoroughfare's proud and beautiful playhouses, the theaters of the Selwyns and Woods and Sam Harris and Ziegfeld, had become brazen film emporiums, specializing in second-run features. Broadway itself, once the street of Rector's and Churchill's and Shanley's, was now cheapened and nightmarish. It was offering palm reading and photos while-U-wait, live turtles and tropical fruit drinks, sheet music, nut fudge, jumbo malteds, hot waffles, ham and eggs, hot dogs, and hamburgers. A screeching, amusement-park bedlam that was somehow without a ferris wheel and a roller coaster, but that presented shooting galleries, bowling alleys, guess-your-weight stands, gypsy tea rooms, rug auctions, electric shoeshines, dance halls—fifty beautiful girls—chop suey, beer on draught, wines and liquors, oyster bars, bus-barkers, and right there at the curb was the man with the giant telescope, ready to show you the craters of the moon for a dime.

During the ten years that had gone by since Al Jolson appeared in *The Jazz Singer*, Hollywood had continued its raiding of the ranks of the legitimate. Ronald Colman could now buy a villa on the Nile and so could Clark Gable. Barbara Stanwyck had walked out on the theater and so had John Cromwell, Robert Montgomery, Jack Oakie, Irene Dunne, Vincent Lawrence, Bette Davis, Joan Blondell, Guy Kibbee, George Cukor. Broadway had undergone, and had recovered from, the Rudy Vallee craze and the "Music Goes Round and Round" mania. Noel Coward had been adopted as America's own; the Critics' Circle had been organized; the "Theater

Magazine" had gone the way of the "Green Book," the "Dramatic Mirror," and the "Clipper," and George M. Cohan had been proclaimed the First Actor. The Algonquin had begun to sell liquor after its long drought, the Cotton Club had moved down from Harlem, and the blond, pale, frail Rita Katzenberg, the theater's number one first-nighter, had suffered, unprotestingly, in Row AA, through scores of dreadful plays. The drama had been ousted from such famous strongholds as the Astor, the New Amsterdam, the Eltinge, the Gaiety, the Globe, the Republic, and the Apollo. Other playhouses, such as the Casino and the Knickerbocker and the Thirty-ninth, had vanished, like the Madison Avenue trolley cars. The night spots of the prohibition era, the Hotsy-Totsy, the Type & Print, the Chez Florence, the Central Park Casino, the Bath Club, and the 300 Club, passed on. But Twenty One, the Stork Club, El Morocco, and Tony Soma's remained, resolutely. . . . The tiny Belmont Theater? It was still in 48th Street the last time I looked, and showing a Spanish movie.

The outstanding plays of the theater's prewar period were *You Can't Take It With You,* by Moss Hart and George S. Kaufman; *Of Mice and Men,* John Steinbeck's trenchant dramatization of his own novel; *Our Town,* by Thornton Wilder; *Abe Lincoln in Illinois,* by Robert E. Sherwood; *The Time of Your Life,* by William Saroyan; *Life With Father,* by Howard Lindsay and Russel Crouse, and Lillian Hellman's two pieces, *The Little Foxes* and *Watch on the Rhine.*

The turbulent and talented William Saroyan, a stocky, thick eye-browed, emotional, and kindly man, given to swift and explosive conversation, and born in 1908 in Fresno, California, of fruit-farming Armenian parentage, burst in upon the American theater with the charming oddity, *My Heart's in the Highlands,* and later came along with the ingratiating *The Time of Your Life,* and the sentimental *Love's Old Sweet Song,* all about a spinsterish lady and an itinerant pitchman, and introducing a Greek wrestler and a swarm of Okies. George Jean Nathan talked Eddie Dowling into producing and appearing in *The Time of Your Life,* which won the Pulitzer Prize, only to have Saroyan heartily (and publicly) reject the $1,000 check. These three plays, when later published together between covers, brought Brooks Atkinson to the observation that Saroyan, "when he writes out of a general relish, usually in isolated scenes, is at his best and makes a definite contribution to the mood of these times," but "when he permits himself to discuss ideas he can write some of the worst nonsense that ever clattered out of a typewriter."

The Hart-Kaufman *You Can't Take It With You,* a convulsive and priceless comedy, revealed two skilled playmakers in brilliant collaboration as they introduced us to the mad, happy, daffy, lovable, unmethodical, but somehow sense-making family called the Sycamores. And gave us, for three delightful acts, the goings on in the seemingly hopeless disarray of the labyrinth that was called, accurately enough, the living room. *You Can't Take It With You* was written in California in six weeks—Kaufman sitting at the typewriter and Hart doing the floor-pacing—about two years after Hart had first mentioned a crazy-family idea to Kaufman.

Their later comedy, *The Man Who Came to Dinner,* was started soon after Alexander Woollcott had been a week-end guest at Hart's place in Bucks County, Pennsylvania—a week end in which life was fairly unendurable for Hart as Woollcott spent most of his time harassing and bullying and torturing and insulting guests and servants. When Monday finally came around—it had been the longest week end of Hart's lifetime—Woollcott suggested that his host come to Philadelphia to see him as an actor and in the role of Binkie Niebuhr, who looked after everybody's problems, in S. N. Behrman's literate and straggling *Wine of Choice.* Wonderful, beamed Hart. Perfectly, positively wonderful. His prayers had been answered. He would have been willing to go to Indo-China to get the barbarian out of the house. During dinner in Philadelphia Woollcott had more drinks than was his custom and he made the pronouncement that it was time Kaufman & Hart wrote a play for him. Hart, in returning to Bucks County, called upon neighbor Kaufman, sank wearily into a chair, and told him of Woollcott's suggestion about the play and of A.W.'s behavior over the week end.

"Wouldn't it have been terrible," said Hart, "if Aleck had broken his leg —and had to stay." They looked at each other. They had their play. Eight months later *The Man Who Came to Dinner* was completed.

Our Town, a touching and affecting study of birth, marriage, and death in the little town of Grover's Corners, New Hampshire, was the first play of the Wisconsin-born Thornton Wilder to reach Broadway. Wilder and Jed Harris knew each other at Yale, and in later years Wilder attended rehearsals of Harris plays. The novelist-playwright prepared a version of

Ibsen's *A Doll's House* for Harris—it was beautifully played by Ruth Gordon—and finished his writing of *Our Town* in Zurich, Switzerland. He returned to New York with his manuscript, and took it to Harris, who accepted it instantly and decided to put it on at once. No other manager saw the script of *Our Town*.

The play was staged in the fashion of *The Yellow Jacket*, with no scenery and just a few props, and was rehearsed with sensitivity and understanding by Harris. Another showman with less confidence in his own ability, and in his own productions, would have abandoned *Our Town* in Boston. It was attacked by that city's press and played to a meager $2,900 on the week. Marc Connelly went to Boston to see the play and his great enthusiasm bolstered Harris's belief in his property. He canceled his second-week booking and brought *Our Town* to New York. It received ovations from the press and won the Pulitzer Prize.

Robert E. Sherwood's exalted biographical drama, *Abe Lincoln in Illinois*, taking Lincoln, in a series of carefully planned scenes, from his early years in New Salem until his departure for the White House, was written after Sherwood had seen Massey as the lank and brooding farmer in the bitter *Ethan Frome*. There, he knew instantly, was his actor to play Lincoln. And it was *Abe Lincoln in Illinois*, plus *There Shall Be No Night*, Sherwood observed later, "that took me out of the theater and into association with Harry Hopkins and the White House for five years."

Abe Lincoln in Illinois started the Playwrights' Company resolutely on its way. This new and vital producing organization was formed at a before-midnight session in a New York bar, with Sherwood, Maxwell Anderson, and Elmer Rice sitting around a table after a particularly stormy session of the council of the Dramatists' Guild of the Authors' League of America. Sherwood, Anderson, and Rice were disturbed by conditions generally; they decided, over their Scotch, that things would be easier if they did their own producing. They knew that Sidney Howard would join them and they'd invite S. N. Behrman.

"And it was all done," Sherwood asserts, "before we knew it. The five of us put up fifty thousand dollars. That was ten thousand dollars a man. We raised another fifty thousand dollars on the outside. . . . Elmer Rice did a magnificent job in staging *Abe Lincoln* and Raymond Massey's performance as Lincoln was remarkable acting. . . . New Salem? I've never been there in my life, or even to Illinois, except between trains."

263

The tall, alert, beret-wearing, Russian-born Oscar Serlin makes this observation: "A producer always starts trying to get Alfred Lunt and Lynn Fontanne for his play, and he is eventually happy to finish up with anybody on the stage. We were happy, and also lucky, to have Howard Lindsay and Dorothy Stickney in the original cast of *Life With Father*."

Serlin, who had been associated with such minor projects as *Broken Dishes* and *Lost Sheep* and *The Guinea Pig*, was working for Paramount when he began to wonder if there wasn't a good play in Clarence Day's essays about his father. He had a meeting with Mrs. Clarence Day but nothing came of it. Mrs. Day suggested another talk, however, and at this second meeting she told Serlin that if the services of the proper dramatist could be obtained she would like to have further discussion.

Serlin later talked it all over with Lindsay and Dorothy Stickney in Hollywood. Certainly, they knew the Day material and loved it, and Lindsay, from out of Waterford, New York, who had trouped in burlesque, tent shows, and *Polly of the Circus*, said that he'd like to appear as Father if there was to be a play. Serlin wasn't quite prepared for that—but would Howard be interested in doing the dramatization and the staging? Why, er—yes! Lindsay called in Crouse and a forty-page scenario was read by Lindsay to the Day family at a session in New Haven, with Serlin and Crouse nervously present. There seemed to be no definite reaction at the close of the reading, and the trio from Broadway made the return trip to New York with something of a where-the-hell-do-we-go-from-here uncertainty. They were told later, however, that Mrs. Day had thought the outline charming, and Lindsay and Crouse settled down to the writing of the play.

The actual writing took only seventeen days—Crouse at the typewriter and Lindsay pacing, and acting out the dialogue as they went along—but it was done after many months of plotting and planning. Plotting and planning as they rode in cabs, as they walked about the streets of New York, as they sat in the park, as they strolled the deck of a trans-Atlantic liner, and as they wandered about the beautiful city of Stockholm, excitedly talking and gesticulating, and drawing stares from puzzled Swedes. In April of 1939 the play was finished, and there was then the matter of getting the right players for the roles of Father and Vinnie. The Lunts turned the play down. So did Walter Connolly, Roland Young, and John Halliday.

So did Walter Huston—twice. Just didn't like it. And long after the fame of *Life With Father* had spread around the world the authors were told why their manuscript had been returned by Alfred Lunt and Lynn Fontanne. It seems that Lunt got excited about the comedy but that Miss Fontanne demurred. Why, yes, Alfred darling, a very nice play, a lovely play, but just think about it for a moment. How could she endure going to the theater night after night wondering whether he was going to be baptized!

With everybody refusing the play, the authors looked at their producer and then at each other, and there was Lindsay, the actor, still standing by. He and Dorothy Stickney offered to do the play for the tryout at Skowhegan, Maine, in mid-August. The tryout went well enough and there was no discussion of a replacement for Lindsay as Father. Script changes were made here and there, Bretaigne Windust was engaged to do the staging for New York, several new players were engaged, and on the evening of November 8, 1939, *Life With Father*, the most successful play in the history of the American theater—its enormous appeal is to be attributed to its universality and to the fact that everyone in the audience at every performance sees in the play something of himself or herself—opened at the Empire. There were two first-night incidents that stay in the minds of the authors and Oscar Serlin. A tray in the hands of a maid smashed to the floor—that seemed to be quite a part of the play—and Richard Sterling, an actor of many years' experience, went up in his lines.

"When I realized that Sterling had blown," Russel Crouse said later, "I hit the floor, but I found Oscar Serlin there ahead of me."

There were some extraordinary performances being given in the American theater about the time that *Life With Father* was settling down to stay until doomsday at the Empire (it passed the long-run mark of *Tobacco Road* before it was withdrawn). Some were extraordinary because of their sheer validity and others—certainly one that I have in mind—because of the background of the players giving them. On the side of validity, there was the restrained and expert playing of Eddie Dowling, once of Woonsocket, Rhode Island, as the mysterious man with money in his pocket in William Saroyan's casual and enormously likable play, *The Time of Your Life*. There was the sharply drawn characterization of Monty Woolley as that malicious and expansive monster, Sheridan Whiteside, in the Hart-Kaufman *Man Who Came to Dinner*. And there was the deliberation and feeling of impending tragedy that Paul Lukas brought to Lillian Hellman's *Watch on the Rhine* with his acting as the implacable anti-Fascist, Kurt Mueller.

And, in the other category, and in another city, Chicago, there was the shocking performance of the actor who had been the greatest of them all —John Barrymore. Here he was, after being absent from the stage for many years, playing in a wild, crackbrained farce, *My Dear Children.* Playing it and enjoying it to the acute distress of playgoers who had seen him, and revered him, in roles of his earlier years. He was now mumbling and roaring and prancing; he was, by turn, droll and earnest and waggish and outlandish. He was pausing every now and then to deliver an aside to the audience—and he was packing the Selwyn Theater. I went to see *My Dear Children* and regretted it.

It was just at this time, too, that a stranger returned to Broadway, a man who had taken many a drink with Barrymore in the days when Jack's in Sixth Avenue was a rendezvous for the celebrated in the theatrical world, when the Hotel Knickerbocker was known as the 42d Street country club. The visitor was Eugene Walter, author of *Paid in Full* and *The Wolf* and *The Easiest Way.*

"Funny," he said, "but I don't know anybody around here any more. I guess I've been in California too long. One of my great troubles out there is that I can't walk into the Brown Derby without meeting a swarm of actors who used to be in my plays, and who'll begin acting out the plays right over the lunch table. . . . But the picture producers are never interested in a man's past, and they never ask, 'What's he done?' George Cohan found that out. They just don't care. They want to know what you can do now. . . . Hell, I wrote a lot of shows for Broadway, but I never really made much money. Playwriting didn't pay then as it does now, and as fast as I took the money in I fed it right out. But so did everybody else in those days. . . . I miss Wilson Mizner. He gave me more laughs than anybody I ever knew."

Eugene Walter's words stay in my mind. So do those of others of that immediate period. . . . "I've played every water tank in this country of ours," said William A. Brady, "and I know about the road. Helen Hayes's tour in *Victoria Regina* is the biggest thing America ever saw. Think of a drama playing to nine thousand dollars for a performance in Des Moines and seven thousand dollars for a performance in Toledo. Hayes is a real trouper. So is Katharine Cornell. She'll die a rich woman unless she gets some fool ideas, as Nat Goodwin did when he decided to play Shylock. . . . The best thing that ever happened to the New York theater was that controversy over the Hamlets of Leslie Howard and John Gielgud. I've seen all the Hamlets since the eighties. Forbes-Robertson was the best, and he underplayed it."

". . . The theater," observed the sententious Jed Harris, "is in a state of stumblebum futility. You have a theater in which a woman, Lillian Hellman, is your most virile playwright, and another woman, Margaret Webster, is your greatest producer of Shakespeare. And then there are a few tired hulks of so-called men hanging around—dead people, still walking around."

". . . I've found out about Ethel Barrymore," commented Herman Shumlin. "She has absolute devotion to her job and is the most professional person I ever met."

". . . Touring agrees with me," said Ethel Barrymore. "America is so exciting I never stop looking. Texas is terrific, and in every way . . . I've often thought of Pinero and *Mid-Channel*, but it would be no good. It reads too old-fashioned. But you can always play Paula Tanqueray. I'll never forget Pinero. He was very wonderful to me when I was young in London."

". . . George Jean Nathan used to say that I wrote weakly but never cheaply," declared Zoe Akins, as she took a gulp of a milk and whisky punch. "My plays have been, for the most part, extravagant productions. I've always felt very shy about introducing politics into a play. I think Rachel Crothers is a sound and gifted person and that Lillian Hellman has one of the greatest talents in the theater. . . . My, how the foreigners can act! I'm talking about George Coulouris and Paul Lukas in *Watch on the Rhine*."

". . . I suppose," observed Buddy De Sylva, song writer and motion-picture executive, born above the sidewalks of New York's Amsterdam Avenue, and part-time resident of Hollywood since it was a bean field, "that I admired Ziegfeld more than I did anybody else. Ziggy was a terrific guy. He made the musical show what it is in the world today. He was the kind of fellow who made people feel honored to have him owe them money."

". . . We have never played," said Lynn Fontanne, "to more wonderful audiences than we got in Seattle. Alfred and I have always liked Beaumont, Texas. San Francisco is marvelous and Youngstown, Ohio, is quite all right. Some of the restaurants in America are terrible; the best are in Seattle and Columbus, Ohio."

". . . I could never be happy playing just one sort of role," admitted Helen Hayes, taking a sip of an after-theater highball. "I don't want always to be the whole cheese. I'm no high priestess; that's silly and difficult. I could never stand to get into a groove. I'm not in the theater merely to make a living, or just to have long runs. I'm also in it for fun."

". . . Haven't played in all the states—not yet," said Katharine Cornell, good-humoredly. "Have never played Nevada, for one. I've appeared in about ninety cities. I adore New Orleans—and Savannah. I'm still to see the Grand Canyon. I do try to get to the art galleries on my tours. And always the parks."

". . . Harry (Henry R. Luce) has always been wonderful about this business of my writing," said Clare Boothe Luce. "He's always been interested and has always been willing to put aside his own affairs and let me yammer about my plays. Harry's mad about the theater—even more stage-struck than I am."

". . . My career?" laughed Alla Nazimova. "I go up and I go down. I've never done Shaw. I played Paula Tanqueray in Russian and in Russia. Shakespeare? I wouldn't dare. I haven't that lilt in my voice. Nora is out for me now—Hedda, too. I'm too old. Anybody who can look twenty-five and act eighteen can play Nora."

And there was the comment of W. Somerset Maugham, as he relaxed in a big chair at Nelson Doubleday's home in Oyster Bay. "I've retired from the theater. I'd be foolish to try to write another play. Success in the theater is for young men. I wrote about thirty plays; twenty were probably successful. For five or six years I was tremendously excited about the theater and then I began to hanker after novels. . . . Poor Jeanne Eagels! How amazing she was in *Rain.* I saw the part played in many cities and in many languages, and no one touched her. Death took a great actress from us."

The decade of the Nineteen Hundred and Thirties was one in which the American dramatist revealed a consuming interest in historical and biographical subjects, but without hesitating to grapple with vital, contemporary issues. There was definitely a trend toward demagogic drama, toward the social-minded theater, and also a widespread appreciation of nostalgia, as revealed in such pieces as *The Star-Wagon, Ah, Wilderness,* and *One Sunday Afternoon.* Several novels put into stage form—*Of Mice and Men* and *Dodsworth,* specifically—provided absorbing theater fare.

If the decade was considerably less dazzling than that of the twenties in the production of new playwrights, if it failed to bring forth another galaxy of exciting new writers, it did, at least, present a dozen or so young dramatists of imagination and integrity. Lillian Hellman, Clifford Odets, and William Saroyan were soaring playmakers; there was also a great deal of quality in the writings of Sidney Kingsley, Lynn Riggs, Paul Osborn, Susan Glaspell, Irwin Shaw, and Edward Chodorov. And there was impressive work in some of the imported plays, such as Paul Vincent Carroll's *Shadow and Substance* and his *White Steed.*

"Two things," comments Louis Kronenberger, "are outstanding in Lillian Hellman's plays: dramatic skill and dramatic force. At her best, Miss Hellman has no equal in the contemporary American theater for sharpness of storytelling or powerfulness of impact. Her conflicts between good and evil, her portrayals of viciousness and greed have that special vividness which only the theater can command, but which the theater, these days, is not very actively commanding."

It was a decade that put stress on the efficacy of ensemble acting, but also one in which numerous individuals distinguished themselves. There were some unforgettable performances: Raymond Massey in *Abe Lincoln in Illinois,* Richard B. Harrison in *The Green Pastures,* Katharine Cornell in *Romeo and Juliet,* Helen Hayes in *Victoria Regina,* Leslie Howard in *The Petrified Forest,* James Dale in *The Green Bay Tree,* Lynn Fontanne in *Elizabeth the Queen,* Alfred Lunt in *Idiot's Delight,* Alice Brady in *Mourning Becomes Electra,* Lloyd Nolan in *One Sunday Afternoon,* Walter Huston in *Dodsworth.* And certainly fine work from Burgess Meredith in *High Tor,* Martha Scott in *Our Town,* Elia Kazan in *Golden Boy,* Tallulah Bankhead in *The Little Foxes,* Josephine Hull in *You Can't Take It With You,* Katharine Hepburn in *The Philadelphia Story,* Grace George in *The Circle* and *Kind Lady,* and from Maurice Evans in his own vivid and uncut *Hamlet* and his own production of *Henry IV, Part I,* in which he came forth as a roistering Falstaff.

The thirties saw the coming and the going of Orson Welles's Mercury Theater; the rise and the decline of the Group Theater, and a somewhat exciting flurry of activity from the WPA Federal Theater, which came through with a creditable presentation of E. P. Conkle's *Prologue to Glory*. During the decade George Gershwin contributed an exalted folk opera in *Porgy and Bess*, Ireland's Abbey Theater provided meritorious productions of such near classics as *The Plough and the Stars, The Playboy of the Western World, Juno and the Paycock*, and there were numerous Shakespearean productions—Katharine Cornell was a tremulous Juliet, John Gielgud a fine Hamlet, and Philip Merivale and Gladys Cooper were utterly tedious as Macbeth and Lady Macbeth.

It was a decade in which Ethel Barrymore tried blackface (in *Scarlet Sister Mary*), Al Jolson returned to the theater as its highest-paid entertainer, in *Wonder Bar*, and some of the country's celebrated players closed out their careers. Death alone stopped Mrs. Fiske. This great actress, after a half century in the theater, was denied a farewell appearance in the New York that she loved. Her final play was a comedy called *Against the Wind;* she was in it for two performances in Cleveland and for sixteen in Chicago. It was during the Chicago engagement that she became mortally ill and was persuaded to discontinue her playing and return to the East for a rest. She never set foot on the stage again, dying in February of 1932 at the age of sixty-six.

William Gillette, tired and aging and resigned to calling it a career, gave up the stage after a one-week, last-gesture appearance in *Three Wise Fools* in New York and retired to the seclusion and the peace of his field-stone castle at Hadlyme, Connecticut. During the final decade of Gillette's life I visited him several times at his fantastic retreat, "Seventh Sister," high above the Connecticut River. There, with his yellow cats, he lived as a recluse in a house he had built exactly as he wanted it, a structure with walls four feet thick, doors of chopped oak with hand-carved latches, mullioned windows, and an enormous open fireplace. And it was his custom, after he had donned blue overalls and put on heavy gloves and an engineer's cap, to take his favored guests for a ride on his famous miniature railroad. Gillette, in inviting me to his hilltop, always insisted that there was to be no interview. He got to know many journalists during his long career but throughout his years he remained press-shy; he had something of a dread of critics, reporters, and such. When he was starred by Arthur Hopkins in Clare Kummer's *A Successful Calamity* in 1917 the reviews were unanimous in their cheering; Hopkins thanked the critics in an advertisement addressed to them and placed in the New York dailies. But

270

when he called backstage to see his star a night or so later, he came upon a stern and disapproving Gillette. "I do not play for critics," said the actor, in a tone of icy precision. "I do not thank them. I do not want you to thank them for me."

And there was one player—an intelligent, somewhat frigid, and singularly able actress—who quit during the thirties when in the best of health, and when she apparently had every reason to want to give ten more years of her life to her career. She just quit. Her name was, and is, Chrystal Herne, daughter of that pioneer in realism, James A. Herne, with whom Gillettte had been contemporaneous. Miss Herne was seemingly discouraged by the plays that had been coming her way. Her last play was the melodrama, *A Room in Red and White*. Its run was brief. Miss Herne gave her usual adroit performance on the final Saturday night, removed her make-up, and walked alone, and slowly, for a half block to the Broadway corner for a taxi, and it was during that little walk, I believe, that she made her decision. She got into a cab, gave the driver her East 57th Street address, settled back against the upholstery, and sighed deeply. Then she smiled, in complete relaxation. She had done her job. She never appeared on the stage again.

The New York theater, operating on a restricted basis in comparison with the wild and frenzied years in which it was overflowing its mid-town boundaries and extending, in its vast profusion and prosperity, to Brooklyn and the Bronx, was now in a reasonably hearty state. The talking pictures had not taken away all the actors, the directors, the playwrights. The Broadway producers were still reading plays, buying plays, casting plays —and they were also reading the day-to-day world headlines of this disturbing prewar period and were wondering what lay ahead. Few of them foresaw the gold-rush delirium, and the theater shortage, that the war years were to bring in.

CHAPTER XVII

Broadway Gold Rush

POLAND reeled under the Nazi invasion. England and France went once more into war. The German hordes overran the Low Countries and turned upon France with paralyzing and resistless fury. France collapsed. Italy, with hideous craftiness and caution, struck from the rear. Unconquerable London fought off the blitz. Hitler swept over the Continent and, in a gigantic blunder, hurled his troops into Russia. The Japs attacked Pearl Harbor—and a stunned and enraged America thundered into the fight.

New York's theatrical district hastily adjusted itself to wartime measures. The Great White Way was doused; the dimout came to the Forties and Fifties. Mid-town Manhattan again swarmed with young men in uniform, the clamorous Stage Door Canteen opened its hospitable doors, and Broadway actresses, walk-ons, and ingénues and stars included, began dancing with the soldiers, singing to the soldiers, and waiting on tables. The thoughts of the theater's service-age males—actors, playwrights, directors, producers—turned from problems of the stage to the matter of personal participation in the great emergency. Many of them soon disappeared from the New York scene, to be gone for the duration.

The New York theater, as war descended upon America, was in a state of shocking mediocrity. Many dramatists were not writing; most of those who were writing were badly off form. Maxwell Anderson's *Candle in the Wind,* depicting the efforts of an American actress to get her French writer-lover out of a Nazi concentration camp, was one of his worst. Frederick Hazlitt Brennan's *Mr. Wookey,* a study of an articulate Cockney at the time of the Dunkirk disaster, was just so much rubbish. *The Land Is Bright,* written by George S. Kaufman and Edna Ferber, was quite the weakest piece to come from these well-organized collaborators. Such

272

offerings of the 1941–1942 season as *Junior Miss, The Moon Is Down, Uncle Harry*, and *Blithe Spirit* were, definitely, run-of-the-mill theater. The theater's best exhibits as of December 7, 1941, were the holdovers, *Life With Father, Lady in the Dark* (Gertrude Lawrence) and *Arsenic and Old Lace*, for which Howard Lindsay and Russel Crouse had tried to bring Maude Adams out of retirement. There were also such new and worth-while exhibits as the Maurice Evans–Judith Anderson *Macbeth*, and a rollicking musical comedy, *Let's Face It*, which introduced a rare comedian in the lean, agile, double-talking Danny Kaye. And a night or two before the millions of a great city were numbed and horrified by the news of Pearl Harbor, a taut, expertly written and skillfully acted melodrama, *Angel Street*, the work of Patrick Hamilton, was submitted to Broadway. It won rave reviews, but you would not have believed it if you had looked in on its theater during the week following the catastrophe in Hawaii. New Yorkers gave up their playgoing that week, and *Angel Street*, which became a tremendous success, almost closed before it got started.

An actor, the able, Brooklyn-born John Halliday, a prospector in the gold fields of Nevada before turning to Broadway, foresaw and foretold, with terrible accuracy, the coming of the Japs in that fateful December. Halliday had gone to Hawaii to make his home and was living in the village of Kaneohe, across the mountains from Waikiki, on the island of Oahu, when I paid him a visit in June of 1941. He took me onto the terrace of his low-swung redwood house, long and rambling, and indicated the Kaneohe naval air station on the Mokapu peninsula, three miles away. "Now look at that spot," he said, in his incisive fashion. "The Japs know about that air station and they've already picked it out for their first bombs. They'll probably blast it before they strike at Pearl Harbor, and when they do I'm going to be standing right here on this terrace watching, and hoping they don't come over this house. The Japs have a date with Hawaii—they'll be here before Christmas."

The theater of the early stages of World War II was one of the adolescent-conscious George Abbott and *Kiss and Tell;* of the square-jawed, sharp-eyed, tough-talking Michael Todd, erstwhile Chicago saloon-keeper, and *Star and Garter;* of the scholarly, suddenly stage-struck Thornton Wilder and *The Skin of Our Teeth;* of the enduring Irving Berlin and his marvelous wartime revue, *This Is the Army;* of the Shuberts in their somewhat bewildering sponsorship of the *Ziegfeld Follies,* and of *Junior Miss* and the energetic and all-over-the-place Max Gordon, described by Lewis Funke in "The New York Times" as "a rotund little man who seems to be in a constant state of detonation."

It was a wartime theater without the services of George M. Cohan. The Yankee Doodle boy, just after receiving from President Roosevelt a gold medal authorized by Congress for the writing of *Over There*—the gesture of an unforgivably tardy government after a time elapse of twenty-three years—had finished his theatrical career wistfully, sadly, tragically. He wrote a new version of *The Tavern* under the title of *The Return of the Vagabond*, a flimsy, warmed-over, and not greatly worked-over little play, and took it hopefully to the place of his birth, Providence. Then to Boston, and then, with steadily mounting misgivings, into New York. He closed it after seven performances and on the final night he said these words: "I'll never come to New York again. They don't want me any more." He was tired, he was ill, he knew that he was through. He went into retirement, a fretful retirement, and passed his days reading, resting, and talking with old friends. On a summer's night in 1942, against the protests of his nurse, he dressed himself and went for an automobile ride up and down Broadway, the street that he had glorified and that had changed so bewilderingly since the days when he strolled it with a straw hat and a bamboo cane. That motor ride gave him his last glimpse of New York's bright lights. In October he became critically ill and on the evening of November 5, 1942, as he feebly touched the hand of Gene Buck, he died.

There was no rush of war plays to the stages of America as there had been during World War I. They now came along slowly, and with varying degrees of effectiveness. Robert E. Sherwood put eloquence and some magnificent writing into his preachment, *There Shall Be No Night*, in which he presented the plight of a high-minded and idealistic scientist caught up in Finland's resistance of Russia. Lillian Hellman, in her sound and superbly sustained *Watch on the Rhine*, showed how the terrors of fascism could jolt the complacency of a genteel, well-to-do American home. Maxwell Anderson wrote a simple, human, and poignant war play in *The Eve of St. Mark* and an indecisive and ungainly one in *Storm Operation*. Edward Chodorov achieved considerable force and dramatic tension in his *Decision*, a drama of conflict on the home front, which recited its story of the blackmailing and the killing, via the methods of Hitlerism, of an incorruptible citizen who was fighting race prejudice and crooked politics. James Gow and Arnaud d'Usseau, new young playwrights, presented, in their *Tomorrow the World*, the study of a twelve-year-old monster, a boy who is brought to an American college town after having been subjected to Nazi indoctrination. Moss Hart crowded some tumultuous theater into his Air Forces propaganda piece, *Winged Victory*, which was enormously successful in New York and in its wanderings about the world.

On the lighter side, there was *O Mistress Mine*, Terence Rattigan's entertaining comedy of an attractive widow, her grown-up son, and her lover, a well-intentioned cabinet minister, and the steadily diverting *Jacobowsky and the Colonel*, a comedy about Jacobowsky, the eternal refugee, a fabulous colonel, and the beautiful woman in the colonel's life. There was a swarm of lesser war plays, such as Irwin Shaw's *Sons and Soldiers* and his *The Assassin*, Terence Rattigan's *Flare Path*, imported from London, and *Counterattack*, based by Janet and Philip Stevenson on a Russian original. (Plays of greater fiber—Paul Osborn's *A Bell for Adano*, Harry Brown's *A Sound of Hunting*, Arthur Laurents's *Home of the Brave*, the James Gow– Arnaud D'Usseau *Deep Are the Roots*, and the *Command Decision* of William Wister Haines—were to come.) The better war plays, as it has been proven twice in the lifetime of so many of us, are written by Americans when their country is back in a world of peace, or something approximating it.

The Theater Guild was having troubling times when America plunged into war. Its season of 1940–1941, one of its bleakest, brought forth only four plays, and two of them were presented in association with Gilbert Miller. The following season did not yield a success. Helen Hayes appeared bravely in Maxwell Anderson's *Candle in the Wind*, and Fredric March and Florence Eldridge found that they could do little with Sophie Treadwell's *Hope for a Harvest*. And along came the drama year of 1942–1943 with Philip Barry given to a great deal of philosophizing and very scanty drama in *Without Love*, and the Lunts appearing in a minor frolic, S. N. Behrman's *The Pirate*. It was a lean, lean period for the Guild. Perhaps it was not on the verge of bankruptcy or dissolution, but something had to happen quickly. Something did.

Ever since the success of *Porgy and Bess* the Guild had been seeking another play for which American music might be written. Theresa Helburn, with a great deal else on her mind, such as the Guild's string of failures, spoke rather casually to Richard Rodgers about turning the Lynn Riggs folk play, *Green Grow the Lilacs,* into a musical piece. Rodgers was only moderately interested, but he became excited about the notion when Oscar Hammerstein II gave his hearty approval, and they went to work. They completed the music, lyrics, and book for a play that bore the title of *Away We Go* and then they set about the casting as the Guild's directors went on a hunt for financial backing, something that they hadn't had to do since the Guild's very beginning. The Guild invested twenty-five thousand of the forty thousand dollars that it had in the bank in the new production and finally, after numerous turndowns, raised the funds necessary for the presentation of *Away We Go.* To some practical-minded showmen, such as Vinton Freedley, and to professional backers, such as Howard Cullman, the project seemed a bad risk. And for several reasons: there were no stars in the new show; the picture rights on the play hadn't been cleared; Richard Rodgers was working for the first time without Lorenz Hart; Oscar Hammerstein hadn't had a hit in ten years—and the Guild was inexperienced in the field of musical comedy. Anyway, *Away We Go* went to New Haven and seemed promising, and in Boston it looked better. It was there that the title was changed to *Oklahoma!* and on the evening of March 31, 1943, *Oklahoma!* struck Broadway with the impact of a hurricane. The musical folk-piece began selling out several nights after the opening and it continued selling out, in New York and elsewhere, for years. It was the biggest hit the Theater Guild had had in 165 productions in a quarter of a century. New York's harassed ticket brokers had to go all the way back to the original *Merry Widow* to mention an attraction for which there had been such an astonishing, and such a sustained, public demand.

Oklahoma!, the most successful musical play in the history of the theater in America—the half-block-long line stretching away from the box office became a familiar sight in 44th Street for many months—was the number one objective for all passing-through G.I.s and all out-of-town civilians as the delirium of wartime spending reached its peak on the island of Manhattan. During the wild splurge nearly every night was New Year's Eve in the Broadway area. Theaters, bars, and restaurants were jammed; so were snack counters and the supper clubs. There was a stampede upon the restaurants, and at 5:30 P.M. thousands were standing in slow-moving din-

276

nertime queues. Hotels sold out nightly; guests slept on cots in parlors and in ballrooms and in chairs in the lobbies. Mid-town Manhattan presented the strange spectacle of playgoers swarming to the stage plays in shirtsleeves. Coatless war workers, without ties, who had seen but few plays in their lives—or perhaps none at all—stepped up to the ticket windows with wads of currency. House treasurers became accustomed to changing fifty-dollar bills, and without their patrons knowing, or caring, anything about the play they were paying to see. However, if there were girls and music in the show, all the better. The tired welder liked to see pretty faces along with his entertainment.

An acute theater shortage, along with a housing shortage, developed. During the thirties the producers became accustomed to being quite particular as to the theaters into which they would put their plays, but it was now the producer who was sitting on the theater operator's doorstep, clamoring for the privilege of exhibiting his wares. The booking jam of 1941–1945 became such that plays were frequently put into rehearsal and given out-of-town presentation with no contracts signed, or promises given, for eventual Broadway shelter.

"But," cried Louis Lotito, astute Broadway showman who had started as an usher, "I still don't know of an instance of any big hit being unable to find a house. There's a theater shortage because theater-building stopped back in the mid-twenties, and a lot of the old houses have disappeared. The thirty-four theaters now used by the legitimate stage in New York are worth today about twenty-seven million dollars. There won't be any more theaters erected until things ease up in the building line."

G.I.s stationed in the New York area, and those who were passing through, got around to Broadway playgoing in odd moments when they weren't frequenting the bars and swarming into the below-the-sidewalks bedlam that was the American Theater Wing's Stage Door Canteen, and they took particular relish in the adventures of one Sergeant Bill Page, who spent a happy week end in the attractive apartment of a pretty young actress. Sergeant Page, envied by untold thousands of his brothers-at-arms, turned up in the delightful war-period comedy that the Britain-born John Van Druten, now an American citizen and a ranch owner, called *The Voice of the Turtle*. Van Druten wrote the comedy at his A.J.C. ranch at Thermal, California.

"When I sat down to write," he told me some months later, "all I had in mind was the main plot line and I knew that at the end of the first act Sally and Bill would go to bed in separate beds and rooms, at the end of Act Two they would go to bed together in the double bed in the bedroom—and I hoped there would be a third act." He sent the play to Alfred de Liagre, Jr., who telephoned his delighted acceptance two hours after reading it.

Van Druten began thinking of Margaret Sullavan for Sally before he had finished the first scene, and he and De Liagre were in complete agreement about her. So they sent her the script. She wired her reply. Yes, yes—she'd love playing Sally, but hadn't they thought of Dorothy McGuire?

"She is free," Miss Sullavan magnanimously added, "and she is really twenty-two."

Several male movie stars turned down the role of Bill Page; they considered the part of Sally just too good. And one of them declined with considerable vehemence. He had been shocked by the play and for months thereafter he deluged the author and the producer with religious literature.

On the afternoon of the day of the New York opening—early December, 1943—Margaret Sullavan and Van Druten took a stroll along Fifth Avenue and she was importunate as she tugged at his arm: "Now, John, even if we're a flop you will make Delly keep the play running over Christmas, won't you? I've promised my children that they can come East and spend Christmas in New York!"

The Voice of the Turtle was in New York at Christmas-time, all right. As played by Miss Sullavan, Elliott Nugent, and Audrey Christie, it became one of the phenomenal plays of the decade. And it failed in London, with Miss Sullavan in the role of Sally, quite as definitely as it succeeded in New York. For all these years, since the days of Pinero, the London theater and the New York theater have been taking seeming delight in reversing each other.

John Van Druten didn't stop with one wartime hit. He went on to give the theater the human and vastly entertaining comedy, *I Remember Mama*, based on Kathryn Forbes's "Mama's Bank Account," submitting it during the 1944–1945 season, which brought the theater surging back with a vitality that was reminiscent of the twenties. Paul Osborn contributed a vibrant drama and a fine war play in *A Bell for Adano*, dramatized from John Hersey's novel of the tribulations and the triumphs of Major Joppolo, representing the Allied Military Government of Occupied Territory in the Sicilian town of Adano. John Patrick, who had been serving with the American Field Service, attached to the British Army, put what he had seen and knew, plus some good characters and sound craftsmanship, into his writing of *The Hasty Heart*, with its locale the convalescent ward of a British general hospital on the Assam-Burma front. John P. Marquand and George S. Kaufman collaborated in the writing of an urbane and expert comedy of manners from Marquand's novel of a Bostonian, *The Late George Apley*. Philip Yordan, new to the trade of playwriting, put vigor and humor into *Anna Lucasta*, superbly played by an all-Negro cast. George Kelly, silent for some seasons, returned to the theater with a caustic study of a preposterous woman in *The Deep Mrs. Sykes*. Two new dramatists, Mary Chase and Tennessee Williams, came along with plays that enriched the native theater. Mrs. Chase's play, *Harvey*, introduced a tall and invisible white rabbit to theatergoing America. Williams's play, *The Glass Menagerie*, presented its pitiful and unforgettable story of crumbled grandeur in the delta country. And it gave to a great actress the finest part she had had in years. Her name was Laurette Taylor.

Mary Coyle Chase, the handsome, Irish-eyed, Denver-born author of *Harvey*, married to a highly respected Denver newspaperman, worked for two years on *Harvey* and wrote eighteen versions. Brock Pemberton patiently waited until he and Mrs. Chase agreed that she had the right version and he then began a search for the actor to play Elwood P. Dowd, the genial, kindly, friend-making lush who goes around with the rabbit. Numerous players declined the role and for such refusals Pemberton later expressed profound gratitude. He found his perfect Dowd in the red-headed, ex-vaudeville headliner, Frank Fay, who had been a master of timing in the two-a-day. *Harvey*, under the title of *The Pooka*, went to Boston for a brief tryout test and it had the gigantic rabbit in the cast until author and producer saw it walk across the stage at the dress rehearsal in Boston. The rabbit, which Mrs. Chase had always wanted, came out that night and was never mentioned again.

Harvey opened in New York to the vast approval of the press—the late and independent-minded Wilella Waldorf entered a sharp dissent—and Mrs. Chase returned to Colorado, bought herself some big, floppy hats, and told her husband and their three boys that the Chases would soon be moving into a beautiful house in Denver's country-club district. And Brock Pemberton, taking all this new success without hysteria, and reporting to his office by ten o'clock every morning and to his theater every night, was deciding to make something of a career of *Harvey*. His friends then had no way of knowing that the alarming day would come when he would get the urge, at the age of sixty, to become an actor, and that he would go all the way to southwestern Virginia, for a week's wage of $46, to play Elwood P. Dowd. When a Kansan gets stage-struck it's something really serious.

Tennessee Williams is an extraordinary young man for many reasons; for one, specifically, he is a writer who actually enjoys putting his thoughts and his words on paper. He went along with his writing before he came in upon the Broadway scene, and as he worked as a waiter, an usher, a night elevator operator, a feather-picker on a pigeon ranch, and as a late-shift employee of a Greenwich Village night club, hired to entertain the stay-ups with recitations of poetry.

Williams, born in Mississippi as Thomas Lanier Williams, the son of a traveling shoe salesman, went to the University of Missouri for three years and later received his B.A. at the State University of Iowa. He knew nothing at all of stage people or behind-the-scenes life when his first play for the professional theater, *Battle of Angels*, was given a Boston tryout by the Theater Guild, with Miriam Hopkins in its leading role. The quick-minded Miss Hopkins, who was often crushingly patronizing in telling Williams that he had written a "nice little play," awed and bewildered the. young dramatist; he was fascinated by her but he was never sure of himself in her presence, and he was frequently baffled by her swiftly changing moods. But Miss Hopkins sensed an enormous poetic talent in Williams; she insisted that the day would come when he would write a fine play, and the disastrous flop of *Battle of Angels* in Boston did not swerve her from this belief.

Williams returned to New Orleans, broke and discouraged, but he was brought back to New York by Audrey Wood, an alert agent, who believed in him completely and sold him to Hollywood for a writing job at $250 per week. The picture people didn't take to Williams and his ideas; he didn't like them at all. He was given a great deal of time to use as he pleased and he used it in writing *The Glass Menagerie*, the tender and tormentingly beautiful play of the frustrated Amanda, living in her many-suitored, white-columned past; of her crippled and pathetic daughter, who cherished a collection of glass animals, and her rebellious and imaginative son, who loathed his job at the warehouse and was planning to walk out on mother and sister and their dingy tenement.

When the manuscript of *The Glass Menagerie* was handed to Eddie Dowling by Mrs. Dowling (Ray Dooley)—she liked it tremendously—he read it with gradually increasing wonder and delight. He was a man who was seldom oversupplied with ready cash—he was a homeowner and a churchgoer and a taxpayer and a day-to-day commuter—and this new play, as he read it a second time, didn't seem to offer great commercial possibilities, but he realized it was one he couldn't resist doing, and at once. He would, of course, play Tom, the son, a poet working in a warehouse. And the actress for the mother? Jane Cowl, perhaps. She could do it, Dowling decided, but he again listened to George Jean Nathan and the role was offered to Laurette Taylor. Miss Taylor, who had lived a strange, confused, and futile life for most of the years since the passing of her husband, Hartley Manners, came through with the finest performance of her career.

Eddie Dowling and Margo Jones did the staging of *The Glass Menagerie*, and it was apparent just at this time that a great surge of new directorial talent was coming in upon the theater. John Van Druten brought the perceptive touch of a true artist to the staging of *The Voice of the Turtle* and *I Remember Mama,* showmanship in direction and in production that contributed immeasurably to the success of both of these plays. Bretaigne Windust, Princeton '29, distinguished himself with *Life With Father* and *Arsenic and Old Lace,* and another Princeton man, Joshua Logan, big, hearty, and Southern-born, brought the sensitivity of a Winchell Smith to the direction of Paul Osborn's affecting fantasy, *On Borrowed Time.* George S. Kaufman, now an experienced hand in the field, put all of his magic into the presentation of *The Late George Apley,* and George Kelly's directorial contributions to his own *The Deep Mrs. Sykes* were undoubtedly more valuable than the services he rendered as a playwright.

There were two other stalwart directors of the period, Garson Kanin and Elia Kazan. Garson Kanin came on from the Hollywood film factories to do a remarkable job in putting on his own famous comedy, *Born Yesterday,* which brought a fabulous thug, a junk king, and his smartened-up blonde, to the native stage. And Elia Kazan, born in Turkey of Greek parentage, started as an actor and, as he turned to direction, fairly overwhelmed Broadway with his brilliance. The slim, lithe, swarthy Kazan, a man with a longish face and a mop of black hair, staged a swarm of hits—*The Skin of*

Our Teeth (he survived conflict with Tallulah Bankhead without blood-shed), *One Touch of Venus, Harriet,* and *Jacobowsky and the Colonel,* and had become, as of the moment, the most in-demand director in the business.

As the theater was becoming more and more director-conscious, George Kelly, who had been staging his own works since his vaudeville days, commented thus: "The crying need of the theater is direction. It's unfortunate that more authors don't interest themselves in it. When an author directs he can give the inflections that are correct; he can at least get what he wrote into the playing. There's a definite humility about good actors; they're good workmen. Actors are divine optimists and I admire their courage. When a director knows his business he can get actors to listen to him, and to go along with him. . . . Me? I've knocked around this business since 1913, when I was on the road with *The Common Law.* I always write at the typewriter. I waste tons of paper and sometimes I write one page twenty times, but when a page is finished it's finished. I don't know anything about this second-draft business. I don't work fast and I may take six months or a year to write a play, but I never go over it."

Al Jolson, as a one-man theater, roamed the world during the war years as an entertainer for the G.I.s, singing before hundreds of thousands under the auspices of USO–Camp Shows. Maurice Evans and Judith Anderson gave Shakespeare to extraordinarily appreciative soldier-audiences with presentation of a wieldy, streamlined *Hamlet* in Hawaii. Gertrude Lawrence and Bob Hope and Fredric March and Ray Bolger brought their magic to the far places, and units of the USO were gratefully applauded in Dakar and Cristobal and Natal, in Sardinia and Naples and Algiers, in Teheran and Cairo, in Nome and Anchorage and in the Aleutians and in the distant islands of the Pacific. And Katharine Cornell put on khaki and made an exciting Continental tour in *The Barretts of Wimpole Street,* co-starred with Brian Aherne, playing Elizabeth Barrett before thousands of young, eager, muddy, just-out-of-combat Americans who had been movie-reared back in the States, and to whom a stage play, with a great star as its heroine, was an experience that left a deep and lasting impression.

And in the Broadway scene, there was no letup in the service of the Stage Door Canteen; there was hardly a "name" player of the stage or screen who did not appear at one time or another—many famous players appeared a dozen times—in the down-one-flight-and-turn-to-the-right basement in New York's 44th Street. Many a country boy in uniform, in New York for the first time in his life, looked up from his pie and coffee to find himself staring into the big and beautiful eyes of Jane Cowl, who had served him.

The theater's professionals, as the war went along, also applied themselves, in odd moments, to their careers. Bobby Clark, of the painted-on eyeglasses, the bouncing cane, and the acrobatic cigar, who has been making the nation's playgoers laugh ever since he came forth in *Mrs. Jarley's Waxworks* at the Eagles' Hall in Springfield, Ohio, in 1902 (he was once stranded in Thomasville, Georgia, with Kalbfield's Greater California Minstrels and ate sugar cane and oranges for two days) had a hilarious time as a numbers-racketeer south of the border in the big musical show, *Mexican Hayride.* Ruth Gordon turned playwright with a glib and witty comedy, *Over Twenty-One,* all about the efforts of a newspaper editor, well over thirty and quite conscious that he was beyond the age of absorption, to win a commission at an officers' training school. Burl Ives, the folk-song specialist, delighted playgoers with his chanting of "Blue Tail Fly," "Foggy, Foggy Dew," and "Big Rock Candy Mountain" in an indifferent and badly organized show called *Sing Out Sweet Land.* Margaret Webster and Cheryl Crawford contributed a creditable production of Shakespeare's long-neglected *The Tempest,* with Arnold Moss revealing himself as an actor who knew how to read Prospero's verse. Paul Robeson came along with a magnetic and thundering performance as Othello, brilliantly supported by José Ferrer as Iago and Uta Hagen as Desdemona. And the American musical play, with *Oklahoma!* and *Carousel* showing the way, suddenly became fresh and vital and alive.

Oklahoma!, which was known as Helburn's Folly during those frantic days when Miss Helburn and others of the Guild were being briskly turned down by many wealthy and supposedly theater-wise New Yorkers, brought about something of a renaissance in the song-and-dance stage. The popularization of the ballet was achieved by *Oklahoma!* and from then on, with Agnes de Mille leading the parade, with such choreographers as Jerome Robbins and Michael Kidd resolutely contributing, the theater became fairly ballet-mad. The ballet dancer, who had been given to periods of protracted idleness and to other periods of aimless wandering about the Continent, became a somebody with the arrival of *Oklahoma!.* It gave her a new stability and a new realm of activity, the Broadway musical stage, and it put money in her pocketbook.

The new-style song-and-dance productions represented an extraordinarily successful blending of the arts of the composer, the lyricist, the dance director, and the scenic designer; dancing began to grow naturally out of plot and action, and to carry the story along. Expert integration was apparent in the distinguished *Carousel* and in such boldly imaginative pieces as the swift-moving *On the Town*, which showed the frenzy and the tension and the jostle of New York City by means of the dance; the beguiling *Finian's Rainbow*, which introduced us to the leprechaun; the whirling and beautiful *Brigadoon*, and on a somewhat lesser plane, the ambitious *Allegro*, which again put Rodgers & Hammerstein into partnership with the Theater Guild.

Finian's Rainbow brought to the stage poetic settings from Jo Mielziner, exciting individual and ensemble dancing, and a mood of whimsicality and complete unreality as it told its story of Finian McLonergan's theft of a crock of gold from the leprechauns in Ireland and the burying of it in the soil of the fabulous state of Missitucky. *Brigadoon*, with exquisite settings from Oliver Smith and colorful costumes from David Ffolkes and a Barrie-like book by Alan Jay Lerner that told of a Scottish village that came to life once in every hundred years, provided an evening in the theater of rare enchantment. And in *Brigadoon*, Agnes de Mille, infusing the story with her dance patterns, achieved the most magical effects brought forth in any of her productions.

The musical stage of the mid-forties turned Elmer Rice's harsh and multitudinous play, *Street Scene*, into a folk opera, and done without dancing chorus, without a change of scene, without comedy, and to the mood-sustaining and frequently exalted music of Kurt Weill. An impressive production, but I wondered, along with Richard Watts, Jr., if *Street Scene* needed all the trimmings. It was better straight. An earlier, but also a post-*Oklahoma!* production, was the tremendously successful *Carmen Jones*, with Oscar Hammerstein writing memorable lyrics, and with the Bizet score modernized and transplanted. Hammerstein casually told his ideas to Billy Rose in a bar one evening, Rose became fascinated, and they went to work. The dapper and articulate Rose, who had made a million on his World's Fair Aquacade, had the greatest night of his life when *Carmen Jones*, rousingly sung by an all-Negro cast, reached New York.

It was during this period of the resurgence and the revivification of the American musical stage that a song-writing genius out of the theater's yesterdays, whose fame went all the way back to Chatham Square, Chinatown, and to the delirium of "Alexander's Ragtime Band" and the madness of "Everybody's Doin' It," came upon the scene with *Annie Get Your Gun*, a song-and-dance play, much of it ingratiatingly old-fashioned, and all of it a tribute to the enduring qualities of the music of the Russian refugee who came into the world as Izzy Baline. Richard Watts, Jr., observed in the "New York Post":

There is a quality in Berlin's music that sets it over and beyond its purely artistic merits. It is a kind of warmheartedness, a sort of human sympathy and unaffected honesty of emotion, which stems from the essential spirit of the man who writes it.

Stage fashions, as has been recorded, run in cycles. There was a time when the theater was surfeited with crook plays and, in another period, with bedroom farces. Romanticism had its day; so did the sociological play, the sex-problem play, the historical play. And the song-and-dance play, in ever-varying form, remains one of the drama's staples. The years of World War II and the immediate postwar period brought the great revival craze into the American theater. Numerous pieces out of the Broadway of long ago, brought back to the stage with new trimmings, found the ticket-buying public tremendously responsive. Some of the old ones, however—such as *The Front Page* and *Craig's Wife* and *Yellow Jack* and *The Chocolate Soldier*—were pretty feeble and were quickly taken off the boards. The Montgomery & Stone hit of 1906, *The Red Mill*, was a joyous success in its mid-forties incarnation, and Bernard Shaw's *Pygmalion*, in a glossy Theater Incorporated production, retained its charm, its sparkle, its paradoxes, its Shavian sense and nonsense. Oscar Wilde's *Lady Windermere's Fan*, all about the notorious Mrs. Erlynne and the carelessness of the Lady Windermere in leaving her fan lying about, was plotty, old-fashioned—and completely delightful, a period piece stylishly played, elaborately costumed, and wrapped in Cecil Beaton's bright, candy-box designs. Wilde's *The Importance of Being Earnest* was also brought buoyantly to life in the diverting, stylized, tongue-in-cheek playing of John Gielgud and his excellent company from London. Wilde's comedy, with all its absurdities and inanities, its deceptions and pretensions, its manners and

285

ill-manners, has remained, for professionals and amateurs alike, one of the enduring plays of the past half century.

Rostand's rueful *Cyrano de Bergerac* found vast prosperity when given a revival by José Ferrer and his associates. The old musical comedy, *Sweethearts,* with its Victor Herbert score, and with the madcap Bobby Clark galloping about the stage, was, to me, one of the period's minor blessings, but it received hearty public support. Irish folk comedy, as represented by J. M. Synge's *Playboy of the Western World,* one of the theater's near classics, retained all of its satiric humor and its quiet magic, and it became apparent, with the return of the playboy and his high tales of the slaughter of his father with a blow from a spade, that audiences have become calmer with the passing years. It was greeted with hisses and tin horns when first done in Dublin, and a New York audience in 1911 expressed violent disapproval with a barrage of missiles, but no eggs or vegetables were thrown by the quietly chuckling playgoers of 1946. Other pieces that were revived during the nostalgia-conscious forties to the considerable delight of a new generation were *Burlesque*—the sentimental comedy of backstage life, in which Bert Lahr, a graduate of the old Burlesque Wheel, distinguished himself with a genuinely moving performance as the inebriated hoofer—and the magnificent *Show Boat.* Notwithstanding the beguilements of *Oklahoma!,* which displaced the Kern-Hammerstein-Ferber musical play in the opinion of many as the finest song-and-dance piece of the native theater, my enthusiasm for *Show Boat* remains undiminished. In all of my years as a playgoer, and it's a total that is beginning to seem mildly startling—from *Mrs. Wiggs of the Cabbage Patch* to *Life With Father,* from *McFadden's Flats* to *Harvey*—I have never been so aware of complete contentment in a theater, of an audience settling back blissfully to enjoy itself to the fullest, as in those moments when Magnolia, the lovely heroine of the Cotton Blossom, begins to sing "Make Believe" or "Why Do I Love You?" Or when the tormented and melancholy Julie, in whose veins there is Negro blood, begins chanting that "fish gotta swim and birds gotta fly," and that she "can't help lovin' dat man. . . ."

Any consideration of the revivals that followed World War II brings to attention, eventually and inevitably, the catastrophic failure of the American Repertory Theater, which had $350,000 and long-range ambitions, and which was doomed after its first blundering Shakespearean production.

Shakespeare, in productions since the turn of the century, has rewarded and has eluded players of the native stage. Shakespearean experimentation has seldom brought on indecisive results; productions have generally succeeded wholeheartedly or they have failed utterly. Annie Russell was a joy as Puck and a disappointment as Beatrice. William Faversham was a colorless Romeo and a rousing Antony in his own production of *Julius Caesar*. Julia Marlowe was a delightul Beatrice and a monotonous Cleopatra. Walter Hampden was a listless Macbeth and an eloquent Wolsey. John Drew was a completely unsatisfactory Benedict. Nat Goodwin failed as Bottom, but Robert Mantell gave a memorable performance in *King John*. The American Repertory Theater made its first mistake in selecting Shakespeare's *Henry VIII*, a ponderous drama, as its first production, and it never recovered from its unimpressive start. The public stayed away from its productions of *What Every Woman Knows* and *John Gabriel Borkman* with a disheartening unanimity, and began responding when *Alice in Wonderland* was delightfully revived. But that came too late. By that time the A.R.T.'s excitement had subsided, its mission was less urgent, its spirit was gone, its money was spent.

Just why did the American Repertory Theater fail? I submit these causes: first, the wrong playhouse; second, the wrong players; third, the wrong plays. And there is also the incontestable fact that classical repertoire has never paid off in the American theater of this century.

CHAPTER XVIII

Consider the Critics

EUGENE O'NEILL, after a twelve-year absence, returned to the theater in October of 1946 with a distinguished play, a four-hour drama of passion, excitement, and violence that had the title of *The Iceman Cometh*. It was a play that was too verbose, too slow in starting, too digressive once it was started, but it was powerful theater, packed with racy and snarling speech, and with characters of enormous vitality. *The Iceman Cometh* was one of the few plays of genuine stature brought to the theater of the century's fourth decade.

O'Neill's locale for *The Iceman Cometh* was a mean, last-resort bar on the lower West Side of New York's Manhattan Island in the year of 1912, a sanctuary for a weird collection of soaks, has-beens, tarts, and half-dead bums—a profane and pipe-dreaming lot given to sustained drunkenness and to frequent self-pity. There, in Harry Hope's foul but hospitable lair, these members of a pathetic family circle sleep off their jags, enjoy their deliriums, and prolong their escape from reality. Harry Hope, the half-soused proprietor and ex-Tammanyite, hasn't been out in the street in twenty years. The habitués of his rooming house and graveyard of a bar are men like himself, and they are his friends. They include Larry, the sardonic philosopher; Ed, the erstwhile circus con-man; Pat McGloin, former police lieutenant, who was kicked off the force, and Willie Oban, who studied law at Harvard. And there is the youth named Parritt, whose mother is in jail in the West, and there are the frowsy streetwalkers, Pearl and Margie and Cora.

They're all there, in Harry Hope's haven for the half-alive, there with their oaths and their cravings, their mumblings and mutterings and boozy meditations, as Hickey, the fast-talking hardware salesman and big spender, arrives. But Hickey is not the good fellow and the hearty drinker that they all knew and liked so well. He's off the stuff, he's selling a line of salvation. He cajoles them, angers them, frightens them, and bewilders them with his promise of peace and contentment. Hickey, who has brought the touch of death with him, goes after them one by one. And, under his proddings, they begin sobering up, deciding to face life. One by one, and with new resolves and false jauntiness, they turn in their room keys to go forth in quest of employment. And Harry Hope, dressed in a black suit, his Sunday best, and making a heroic effort, stumbles through the swinging doors to take that walk around his ward, something he's been promising himself for twenty years. But he's back quickly. Automobiles have come to New York's streets since he was last outside and he was almost struck by one of the blasted things.

They all come back. They slink back, one at a time, and they reach for the bottle, but the stuff no longer has a kick. They can't pass out. They sit around dejectedly, bewilderedly, and it is then that Hickey returns and goes into his confession. He murdered his wife as she slept and he has summoned the police, who are now standing by. Hickey has two converts to death, the boy Parritt and old Larry, but the others are given release as he is led away. The stuff in the bottle has a wallop again. They go back to it, and to their pipe dreams. And to which, O'Neill argues, all men are entitled, contending that anyone disrupting them is up to no good in the world.

O'Neill arrived with his diffuse but prodigious drama at a time when some of the theater's other high-powered dramatists were turning in awkward and haphazard plays. Robert E. Sherwood contributed a singularly unimpressive play in *The Rugged Path,* in which a liberal-minded newspaper editor, seeking a cause for living and a cause for dying, found heroic death in combat action in the Pacific after he had given up his job to join the Navy. It was a long-spun and roundabout drama that contained the thought of an intellectual playwright and the prose of a dramatist with a talent for self-expression, but it came through as a message and not a play. Moss Hart put some of his best writing into *Christopher Blake* but he ruined his play with sheer repetitiousness, and a swarm of actors and a lot of expensive scenery didn't help. It was a play of the divorce courts and there was one unforgettable scene, that in which a twelve-year-old boy has to choose between his parents. John Van Druten, who had come to be regarded as infallible since *The Voice of the Turtle* and *I Remember Mama*, lost the trick in his writing of love, sex, and infidelity in *The Mermaids Singing*, the story of a famous and middle-aged playwright, married and with two daughters, who was seeking a final illicit fling. Two acts were good enough but Van Druten had no third act; he knew it in New Haven and he was sharply told of it as his play was submitted to New York. George S. Kaufman came along, as co-author, with Nunnally Johnson and Arthur Schwartz, of a minor musical comedy, and Mary Chase, author of the incredible *Harvey*, served notice on embryonic dramatists that a successful playwright can also have a detonating flop. Her *The Next Half Hour*, a study of Irish superstitions and folklore, wasn't deserving of a production.

But all was not too dismal in the theater's postwar seasons of 1945–1946 and 1946–1947. Those happy collaborators, Howard Lindsay and Russel Crouse, gave the stage a knowing and expert comedy of the political scene in *State of the Union*. Elmer Rice, done with his problems and his preachments for the moment, turned out an engaging piece in *Dream Girl*, and Lillian Hellman again wrote fascinatingly of the rapacious Hubbards in *Another Part of the Forest*, showing them as they were twenty years prior to *The Little Foxes*, showing them as the wily Ben blackmailed the tyrannical father, a Civil War profiteer, and became head of the family. Miss Hellman put all of her adroitness into her drawing of her despicable clan— the fanatical father, the half-demented mother, the ruthless Ben, the weakling Oscar, the calculating Regina. She achieved a vigorous drama, bringing in elementals out of melodrama of long ago. A thoroughly creditable job of playwriting, *Another Part of the Forest*, but a lesser play than *The Little Foxes*.

And to this season of the outcasts of O'Neill, the home-destroying husband and wife of Moss Hart, the blackguards of Lillian Hellman, Maxwell Anderson contributed an exalted drama of Joan of Arc; Ingrid Bergman was tremulous and eloquent and tremendously moving as the Maid of Orleans, played through the years by actresses from Bernhardt to Cornell. And a new young playwright emerged in the tall, dark, rawboned Arthur Miller, who gave the theater *All My Sons*. Miller was thirty-two years old, New York–born, and graduated from the University of Michigan in 1938. He wrote a play called *The Man Who Had All the Luck* that brought forth engaging characters; one of them was a big, hulking boy who wanted to be

Important Dramatists, 1920–1950

1. Clifford Odets   2. Tennessee Williams   3. Maxwell Anderson   4. Paul Green   5. Elmer Rice
6. Lillian Hellman   7. Eugene O'Neill   8. Philip Barry   9. Marc Connelly   10. Robert E. Sherwood
11. George Kelly   12. Noel Coward   13. George S. Kaufman   14. William Saroyan   15. Moss Hart
16. John Van Druten

The White Rabbit Is Invisible

But his pal, Elwood P. Dowd (Frank Fay), is getting solicitous attention from Josephine Hull in Mary Chase's comedy-fantasy, *Harvey*, one of the ten biggest hits of the twentieth century (New York Sun)

America's Most Popular Musical Play

Alfred Drake and Joan Roberts in the surrey with the fringe on top in a scene from *Oklahoma!*, the all-time wonder of this century's song-and-dance theater—1943 until 1963, undoubtedly (Vandamm Studio).

a big-league pitcher but who lacked the brains to go along with his physique. But this first play lost itself in sermonizing and in weird goings on about a mink farm. It had one of those three- or four-performance runs which have been known to drive young and promising dramatists from the theater forever.

Not Miller, however. He sat down over a ten-year-old portable typewriter in a bare-walled room of his Brooklyn apartment and worked for a year on the drama that was to be known as *All My Sons*. He finished the play and sent it around. Herman Shumlin was interested, but not sufficiently to buy it. The Theater Guild liked the play and wanted to talk to Miller about it, but the new firm of Harold Clurman, Elia Kazan, and Walter Fried showed the sort of enthusiasm he had been hoping for—and these showmen got *All My Sons*. Arthur Miller revealed, in his writings of the tragedy of Joe Keller, the middle-class, family-loving airplane-parts manufacturer whose shipment of cracked cylinder heads sent twenty-one combat flyers to their death—Joe sought to excuse his criminal act on the grounds of practicality and a yearning to provide for his family at the expense of society in general—a sharp sense of dramatic situation, a feeling for character, and a talent for trenchant dialogue.

Something of a Jean-Paul Sartre vogue was created when this Parisian dramatist's *No Exit* was done in New York. An even better Sartre play was revealed in *The Respectful Prostitute,* a melodrama of racial strife and bigotry in a Southern town, and the restoration of George Bernard Shaw's *Man and Superman* served to remind playgoers that this comedy is one of the finest of the Shavian works and, when brightly played, is one of the most amusing plays written in the English language.

But the native dramatists dominated the American theatrical scene in the second half of the forties. George Kelly continued his merciless examination of feminine foibles in *The Fatal Weakness,* in which he presented the case of Ollie Espenshade who discovered, after twenty-seven years of married life, that her husband was having a fling—and enjoying it. Ruth Gordon followed her flippant and popular *Over Twenty-One* with a charming, entirely out-of-memory comedy, *Years Ago,* in which she wrote of her own girlhood at Wollaston, Massachusetts, and of her yearnings for a stage career. William Wister Haines, a new dramatist, turned in an excellent war play in *Command Decision,* an Air Force drama depicting the agony suffered by a fiery Brigadier General as he sent forth his combat fliers on precision-bombing missions that were taking a dreadful toll of human life.

Tennessee Williams, giving proof of his sturdiness and serving notice that he was not to be considered a one-play dramatist, startled the theater with the power of his rueful, violent, and fascinating play called *A Streetcar Named Desire,* which took its title from the name of a trolley car that careened and rattled through the New Orleans Vieux Carré, in which he had lived.

Williams wrote of the sisters Du Bois, Stella and Blanche, who had known better days. Stella, the younger and more practical, is married to a Polish boy—a crude, brawling, gentle, hard-working ex-G.I., who will smash up the flat at one minute and come to her, tearful and penitent, the next. Blanche is the dreamer. The family's Mississippi plantation is gone, but Blanche lives on in a world of unreality. She comes to visit Stella and her young brute of a husband in their squalid New Orleans rooms, and there is no longer any peace for the Kowalskis. Playwright Williams, in scenes of increasing tension, reveals that Blanche, for all of her airs and her scented baths and her paste jewels and pathetic finery, was fired from her job as a schoolteacher and driven out of Laurel as the town trollop. And when her new and inarticulate suitor, who had regarded her as the nicest girl he had ever known, comes to be revolted by the truth of her past, the author defends Blanche as a fallen creature of tragic circumstances, whose youthful marriage was disastrous and whose subsequent promiscuity was brought on by desperate loneliness.

A great deal of the sharpness that came through in the playing of *A Streetcar Named Desire,* described as a "savagely arresting tragedy" by Howard Barnes in the "Herald Tribune," is to be attributed to the driving direction of Elia Kazan, who insisted upon consulting Tennessee Williams on all details as rehearsals went along, thereby giving the dramatist new confidence and a feeling of being a necessary part of the proceedings. Stage directors of the theater's earlier years were seldom like that; they were generally scornful of the author, regarding him as a nuisance and not wanted about the place.

Kazan had distinguished himself with the direction of *A Streetcar Named Desire* when the dark and hearty extrovert, Joshua Logan, put on *Mister Roberts,* the uproarious comedy of the boredom of young Americans who found themselves in the crew of a Navy cargo ship on dreary wartime missions in the noncombat areas of the tropical Pacific. *Mister Roberts* was accepted by the critics as a play that provided an eloquent demonstration of what the theater could do when it really tried. It was John Chapman's decision in the "Daily News" that "everything which is wonderful and happy about the theater—good writing, skilled acting, masterful staging"—came together in *Mister Roberts,* and the equally jubilant Robert Garland, writing in the "New York Journal-American," told his readers that "with the radio growing more and more afraid of its own voice and the movies growing more and more afraid of their own shadows, it's wonderful to realize that the theater can still stand up and speak out like a man. . . . *Mister Roberts* puts those upstarts, the radio and the movies, in their obviously inferior places."

Further evidence of the magnificence that can be achieved by the theater when it really tries came with the submission, early in 1949, of Arthur Miller's merciless and withering drama, *Death of a Salesman.* Here is the tragedy of a weary drummer and of his relationship with his two sons—a play that is devastating in its impact, numbing in its sheer power, crowded with bits and pieces of family life, so stark and so true in its depiction of the American scene, so full of pathos and vehemence and tenderness and pitilessness, that only a playgoer of vast insensitivity can sit through a performance of it without being profoundly moved.

It's from such men as Joshua Logan, Tennessee Williams, Arthur Miller, and Elia Kazan and, of course, Richard Rodgers and Oscar Hammerstein II, that the theater is asking, and expecting, a great deal during years to come.

This chronicle, in following the fascinating course of the theater through half a century, has considered the activities of playwrights, producers, actors, actresses, directors, scenic designers, composers, and hoofers. There is now a pause for some attention to the dramatic critics, who have a way of giving a show of their own, and it's frequently a good one. The personnel of the critical fraternity changes from decade to decade, but it's a well-established fact that most dramatic critics live long, and that once a man is established in a New York reviewing job it is not easy to dislodge him. Some critics, and good ones, have ceased functioning only because their newspapers ceased to exist.

A dramatic critic is a man who goes to the theater on free seats, at the invitation of the management, to review, to analyze, to report upon, to particularize, and to give his own personal reactions to the play that is enacted upon the stage. But the critic, for all his power—and it's a power that is frequently exaggerated—has never been immune from attack. Throughout the half century to which I have been devoting these pages critic-baiting has remained a lively metropolitan pastime. William A. Brady snarled when the gentlemen of the aisle seats blasted a play of his called *The New South*. A. H. Woods, stung by the reviews of *The Green Hat* and *The Shanghai Gesture*, issued a challenge to the press, telling his detractors to pick a play and that he would produce it and that if it became a success he would build them a clubhouse. Edgar Selwyn lost all his suavity, plus his sense of humor, as he talked back to the critics; the Shuberts went to court; Arthur Hopkins charged the press with incompetence; Elmer Rice threatened to retire from playwriting, and Maxwell Anderson, defending the weakest play of his entire career (*Truckline Café*), consigned the entire clan to the Jukes-family category. Such controversy has always served to enliven the theatrical scene, and a critic is a man who must take it as well as give it.

Dramatic critics have always seemed more illustrious when considered in retrospect—the bestowal of respect and recognition is generally withheld until a critic is dead or is in unoffending retirement—and there has never been a reviewing coterie of any period that has not been accused of inefficiency and brazen stupidity. William Winter, Alan Dale, and Louis V. De Foe were covering the plays in New York just after the century turned, and they were often adjudged as malicious and inhuman men who held an abomination for the theater. A decade later the critics included Adolph Klauber, Lawrence Reamer, Charles Darnton, Rennold Wolf, and Burns Mantle; they were not spared charges of viciousness and imbecility. The formidable critical fraternity of the twenties—Hammond, Woollcott, Broun, Atkinson, Benchley, Gabriel, Brown, and Anderson and the like —drew the return fire of infuriated playwrights and managers, and still later, when such men as Watts, Krutch, Winchell, Garland, Gibbs, and Arthur Pollock were reporting at the first nights, they all came to realize that a wounded producer had all the savagery of a cornered animal.

Some of the foregoing commentators on the drama have now become legendary figures. There is always that tendency toward canonization of a critic who is no longer on combat duty, and I readily concede that the theater for the first four decades of the century knew some brilliant practitioners in the field of dramatic criticism. But I also contend that there are members of the New York Critics' Circle, as of the season of 1949–1950, whose lucidity is comparable to that of the most discerning reviewers of other years; that they're just as sagacious and just as theater-loving, and that an Atkinson-Watts-Chapman-Barnes-Garland-Coleman-Hawkins-Kronenberger verdict on a play is likely to be as sound, quite as skillfully worded, and probably a great deal more to the point, than the critiques of the giants of the theater's bygone seasons.

Take a backward glance for a moment. The aisle seats at the New York first nights over the fifty-year period have been graced by some able and picturesque men. William Winter, for whom Belasco could do no wrong, had a profound knowledge of the theater, a vast understanding of the classic drama. He was serious, verbose, and scholarly, and often given to indignation and vituperation. Edward A. Dithmar, who reviewed the plays for "The New York Times," was a student of the theater with an impressive literary background. Alan Dale—born Alfred J. Cohen in Birmingham, England—had flippancy, a smart-alecky quality, and showmanship of a sort. James Gibbons Huneker, the "Sun's" critic, was equally facile in writing of music, painting, sculpture, dancing, or literature. J. Ranken Towse, once a spear-carrier on the London stage, liked to recall performances of the grand-style actors, Booth and McCullough and Salvini, and he believed in using one thousand words when one hundred would have done as well. He had remarkable endurance, as fifty years of first nights will attest. Louis V. De Foe, the "Morning World's" authority on the drama, was an intelligent reviewer and a man of impressive bearing; he would have been engaged for the role of a Cabinet Minister by a type-casting director. James A. Metcalfe, with the old "Life" for years, was never an important critic. Charles Darnton was a great big fat man who enjoyed himself when seeing the musical plays. Lawrence Reamer wrote in a discursive and laborious style—a cultured man with a great deal of charm, who liked music better than he did the theater.

The "Morning Telegraph's" representative at the first nights for some years was Rennold Wolf, raconteur and after-dinner speaker; in his reviewing he was cynical, humorous, and frequently bitter. Acton Davies was blond, chubby, and readable in his pieces for the "Evening Sun," and he was of a heroism not always associated with men of his calling. He quit the Broadway scene at the time of the Spanish-American War to become a war correspondent, and there came the afternoon when a man on his ship off the coast of Cuba fell overboard. Davies quickly tore off his shoes and leaped into the sea and saved him.

Burns Mantle, who gave distinguished year-to-year service to the theater with his "Best Plays" series, was a steadying critic, fair-minded and unsensational, and always aware of his responsibility to his readers. Louis Sherwin did some excellent reviewing and writing for the old "New York Globe," one of the papers extinguished by Frank A. Munsey. Stark Young, who served the "Times" for a brief period, was a novelist, an essayist, a teacher, and never a man for the exacting rigors of daily criticism, but he wrote charmingly, skillfully and with great seriousness. Clayton Hamilton was a student of stagecraft with a wide knowledge of the drama. Walter Prichard Eaton was a tremendously perceptive critic—intelligent, theater-wise, self-important, and never too readable. Bostonians took an understandable pride in the writings and services of H.T.P. (Henry Taylor Parker) of the "Transcript"—a cantankerous, windy, authoritative, and outspoken commentator on music as well as the drama.

Two men of enormous stamina, of mystifying indestructibility, who are working critics at the moment of this writing, are George Jean Nathan and Ashton Stevens. Nathan was, for many years, a revolutionizing force in the theater—a trend-changer, a champion of new dramatists, a spokesman for the theater in revolt which came along at the time of Eugene O'Neill's emergence. He performed a genuine service in his blastings against artificiality, in bringing about a liberation from hokum, in raising the standards of American playgoers. The Illinois sage, Ashton Stevens, is an alert, slender, California-born journalist in his middle seventies; he has put in fifty years of playgoing in San Francisco, New York, and Chicago, and it's his contention that a critic has no right to be dull, regardless of the type of play he is writing about. It was Stevens who made the observation many years ago that "dull people don't like Mrs. Fiske's acting."

Gilbert W. Gabriel is a commentator on the state of the drama who is capable of sharp judgments and vivid phrasing and has a definite creative talent of his own. He writes easily, often flippantly, and frequently achieves a sheer brilliance of prose. Joseph Wood Krutch is a learned and respected critic and a stimulating writer. Lewis Nichols, who has turned to the freelance field, rendered valiant service as drama critic of "The New York Times" during Brooks Atkinson's absence as a foreign wartime correspondent. Walter Winchell gave up play reviewing some years ago but he occasionally takes a whirl at first-nighting, and his endorsement of a play, whether he has seen it or not, is eagerly sought by the Broadway press representatives. He is quoted in the amusement advertisements with great frequency and it is a fact beyond any dispute that his approval of a play, via his column or his broadcasts, will send playgoers hurtling toward a box office, just as his championship of a book creates an instantaneous flurry in the bookstore. Winchell, commanding an enormous reading and listening public, is a national craze, an American obsession, just as the Turkey Trot was, and he has lasted longer. Many of those who are most scornful of his pronouncements, his revelations, and his prophecies are those who are most avid in the reading of his every printed word, and who couldn't be dragged from the radio when he is on the air. Therefore, when he breathlessly tells the world that a particular show is Broadway's newest sweetheart, his following accepts the recommendation as gospel—and the play receives a sudden surge of new business.

The men who hold the daily-reviewing jobs in the New York field as the fifth decade of the twentieth century is nearing an end range in age from the late thirties to the middle fifties. One of them, with a fondness for the sea, has sailed a 46-foot auxiliary schooner along the Maine coast. Another is a disciple of Thoreau. One has a passion for eighteenth-century literature, another is an expert cook and an ex-photographer. The critics of the metropolitan dailies and those of the theater-minded periodicals like their jobs and guard them jealously. They vary in writing ability and in keenness of critical judgment, and they are all occasionally intemperate in their praise as well as in their abuse, but over the course of a season the plays that these men have liked are generally the plays that are worth seeing.

There has been no critic in the New York scene since the drama flourished in downtown John Street who has surpassed Alexander Woollcott, a man of many faulty judgments and undisciplined emotionalism, in sheer readability; few engaged in dramatic criticism in my time have written with wit and skill beyond that of Wolcott Gibbs. One of the most discerning and outspoken of the new-school critics is Claudia Cassidy of the "Chicago Tribune." Robert Sensenderfer of the "Philadelphia Evening Bulletin" is a reviewer with an undiminishing passion for the stage, and the "Philadelphia Inquirer" has a critic of sharp and sound judgments in Edwin H. Schloss. Boston has a good man in Elliott Norton, and Baltimore has another in Donald Kirkley. William F. McDermott of Cleveland is an able and long-in-service commentator. New York's John Mason Brown is a man of enormous erudition, who combines graceful and tasteful writing with his book learning. John Chapman of the "Daily News" is an outspoken, self-styled drama reporter with a genuine crusading fervor. Richard Watts, Jr., of the "New York Post," writes engagingly, with ease, force, and clarity, and he is a critic with a consuming devotion to the theater, and one of extraordinarily perceptive judgments. Brooks Atkinson, the "Times's" moderator at the first nights, has scrupulous theater manners, and his readable and fluently phrased must-make-the-deadline reviews are followed by an enormous public. He is the most avidly read of all the present-day dramatic critics, and has more influence on theatergoers than any other reviewer in America. I've yet to meet Louis Kronenberger's superior in assaying the contents of a play, in presenting one's reasons for its merit or its insufficiency, which he always does in sharp and stimulating prose. Critic Robert Garland learned his theater from years of Baltimore playgoing, and he is one of its resolute champions; his reviews have raciness and vitality, and to him an evening not spent in seeing a play is an evening wasted.

Some critics are readable; others are given to slow-gaited and unexciting verbiage. Some are afflicted with psychoneurosis, and others are well-adjusted, calm gentlemen who are enjoying their lives and the work that has been assigned to them. Some have practiced their calling for three-quarters of a lifetime, but others have finished reviewing careers very quickly. There was the case of a "New York Herald Tribune" staff member of the mid-twenties who was sent to cover the Shubert operetta, *The Student Prince*. He had been told that if he made a good job of that review there would be many more assignments for him. He roasted *The Student Prince*. The Shuberts, very tough in those days, raised hell at the "Herald Tribune" office. Young Mr. S. was instantly retired from dramatic criticism.

I've known some critics who had no actual fondness for the theater; some who frequently softened their punches for personal reasons, but I've never come upon an instance of actual corruption. There are the legends, of course, that one celebrated reviewer of years ago was on a producer's payroll, and that the wife of another was forever having plays accepted by managers who never had the slightest thought of producing them. There are dramatic critics—some of them of the 1949–1950 contingent—who have come into theater-reporting via the City Room. There have been others who wrote about music and others about books before taking to covering the plays. And one, Heywood Broun, was a baseball writer. Consider the case of James E. Craig, who came to New York in the spring of 1921 to be City Editor of the "Evening Mail." It was as he held that all-demanding post that he made the observation to Pop Niles, the Managing Editor, that any damn fool who could write the English language had all the qualifications necessary to be a dramatic critic. Niles remembered Craig's words. When Burns Mantle resigned at the "Mail" to go to the "Daily News" Jim Craig was told to begin going to the plays. This was a day and time when Frank A. Munsey was buying up and killing off newspapers, and Craig's appetite was completely taken away at dinner one evening when C. P. Greneker, the Shuberts's formidable press representative, remarked that the "Mail" had been sold to Munsey during the afternoon.

"How does that leave you, Mr. Craig?" asked Greneker.

"I guess it leaves me out on a limb," said Craig.

"Well," said Greneker, "if they don't take care of you, come to me and we will."

That's one instance of humanity on the part of a supposedly insensible Broadway. There have been countless others. When Samuel Hoffenstein was fired from the "Evening Sun" because of his review of *Marie-Odile* Al Woods got him on the telephone.

"I'm offering you a job, Sam," he bellowed. "How much were they paying you?"

"Seventy-five dollars a week," lied Hoffenstein, boosting the figure by fifteen dollars.

"I won't give you that, sucker, but I will give you one hundred and fifty."

Hoffenstein went to work for Woods.

CHAPTER XIX

The Show Goes On

WHEN I first set foot upon the overpowering island of Manhattan in the late fall of 1919, young and terrified and just up from the City Room of the "Atlanta Journal," 42d Street was the most spectacular theatrical thoroughfare in the world. Maxfield Parrish's Old King Cole was his jolly self in the Knickerbocker bar, Caruso was occupying half a floor in that gaudy hotel, Murray's Roman Gardens was just down the street, the Hippodrome was around the corner, and a one-set play could be produced in New York for from five thousand to ten thousand dollars. There has been a vast change in the landmarks and in the personnel of America's theatrical capital in three decades, and strange things have been happening in the theater's economic division.

Costs of costume fabrics, and the costs of the building, painting, and hauling of scenery and the hire of stagehands have soared unbelievably—there was a sharp rise during the war years, this to be attributed to the shortage of wartime labor and the scarcity of materials—and there are literal-minded economic experts who often wonder why anybody is in the theatrical business at all. And yet, plays are still being written, plays are being bought, bonds are posted, directors and actors are engaged, bookings are made, rehearsals are held, and productions, in one way and another get to Broadway—for an immediate triumph or a quick collapse. The theater is in a hit-or-nothing era. Many a professional script reader will testify that there is now far more technical skill in the plays going from office to office than there was twenty years ago, but the producers have become extraordinarily cautious. They're looking for failure-proof products. If a play sent along by an agent with a plea for immediate reading does succeed in capturing a manager's interest, he is likely to speak to himself in this fashion: "Yes, there's fine stuff in this play. I like it. It's something I'd like to do. But it would cost a lot—and would anybody come to see it?" So the managers, in understandable wariness, remain inactive—and continue reading.

Now let me hastily assure you that this chapter is not to be a long and sustained wail—the note that I shall try to sound is one of unconquerable optimism—but the disturbing increase in the costs of play production within twenty years constitutes a phase of the theater that must be examined in these final pages. Francis Wilson, the sprightly comedian, once produced the farce *The Bachelor's Baby*, for a matinee performance in Baltimore for eighty-seven dollars. The Theater Guild, when it was going in grimly for experimentation and expressionism, put on *From Morn to Midnight* for two thousand dollars. William A. Brady did his revival of *What Every Woman Knows* for five thousand and *Street Scene* for eight thousand—or less. Lillian Hellman's *The Children's Hour* cost Herman Shumlin only eight thousand, and Jed Harris spent less in bringing in *The Green Bay Tree*. The Moss Hart–George S. Kaufman *You Can't Take It With You* came to Broadway with a total gross expenditure of sixteen thousand dollars, inclusive of a five-thousand-dollar loss for the two-week, out-of-town break-in, and Hart's *Christopher Blake*, produced less than ten years later, cost $183,000. The American Repertory Theater's *Alice in Wonderland* (presented with Rita Hassan), acclaimed by the press, played in one week to the fine gross of $21,250.49 and earned a profit on the week of $1.22, the week's expenses including the excessive charges of moving the production from one New York theater to another.

Go into the arithmetic of present-day musical productions and the figures will get you fairly dizzy; it's no wonder that the showmen who specialize in the song-and-dance field go around mumbling to themselves and shaking their heads. Vinton Freedley once put on *Hold Everything*, a big hit, for $63,000 and *Anything Goes* for a neat $61,000, inclusive of room-service charges at Boston's Ritz-Carlton for himself and Lindsay & Crouse. Either of those productions would cost $150,000 today. The Scottish musical play, *Brigadoon*, beautifully produced by Cheryl Crawford, reached its New York theater after an outlay of $167,000, and the Rodgers & Hammerstein *Allegro* cost considerably more. Some of the musical plays that failed utterly—such as *Mr. Strauss Goes to Boston*, *Polonaise*, and *The Duchess Misbehaves*—were in the $200,000–$300,000 category. All of which has caused such showmen as Freedley and Laurence

301

Schwab, producer of *Good News* and *Follow Thru,* enormous hits of another day, to forswear the musical comedy field.

"Never again," laments Schwab. "Never for me. There's no longer any money in the big musicals except for the authors, and no reason for doing one of them unless there's a dame involved, some girl a rich producer wants to bring out. Not for me—I'll take the palms of Miami."

And William A. Brady, dean of the big-time showmen, adds these words: "New people in the theater, not knowing the game, have put up the costs through sheer ignorance. . . . In the old days we didn't throw away stuff. We could make fine settings out of old scenery, but today the designers just won't do it. Theatrical storehouses are things of the past. Why, I once had one in Fort Lee, New Jersey, with scenery for fifty productions."

When the century turned New York City was making use of twenty-odd theaters for stage productions; the rush of building did not begin until around 1906. The new playhouses increased the total to forty, and this total worked up to fifty, to sixty, and to almost seventy; the shrinkage began during the depression, and the Broadway area will go into the century's second half with thirty-odd playhouses at the command of the living stage. A two-dollar bill was all that was needed for the best seat to a Broadway play in 1900. The $2.50 top for dramatic plays was established in 1919, and the prices continued rising until the box-office top for non-musical plays was $4, plus tax, and the musical productions got $6, plus tax. The box-office scales dropped after the panic of 1929, and began climbing again with the beginnning of World War II. Now they are right back at such levels that the theater is losing the business of millions of potential playgoers. And the people of the white-collar trade, as Brock Pemberton points out, who became accustomed to buying orchestra seats during the boom years, won't shift to the lower-priced upstairs seats; they just quit going to the plays.

The theater, in a half century, has undergone startling and undeterminable changes in trends, in conditions, in policies, in tastes, in customs. The chorus girl is no longer the plodding, unimaginative, and underpaid member of the line that she was in the era of *The Greenwich Village Follies* and *Rose-Marie.* She is now career-minded and she is decently paid. In 1919 Chorus Equity established a minimum of $30 weekly in New York and $35 on tour; the minimum has soared to $75 in New York and $80 on tour. The play producer of other years was a man who bought a play with his own money, worked with the author on the revision of the script, supervised the casting, and frequently attended to the direction. But the producer, under the conditions of the past fifteen years, has become, in many cases, merely a front man; a money-raiser, an organizer, a promoter, a salesman, who has his name on the billing but not a dollar of his own in the show.

Playhouses used to belong to individual managers; they are now owned and operated by showmen working in combination, and by banks, real-estate corporations, and motion-picture companies. The matinee idol is no more. The minstrel man is extinct, and it's a passing that is saddening. Elegance has vanished from the New York first nights; the grace of other years is missing, and the cry of "Author!" is seldom heard at the fall of the final curtain. The theater retains the services of players who have the leading-man and leading-woman status, but the nonexistence of comedians is a cause for tears. There have been no replacements for such master comics as James T. Powers, Frank Daniels, Eddie Foy, for Sam Bernard, Leon Errol, and W. C. Fields. The drawing-room comedy is now obsolete, and the romantic play, of the school of E. H. Sothern, Otis Skinner, Kyrle Bellew, and William Faversham, has been gone these many years. Audiences have toughened since those days when the staircase scene in *Sapho* was a sensation, since playgoers shuddered as Clyde Fitch's dope fiend in *The City* screamed his "you're a goddam liar" across the footlights. Audiences now like to be jolted, and relish the violence offered by such a play as *A Streetcar Named Desire*.

It is heartening that Shakespeare retains a remarkable vitality at the box office. A well-done *Hamlet* or *Othello* or *Macbeth* will still pack a playhouse. The postwar revival craze, brought about to a certain extent by the nonactivity of the living dramatists, brought on a sudden and widespread appreciation of the dead ones. A new-found public developed for the classics, with the theater presenting the strange spectacle of playgoers in a stampede to see the works of Sophocles, Bernard Shaw, Ibsen, and Wilde. There have been few plays of this generation that enthralled audiences as the Old Vic's *Oedipus* did, or that set them to cheering as they cheered for Judith Anderson in her playing of the wanton and hellish Medea of Euripides.

There is, in the theater of 1949–1950, that Hollywood situation. There has always been that Hollywood situation since the desertion of John

303

Barrymore in the early twenties gave it a certain seriousness. The majority of the leaders in the motion-picture industry are men without feeling for the theater, without knowledge of its glories through the years, without appreciation of it as a factor in the cultural development of a nation. Many of the movie-makers are actually contemptuous of the stage, and they have been unconscionable in their raidings of its talent, in their buccaneering and their plundering. They see little reason for the theater's existence save as a supply depot for the studios, and they are ever willing to avail themselves of its prize products, to buy up and buy out its best plays at fabulous prices, to pay fortunes for the employment of its ablest players and playwrights and directors. Hollywood disrupts promising stage careers as they are in the making. "Broadway," observed the late and astute William Harris, Jr., "has become merely a Poli stock tryout."

The bright young women of the stage who have yielded to the screen's inducements have become ruthless in the use that they make of the theater. The return of an interesting young actress to the field in which she got her start, the living theater, can no longer be accepted as a defiance of talking pictures, as a move to redeem herself and to go on with her life as she had originally planned it. The sudden reappearance of the glamour girl in the Broadway scene is now being taken for what it is: merely a ruse on her part to try for a one-play stage success and thereby give her prestige in the studios a greatly needed upswing. The disservice that the all-devouring Hollywood does the theater is by no means confined to the fact that it is continually robbing the stage of exciting young players and brainy young dramatists for periods ranging from six months to six years. There is the larger truth, certainly in the case of the playwright, that he suffers a deterioration in a land that seemed, in the beginning, all gold. He loses a vital something that gave him his importance before he rolled across the plains in *Super Chief* comfort, and when he returns to the theater, in all penitence, he is of no value.

The wailing about the state of the theater has gone on throughout the years. Nearly fifty years ago William Winter proclaimed that "the race of actors is slowly dying out" and that the theater had "fallen into the clutches of sordid, money-grabbing tradesmen, who have degraded it." Twenty years later the "Theater Magazine" solemnly reminded its readers that "our stage is in a parlous state" and that the "real estate speculators, the panderers, and the money changers must be driven from the dramatic temple." The theater then went on to enjoy the most prosperous and the most important decade in its entire history. The theater of 1949–1950 is in the grip of prohibitive costs and it is frantically in the need of the development of young playwrights and players—there are many who yearn for the return of that extraordinary training school, the old-time stock company—but it is also one of no governmental interference, one with an open-minded and steadily cooperative press, with a censorship that asserts itself in only occasional outbursts in the cautious city of Boston, and one that is likely to break forth into magnificence at any time with a *South Pacific* or a *Glass Menagerie*, or a transcendant Shakespearean production, such as the uncut *Hamlet* of Maurice Evans and Margaret Webster, or the *Macbeth* done by Evans and Judith Anderson.

For me, the theater is hypnotic and ever-present. It has been an obsession since my wide-eyed, gallery-seat years. A good play, to my notion, is always to be preferred to a great movie, or to an evening at the opera or the concert hall or the circus. My playgoing adventures must have begun around 1909. I never saw Booth or Barrett or Joseph Jefferson. I missed Nat Goodwin in *Nathan Hale* and Kate Claxton in *The Two Orphans* and I feel grossly cheated in not having gazed upon Maude Adams as she brought her enchantment to *The Little Minister*. But there have been many richly rewarding evenings—and matinees, of course, in early years —through four decades of relentless attendance in the playhouses. Those who relished John McCullough in *Virginius* and Mary Anderson in *The Hunchback* and Fanny Davenport in *Old Heads and Young Hearts* were denied Louis Wolheim as the haggard Captain Flagg in *What Price Glory*, Jeanne Eagels as the tortured Sadie Thompson in *Rain*, Joyce Redman as the reeling Doll Tearsheet in *Henry IV*, and Lionel Barrymore as the aroused and suddenly eloquent Milt Shanks in *The Copperhead*—performances that I cherish.

And I shall never forget the magic of Laurette Taylor in *The Glass Menagerie*, the supreme art of Josephine Hull in *Arsenic and Old Lace*, the croakings of Dudley Digges in *The Iceman Cometh*, the drawling and the moaning of the burnt-cork partnership of Moran & Mack in *The Greenwich Village Follies*, the sack-sipping of Ralph Richardson as Sir John Falstaff, the wise, witty, and disreputable old knight in *Henry IV*, and the tremulousness of Irene Timmons, a stock actress out of the long ago, as the lovely heroine of Israel Zangwill's sentimental comedy, *Merely Mary Ann.* The life span of the true theater-lover should be at least a century and a half.

It is my feeling that a genuine cooperation from all sides is needed in the theater's fight against paralyzing production costs, and that the unions will have to take the gamble, along with everybody else. If a play earns a large profit all the money necessary to meet union demands will be available; if it does not it will be up to them to go along on what the production can afford; their all-or-nothing policy is ruinous to the theater and to themselves. One quite rational producer, in commenting recently upon the frightening expenditures necessary to get a play on the stage, made the observation that the theater is not dying; it is merely committing suicide. Another, deploring the scarcity of good plays and new playwrights, decided that "the theater is a business with all the customers in the world —and nothing on the shelves."

America has never been more theater-minded than it is as the half-century mark approaches. There are countless indications of a genuine theater hunger existing throughout the nation. The country is swarming with acting groups. The university theater is on the upswing and is to be regarded as a source for the development of playwrights and players of the future, but Community Theaters of a professional order, of definite purpose and standing and class, are needed to give the drama its place as a cultural and national force.

Shakespeare, played by on-from-Broadway professionals, has been taken to the midlands by truck and bus and given college-sponsored presentations. The American National Theater and Academy, granted a charter by an act of Congress, is striving to spread the doctrine of the living theater to the remote corners of the country. It is working toward decentralization and the establishment of a professional state theater in every one of the forty-eight states, thus reaching a vast and untapped audience for the years to come. "Decentralization," as Walter Prichard Eaton has observed in "The New York Times," "does not mean that New York will cease to be the ultimate goal of talent, as well as the production heart of our theater. It means that New York will not be the only goal nor the only production

Stars of the Musical Stage, 1905–1950

1. Bert Lahr   2. William Gaxton   3. Victor Moore
4. Paul Hartman   5. Mary Martin   6. Beatrice Lillie   7. Grace Hartman   8. Ray Bolger   9. Alfred
Drake   10. Ethel Merman   11. Nanette Fabray

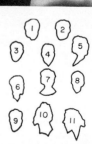

A Streetcar Named Desire

A moment of violence from Tennessee Williams's poignant and fascinating study of the disintegration of a Southern belle—the play which won the New York drama Critics' Circle award and was also the Pulitzer committee selection for the season of 1947–1948 (Eileen Darby).

Death of a Salesman

Lee J. Cobb and Mildred Dunnock in a scene from Arthur Miller's merciless and withering drama of the life and times of Willy Loman—Broadway's great dramatic hit of 1949 (Eileen Darby).

center. It means finding a way with local theaters and companies to bring living drama back to the country, to encourage the development of regional playwrights, and to offer a chance for employment to the young but now pretty discouraged theater aspirants."

New York City, aside from its large-scale Broadway activity, has become one vast laboratory for the living theater, with swarms of dramatic groups—some of them professional—earnestly at work. New York's professional theater of future decades will be one that will break out of its midtown-Manhattan boundaries. And I am making the prediction that the building code will be altered to permit the construction of playhouses on the ground floors of skyscrapers and that the day will come when the theaters will be equipped with bars—trim, tidy, well-stocked bars—to accommodate the thirsty during the entr'acte stampede. As in London. The American showmen, since the days of Augustin Daly, have grumbled about the absence of the pubs.

The theater, the most fascinating business in the world—and the greatest gamble—can be wonderful. It can be cruel. Many great people of the stage—producers, playwrights, actors, actresses—have died in bitter poverty. The relief rolls of that fine organization, the Actors' Fund of America, tell their saddening stories of the straitened circumstances of celebrated figures of bygone seasons. A famous woman star of the Broadway theater of yesterday is living alone, almost penniless, in a small New York hotel as these lines are being written. Many players who knew wonderful years in the theater are now grateful for bits and walk-ons in the Hollywood films. It's one of the adages of the theater—and an adage that has its foundation in grim truth—that most managers die broke: A. M. Palmer, Theodore Liebler, George C. Tyler, C. B. Dillingham, Florenz Ziegfeld. Charles Frohman produced countless plays, managed the foremost stars, and had enormous success for nearly a quarter of a century, but when an accounting was taken of his estate, after all bills had been paid, it was found that he left only $451.78.

But if you are disturbed about the state of the living stage, you might well save your tears. The theater has great powers of resistance and recuperation. It has been violated by Hollywood, it has been abused by the crafts-unions, it has been deplored by the critics, and given up for dead by some of its own people, the actors and the managers and the playwrights.

But it fights back. If it ever disappears entirely from the city of New York, driven out by production costs or by an atomic war, it will turn up in Wichita and in Santa Fe and in Atlanta and in Grand Forks. The theater, I suspect, will be an undiminished force in this republic when the year of 2050 comes around.

I regret that I won't be here.

MONTAGE PICTURE CREDITS

PAGE 2
1. Ira L. Hill
2. Collection of Joseph Cameron Cross
3. Daniel Blum Collection
4. Apeda Studio
5. Daniel Blum Collection
6. Culver Service
7. Culver Service
8. Daniel Blum Collection
10. Culver Service
12. New York Sun

PAGE 3
6. Daniel Blum Collection
7. Pinchot

PAGE 19
1. Mattie Edwards Hewitt
3. Culver Service
4. Ira D. Schwartz
6. Culver Service
7. Underwood and Underwood
11. Apeda Studio
12. Culver Service
13. Culver Service

PAGE 35
1. Culver Service
3. Florence Vandamm
5. Associated Press Photo
6. Matzene, Chicago
7. White Studio
10. Culver Service
12. Culver Service

PAGE 51
1. Byron
2. Daniel Blum Collection

3. Daniel Blum Collection
4. Sarony
5. Daniel Blum Collection
7. Daniel Blum Collection
8. Sarony
9. Gould and Marsden

PAGE 130
4. Culver Service
5. Culver Service
6. Keystone
7. Culver Service
8. Associated Press
9. Culver Service

PAGE 146
1. Apeda Studio
2. Sarony
4. White Studio
6. De Barron
7. Daniel Blum Collection
9. Dorothy Wilding
10. White Studio
12. Wide World
13. White Studio

PAGE 147
2. White Studio
5. Culver Service

PAGE 162
2. De Mirijian
3. Harold Stein
4. Harold Stein
5. Vandamm Studio
6. Vandamm Studio
7. White Studio
9. White Studio
10. White Studio

309

INDEX

A

Abbey Theater, 270
Abbott, George, 243, 273
   Broadway collaborator and director, 210
Abe Lincoln in Illinois, 261, 263, 269
Abie's Irish Rose, 126, 189–192
Abraham Lincoln, 173, 180
Academy of Music, 7, 24
   stock company and Priscilla Knowles, 135
Acquittal, The, 175
Actors, 87, 97, 110, 135, 252, 307
   memorable performances, 1910–1920, 177
   of mid-1800s, 5–6
   and motion pictures, 137, 170, 231, 232, 304
   outstanding, of 1920–1930, 235
   pay of, 44–45, 62, 76, 78, 85, 114, 134
   revue stars of 1920s, 208
   stars and star system, 2, 17, 18, 62, 184, 303
   in stock companies, 135
   strike of, 170–172
   war aid and service, 282–283
     in World War I, 155
   women, of 1900–1910, 56–57
   of 1910–1912, 106
Actors' Equity Association, 172, 173
   strike of, 170–172
   Sunday performance ban and effect on Civic Repertory, 215
Actors' Fidelity League, 171, 173
Actors' Fund of America, 48, 307
Actors' Fund Home, 92
Actors' summer colony, Nantucket, 60
Adams, Franklin P., 167
Adams, Maude, 62–65, 78, 88, 145, 184, 273, 305
   early career, 62–65
   her Juliet, 11
   Legend of Leonora, The, 130
   Peter Pan playbill, 63
   in *Peter Pan*, 64
   return to stage on tour as Portia, 246
Adding Machine, The, 224
Ade, George, 52–53
Adelaide & Hughes, 166

Adler, Luther and Stella, 249
Admirable Crichton, The, 47
Adrea, 40
Affairs of Anatol, The, 96
   John Barrymore's five leading women, 119
Against the Wind, 270
Ah, Wilderness, 255–256; 269
Aherne, Brian, 282
Akins, Zoe, 204, 245, 267
   The Old Maid, 248
Albee, E. F., 162, 164, 165, 166
Albertson, Lillian, on Eugene Walter and *Paid in Full*, 82
Aldrich, Charles T., 163
Aldrich, Richard, 243
"Alexander's Ragtime Band," 102
   story of song's introduction, 131–132
Algonquin, the fabulous inn, 105, 261
Alias Jimmy Valentine, 101, 105, 106, 135
Alice in Wonderland, 215, 287, 301
Alice of Old Vincennes, 102
Alien Corn, 254–255
Alison, George, 134
Alison's House, 245
All My Sons, 290–291
Allegiance, 154
Allegro, 284, 301
Allen, Kelcey, on *Abie's Irish Rose*, 191
   on *Street Scene*, 225
Allen, Viola, 2, 3, 6, 26, 65
Altar of Friendship, The, 41
Ambush, 188
"American Magazine," 113
American National Theater and Academy, 306
American Repertory Theater, 286–287, 301
American Theater Wing, 277
Americana, 244
Ames, Winthrop, 96, 111, 112, 118, 140, 143, 158, 176, 180, 216–217, 224, 229, 232, 242
   and *The Affairs of Anatol*, 119
   aides Johnson Briscoe and Guthrie Mc-Clintic, 96
   In the Next Room, 217
   Merchant of Venice, The, 220
   and New Theater, 93–95
Ames workshop, 96

316

Dances, Castle walk, turkey trot and the
tango, 133
Hoffman, Gertrude, 165
Roshanara, 165
soft-shoe, 163
song-and-dance shows (see Musical
comedy)
Dane, Clemence, 186
Daniel Frawley stock company, 57
Daniels, Frank, 303
Darewski, Herman, 154
D'Armond, Isabel, 164
Darnton, Charles, 294, 295
The Easiest Way, 91
Daughters of Men, The, 89
Davenport, Fanny Lily Gipsy, 6, 305
David Harum, 17
Davies, Acton, 34, 83, 101, 295
Davis, Bette, 218, 260
Davis, Donald, 257
Davis, Owen, 18, 111, 257
Detour, The, 187
Icebound, 187
and melodrama, 102, 103, 104
Sinners, 143
Davis, Richard Harding, 31
Dawn, Hazel, 106, 150, 160
Pink Lady role of, 107
Dawn of a Tomorrow, The, 58
Day, Clarence, Jr., 264
Day, Mrs. Clarence, Jr., and genesis of
Life With Father, 264
Day, Edith, in *Irene,* 173
Day, Juliette, 108
Dayne, Blanche, 164
Dayton, Katharine, 255
Dead End, 257
Dean, Julia, 83, 112
De Angelis, Jefferson, 38
Dear Brutus, 159
Dear Queen, The, 248
Death of a Salesman, 293
Decision, 274
Déclassée, 173, 204
De Cordoba, Pedro, 94
Deep Are the Roots, 275
Deep Mrs. Sykes, The, 279, 281
Deep Purple, The, 105–106, 114
Defender, The, 30
De Foe, Louis V., 31, 101, 294, 295
De Kruif, Paul, 254
De Lawd in *The Green Pastures,* 239–
240
De Liagre, Alfred, Jr., 243
Del Bondio, J. H., 45
Dellenbaugh, Harriet Otis, 94
Delmonico's, 7, 101
De Long, George, 29

De Mille, Agnes, 283–284
De Mille, Cecil, 69
De Mille, William, 69, 136, 165
De Navarro, Antonio F., 49
Design for Living, 244
Desire Under the Elms, 204
Deslys, Mlle. Gaby, 112, 113, 114, 177
De Sylva, Buddy, 267
Detour, The, 18, 187
Devil, The, 75, 112
Dictator, The, 31, 138
Digges, Dudley, 113, 169, 177, 180, 205,
305
Dillingham, Charles, 5, 30, 42, 47, 51,
81, 101, 145, 152, 307
and Katharine Cornell, 186
and *Spring Maid,* 106–107
and *Watch Your Step,* 132–133
Dietz, Howard, 245
Diff'rent, 188
Dillman, Hugh, and *Rain,* 195
Dinehart, Alan, 165
Diplomacy, 57
Disraeli, 112, 113, 127, 176
Dithmar, Edward A., 9, 295
Ditrichstein, Leo, 109, 140
Divorçons, 30
Dix, Beulah Marie, 33
Dixey, Henry E., 111
Dixon, Thomas, Jr., 66, 137
Dockstader, Lew, 166
Doctor's Dilemma, The, 141, 142
Dodd, Lee Wilson, 218
Dodson, J. E., 91
Dodsworth, 257, 269
Doing Our Bit, 154
Dollar Princess, The, 107
Doll's House, A, 69, 263
Donnelly, Dorothy, 106, *Candida,* 46–
47
Donnelly, Henry V., 26
Dooley, Johnny, 166
Dooley, Ray (Mrs. Edward Dowling),
166, 208, 281
Doro, Marie, 30, 137
in *Morals of Marcus, The,* 76
in revivals of *Diplomacy* and *Oliver
Twist,* 57
Dostoevski, 202
Dove, Billie, 208
Dover Road, The, 96
Dowling, Eddie, and *The Glass Menag-
erie,* 281
and *The Time of Your Life,* 265
Doyle, James W., 135
Doyle & Dixon, 166
Drake, William A., 240
Dramatic critics (see Theater, critics)

322

324

Moran & Mack, 305
More than Queen, 25
Morgan, Edward J., 13
Morgan, Helen, 230
Morgan, J. P., 87, 95
Morley, Victor, 165
Morosco, Oliver, 116–118, 151, 190
Morosco Theater, 116, 176
Morris, Clara, 6, 164
Morro Castle, liner, 258
Morse, Frank P., 68
Morton, Michael, 130
Moscow Art Theater, 183, 202
Moses, Harry, 240, 243
Moskvin, Ivan, 202
Moss, Arnold, 283
Motion Pictures, 25, 102, 134, 136, 137, 170, 178, 183, 232, 246, 260, 266, 303, 304
Mourning Becomes Electra, 240, 269
Mr. Strauss Goes to Boston, 301
Mr. Wookey, 272
Mrs. Black Is Back, 60
Mrs. Bumpstead-Leigh, 114
Mrs. Dane's Defense, 17
Mrs. Jarley's Wax Works, 283
Mrs. Temple's Telegram, 135
Mrs. Warren's Profession, 27, 54
Mrs. Wiggs of the Cabbage Patch, 54, 66
Munsey, Frank A., 296
Murdock, Ann, 138
Murdock, John J., 164
Murfin, Jane, 153
Murray, Marion, 166
Murray Hill Stock Company, 90
Murray Hill Theater, 26
Murray's Roman Gardens, 300
Music Box Revue, 183, 208
Music Box Theater, 183
"Music Goes Round and Round," 260
Music Master, The, 54
Musical comedy and the revue, 74–75, 207–209, 234, 245
 and the "book" show, 208
 in 1920s, 207–209
 Oklahoma!, 275–276, 283–284
 soaring production costs of, 301–302
My Dear Children, 266
My Heart's in the Highlands, 261
My Wife, 88
Myself Bettina, 50

N

"Nancy Brown," song hit, 56
Nash, Mary, 96, 150
Nathan, George Jean, 65, 128, 158, 188, 189, 261, 296

Nathan, George Jean, on *Abie's Irish Rose,* 191
 and *Glass Menagerie,* 281
 and *Rain,* 194
Nathan Hale, 1, 8, 10, 25, 305
Naudain, May, 166
Naughty Anthony, 16
Nazimova, Alla, 69, 70, 160, 164, 165, 214, 241, 268
Nearly Married, 138
Neighborhood Playhouse, 208
Neilson, Adelaide, 6
Nellie, the Beautiful Cloak Model, 18, 102
Neptune's Daughter (motion picture), 141
Nesbit, Evelyn (*see* Thaw, Evelyn Nesbit)
Nethersole, Olga, 25, 164
 in *Sapho,* 26–28
Neutrality as observed by the theater, 153
Never Say Die, 138
New Amsterdam Theater, 261
New South, The, 294
New Theater, 93–95, 161, 205
New York, 111
"New York Clipper," 209, 261
"New York Daily News," 251
"New York Dramatic Mirror," 9, 10, 11, 36, 261
"New York Evening Post," 35–36
"New York Evening Sun," 143
"New York Herald," 3–4, 128
New York Idea, The, 31, 98, 149
"New York Press," 70–71
"New York Sun," 2, 20, 69, 97, 160
"New York Times," 143–144
"New York Tribune," 97
"New York World," 8
Next Half Hour, The, 290
Nice People, 150, 185
Nicolai, George H., 102
Nichols, Anne, and "Abie," 189–192
Nichols, Lewis, 296
Nichols, Robert, 230
Nigger, The, 84, 94, 101
Night Boat, The, 175
Night of the Party, The, 38
Night spots of the prohibition era, 261
Nillson, Carlotta, 66
Nirdlinger, Samuel F., 7
No Exit, 291
No More Ladies, 257
No, No, Nanette, 209
Nolan, Agnes, 71
Nolan, Lloyd, 269
Norton, Elliot, critic, 298
Norworth, Jack, 164
Nothing but the Truth, 138

Rule of Three, The, 138
Running for Office, 26
R.U.R., 205, 234
Russell, Annie, 3, 81, 94, 287
Russell, Lillian, 4, 49–50, 65, 88, 163
Rutherford and Son, 176
Ryan, Mary, 93, 126, 173
Ryley, Thomas W., and Sextette, 28
Ryskind, Morrie, 240, 241

S

Sabine Woman, A, 67
Sag Harbor, 11
St. Claire, Winifred, 134
St. Elmo, 66, 102
St. Joan, 205
St. John, Marguerite, 113
Sally, 209
Salomy Jane, 57, 73
Salvation Nell, 84, 85
Salvini, Tommaso, 6
Sam S. Shubert Memorial Theater, 39
Sam T. Jack's (burlesque), 3
Sampson, William, 90
Samson, 86
Samuels, Ray, 164
Sandow, the Strong Man, 74
Santley, Joseph, 166
Sapho, 19, 25, 26–28, 140, 303
Saratoga, 16
Sarony, stage photographer, 1
Saroyan, William, 261–262, 269
Sartre, Jean-Paul, 291
Saturday Night, 214
Saturday's Children, 211
Sauce for the Goose, 111, 149
Savage, Henry W., 8, 73, 75, 76, 107, 242
    on the critics, 108, 177
    Merry Widow, The, 73, 75–76
    opposition to Syndicate, 8, 109
Savannah, Georgia, 53, 59
Saved from the Sea, 113
Savo, Jimmy, 164
Savoy, Bert, impersonator, 177
Sawyer, Joan, 164
Scandals, 175, 207, 208
Scarborough, George, 128, 173, 183
Scarecrow, The, 140
Scarlet Sister Mary, 270
Scenery and scenic design (see Theater,
    stagecraft)
Schaffer, Sylvester, 165
Scheff, Fritzi, 164
Schenck, Joe, 164
Schildkraut, Joseph, 180, 214
Schloss, Edward, critic, 298
Schwab, Laurence, 301–302

Schwartz, Arthur, 245, 290
Scott, Cyril, 28, 101, 137
Scott, Martha, 269
Sea Gull, The, 148
Sears, Zelda, 54, 140
Second in Command, The, 78
Second Mrs. Tanqueray, The, 139, 203
Secret Service, 2, 22, 23, 86
See Naples and Die, 225
Seeley, Blossom, 164
Selwyn, Arch, 81, 86–87, 89, 122–123, 243
    and Twin Beds promotion, 138
Selwyn, Edgar, 86–87, 105, 122, 152, 153,
    189, and the critics, 294
Selwyn & Company, 140, 153
Sennett, Mack, 231
Sensenderfer, Robert, critic, 297
Serlin, Oscar, 226–227, 264–265
Serrano, Vincent, 86
Servant in the House, The, 72, 83, 88, 140,
    184
Seven Days, 81, 92, 101, 115, 126
Seven Days' Leave, 154
Seven Keys to Baldpate, 124–125, 138, 176
Seven Sisters, 48
Seventeen, 174
Sex, 218, 236
Shadow and Substance, 269
Shakespearean performances (see The-
    ater)
Shame Woman, The, 237
Shanghai Gesture, The, 220–221, 294
Shanley's, 101
Shannon, Effie, 121, 154
Sharkey, Tom, 12, 23
Shaw, George Bernard, 25, 46, 99
Shaw, Irwin, 248, 255, 269, 275
Shaw, Mary, 54
She, 78
Sheldon, Edward, 84, 85, 94, 105, 130,
    146, 170
    and Justice, 157
Shenandoah, 2, 16
Shepherd of the Hills, The, 136
Shepherd King, The, 112
Shepley, Ruth, 139
Sherlock Holmes, 11, 17, 230–231
    playbill, 21, 41
Sherman, Lowell, 134, 173
Sherriff, R. C., 230
Sherwin, Louis, 156, 296
Sherwood, Robert, 240, 261, 263, 274,
    289
    Abe Lincoln in Illinois, 85, 263
    Idiot's Delight, 253–254
    Petrified Forest, 253
    Road to Rome, 217–218
Shields, Ren, 30

333

338